The Global Transform

The 'long nineteenth century' (1776–1914) was a period of political, economic, military and cultural revolutions that re-forged both domestic and international societies. Neither existing international histories nor international relations texts sufficiently register the scale and impact of this 'global transformation', yet it is the consequences of these multiple revolutions that provide the material and ideational foundations of modern international relations. Global modernity reconstituted the mode of power that underpinned international order and opened a power gap between those who harnessed the revolutions of modernity and those who were denied access to them. This gap dominated international relations for two centuries and is only now being closed. By taking the global transformation as the starting point for international relations, this book repositions the roots of the discipline and establishes a new way of both understanding and teaching the relationship between world history and international relations.

BARRY BUZAN is Emeritus Professor in the Department of International Relations at the London School of Economics and Political Science, a Senior Fellow at LSE IDEAS and a Fellow of the British Academy. Among his books are *International Systems in World History* (2000, with Richard Little); *Regions and Powers* (Cambridge, 2003, with Ole Wæver); *From International to World Society?* (Cambridge, 2004, with Ole Wæver); *The Evolution of International Security Studies* (Cambridge, 2009, with Lene Hansen); and *An Introduction to the English School of International Relations* (2014).

GEORGE LAWSON is an Associate Professor of International Relations in the Department of International Relations at the London School of Economics and Political Science. His research focuses on the interface between International Relations and Historical Sociology, and on processes of radical change, most notably revolutions. He is the author of *Negotiated Revolutions* (2005) and editor of *The Global 1989* (Cambridge, 2010, with Chris Armbruster and Michael Cox).

Cambridge Studies in International Relations: 135

The Global Transformation

Cambridge Studies in International Relations

Series list continues after index

The Global Transformation

History, Modernity and the Making
of International Relations

BARRY BUZAN AND GEORGE LAWSON

CAMBRIDGE
UNIVERSITY PRESS

CAMBRIDGE
UNIVERSITY PRESS

University Printing House, Cambridge CB2 8BS, United Kingdom

Cambridge University Press is part of the University of Cambridge.

It furthers the University's mission by disseminating knowledge in the pursuit of education, learning and research at the highest international levels of excellence.

www.cambridge.org
Information on this title: www.cambridge.org/9781107630802

First published 2015
4th printing 2016

Printed in the United Kingdom by Clays, St Ives plc

A catalogue record for this publication is available from the British Library

Library of Congress Cataloguing in Publication data
Buzan, Barry.
The global transformation : history, modernity and the making of international relations / Barry Buzan, George Lawson.
    pages   cm. – (Cambridge studies in international relations ; 135)
ISBN 978-1-107-63080-2 (paperback)
1. International relations – History – 19th century.   2. World politics – History – 19th century.   I. Lawson, George, 1972–   II. Title.
JZ1318.B894 2015
327.09′034–dc23

2014032245

ISBN 978-1-107-03557-7 Hardback
ISBN 978-1-107-63080-2 Paperback

To Fred Halliday and Justin Rosenberg,
for pointing the way.

Contents

Figures

Tables

.

Preface

This project originated in our shared interest in modernity and our shared frustration at the lack of awareness of its importance in International Relations (IR). Working together at the LSE gave us the opportunity to talk about the book's main ideas, and both of us were in different ways guided towards this project by the influence of Fred Halliday and Justin Rosenberg. Fred always made a big deal of the nineteenth-century disjuncture, even though most people in IR were resistant to his promptings. Justin's work on both modernity and uneven and combined development provided another shared stimulus. We dedicate this book to both of them, and hope that it might stand as a vindication of Fred's campaign to turn the IR supertanker.

We would like to thank Carmen Gayoso, Mark Kersten and Luca Tardelli for their extremely helpful research assistance, and for always delivering more than we asked for. Luca in particular has worked on a number of different parts of the book, providing both materials and insights that have greatly strengthened our argument. Kirsten Ainley gave us good advice on the history of International Law. Especially big thanks to Mathias Albert, Tarak Barkawi, Pinar Bilgin, Andrew Linklater, Richard Little, Jeppe Mulich and Justin Rosenberg for reading the whole manuscript and providing comments on it, and to Vivien Barr and Harvey Chisick for comments on particular aspects of our argument. Thanks also to the Cambridge University Press reviewers who commented on the proposal and the manuscript. Whether or not we agreed with all the comments we received, our community of scholars made us think hard about what we wanted to say, and we are deeply grateful for their collegial insight and support. Our gratitude also to Cambridge University Press, particularly Carrie Parkinson for being extremely helpful with the production process, and John Haslam for his encouragement, and sometimes tolerance, of our project.

Along the way the research for this book spun off three journal articles: Barry Buzan and George Lawson (2013) 'The Global Transformation: The Nineteenth Century and the Making of Modern International Relations', *International Studies Quarterly*, 57(3): 620–34; Barry Buzan and George Lawson (2014a) 'Rethinking Benchmark Dates in International Relations', *European Journal of International Relations*, 20(2): 437–62; and Barry Buzan and George Lawson (2014b) 'Capitalism and the Emergent World Order', *International Affairs*, 90(1): 71–91. Readers familiar with these articles will find arguments from them scattered throughout this book. During the course of writing the book, we presented parts of the argument at LSE, Sussex University, Copenhagen University, the University of British Columbia, Korea University and Zhejiang University, plus various conferences, including those held by the International Studies Association, the American Political Science Association, the European International Studies Association, the British International Studies Association and the Social Science History Association. We thank colleagues who took part in these events – the book is much richer for their engagements.

Our hope is that this is one of those books where the argument is so obvious that people will react by saying: 'Of course!' But if our argument is unlikely to be quite as easy a sell as that, we do at least hope to convince our IR colleagues to take modernity more seriously. Lest we forget, IR owes its origins to the global transformation, as does the term 'international', which Jeremy Bentham coined in 1789 to refer to the legal transactions between sovereigns. We also hope that sociologists and historians find that the book has something to offer their debates. Neither sociologists nor historians have done sufficient justice to the global features of modernity. This mutual neglect provides the opportunity for a productive conversation to take place between IR specialists, historians and sociologists around the subject of 'global modernity'. Our aim is for this book to contribute to just such a conversation.

This is not one of those books where we have carved out discrete spheres of influence. Although some parts of the text bear the hallmarks of one of us more than the other, everything in the book is the result of extensive discussion, collaboration and co-authorship. Both of us wrote with the other 'on their shoulder', and the back and forth we had on the manuscript made writing it an enjoyable, if sometimes exhausting, process. We offer our heartfelt thanks to our families for putting up with us as we worked long hours and mused to the point of obsession over the global transformation. We would like to say that Deborah, Kirsten, Jake and Xavi have been patient. But we're not sure we'd love them as much if they had been.

Barry Buzan

George Lawson

Abbreviations

ABM	anti-ballistic missile
ASEAN	Association of Southeast Asian Nations
AU	African Union
BRIC	Brazil, Russia, India, China
CIS	Commonwealth of Independent States
CPI	Consumer Price Index
DPT	Democratic Peace Theory
ECOWAS	Economic Community of West African States
ETA	Euskadi Ta Askatasuna (Basque Homeland and Freedom)
EU	European Union
FDI	foreign direct investment
G7	Group of Seven
G8	Group of Eight
G20	Group of Twenty
G77	Group of Seventy-Seven
GATT	General Agreement on Tariffs and Trade
GDP	gross domestic product
GEG	global economic governance
GNP	gross national product
ICBM	intercontinental ballistic missile
ICJ	International Court of Justice
ICSU	International Council of Scientific Unions
IFI	international financial institution
IGO	intergovernmental organization
ILO	International Labour Organization
IMF	International Monetary Fund
INGO	international non-governmental organization
IPCC	Intergovernmental Panel on Climate Change
IPE	International Political Economy
IR	International Relations

IRA	Irish Republican Army
ISI	import substitution industrialization
IT	information technology
IUCN	International Union for the Conservation of Nature and Natural Resources
IWA	International Workingmen's Association
NAFTA	North American Free Trade Association
NSA	non-state actor
OECD	Organisation for Economic Co-operation and Development
OPEC	Organization of the Petroleum Exporting Countries
Oxfam	Oxford Committee for Famine Relief
PCIJ	Permanent Court of International Justice
R&D	research and development
RMA	revolution in military affairs
RMB	renminbi
RPG	rocket-propelled grenade
SADC	Southern African Development Community
SARC	South Asian Regional Cooperation
SCO	Shanghai Cooperation Organization
SOE	state-owned enterprise
TNC	transnational corporation
TPP	Trans-Pacific Partnership
TTIP	Transatlantic Trade and Investment Partnership
UCD	uneven and combined development
UDHR	Universal Declaration of Human Rights
UN	United Nations
UNESCO	United Nations Educational, Scientific and Cultural Organization
UPU	Universal Postal Union
WMD	weapons of mass destruction
WTO	World Trade Organization
YMCA	Young Men's Christian Association

Introduction

The Global Transformation and IR

During the nineteenth century, a 'global transformation' remade the basic structure of international order. This transformation was profound, involving a complex configuration of industrialization, rational state-building and ideologies of progress.[1] Because this transformation happened unevenly, it changed the distribution of power by generating a shift from a 'polycentric world with no dominant centre' to a 'core–periphery' order in which the centre of gravity resided in the West (Pomeranz, 2000: 4). Acquiring the new configuration meant undergoing wide-ranging political, economic and cultural transformations, and polities that underwent those transformations held enormous advantages over those that did not. Although oscillations of power are nothing new in human history (Morris, 2010), the global transformation opened up a vastly expanded pool of resources, making the power gap both much bigger and much more difficult to emulate. In this sense, as well as marking a shift in the distribution of power, the global transformation also changed the basic sources, or *mode of power*,[2] stimulating the emergence of global modernity.[3]

[1] By configuration, we mean a set of interlinked events and processes that concatenate in historically specific form. The basic assumption of this approach is that big events do not require big causes. Rather, social transformations arise from the conjunctural intersection of sequences of events and processes that are causally, but contingently, interrelated. On this issue, see Lebow (2010).
[2] By 'mode of power', we mean the material and ideational relations that are generative of both actors and the ways in which power is exercised. As we note above, during the global transformation, three dynamics (industrialization, rational statehood and 'ideologies of progress') combined to generate a new basis for how power was constituted, organized and expressed – we refer to this as a shift in the 'mode of power'. Contra most IR approaches, changes in the mode of power are more significant than changes in the distribution of power, affecting not just outcomes, but the basis for how interactions take place and are understood. We consider the consequences of thinking about power in this way in Chapter 10.
[3] We outline what we mean by 'global modernity' later in this chapter. For now, it is worth noting that, for many social scientific disciplines, modernity serves as the

1

Global modernity pulled the world into a single system, within which the consequences of the changes in the mode and distribution of power were widely and deeply felt. The world had been an *economic international system* since the European voyages of discovery during the fifteenth and sixteenth centuries opened up sea-lanes around Africa, and across the Atlantic and Pacific Oceans (Buzan and Little, 2000: 96). Eurasia had been an economic system for two millennia. But the global ties binding such systems were thin, slow and limited in scope. Not until the nineteenth century did the world become a global system in which core states could quickly and decisively project the new mode of power around the world. In this way, multiple regional international systems were engulfed in a *full international system* in which all parts of the world were closely connected not just economically and culturally, but also in military-political terms (Buzan and Little, 2000; Osterhammel, 2014: 392–402).[4]

If the first effect of the global transformation was to foster the emergence of a full international system, the second effect was to generate a host of new actors: rational nation-states, transnational corporations, and standing intergovernmental and non-governmental

basic foundation of their enquiry. In broadly Durkheimian terms, this transformation can be understood as a shift from social orders defined by stratificatory social differentiation to those dominated by functional differentiation. Stratification is about hierarchies of rank and class – it is characteristic of social orders defined by dynasticism and caste. Functional differentiation is about the coherence and interdependence of specialized types of activity, the creation of a complex division of labour, and the rise of legal, political, military, economic, scientific, religious and other specialized roles. From this perspective, functional differentiation is the central characteristic of modernity (see Buzan and Albert, 2010; Albert and Buzan, 2011; Albert et al., 2013).

[4] This prompts a supplementary question about what 'international' means. Sociologists tend to avoid this question by thinking of society as a unitary construction, while world historians usually have little sense of 'the international' as a distinct realm. In IR, thinking about 'the international' tends to start, even if it does not finish, with the issue of political multiplicity, whether this is understood as the 'logic of anarchy', the 'problem of difference', or variants thereof. Our view, following Rosenberg (2006: 308), is that the international is 'that dimension of social reality which arises specifically from the co-existence within it of more than one society'. Such a definition accepts the 'fact' of political multiplicity, but also stresses the importance of interactions between societies, whether these consist of the spread of ideas, the transfer of technologies, trading networks, security alliances, or practices of subjugation and emulation. The simultaneous existence of multiplicity and interactivity engenders a distinct field of enquiry – international relations.

organizations became leading participants in international affairs. Taken together, these changes in global structure and international actors meant that 'the nineteenth century saw the birth of international relations as we know it today' (Osterhammel, 2014: 393). Yet the discipline of IR pays surprisingly little attention to such changes. This book examines the reasons for IR's failure to grasp the full significance of the global transformation and argues that this shortcoming creates major problems for how the discipline understands both itself and its subject matter.

Our argument is that the global transformation generated four basic, but linked, types of change in international relations.

1. Industrialization and the extension of the market to a global scale produced major increases in interaction capacity, bringing all parts of the international system into closer contact with each other.[5] At the same time, the new mode of power associated with industrialization and marketization produced major inequalities between societies. The result was a system that was simultaneously both intensely connected and deeply divided.
2. The reconstitution of power associated with the emergence of modernity was sustained by processes of rational state-formation, in which capacities were both caged within nation-states and extended outwards into 'alien spaces'. Nation-building went hand-in-hand with imperialism. The result was a bifurcated international system in which rule-based order was reserved for 'civilized' peoples, and territorial annexation rendered for 'barbarians' and 'savages'. This core–periphery structure took global form, sustained by a large and durable power gap between those most enabled by the configuration of global modernity and those most disadvantaged by it.
3. The new ideologies that rose to prominence during the nineteenth century, most notably liberalism, nationalism, socialism and 'scientific' racism, generated new entities, actors and institutions (e.g. settlers, civil society, limited companies) and either reconstituted old ones (e.g. the state), or undermined them (e.g. dynasticism). These ideologies, closely bound up with notions of progress, provided new legitimating strategies for how international relations was practised.

[5] Interaction capacity is defined as the physical and organizational capability of a system to move ideas, goods, people, money and armed force across the system (Buzan and Little, 2000: 80–4). This issue is discussed in depth in Chapter 3.

4. The tripartite configuration that lay behind the global transformation (industrialization, rational state-building and ideologies of progress) not only generated a core–periphery global order, but also destabilized great power relations by exposing the balance of power to the pressures of rapid technological and social change, with the consequence of making balancing dynamics much more volatile. Concerns about the rise and fall of those powers that harnessed – or failed to harness – modernity began in the nineteenth century. This dynamic remains a major feature of great power relations in the contemporary world.

These changes need to be understood in relation both to what came before the global transformation and what came after. In terms of what came before, our argument is that the scale and depth of these changes amounted to a material and ideational transformation of the international system. The main changes that distinguish global modernity from previous periods in world history include the following:

- Agrarian political economies based on land as wealth, and with cycles of prosperity and famine based on harvests, were superseded by industrial political economies based on capitalist accumulation, and featuring boom and bust trade cycles. At the same time, rapid and frequent technological transformations replaced slow and intermittent technological changes.[6]
- Expectations of historical progress underpinned the emergence of industrial societies. New ideologies challenged personalized, composite polities and reshaped the territorial sovereign state by vesting sovereignty in the people and linking territory to the nation.
- Rational states legitimized by these ideologies replaced absolutist polities, developing new bureaucratic structures that increased infrastructural capacities and provided the means for extending state power both at home and internationally.

---

[6] As graphically shown by Diamond (1998), there were enormous differences of technology both within and across the agrarian era. This period witnessed major technological developments from iron and guns to clocks and windmills, and it was also a time of major ideational developments, most notably the advent of the Axial Age religions. But while the agrarian era was far from 'static', its pace of change was both slower and less compressed than the rapid, incessant change that has marked the period since the nineteenth century. The revolutions of modernity accelerated historical development.

- The configuration of industrialization, rational state-building and ideologies of progress became the criteria by which great powers were defined.
- As a result of this new configuration, a relatively even distribution of global power was replaced by a radically uneven distribution of power in favour of the West.

The nineteenth century is thus close kin to the twentieth and twenty-first centuries, and quite distinct from previous periods of world history.

The marginalization of the global transformation in IR sets the discipline on tenuous foundations. Indeed, it can be argued that the current benchmark dates around which IR is organized omit the principal dynamics that established the modern international order (Buzan and Lawson, 2014a). These benchmarks usually include: the opening of the sea-lanes from Europe to the Americas and the Indian Ocean in the late fifteenth century (Buzan and Little, 2000: 401–2); the emergence of modern notions of sovereignty codified in the Treaty of Augsburg and, it is often argued, reaffirmed in the Peace of Westphalia (Spruyt, 1994; Ikenberry, 2001; Philpott, 2001); the two World Wars and the Cold War as major contestations over world power during the twentieth century (Lundestad, 2005; Mayer, 2010); and the shake-up to dynamics of polarity initiated by the end of the Cold War (Mearsheimer, 1990; Waltz, 2000; Brooks and Wohlforth, 2008). These commonly held 'turning points' are not so much wrong as incomplete, under-theorized and cumulatively misleading (Buzan and Lawson, 2014a). They emphasize the distribution of power without focusing on the underlying mode of power. They pay little or no attention to changes in the density and connectedness of the international system. They focus on the impact of wars without examining the social developments that gave rise to them. And they omit the range of nineteenth-century political, economic and ideological transformations that set in place core features of modern international relations. Once the magnitude of the changes initiated during the nineteenth century is recognized, it becomes clear that we are not living in a world where the principal dynamics are defined by the outcomes of 1500, 1648, 1919, 1945 or 1989. We are living now, and are likely to be living for some time yet, in a world defined predominantly by the downstream consequences of the nineteenth-century global transformation. If IR is to gain a better grasp of its core areas of enquiry, this global transformation needs to become central to its field of vision.

Establishing the Argument: Six Assumptions and Two Claims

There are six main assumptions that underlie our claims. First, our understanding of the nineteenth century shares affinities to Eric Hobsbawm's (1987: 8) concept of 'the long nineteenth century', sandwiched between the 'Atlantic Revolutions' that began in America, France and Haiti on the one hand, and the First World War on the other. We include some aspects of modernity that were established during the late eighteenth century, but which matured principally in the nineteenth century (such as industrialization), and we also include some dynamics that are more associated with the early decades of the twentieth century (such as changes in the organization of violence). As such, we use 'the long nineteenth century' as an analytical shorthand for a range of transformations that shaped the modern world. We show how much of IR's contemporary agenda stems from these changes and what benefits would accrue to IR from making the global transformation more central to its enquiries.

Second, as noted in the previous section, we understand the global transformation as constituted by three interlinked processes: industrialization, the rational state and ideologies of progress. By industrialization we mean both the commercialization of agriculture and the two-stage industrial revolution,[7] which together generated an intensely connected global market. The extension of the market brought new opportunities for accumulating power, not least because of the close relationship between industrialization and dispossession. Indeed, industrialization in some states (such as Britain) was deeply interwoven with the forceful de-industrialization of others (such as India). By rational state-building, we mean the process by which administrative and bureaucratic competences were accumulated and 'caged' within national territories (Mann, 1988). This process was not pristine. Rather, as we show, processes of rational state-building and imperialism were co-implicated. Finally, by 'ideologies of progress', we mean systematic schemas of thought, specifically modern liberalism, socialism, nationalism and 'scientific' racism, which were rooted in ideals of progress and, in particular, associated with Enlightenment

---

[7] The first stage was defined by iron and steam, the second by steel, electricity, chemicals and internal combustion engines. Both stages are discussed in Chapter 5.

notions of classification, improvement and control. Once again, there was a dark side to these ideologies – the promise of progress was linked closely to a 'standard of civilization' which, along with 'scientific' racism, served as the legitimating currency for coercive practices against 'barbarians' (understood as peoples with an urban 'high culture') and 'savages' (understood as peoples without an urban 'high culture') (Gong, 1984; Keene, 2002; Anghie, 2004; Suzuki, 2009; Hobson, 2012). These three components of the global transformation were mutually reinforcing. For example, European colonialism was legitimized by one or more of the ideologies of progress, and enabled through military superiority, mechanisms of state control and infrastructural developments that had their roots in industrialization.

Third, we emphasize the role played by inter-societal interactions in generating the global transformation. We reject the view that modernity was a uniquely European development arising from endogenous, self-generating civilizational qualities (e.g. Jones, 1981; Landes, 1998; North et al., 2009). We do so primarily on empirical grounds – as later chapters show, these claims do not stand up to scrutiny. At the same time, there seems little point replacing unsatisfactory Eurocentric approaches with equally unsatisfying Sino-centric (e.g. Frank, 1998) or Eurasian-centric (e.g. Morris, 2013) explanations. Instead, we emphasize the 'entangled histories' and 'multiple vectors' that combined to vault Western states into a position of pre-eminence (De Vries, 2013: 46). Specifically, we highlight the ways in which the configuration of modernity, constituted by inter-societal processes, cohered in parts of northwestern Europe during the long nineteenth century and thereafter sustained a core–periphery global order. Modernity was a global process both in terms of origins and outcomes, hence our preferred term: *global modernity*. We use global modernity rather than alternatives such as 'multiple modernities' (Eisenstadt, 2000) for two reasons: first, because the latter retains a sense of Europe as the original, definitive modern experience – it is analytically prior to the regional variations that are compared to it; and second, because the concept of multiple modernities rests on a comparison of internally driven modernities, mediated by cultural differences, rather than deriving from the transnational interconnections that produced the modern mode of power (Bhambra, 2007: 65–72 and 2013: 301–3; see also Blumi, 2012).

Fourth, modernity should be seen as a protracted, uneven process rather than as a singular moment of sharp discontinuity – there is no hard-and-fast distinction to be made between modern and pre-modern eras (Teschke, 2003: 43, 265). It is important to note that capitalism as a term did not attain wide currency until the 1860s, while agriculture, sailing ships and non-carbon-based production remained important components of almost every economy deep into the twentieth century. Many agrarian social hierarchies proved resilient – the nobility, gentry and landholding classes remained influential throughout the nineteenth century (Tombs, 2000: 30–1; Bayly, 2004: 451). And empires were not weakened but rebooted by the power differentials ushered in by the global transformation, remaining a central site of political authority up to, and in some cases beyond, the Second World War (Darwin, 2007; Burbank and Cooper, 2010: 20–1; Ballantyne and Burton, 2012: 285–6). In similar vein, we are not arguing that there was a single modern project that was instituted around the world, nor that modernity represents a necessary stage in a linear historical storyline, and still less that the nineteenth century contained a nascent 'modernity formula' that was waiting to be realized (Blumi, 2012: 4, 175). In many respects, our argument is the reverse of these claims – modernity was a contingent concatenation of social forces, a complex jumble of myriad events and processes. Once this concatenation had formed, it constituted a mode of power that contained massive transformative potential. This mode of power had deep roots, some of which went back centuries. But it was only in the nineteenth century that the whole package coalesced in a small group of polities from where both its effect (a revolutionary configuration in the mode of power) and its challenge (how other societies responded to this configuration) became the principal dynamic through which international relations was conceived and practised. As this book shows, these issues still define the basic structure of international relations and many of its principal issue-areas.

Fifth, we argue that the global transformation can be characterized by both the intensification of differential development and heightened interactions between societies. In other words, particular experiences of the configuration we highlight were accentuated by increasingly dense connections between societies. The result was 'differential integration' into global modernity (Halliday, 2002a). Intensified trade, improved transport and communication systems, and practices such as colonialism generated a denser, more integrated international order. As a consequence, levels of interdependence rose, making societies more exposed to developments elsewhere. However, during the nineteenth century, the development gap between societies opened more widely than ever before. Unevenness has always been a fact of historical development (Rosenberg, 2010), but never was unevenness experienced on this scale, with this intensity, or in a context of such close, inescapable interdependence. Those convinced of their cultural superiority and with access to advanced weapons, industrial production, medicine and new forms of bureaucratic organization gained a pronounced advantage over those with limited access to these sources of power. After around 1800, these dynamics fostered a substantial power gap between a handful of 'core' polities and a much larger group of 'peripheral' polities. In principle, this power gap could be closed: those with access to the configuration that sustained the global transformation could move from periphery to core. In practice, this move was made exceptionally difficult not only by the depth of the transformative package, but also by practices of imperialism and other forms of coercive interventionism that reinforced the advantages of the core. The result was the formation of a core–periphery international order in which the leading edge was located in the West. This hierarchical international order lasted from the early nineteenth century until the early years of the twenty-first century. In the contemporary world, it is being replaced by a more decentred global order in which those states that were once on the receiving end of the global transformation are employing its mode of power to reassert their position in international society.

Finally, we do not use the terms 'core' and 'periphery' along the lines popularized by world systems analysts, i.e. as an 'axial division of labour' premised on unequal exchange between a low profit, high-competition, labour-intensive periphery and a high profit, quasi-monopolistic, capital-intensive core (Wallerstein, 2011b: xiv). First, we see the dividing line between core and periphery as premised on access to the entire modern configuration of power (industrialization, rational statehood and ideologies of progress) rather than just one aspect of it. Second, Wallerstein's view is too homogenizing: there are peripheries in the core and cores in the periphery – the geography of capitalism is lumpier than Wallerstein and his colleagues allow (Galtung, 1971). Third, we do not follow world systems analysts in seeing historical development as a cycle or wave, lasting roughly 50 years, in which capitalist accumulation goes through certain elemental stages: monopoly, competition, falling prices, reduced profits, stagnation, geographical relocation, incorporation of resistance, and the emergence of new monopolies (Wallerstein, 2011b: xiv). This analytic is premised on a reproductive logic (a system of permanently unequal exchange in which surplus value is transferred from the periphery to the core) that has difficulty explaining movement from the periphery to the core, a process that, as we note above, is a central feature of contemporary international relations. Finally, in contrast to world systems theorists, our use of 'core' and 'periphery' is analytical rather than explanatory – we deploy these terms to delineate polities according to their relationship to the modern mode of power. This allows us to capture the central features of the core–periphery international order that emerged during the long nineteenth century and chart its partial erosion over recent decades.

These six assumptions produce two main claims. First, a set of dynamics established during the nineteenth century intertwined in a powerful configuration that reshaped the basis of international order in such a way as to define a new era. Second, this order not only transformed international relations during the long nineteenth century, it also underpins core aspects of contemporary international relations. As such, our contention is that the global transformation is central to understanding both the emergence of modern international relations and the principal features of contemporary international order. If this claim stands up, then IR needs to rethink many of its principal areas of interest and reconsider how it defines much of its contemporary agenda. As we show in the chapters that follow, many central concerns of the discipline, from dynamics of war-making to debates about the changing character of sovereignty, have their roots in the global transformation. Marginalizing modernity means that IR rests on unstable foundations.

Structure

Our argument unfolds in three sections. The first section establishes the foundations for the book as a whole. In Chapter 1, we outline the principal features of the global transformation, showing how industrialization, the emergence of rational states and ideologies of progress transformed the structure of international order during the long nineteenth century. This chapter also provides the basis for our claim that core aspects of contemporary international relations can be understood as an ongoing working-out of dynamics unleashed during this period. Our aim is not to make a novel theoretical argument regarding the causes of the global transformation – that would require a different book. Rather, we use scholarship in economic history, world history and historical sociology to build a composite picture of the global transformation, focusing on the ways in which its nexus of intertwined dynamics served to drive the development of modern international relations. We do not introduce these literatures as parallel tracks or providers of diverting background material. Rather, we synthesize these fields of enquiry, explicitly linking debates in IR to those in cognate disciplines. The result is a shared conversation about how to conceptualize, historicize and theorize global modernity.

Chapter 2 examines the ways in which IR scholarship currently approaches the nineteenth century. It is not our claim that *all* IR scholarship ignores the nineteenth century – it is relatively easy to find work that refers to the Concert of Europe or to the rise of the firm, and which interrogates the thought of nineteenth-century figures such as Clausewitz, Marx and Nietzsche. However, for the most part, the global transformation is treated in one of three ways: as an absence; as a point of data accumulation; or as a fragment in a wider research programme. As such, our intervention is motivated by the failure of IR as a *discipline* to understand the nineteenth century as home to a *systemic* transformation. We examine the reasons for this lacuna and establish why it creates difficulties for effective theorization of both the emergence and institutionalization of modern international relations.

The second section of the book provides the empirical ballast for our theoretical claims. Each chapter looks at a particular meme associated with international relations, in order to: (a) show how this issue was transformed by nineteenth-century developments; and (b) trace the downstream effects of this transformation to the present day. The aim of these chapters is to highlight principal storylines and key processes that are crucial to how we think about international relations. In other words, we develop an analytical narrative that illustrates the significance of nineteenth-century processes to twentieth- and twenty-first-century international relations. Such an enterprise necessarily simplifies detail and compresses complexity. We make no attempt to compete with area studies and issue experts, or with those who carry out fine-tuned, granular historical analysis. There are, as there always must be in an exercise of this kind, historical gaps in our account. Our contribution is the overview itself, which we see as providing stronger foundations for the discipline than any currently provided.

Chapter 3 focuses on the 'shrinking of the planet', which many globalization theorists link to twentieth-century changes in finance, trade, communication technologies and global governance. We show how these modern forms of interaction capacity not only originated in nineteenth-century developments, but also had dramatic impacts on international relations at the time. We then chart their ongoing impact on the contemporary international order. Chapter 4 examines the emergence of modern ideologies of progress – liberalism, nationalism, socialism and 'scientific' racism – again unpacking their nineteenth-century origins and highlighting their role in the formation of contemporary international order. Chapter 5 explores the ways in which polities were transformed during the global transformation, rooting the development of rational states in the intensification of imperialism, the revolutionary challenge, and the relationship between states and markets. Chapters 6 and 7 discuss the emergence, development and partial erosion of a distinctively modern core–periphery international order. Chapter 6 examines the establishment of extreme inequality between core and periphery during the nineteenth century and explores the ways in which elements of this inequality have been sustained during the twentieth and twenty-first centuries. Chapter 7 looks at how, when and where the gap between core and periphery has narrowed or closed, particularly since 1945. Chapter 8 turns to the specific issue of how the global transformation impacted on great powers and their interrelations, and how this carried through to contemporary international relations by transforming the nature and utility of war.

The final section of the book is made up of two chapters that focus on the implications of our argument. Chapter 9 studies the ways in which our argument both disrupts and adds value to contemporary debates in international relations, including reassessment of the proposed power shift from the Atlantic region to Asia, the competition between varieties of capitalist states, and the possibility of a world without superpowers. Our argument is that the trajectory of the revolutions of modernity has been from a nineteenth- and twentieth-century world of 'centred globalism' to one of 'decentred globalism'. Contemporary international order is highly globalized. But the power gap that marked international relations over the past 200 years is beginning to close – international order is becoming increasingly decentred. Decentred globalism provides a foundation for international affairs quite unlike the core–periphery global order of the past two centuries. It also provides a backdrop quite unlike the world before the nineteenth century, in which there were many centres of power, but these were only lightly connected with each other. Chapter 9 surveys the main dynamics that sustain a world of decentred globalism.

The book's final chapter outlines the consequences of our argument for IR as a discipline. It notes the ways in which a fuller understanding of the global transformation reshapes the ways that the discipline should think about six issue-areas: power, security, globalization, ideational structure, periodization and history. It concludes by looking at how a fuller engagement with the global transformation affects IR's self-understanding as a discipline.

keep this in mind for a possible final

PART I

The Global Transformation and IR

This section establishes several themes that serve as the backdrop to the more detailed discussions that animate later parts of the book. Chapter 1 addresses world historical transformations as a general phenomenon, showing how the nineteenth-century global transformation fits into broader patterns of macro-historical change. Chapter 2 sketches out the limited ways in which IR scholarship currently examines the nineteenth century, why its appreciation of the global transformation is weak compared to cognate disciplines, and why IR's failure to give global modernity systematic attention is a problem both for how the discipline theorizes its subject matter and how it understands the nature of macro-historical transformations.

1 | *The Global Transformation*

Introduction

As noted in the Introduction, the global transformation was asynchronous and interactive, produced by the 'promiscuous interconnections' of peoples, institutions and practices on a worldwide scale (Bayly, 2004: 5; Hobson, 2004: 304). These promiscuous interconnections so transformed the means by which power was accumulated and expressed that it generated 'the first ever global hierarchy of physical, economic and cultural power' (Darwin, 2007: 298), a 'single power network' with its centre in northwestern Europe (Mann, 1993: 11). The contemporary international order sits downstream from this first global power hierarchy and is largely constructed in the terms and forms established by it.

This chapter takes a closer look at these dynamics. The first section examines previous macro-transformations in world history. Second, we demonstrate how the range of dynamics that emerged during the nineteenth century intertwined in a powerful configuration that reshaped the bases of international order sufficiently to justify comparison with these previous transformations. The third part shows that this configuration continues to serve as the underpinning for much of contemporary international relations.

The General Nature of World Historical Transformations

Our argument could be read as making the case for the long nineteenth century as containing a series of transformations sufficient to warrant being seen as an epochal shift. We are not wholly opposed to such a reading. But we do not want to be drawn into the range of controversies that surround debates around macro-periodization (Buzan and Little, 2000: 389–406). We focus instead on how global modernity constituted a transformation broadly comparable to the shift from hunter-gathering to agriculture that started around 12,000 years ago. This comparison is well established, particularly in arguments that see shifts in 'mode of production' as turning points in world history (e.g. Hobsbawm, 1962: 13; Gellner, 1988: 16). These two transformations are unquestionably major developments in world history. As such, comparing them offers some pointers as to how such world historical transformations take place.

Before the emergence of agriculture, the limited productivity of hunter-gathering could sustain only a small human population that was mainly organized into bands of a few dozen people. The lifestyle was mobile and hand-to-mouth, and the social structure had little by way of hierarchy or functional specialization. Hunter-gathering was fundamentally a political economy of subsistence, but there was nevertheless some trading and other forms of exchange between bands. Over time, this relay trade could move prestige goods such as amber and arrowheads over long distances (Buzan and Little, 2000: 111–62).

Agriculture, by contrast, was a vastly more productive political economy capable of producing surpluses that could be used to support more complex forms of society. Cultivating the land generated a sedentary, settled lifestyle that had implications for everything from frequency of childbirth to property rights (Mann, 1986: 34–102; Fagan, 1993: 117–41). Surplus production supported a larger and more stratified population, and could be stored, controlled, traded, stolen and fought over. The expanding population organized itself into larger units, which became both increasingly hierarchical and more functionally specialized. Agricultural societies formed an expanding leading edge, steadily dominating more of the planet and marginalizing hunter-gathering communities (Buzan and Little, 2000: 111–240). This process eventually generated a second major transformation around 6,000 years ago with the emergence of cities, city-states and, eventually, empires. These developments marked a dramatic shift in the scale and complexity of human organization. Increasing productivity sustained a rising human population grouped into larger settlements. In some places, agriculture provided incentives for the larger and more complex forms of social order necessary to build and maintain complex irrigation systems. The same was true of trading circuits, which facilitated the emergence of larger, more specialized social orders, not only to conduct trade, but also to manufacture trade goods. These developments precipitated the rise of cities. And cities, in turn, helped to sustain larger, more complex societies, which featured a step-level increase in both hierarchy and functional specialization. Urban societies had kings, priests, artisans, soldiers, merchants and bureaucrats, along with organized religions, money, writing and calendars. These cities and their trading, cultural and diplomatic networks became the building blocks of the agrarian empires that dominated the ancient and classical worlds. Several of the religions and cultures they fostered are still a major presence in world affairs.

A related form of agrarian order – pastoralism – developed around 4,000 years ago mainly amongst steppe peoples (Khazanov, 1984; Buzan and Little, 2000: 183–8; Neumann and Wigen, 2013). Pastoralism was based on a nomadic lifestyle and a political economy of animal herding. Pastoralists developed the use of horses as riding animals and this underpinned the power of what the 'civilized' agrarian world knew as 'barbarian' tribes. The division of labour between farmers and herders generated trade between them, but the military effectiveness of 'barbarians' meant that they could raid as well as trade. Sometimes they were able to form empires of their own, like the Mongols, or overrun and destroy agrarian empires, as happened to Rome. More frequently, they were able to conquer agrarian territories and become the ruling elite of agrarian empires, such as the Ottomans, the Mongols, the Qing and the early Arab empires that ruled Mesopotamia, Egypt, North Africa and Spain.

If one thinks in broad terms about these transformations, four characteristics stand out. First, they triggered basic changes in both the scale of social orders and their mode of organization. In other words, social relations underwent a revolutionary transformation. In general, social orders became larger, more complex and more differentiated, for example into distinct political units (such as city-states and empires), into hierarchies of status and rank, and into distinct social roles (priest, soldier, artisan, farmer, etc.). In this way, social life became both larger in scale and more complex in its forms of differentiation. This increase in 'social density' meant an extension in the collective power of social orders to exploit both populations and nature (Mann, 1993: 13–14; Johnson and Earle, 2000).

Second, major transformations of this kind have a distinct point or points of origin in which a particular configuration emerges and is sustained. And this configuration is produced and reproduced through inter-societal interactions. Morris (2010: ch. 2) charts how settled agriculture spread from the hilly flanks of Mesopotamia north-west

into Europe, and from other originating cores, as in China, to wider
zones. Further changes spread outwards from the leading edge or edges.
The pace of spread varied according to the mediating effects of social
and physical environments. Agriculture was slow to spread to less
productive soils and climates, and some modes of social order were
more receptive to it than others. In short: unevenness is a basic fact of
historical development (Rosenberg, 2010 and 2013). Different peoples
and places encounter macro-transformations at different times and
under different circumstances.

Related to this is a third characteristic: as well as being uneven in
origin, new power configurations are uneven in terms of outcomes.
Each social order that encounters the new configuration has its own
way of adapting to it. The 'whip of external necessity' (Trotsky, 1997
[1932]: 27) produced by a new power configuration has often been
coercive, occurring through force of arms. At other times, inter-societal
dynamics have taken the form of emulation. Some societies do not take
on the new configuration at all, either because of internal resistance to
the changes it required, or because of attempts by leading-edge polities
to maintain inequalities between them by denying access to elements of
the transformation. Others succeed in developing indigenous versions
of the new configuration. These 'late' developers are not carbon copies
of the original adopters, but develop their own distinctive characteristics. In this sense, the interactions between different social orders
produce not convergence, but (often unstable) amalgams of new and
old. These 'contradictory fusions' make clear that historical development is not linear or sequential, but jumbled and, often, compressed
(Rosenberg, 2010).

The fourth lesson is that increases in productivity and population,
plus increases in the complexity of social orders and physical technologies, have produced a denser, more deeply connected international order. The expanded scale, complexity and technological
capacities of agrarian polities meant that they had more intense
relationships with both their neighbours and peoples further away
than their predecessors. Those relationships were military, political,
economic or cultural, or some mixture of these. In this way, levels of
interdependence within the international sphere have increased over
time, meaning that every society has become less self-contained and
more exposed to developments elsewhere. As societies became larger
in scale and more functionally differentiated, differences between

them were accentuated and interactions between them intensified. Late developers could not escape the influence of earlier adopters. Unevenness and combination were mutually constitutive and mutually reinforcing features of macro-historical transformations.[1]

The nineteenth-century configuration of industrialization, rational state-building and ideologies of progress displays all of these characteristics. Because we are little more than a couple of centuries into global modernity, it is difficult to discern the extent to which it compares with previous macro-transformations. But even with a relatively limited perspective through which to work, the basic pattern of the global transformation shares many similarities to those triggered by the shift from hunter-gathering bands to agriculture and cities.

First, if macro-transformations unleash new resources that both support increases in population and create new sources of wealth and power, this was experienced during the global transformation as a new

---

[1] Our understanding of development as 'uneven' and 'combined' draws heavily on the work of Justin Rosenberg (2010 and 2013). As we noted briefly in the Introduction, unevenness is a constant, necessary feature of the social world. Throughout human history, social orders have existed alongside others with differing geographical and historical endowments. But this unevenness is only part of the story. Social orders also exist in combination with others – that is, they trade, coerce, emulate, borrow and steal from others. The interactions between these diversely situated social orders are what drive historical development: powerful polities coerce weaker polities; those who experience their social order as 'backward' attempt to 'catch up' with those considered to be more powerful, and so on. During the global transformation, degrees of combination intensified because of both technological breakthroughs (such as steamships, railways and electronic means of communication from the telegraph to the internet) and social practices (such as imperialism, colonialism and the expansion of the market). Yet such developments also heightened degrees of unevenness between those in possession of the new mode of power and those without it. The global transformation produced both convergence and divergence simultaneously. This optic stands as an alternative to Waltz's (1979: 76) formula of homogenization into like units through 'socialization and competition', world polity approaches that see modernity as heightening homogenization through top-down diffusionary mechanisms (e.g. Meyer et al., 1997), and world systems theory, which focuses on the structural differentiation wrought by market expansion (e.g. Wallerstein, 1979 and 1983). In contrast to these approaches, the analytic of uneven and combined development (UCD) stresses the ways in which the timing and circumstances of interactions between diversely situated social orders generate *varied* outcomes. In this way historical development is seen as multilinear rather than linear, variegated rather than singular, and uneven rather than smooth. The following chapters show the utility of this framework to analysing historical development since the nineteenth century.

mode of power. From this point on, great powers were defined by the mode of power constituted by the configuration of industrialization, rational state-building and ideologies of progress. The modern mode of power generated a new basis for how power was constituted, organized and expressed, transforming the ways in which interactions in the international sphere took place and were understood.

Second, as noted above, macro-transformations contain a leading edge or edges where the transformation coheres first, creating deep changes in social orders, including substantial increases in complexity and differentiation. The leading edge of global modernity was located in north-west Europe, spreading over the next few decades into a broader Atlantic region that we capture through the generic label *the West*. The West is a clumsy term, but it is the least bad option available, embracing not just Europe (with particular emphasis on the northern and western parts of the continent), but also the Americas (with particular emphasis on the United States).[2] As also noted above, leading-edge polities transmit – and often impose – their new mode of power on other parts of the world. The main dynamics that underpinned these processes during the long nineteenth century were capitalism, imperialism and ideologies of progress. For example, British development relied on its position as the imperial centre of an Atlantic economy nurtured by the raw materials wrought from slavery, indentured labour and the plantation system (Gilroy, 1993: 2; Blackburn, 1997: 510, 530, 581; Frank, 1998: 277–8). Most people in Britain saw the extension of the market and imperial practices as 'progressive', attendant on a worldview that divided the world into categories of 'civilized', 'barbarian' and 'savage'. Such distinctions were crucial to the transmission of the new mode of power.

Third, as with previous major transformations, global modernity was uneven in terms of both origins and outcomes. The intensification of the new mode of power resulted in uneven development, uneven both because the new mode of power cohered in some societies earlier than others and because leading-edge states could impose themselves

---

[2] By using the West as our point of reference, we sidestep debates about the precise location and nomenclature of global modernity's early adopters. Readers curious about these debates can take their pick from a range of options, including: Europe (e.g. Jones, 1981); the Anglo-world (e.g. Belich, 2009); the North Atlantic (e.g. Pomeranz, 2000); or the North Sea Area (e.g. Broadberry, 2014).

on those without access to it. For example, during the nineteenth century, German industrialization was not a replica of British development, but took distinct form, even as it borrowed from the British experience. Likewise Soviet, or more recently Chinese, development also maintained its own 'characteristics', combining new technologies and productive forces alongside inherited social formations. In short, development over the past two centuries has been multilinear rather than linear, proceeding in fits and starts rather than through smooth gradations, and with many variations in terms of outcomes. One indicator of the ways in which polities adapted in diverse ways to the global transformation is the variety of ideologies that have emerged to define different assemblages of economy, politics and culture in the modern world: liberalism, social democracy, conservatism, socialism, communism, fascism, patrimonialism, and more.

Fourth, as with previous macro-transformations, the global transformation has produced larger, more complex social orders bound together in denser, more interdependent ways. Since the nineteenth century, development, despite its unevenness and diversity, has become increasingly combined. Industrialization produced a single world economy for the first time. This global economy was enabled by improved technologies of transportation and communication, technologies that also made war and politics global, producing an integrated, hierarchical, global order. During the global transformation, therefore, the development gap between polities opened more widely than ever before and, at the same time (and for the same reasons), the planet was bound together more tightly than in previous eras.

While the relative depth of political, economic and cultural transformations generated by the shift to agricultural societies was comparable to that generated by the emergence of global modernity, the agrarian transformation happened slowly – its impact was spread out over millennia. By contrast, the global transformation has been compressed into a compact time span, with major changes happening on a scale of decades rather than centuries. This disjuncture, and the acceleration of historical development that ensued from it, are what defines the commonality between the nineteenth century and the contemporary world. It is also what distinguishes this period from those that preceded it.

of it mined in the Americas, was shipped to the Philippines to finance European trade with China (Barrett, 1990: 249). Equally importantly, as subsequent chapters relate, the position of leading-edge societies was sustained by a range of coercive practices, including colonialism, the deliberate de-industrialization of other societies, and the forcible dispossession of land and resources. The result of these practices was that parts of the West gained a considerable power advantage over many other parts of the world.

The power advantage gained by Britain and a handful of other states during the nineteenth century represented a major change from earlier periods. For many centuries, the high cultures of Asia were held in respect, even awe, in many parts of Europe; the West interacted with Asian powers sometimes as political equals and, at other times, as supplicants (Lach, 1965: 825; Jones, 2001; Darwin, 2007: 117). India's merchant class produced garments that 'clothed the world' (Bayly, 1983; Chaudhuri, 1985; Parthasarathi, 2011: 22), while the sophistication of Chinese administration and commercial practices was widely admired (Wong, 1997). Between 1600 and 1800, India and China were so dominant in manufacturing and many areas of technology that Western take-off is sometimes linked to its relative 'backwardness' – the desire to emulate more advanced practices acted as a spur to European industrialization (Parthasarathi, 2011: 10).

Up to around 1800, therefore, the principal points of wealth differentiation were within rather than between societies (Davis, 2002: 16). There were not major differences in living standards amongst the most developed parts of the world: in the late eighteenth century, GDP per capita levels in the Yangtze River Delta of China were around 10% lower than the wealthiest parts of Europe, less than the differences in the contemporary world between most of the EU and the US (Bayly, 2004: 2; van Zanden, 2004: 120–1). In 1750, the Yangtze region produced as much cloth per capita as Britain did in 1800 (Pomeranz, 2000: 18). Overall, a range of quality of life indicators, from levels of life expectancy to calorie intakes, indicates a basic equivalence between China and Europe up to the start of the nineteenth century (Hobson, 2004: 76).

A century later, the most advanced areas of Europe and the United States held between a tenfold and twelvefold advantage in levels of GDP per capita over their Chinese equivalents (Bayly, 2004: 2;

van Zanden, 2004: 121). In 1820, Asian powers produced 60.7% of the world's GDP, and Europe and its offshoots (mainly the United States) only 34.2%; by 1913, Europe and its offshoots held 68.3% of global GDP and Asia only 24.5% (Maddison, 2001: 127, 263). Between 1800 and 1900, China's share of global production dropped from 33% to 6%, India's from 20% to 2%, and today's 'Third World' from 75% to 7% (Christian, 2004: 463). During the same period, Europe's share of global manufacturing rose from 16% to 62% (Ferguson, 2001: 122). Between 1870 and 1939, levels of life expectancy rose from 45 to 65 in northwestern Europe and the United States; yet, there was no increase in life expectancy in Africa, Latin America or Asia, with the exception of Japan (Topik and Wells, 2012: 602–3; Osterhammel, 2014: 170–2). The rapid turnaround during the nineteenth century represents a major swing in global power.

The extent of this volte-face is captured in Table 1.1, which uses modern notions of 'developed' and 'Third World' to gauge the gap in production and wealth generated by the emergence of modernity during the long nineteenth century. As the table shows, from a position of slight difference between polities in 1750 in terms of GNP per capita, 'developed' states opened up a gap over 'Third World' states of nearly 350% by 1913. And from holding less than a third of the total GNP of today's 'Third World' countries in 1750, by 1913, 'developed' countries held almost double the GNP of the 'Third World'.

Table 1.1: *GNP/GNP per capita, 1750–1913*

	Total GNP (billions)			GNP per capita (dollars)		
	Developed countries	Third World	World	Developed countries	Third World	World
1750	35	112	147	182	188	187
1800	47	137	184	198	188	191
1830	67	150	217	237	183	197
1860	118	159	277	324	174	220
1880	180	164	344	406	176	250
1900	297	184	481	540	175	301
1913	430	217	647	662	192	364

Source: Bairoch, 1981: 7–8, 12.

Why

There are a number of explanations for the 'great divergence' between East and West (Pomeranz, 2000; Osterhammel, 2014: 637–51). At the risk of oversimplification, it is possible to highlight four main modes of explanation: accounts that stress economic advantages; those that focus on political processes; those that emphasize ideational factors; and those focusing on material factors of geography, environment and technology.

Economic accounts are divided between liberals and Marxists. Liberals underline several features of the rise of the West: the role of impersonal institutions in guaranteeing free trade and competitive markets; the legal protection offered by liberal states to finance and industry; and the capacity of liberal constitutions to restrict levels of domestic conflict (North et al., 2009: 2–3, 21–2, 121–2, 129–30, 188). Liberal accounts also stress the superior accountancy practices of Europeans, particularly double entry bookkeeping which, it is argued, allowed for a clear evaluation of profit, thereby enabling joint-stock companies to provide credit in depersonalized, rationalized form – the hallmark of commercial capitalism (North et al., 2009: 1–2; Weber, 2001 [1905]). Europeans also enjoyed better access to credit and bills of exchange, which provided predictability to market interactions and incentivized the development of long-term syndicated debt (e.g. Kennedy, 1989: 22–4). Marxists focus on the ways in which, in north-western Europe, a system of generalized commodification and commercial exchange extracted productive labour as surplus value, realized this through the wage contract, and returned it as profit (e.g. Anderson, 1974: 26, 403; Halperin, 2013: 32). This set off a 'capital intensive' path oriented around private property regimes that enabled capital to be released for investment in manufacturing and finance (Brenner, 1985).

A second literature focuses mainly on political dynamics, stressing the particular conditions of state-formation that allowed European states to construct trustworthy, inclusive political institutions (Acemoglu and Robinson, 2012: 43, 81), negotiate effectively between elites (Spruyt, 1994: 31, 180), and generate superior revenue flows through efficient taxation regimes (Tilly, 1975: 73–4). Some of this literature stresses the active role played by states in assuring favourable conditions for industrialization to take hold, ranging from restricting domestic labour mobility to protecting nascent industries (Parthasarathi, 2011: 10–11,

145, 151–2). Other accounts concentrate on shifts in the means of coercion and, in particular, on the frequency of European interstate wars: European powers were involved in interstate wars in nearly 75% of the years between 1494 and 1975 (Mann, 2012: 24; also see Mann, 1993: 1). The frequency of European interstate war, it is argued, led to technological and tactical advances, the development of standing armies, and the expansion of permanent bureaucracies (e.g. Howard, 1976; Kennedy, 1989: 26; Tilly, 1990: 14–16; Bobbitt, 2002: 69–70, 346; Rosenthal and Wong, 2011: 228–9; Morris, 2014). In this way, nineteenth-century states combined their need for taxation (in order to fight increasingly costly wars) with support for financial institutions that could, in turn, deliver the funds required for investment in navigation, shipbuilding and armaments (Burbank and Cooper, 2010: 176; Stasavage, 2011: 3–4, 156). 'War and preparation for war' gave European states a decisive advantage over polities in other parts of the world (Tilly, 1990: 31; also see Hintze, 1975 [1906]), even if these advantages were both unintentional and unanticipated (Rosenthal and Wong, 2011: 230; Morris 2014).

A third set of explanations highlights the role of ideational schemas in the breakthrough to modernity, whether this is considered to have occurred via scientific advances associated with the Enlightenment (e.g. Gellner, 1988: 113–16; Jacob, 1997; Mokyr, 2009; Israel, 2010), the swamping of diverse forms of reasoning by 'means–ends' rationality (e.g. Polanyi, 2001 [1944]; Weber, 2001 [1905]; Foucault, 2002 [1969]), the 'disciplinary' role played by religions, such as Calvinism, which influenced the routines of modern armies, court systems and welfare regimes (e.g. Gorski, 2003; also see Weber, 2001 [1905]), new ideas of authoritative rule that led to the reconstruction of notions of political space as exclusive, linear and homogeneous (e.g. Ruggie, 1993; Branch, 2014), the emergence of 'secular religions' such as nationalism (e.g. Mayall, 1990; Hall, 1999), or the ways in which 'the native personality' was 'recognized' through unequal legal practices such as protectorates and, later, mandates (e.g. Anghie, 2004: 65–97).

A fourth set of approaches concentrate on the geographical, demographic and technological advantages enjoyed by the West. Jones (1981: xiv, 4, 226) highlights the environmental advantages of a temperate climate that was inhospitable to parasites and a range of demographic factors, most notably later marriage habits in Europe than in Asia, which led to lower fertility rates and, in turn, lower population densities (also see Broadberry, 2014). Geographical factors are also cited as the precursors to the rise of distinct and varied cultures able to protect themselves within a diverse physical topography (Chirot, 1985; Jones, 1987: 104–26). Other accounts stress the knock-on effects of deforestation in Britain that, it is argued, incentivized the development of alternative energy sources to wood (such as coal) and new energy-grabbing techniques (such as iron smelting) (Parthasarathi, 2011: 2). This argument links to approaches that see British industrialization as originating in the unusual, and fortunate, co-location of coal and iron (Goldstone, 2002). The cheapness of these materials in Britain, added to the country's expensive labour, produced a capital-intensive society that made 'macro-inventions', such as steam engines and cotton spinning machinery, particularly profitable (Allen, 2009: 136). These macro-inventions were an opportunity for employers to reduce the costs of labour, something unnecessary in societies where labour was cheap and energy was expensive (such as China and Japan). It was only when energy costs came down during the course of the nineteenth century that industrial technologies diffused, providing labour-intensive societies with sufficient cause – and opportunity – to follow Britain's lead (Allen, 2009; also see Sugihara, 2013).

As discussed in the Introduction, our argument is that global modernity arose from a configuration of industrialization, rational state-building and ideologies of progress. We outline how this configuration generated global modernity both below and in subsequent chapters. For now, it is worth noting the inter-societal 'system of linkages' that helped to constitute global modernity (Wolf, 1997: 5, 71). First, European success was predicated on imperialism and, in particular, on imperial 'circulatory systems' (Gilroy, 1993: ch. 3). Germany's colonies in East Africa were forced into producing cotton for export just as Dutch Indonesia became a vehicle for the production of sugar, tobacco and, later, rubber. In similar vein, after the East India Company was ceded the right to administer and raise taxes in Bengal, they made the cultivation of opium obligatory, subsequently exporting it to China in a trading system propped up by force of arms. Through imperialism, European powers exchanged raw materials for manufactured goods and used violence to ensure low production prices (Pomeranz, 2000: 54). Although the gains from these circuits are difficult to measure precisely, they were certainly profitable (for a sceptical view, see O'Brien, 1988 and 2004). The Atlantic slave trade, for example, returned profits to British investors at an average rate of 9.5% at the turn of the nineteenth century (Blackburn, 1997: 510). By 1913, the Dutch received 700 million guilders per year in revenue from the Indonesian plantation system (Maddison, 2007b: 135).

Second, European polities assumed control, often coercively, of the trade of commodities as diverse as sandalwood, tea, otter skins and sea cucumbers, as well as those in silver, cotton and opium. As noted above, Europeans used silver from the Americas and opium from India in order to buy entry into Asian economies. This led to radically unequal patterns of trade: while Britain provided 50% of Argentina's imports and exports, and virtually all of its capital investment, in 1900, Argentina provided just 10% of Britain's imports and exports (Mann, 2012: 39). By 1913, half of Argentina's economy was foreign-owned (Frieden, 2006: 20). It also led to radically unequal patterns of growth: whereas India's GDP grew at an average of 0.2% per year in the century before independence, Britain's grew at ten times this rate – India provided a 'colonial tribute' to Britain in that its surpluses were expatriated to London where they were used to maintain sterling and reduce balance of payments deficits (Silver and Arrighi, 2003: 338). These disparities forged transnational networks that were fundamental to the global extension of the market – Indian *nawabs* and Argentinian comprador elites were as implicated in global modernity as British industrialists and engineers (Burbank and Cooper, 2010: 238).

Third, European advances arose from the emulation and fusion of non-European ideas and technologies: the techniques used in the production of Indian wootz steel, for example, were replicated by Benjamin Huntsman in his Sheffield workshop, while technologies used in the cotton industry drew heavily on earlier Chinese advances (McNeill, 1991: xvi; Hobson, 2004: 211–13; Riello, 2013). These ideas and technologies were carried, in part, via migration: over 50 million Europeans emigrated between 1800 and 1914, most of them to the United States – by 1914, half of the population of the US was foreign born (Crosby, 2004: 301; Hoerder, 2011: 279). Six million Europeans emigrated to Argentina between 1857 and 1930; at the onset of the First World War, one-third of Argentinians, and half the population of Buenos Aires, had been born outside the country (Crosby, 2004: 301). A 'settler revolution', particularly pronounced within the Anglophone world, acted as a 'caucasian tsunami', integrating metropolitan and frontier zones, and establishing powerful new transnational linkages (Crosby, 2004: 300; Belich, 2009; Schwarz, 2011). At the same time, up to 37 million labourers left India, China, Malaya and Java during the nineteenth and early twentieth centuries (Davis, 2002: 208; Castles et al., 2014: 88), many of them serving as indentured labour in imperial possessions. Global modernity was fuelled by a worldwide intensification in the circulation of peoples, ideas, resources and technologies. Indeed, it could be argued that global modernity was predicated on Indian textiles, Chinese porcelain, African slaves and colonial labour (Wolf, 1997: 3–4). These inter-societal interactions helped to produce a new configuration of power with its centre in northwestern Europe.

When

The global transformation was not a 'big bang'. In fact, the emergence of industrialization, the rational state and ideologies of progress was gradual and uneven. Aspects of industrialization, for example, were formed in small-scale 'industrious revolutions' in which households became centres for the consumption of global products ranging from Javanese spices to Chinese tea (De Vries, 2008; Broadberry, 2014). Even central nodal points of the global transformation, such as London and Lancashire, contained acute pockets of deprivation. Some British regions, most notably East Anglia and the West Country, experienced a decline rather than growth during the nineteenth century, as did many parts of Europe, including Flanders, Southern Italy and Western France (Wolf, 1997: 297). Even within core metropolitan zones, therefore, experiences of the global transformation were uneven.

Such issues have fostered considerable debate over both the extent and timing of the global transformation and, in particular, the significance of the shift to industrialization. Some scholarship has pushed the basic transformation of European societies to a later period, usually the first part of the twentieth century (e.g. Mayer, 2010); others have traced 'world capitalism' back to the late fifteenth century (e.g. Wallerstein, 1983: 19) or even earlier (e.g. Mann, 1986: 374; Abu-Lughod, 1989; Frank and Gills, 1993). It is certainly the case that trade routes connected entrepôts such as Malacca, Samarkand, Hangzhou, Genoa and the Malabar Coast well before the nineteenth century. Long-distance commodity chains operating for many centuries leading up to the global transformation established trading networks in silks, cotton, sugar, tea, linen, porcelain and spices. In part, these networks were sustained by 'ecological transfers' between the Americas and Europe: maize, potatoes, tomatoes, beans and tobacco were imported from the 'New World', while horses, cattle, pigs, chickens, sheep, mules, oxen, vines, wheat, rice and coffee travelled in the opposite direction (Maddison, 2005: 2).[4] These ecological exchanges played a major role in increasing productivity, and both widening and deepening trade networks. So too did the trafficking in African slaves, which fostered a 'triangular trade' in which the demand for sugar in London furnished the plantation system in the Caribbean, which was supplied by African slaves and North American provisions (Blackburn, 1997: 4, 510). Capitalist accumulation did not arrive in the nineteenth century unannounced.

However, even if commercial capitalist logics – 'relentless accumulation' and commodification (Wallerstein, 1983: 14–16) – shared affinities with industrial capitalism, the system of the fifteenth–eighteenth centuries operated on a markedly different scale and intensity from its nineteenth-century successor. Most notably, the degree of intensification in terms of simultaneously differential and interactive development that characterized the nineteenth century was distinct from previous capitalist systems. Until the deepening of interaction capacity that took place during the long nineteenth century, most economic activities took part in 'microeconomies' with a 20-mile circumference (Schwartz, 2000: 14). Those activities that went beyond the micro-scale, such as long-distance trading 'corridors', were only lightly connected (Frank and Gills, 1993: 86). Commodity chains were an uneven archipelago of cities, caravans and trade fairs. The nineteenth-century marketization of social relations fuelled the growth of a global system of much more densely connected networks, governed through the price mechanism and structured via hierarchical core–periphery relations. Western states established dependencies around the world that forcibly restructured local economies, turning them into specialist export-intensive vehicles for the metropole. To take one example, Indian textiles were either banned from Britain or levied with high tariffs,

---

[4] Perhaps the most important ecological transfers were diseases. Smallpox, measles, influenza and yellow fever had killed two-thirds of the population of the Americas by the middle of the sixteenth century.

while British manufacturing products were forcibly imported into India without duty (Wolf, 1997: 251). Between 1814 and 1828, British cloth exports to India rose from 800,000 yards to over 40 million yards, while during the same period, Indian cloth exports to Britain halved (Goody, 1996: 131).

Alongside the debates about the 'when' of industrialization lie similar questions about the emergence of the rational state. As with debates about the emergence of industrialization, it is clear that a range of antecedent processes enabled the rise of the rational state during the nineteenth century. Some scholarship sees rational states as emerging before the nineteenth century, pointing to the impact on state administrative capacities of the 'military revolution' of the sixteenth and seventeenth centuries (Howard, 1976; Mann, 1986: 445–6 and 1993: 1; Downing, 1992: ch. 3) and the eighteenth-century development of states as calculating 'power containers' responsible for the certification of fiduciary money (Giddens, 1985: 13, 126–8, 153). Others see the British 'fiscal-military juggernaut' that emerged from the Glorious Revolution and the War of the Spanish Succession as the first modern state, constituting a system of governance that was thereafter emulated by many of its rivals (Brewer, 1990: 251; Pincus, 2009).

However, it was only during the nineteenth century that leading-edge states began to claim monopolistic control over the use of legitimate force within a particular territory. Such claims were not easily realized. In the eighteenth century, institutions such as the Dutch East India Company held a constitutional warrant to 'make war, conclude treaties, acquire territory and build fortresses' (Thomson, 1994: 10–11). These companies remained influential throughout the nineteenth century: the British parliament provided a concession of several million acres of land to the British North Borneo Company as late as 1881, while the Imperial British East Africa Company and the British South Africa Company also held 'state-like powers of governance' (Phillips and Sharman, forthcoming: 239–40). As these examples illustrate, such companies were not 'private actors' whose remit was restricted to trade and other commercial matters. Rather, they were formal political institutions – 'company-states' – that enjoyed the authority to: 'erect and administer law; collect taxes; provide protection; inflict punishment; regulate economic, religious and civic life; conduct diplomacy and wage war; make claims to jurisdiction over land and sea', and more (Stern, 2011: 3–6).

Despite the extensive powers held by company-states such as the British East India Company and the Vereenigde Oostindische Compagnie, and their persistence into the nineteenth century, this period saw the ceding of a range of responsibilities to rational states (Stern, 2011: 209–14). Polities in the core sought control over competences previously reserved for either local intermediaries (such as policing and taxation) or company-states (the East India Company's commercial monopoly on Asian trade was withdrawn in 1813) (Tilly, 1990: 23–9; Darwin, 2012: 168). A range of international agreements sought to eliminate privateering and restricted the use of mercenaries. After the French Revolution, armies and navies became more distinctly national, coming under the direct fiscal control of the state. Although nation-states coexisted with other polity forms, including company-states, empires, dependencies and colonies – and many polities were both states and empires simultaneously – there was a notable 'caging' of competences within states, itself enabled by the rise of nationalism and popular sovereignty (Mann, 1988). These ideologies legitimized state borders and presented the outside world as an alien space. Imperial expansion into these alien spaces went hand-in-hand with the emergence of the sovereign nation-state. Both were seen as the 'progressive' hallmarks of 'civilized' states (Anghie, 2004: 310–20).

The nineteenth-century transformation in material capabilities was co-implicated with a transformation in ideational frameworks. During the nineteenth century, the basic framework of ideas that governed and, in part, constituted international relations underwent a marked change. Legitimating ideas such as dynasticism and divine right were weakened. In their place, a novel set of 'ideologies of progress' helped to transform both domestic and international orders. Nationalism redefined sovereignty, territoriality and citizenship, providing a potent new source of legitimacy. Nationalism's noxious sibling, 'scientific' racism, framed a pungently unequal view of social relations. Europeans reinvented African clans such as the Ashanti, Yoruba and Zulus as ancient tribes, transformed the Indian caste system into a rigid, stratified order (Dirks, 2011), racially demarcated zones within imperial territories, and homogenized indigenous peoples, such as Native Americans, into a monolithic category of 'Indians' in order to demonstrate the 'backwardness' of 'uncivilized' peoples (Quijano, 2000: 219). No system in world history so united the planet, while simultaneously wrenching it apart. Liberalism relied on a view of the 'possessive individual' and legitimized the rise of the bourgeoisie (Macpherson, 1962). Socialism challenged liberalism by seeing the industrial proletariat rather than the bourgeoisie as the principal agents of progressive change, and by prioritizing collective emancipation over individual rights. Behind these schemas was the idea of progress itself, combining material advances in science and technology with the desire to 'control' nature and 'improve' not only the human condition, but also the human stock (Drayton, 2000). Taken together, ideologies of progress made peace seem attainable in a way that had been unthinkable before the nineteenth century. But they also provided new rationales for war and imperialism. To appreciate the scale of their impact, one has only to ask what the history of the twentieth century would have looked like in the absence of nationalism, 'scientific' racism, liberalism and socialism. Quite different indeed.

It is commonplace to think of the twentieth century as the period in which titanic struggles about ideology dominated world politics. The conflict between liberalism, communism and fascism often takes centre stage in this narrative. It is less common to track these ideologies back to their (mainly) nineteenth-century origins. Yet the global transformation decisively set the stage for twentieth-century conflicts (Hobsbawm, 1962; Nisbet, 1969; Elias, 1978; Christian, 2004: 421), establishing changes in class alignment (a declining aristocracy, a rising bourgeoisie, an emerging proletariat) and a series of ideologies that cast social relations in a new light. These ideologies transformed the legitimating principles of social orders around the world, reshaping how states constructed their identities and related to each other internationally.

As noted above, debates about periodization generate often fierce debates about turning points, cumulative vs. disjunctural changes, and the nature of temporality itself.[5] It is clear that many of the developments that enabled global modernity can be traced back well before the nineteenth century. Our point is not that everything changed during the long nineteenth century. Nor do we want to argue that modernity is a year zero, a moment of 'all change', or a single point in time before which things were radically different. Rather, our contention is that, during the long nineteenth century, a concatenation of dynamics combined to produce a major transformation in terms not only of how

---

[5] For a discussion of these debates and how they make it difficult to establish a clear temporality of the nineteenth century, see Osterhammel (2014: 45–76).

social orders were organized and conceived, but also how polities and peoples related to each other. Significant changes were underway well before the last quarter of the nineteenth century. But, from the early-to-middle decades of the nineteenth century, these changes combined to generate a new mode of power that, in turn, reconstituted the foundations of international order.

How

The configuration of global modernity was a powerful 'social invention' (Mann, 1986: 525), capable of delivering 'progress' domestically (through linking industrialization with state capacity, infrastructural change and scientific research) and internationally (through coercive interventions in trade, production and financial regimes, as well as through the acquisition of new territories).

In this way, the 'European miracle' should be seen as 'capital-intensive, energy-intensive and land-gobbling' (Pomeranz, 2000: 207). It was capital-intensive because it rested on technologies that heightened productivity and thereby released capital for investment and trade (Sugihara, 2013). It was energy-intensive because it incorporated a revolution in energy enabled by the proximity and relative cheapness of coal and iron (Goldstone, 2002). And it was land-gobbling because it was predicated on a major expansion of imperialism – between 1815 and 1865, Britain conquered new territories at an average rate of 100,000 square miles per year (Kennedy, 1989: 199).[6] Between 1878 and 1913, European states claimed 8.6 million square miles of overseas territory, amounting to one-sixth of the Earth's land surface (Abernathy, 2000: 81). By the outbreak of the First World War, 80% of the world's land surface, not including uninhabited Antarctica, was under the control of European powers or colonists of European origin (Blanning, 2000: 246). The mode of power that underpinned global modernity enabled a handful of states to treat the whole world as their region.

Before the nineteenth century, Europe played a relatively peripheral role in the Eurasian trading system (Pomeranz, 2000: 4; Bayly, 2004: 2; Hobson, 2004: ch. 7; Darwin, 2007: 194; Morris, 2010: 557). As a result, many of the goods, ideas and processes that enabled the rise of

---

[6] For purposes of comparison: the current land area of Great Britain is 80,823 square miles.

Europe originated outside the region, from Indian textiles to Chinese bureaucracy. Once established, Western industrial powers began to establish a global economy in which its trade, production and finance reshaped peripheral societies. The visible hand of state power was crucial to this dynamic. As noted above, the British government tripled duties on Indian goods during the 1790s and raised them by a factor of nine in the first two decades of the nineteenth century (Darwin, 2007: 195). At the same time, the British Raj taxed Indians to pay for a sepoy army that was deployed in conflicts throughout the empire (Darwin, 2007: 16; Metcalf, 2007: 1–15). Banking flourished alongside colonialism, not least because of high rates of lending for imperial infrastructural projects. The London Stock Exchange also thrived on imperial expansion, trading government bonds and securities that were used to finance the construction of railways and other projects around the world. British foreign investment flows doubled between 1880 and 1894, and quadrupled between 1894 and 1913 (Sassen, 2006: 136, fn. 113). At the outbreak of the First World War, half of Britain's assets were held overseas. This capital investment was unevenly spread: of British overseas investment, 70% went to the settler colonies; by 1913, British investments in Australia (with a population of 6 million) were 50% higher than those made in India (with a population of 300 million) (Belich, 2009: 115). Imports were similarly uneven – during the long nineteenth century, the value of British imports from the US was usually greater than the value of its entire trade with Asia (Darwin, 2012: 168).

The uneven extension of the market through imperialism and finance capitalism generated a core–periphery order in which the ebbs and flows of metropolitan markets, commodity speculations and price fluctuations controlled the survival chances of millions of people around the world. As Davis (2002: 9) notes: 'Millions died, not outside the "modern world system", but in the very process of being forcibly incorporated into its economic and political structures.' The opening-up of new areas of production in the Americas, Russia and elsewhere greatly increased agricultural exports, intensifying competition and repressing agricultural incomes (Davis, 2002: 63; Osterhammel, 2014: 124–7). The industrial core adapted production and trade in the periphery to its needs, setting up the modern hierarchy between providers of primary and secondary products (Mann, 2012: 43). While peripheral countries could be the central producers of primary products, as India was with tea, Burma with jute, Malaya with rubber, Nigeria with palm oil, Bolivia with tin and Brazil with coffee, core states maintained their advantage in high-value exports, capital goods and finance. This division of labour and its accompanying upheavals was first established in the nineteenth century; it came to dominate the global political economy in the twentieth century.

The role of industrialization in generating a core–periphery world market was conjoined with the emergence of the rational state. Prior to modernity, economic relations were generally political tools through which elites exerted their authority: property and title went hand-in-hand with administrative offices; taxation was often contracted out to private entrepreneurs; and landlord–peasant relations were conducted directly through mechanisms such as *corvée* (Anderson, 1974: 417–22). During the global transformation, the shift to economies mediated by prices, wage-contracts and commodities generated a condition in which states provided the legal frameworks that sustained market transactions, and assumed many of the regulative and coercive functions that underpinned capitalist expansion. We discuss the changing relationship between states and markets in more detail in Chapter 5.

Also key to the emergence of the rational state were improvements in infrastructure; we detail the impact of railways and the telegraph in Chapter 3. For now, it is worth noting the role played by railways in linking areas of production with ports, both in the core and the periphery (Topik and Wells, 2012: 651). The result was increasing state coordination of both domestic and foreign affairs, fuelled partly by improvements in infrastructural capabilities and partly by the emergence of powerful ideologies such as nationalism. Nationalism shifted the locus of sovereignty from ruler to people, identifying the territory of the state with the people rather than seeing it as determined by hereditary rights or dynastic inheritance. As Chapter 4 makes clear, nationalism facilitated the overcoming of local identities, increasing the social cohesion of the state through the cultivation of national languages, themselves the result of national education systems and the advent, in many places, of national military service. Crucially, nationalism affected both *how* wars were fought (by opening up the possibility of mass mobilization) and *why* they were fought (to defend nations and to pursue territorial claims on behalf of 'misplaced' peoples). Nationalism drove the unification of some states (e.g. Germany and Italy), acted as the glue of 'modernizing missions' (e.g. Japan) and undermined multinational empires (e.g. the Spanish Empire in Latin America, the Austro-Hungarian Empire in Southeast Europe, and the Ottoman Empire in Europe, North Africa and the Middle East). National armies also became responsible for domestic pacification, serving to clarify the frontiers of states by crushing internal rebellions and dissenters (Black, 2009). During the long nineteenth century, nationalism became the reference point for virtually all territorial claims.

Rational states were sustained, therefore, by industrialization, infrastructural developments and nationalism. They also grew through imperialism: the modern, professional civil service was formed in India before being exported to Britain (Metcalf, 2007: 32–45); techniques of surveillance, such as fingerprinting and file cards,[7] were developed in the colonies and subsequently imported by the metropole; cartographic techniques used to map colonial spaces were reimported into Europe to serve as the basis for territorial claims (Branch, 2012 and 2014: ch. 5); and imperial armies acted as the shock troops in conflicts in many parts of the world (Bayly, 2004: 256). Domestically, rational states provided facilitative institutional frameworks for the development of industry, technological innovations, weaponry and science; abroad, they provided sustenance for imperial policies. Both functions were underpinned by ideologies of progress.

Notions of progress underpinned the expansion of trade, the growth of the rational state and a range of policies from scientific research to the promotion of cultural fairs (McNeill, 1991: 729). Beginning in the 1850s, 'great international exhibitions' provided showcases for state progress: in 1876, 10 million people visited the international exhibition in Philadelphia to witness 'the progress of the age', including the first ever 'Women's Pavilion' at an international exposition; in 1889, the Exposition Universelle in Paris welcomed over 30 million visitors and left an enduring legacy in the form of the Eiffel Tower (Hobsbawm, 1975: 49; Osterhammel, 2014: 15). Industrialization consolidated expectations of progress by normalizing the idea of permanent social change – innovation and research became a feature of both state and

---

[7] These systems were often remarkably thorough. The US-constructed police force in Manila, for example, generated file cards consisting of photos and a range of information for 70% of the city's population (Ballantyne and Burton, 2012: 351). These systems should be seen as the forerunners to contemporary modes of military surveillance, such as smart cards and handheld biometric devices (Ansorge and Barkawi, 2014).

private activity. German research labs led the way, pioneering developments in chemicals, pharmaceuticals, optics and electronics. Private labs followed: General Electric set up a research lab in commercial dynamos in 1900, followed by DuPont's chemicals lab in 1902.[8] Transnational research institutes such as the Institut Pasteur developed vaccines for typhoid, cholera, smallpox, plague, tetanus, diphtheria, and more. During the same period, formal academic disciplines emerged for the first time, aiming to systematize branches of knowledge (Gellner, 1988: 116; Osterhammel, 2014: 779–824). 'Expert systems' of licensing and regulation gathered information and codified data (Giddens, 1985: 181; see also Hacking, 1990; Israel, 2010; Wallerstein, 2011a; Rosenberg, 2012). These developments are the subject of Chapter 4.

The idea of progress went further than the professionalization of research and the production of academic knowledge. The late eighteenth and early nineteenth centuries saw the emergence of 'world history' for the first time, a move that encompassed both the idea that it was possible to think 'globally about history' and that it was possible to think 'historically about the globe' (Armitage, 2013: 37). In this sense, progress provided an explanation of world historical development that was not just to be analysed, but also imposed on societies around the world (Wallerstein, 1983: 98–110). Major nineteenth-century ideologies, from liberalism to socialism, contained an inbuilt drive towards the improvement of the human condition. Even the 'scientific' version of racism that became increasingly prominent in the last quarter of the century contained its own vision of 'progress'. Some advocates of scientific racism supported a 'forward policy' in which European imperialism was hardened, both to safeguard white gains and to combat miscegenation with 'backward' peoples (Darwin, 2009: 66–7; Hobson, 2012). In comparable vein, ideas of progress were bound up with the experience of empire, based on a comparison

---

[8] These private laboratories produced a great diversity of products, including consumer goods from Coca-Cola to Heinz Ketchup, and from Lever's Margarine to Kellogg's Corn Flakes. The increasing consumerism of late nineteenth- and early twentieth-century societies, and the advent of mass marketing campaigns that accompanied this development, meant that such inventions were often extremely successful – sales of Coca-Cola, launched in 1886, rose from 1,500 gallons in 1887 to 6,750,000 gallons in 1919 (Osterhammel, 2014: 233).

between core and periphery that reflected a metropolitan sense of superiority. These processes helped to forge modern notions of difference by determining which areas of the globe lay outside the 'civilized' realm of white, Christian peoples (Armitage, 2013: 40–1). The notion of the 'standard of civilization' served as the legitimating currency of European colonialism.

The standard of civilization fostered a bifurcated international order in which Western powers practised sovereign equality amongst themselves, while imposing varying degrees of inferior status on others (Gong, 1984; Anghie, 2004: ch. 2; Suzuki, 2005: 86–7; Bowden, 2009). Inequality came in many forms: unequal treaties and extraterritorial rights for those polities left nominally independent (like the Ottoman Empire, Japan and China); partial takeovers, such as protectorates, in which most local government was allowed to continue, but finance, defence and foreign policy were handled by a Western power (as in the case of Sudan); and formal colonization, resulting in elimination as an independent entity (as in India after the 1857 uprising). It is no surprise, therefore, that those states, like Japan, which sought to emulate European power, underwent both a restructuring of domestic society through industrialization and state rationalization, and a reorientation of foreign policy towards 'progressive' imperialism: Japan invaded Taiwan in 1874 (annexing it formally in 1895), fought wars for overseas territory with both China (1894–5) and Russia (1904–5), and annexed Korea in 1910 (Suzuki, 2005: 138). Undertaking a 'modernizing mission' meant that Japan extended the same arrogance towards its neighbours that the Europeans felt towards 'barbarians' and 'savages'. Becoming a 'civilized' member of international society meant not just abiding by European legal frameworks, diplomatic rules and norms; it also meant becoming an imperial power.

Imperialism, therefore, was closely bound up with ideas of progress that were themselves interwoven with industrialization and the emergence of the rational state. The result was a powerful configuration that transformed both domestic societies and international order. By the end of the nineteenth century, four states (Britain, France, Germany and the United States) provided two-thirds of the world's industrial production (Sassen, 2006: 133). By the outbreak of the First World War, one of these powers (Britain) claimed nearly a quarter of the world's territory (Abernathy, 2000: 84).

The Impact of the Global Transformation on International Relations

The global transformation had three major effects on international relations. First, the spread of industry, finance, railways and the telegraph, along with practices of colonialism, bound peoples and states together within a more closely integrated global system. The consequence was the fostering of a more interconnected human community, or at least a world society based on some common knowledge and mutual awareness. Second, the global transformation created a disjuncture between those social orders that acquired the configuration of global modernity and those who either failed to acquire, or who were denied, the new mode of power. Because this mode of power allowed the core to open up distant societies and extend market relations globally, interactions did not take place on equal terms. The global transformation bifurcated the world between a small core of strong, rich states and a large periphery of weak, poor, often colonized peoples. Third, global modernity caused upheaval in the ranks of the great powers. Specifically, it promoted early adopters (Britain and, in the last quarter of the nineteenth century, Germany, the United States and Japan) and demoted others who did not make the initial transformation (China, the Ottoman Empire, Russia). More generally, by making power conditional on the new configuration of industrialization, the rational state and ideologies of progress, the global transformation induced volatility into balancing dynamics. This volatility has remained a central feature of international relations in the present day, serially reproduced in fears (or hopes) over 'the rise of' (Germany, Japan, China, India, etc.) and/or 'the decline of' (Britain, France, the United States, Russia, etc.). The rise and decline of great powers is nothing new in world history, but the global transformation both speeded up this process and changed the bases on which it took place. The impact of the configuration we highlight on the differentiation of power has thus been one of the central dynamics underpinning power politics from the nineteenth century until the present day.

In this way, during the nineteenth century, global modernity transformed the conditions of international relations as much as it transformed other aspects of social relations. This means that there is a basic similarity between the nineteenth century, the twentieth century, and that part of the twenty-first century we have experienced so far.

As discussed in the previous section, it is not our claim that there are *no* continuities between the modern world and earlier times. The idea of the sovereign state has been around since the sixteenth century, there have been cities that serve as hubs of political power, culture and economic exchange for many centuries, while major religions are carry-overs from the Axial Age. But even these continuities have been redefined by global modernity. In the case of the state, nationalism reforged notions of territory and community. In the case of cities, modernity hugely expanded their number and scale. In the case of religions, resistance to colonial rule during the nineteenth century prompted a revival of Islam, Hinduism and other religions, which played a major role in redefining them as 'world religions', providing the means for these religions to extend their reach through the provision of schooling and centralized training, the translation of texts and the funding of periodicals (Bayly, 2004: 313–14).[9]

The global transformation, therefore, profoundly influenced the construction of the modern international order. This period set the material conditions under which a global international system came into being. It forged the ideologies for which tens of millions of people fought and died. And it generated the many inequalities within the international order – political, military, economic and cultural – that continue to define contemporary international relations. It is no exaggeration to say that the capabilities and ideas that developed during the nineteenth century, and the events and processes that followed from them, provide much of the foundation for modern international relations.

Given the importance of these dynamics, it is little surprise that many social sciences see the global transformation as their starting point. Indeed, it can be said that modern social science was established to examine the causes, character and outcomes of the global transformation. Concomitantly, it may be that the residual role IR plays within the contemporary academy is, at least in part, related to its failure to provide compelling accounts of global modernity. IR's failure in this regard means that the discipline is missing out on one of its core

---

[9] Another example of continuity is gender relations, which remained broadly patriarchal throughout the century. Indeed, Victorian society (in particular) and colonial society (in general) reinforced gender differences through powerful practices and rhetorical tropes. On these issues, see McClintock (1995), Levine (2004), Woollacott (2006) and Towns (2010).

contributions to social science. In the next chapter, we survey the ways in which IR approaches the nineteenth century and outline the parameters of a fruitful exchange between IR, world history, economic history and historical sociology around the multiple vectors of the global transformation.

2 | IR and the Nineteenth Century

Introduction

This chapter addresses the question of why IR pays so little attention to the global transformation. First, we look at a range of IR authors whose understandings of the importance of the nineteenth century reflect ours, but whose views on this point are marginal within the discipline. Second, we explore three approaches to the nineteenth century in IR: as an absence; as a source of data; and as a fragment of a wider research programme. Finally, we examine why IR has largely forgotten the nineteenth century and why this is a problem.

Understanding the Nineteenth Century in IR

It is not the case that *no* IR scholarship recognizes the significance of the nineteenth century. Interestingly, such recognition stretches across the theoretical spectrum. From a Marxian perspective, Fred Halliday (2009: 19) recognized 'the radical difference, and rupture, that divides the modern, roughly post-1800 world from that which precedes it'. Halliday also noted in disciplines outside IR 'the insistence of writers such as Karl Polanyi in economic history, of Ernest Gellner in sociology and of Eric Hobsbawm in history on the great divide that separates the pre-modern and modern worlds'. From a broadly post-structural perspective, Ole Wæver (1997: 7–8) observes that 'the nineteenth century is strangely absent [from IR] despite the fact that it is actually in the late eighteenth- and nineteenth-century works that one is best able to find its connecting lines, continuous ideas and real inspirations'. From an English School perspective, Little (2014) argues that many of the contributors to Bull and Watson's (1984a) *The Expansion of International Society*, including the editors, were fully aware that the nineteenth-century transformation in power and wealth, and the associated transformations in the states and international society of Europe, underpinned a basic change in Europe's relationship with Africa and Asia. From a Realist perspective, Hans Morgenthau (1978) argued that the period 1789–1919 constituted an important transformation from inter-dynastic to international politics (Little, 2007: 109–18). And, writing from a liberal perspective, John Ikenberry (2009: 71) notes that:

The most important transformation in world politics unfolding over the last two centuries has been what might be called the 'liberal ascendency'. This has involved the extraordinary rise of the liberal democratic states from weakness and obscurity in the late eighteenth century into the world's most powerful and wealthy states, propelling the West and the liberal capitalist system of economics and politics to world pre-eminence.

Historical sociology is perhaps the approach that comes closest to our emphasis on the importance of the global transformation. John Hobson (2012), for example, claims that much contemporary IR thinking replicates nineteenth-century views about Western superiority (see also Salter, 2002). Ayse Zarakol (2011: esp. 38–56) argues that the revolutions of modernity set the terms for the social hierarchy between the West and outsiders that has defined aspects of the modern international agenda from the 'standard of civilization' in the nineteenth century to the differentiations of 'development' and 'good governance' today. More fundamentally, Andreas Osiander (2001a) argues that IR is itself a product of the global transformation. For Osiander, industrialization increased the wealth and military power of Western states, while at the same time making them much more dependent on trade for their prosperity and much more vulnerable to attack. These changes disturbed the traditional utility of war, creating a crisis of the state that, in turn, generated a novel international *problématique*. Osiander (2001a: 14–15) concludes that: 'The ultimate cause of the appearance of systematic IR thought from the late nineteenth century onwards is the crisis of the state brought about by the process of industrialization.' Like Halliday, Osiander argues that, as a consequence of these origins, IR is constitutionally incapable of analysing periods in world history before the global transformation. We return to this question of comparability across historical periods in Chapter 10.

Three Approaches to the Nineteenth Century in IR

Despite these scattered prompts, IR *as a discipline* pays relatively little attention to either the nineteenth century as a transformational period or to the specific configuration of industrialization, rational state-building and ideologies of progress we see as constitutive of global modernity (Rosenberg, 1994: 162; Zarakol, 2011: 5). When the nineteenth century does appear in IR it is usually in one of the following three ways.

The Nineteenth Century as an Absence

The first way that IR approaches the nineteenth century is by ignoring it. Perhaps surprisingly given its prominence in neighbouring disciplines, most of mainstream IR relegates the global transformation into a more or less undifferentiated space between the benchmark dates of 1648 (the Peace of Westphalia) and 1919 (the settlement of the First World War and the supposed founding of IR as a discipline). This reduces the global transformation to little more than 'business as usual', a time when nothing much happened beyond some changes to the distribution of power and great power alignments.

At one end of this intellectual void is the 1648 Peace of Westphalia. As is by now well rehearsed, Westphalia is usually considered to be the intellectual basis for the discipline, establishing a 'revolution in sovereignty' through the principle of *cuius regio, eius religio*, which is taken to be a 'historical faultline' in the formation of modern international order (Philpott, 2001: 30, 77). Constructivists, in particular, see Westphalia as marking a fundamental shift from feudal heteronomy to modern sovereign rule through the emergence of principles of exclusive territoriality, non-intervention and legal equality (e.g. Ruggie, 1983: 271–9). However, Westphalia is also given prominent attention by Realists (e.g. Morgenthau, 1978), English School theorists (e.g. Watson, 1992) and liberal cosmopolitans (e.g. Held et al., 1999).

Regardless of the cross-paradigmatic hold of Westphalia, its centrality to the formation of modern international order is questionable. Most obviously, Westphalia did not fundamentally alter the ground-rules of European international order. Neither sovereignty, non-intervention nor the principle of *cuius regio, eius religio* were mentioned in the treaties (Osiander, 2001b: 266; Carvalho et al., 2011: 740). Rather,

Westphalia was part of a long-running battle for the leadership of dynastic European Christianity – its main concerns were to safeguard the internal affairs of the Holy Roman Empire and to reward the victors of the Wars of Religion (France and Sweden) (Osiander, 2001b: 266). Indeed, Westphalia set limits to the idea of sovereignty established at the 1555 Peace of Augsburg, for example by retracting the rights of polities to choose their own confession. Instead, Westphalia decreed that each territory would retain the religion it held on 1 January 1624 (Teschke, 2003: 241; Carvalho et al., 2011: 740). More generally, Westphalia did not lead to the development of sovereignty in a modern sense – European order after 1648 remained a 'patchwork' of marriage, inheritance and hereditary claims rather than constituting a formal states system (Osiander, 2001b: 278; Teschke, 2003: 217; Nexon, 2009: 265; Branch, 2014: 125–8). It is unsurprising, therefore, to find imperial rivalries, hereditary succession and religious conflicts at the heart of European wars over subsequent centuries. Although German principalities assumed more control over their own affairs after 1648, this was within a dual constitutional structure that stressed loyalty to the Empire (*reichstreue*) and that was sustained by a court system in which imperial courts adjudicated over both interstate disputes and internal affairs (Teschke, 2003: 242–3). Overall, Westphalia was less a 'watershed' than an affirmation of existing practices, including the centrality of imperial confederation, dynastic order and patrimonial rule (Nexon, 2009: 278–80).

At the other end of the void is the First World War, often viewed as the beginning of a new era. Much IR scholarship jumps from the intellectual 'big bang' of Westphalia to the establishment of IR as a discipline after the First World War (Carvalho et al., 2011: 749). The 1914–18 war serves as an important reference point for a great deal of IR theory ranging from the specific (arms racing) to the general (polarity), which along with its link to 'the German problem' does at least provide some links to nineteenth-century developments. But for the most part, the First World War is taken to be a foundational event from which IR looks forward rather than backwards.

However, equating the First World War with the institutionalization of IR is as problematic as linking the intellectual agenda of the discipline with Westphalia. A starting date of 1919 occludes the fact that international thought became increasingly systematic during the last part of the nineteenth century. It was taught in some US Political Science departments (such as Columbia), and fuelled major debates in both Europe and the United States (Knutsen, 1997; Schmidt, 1998; Carvalho et al., 2011: 749).[1] As we show in Chapter 4, the shift from thinking about (European) international relations in terms of dynastic interests, and towards the modern conceptualization of balance of power and state/national interest, was largely a product of the early nineteenth century. During the nineteenth century, the modern rational state emerged through the fusion of nationalism with popular sovereignty, sovereign equality, a professional bureaucracy, and suchlike. This generated distinctive forms of multilateral diplomacy and power politics. Alongside this dynamic, and interwoven with it, was the rise of liberal understandings of economics and, in particular, the idea that both prosperity and peace arose from pursuing free trade. In other words, as will become clear in Chapter 4, the basic framings for modern ways of thinking about international relations were being put into place during the nineteenth century. As Ole Wæver (1997: 8) astutely observes: 'Equipped with Ranke's essay on the great powers, Clausewitz, Bentham's works, maybe Cobden and finally Kant, it is difficult to be surprised by much in twentieth-century IR except for the form, the scientific wrapping, of much of it.'

The same is true of positive international law and intergovernmental organizations. During the long nineteenth century, the impact of rapidly rising interaction capacity increased the flows of international trade, travel and communication. These flows, along with increasing capacities for the organization of violence, augmented the need for treaties and conventions as tools of regulation. IGOs and international non-governmental organizations (INGOs) both reflected and amplified the development of positive international law. If states wanted to go to war, they could. But if they wanted to pursue commerce and peace, then an ever-denser sphere of international rules and regulations over commerce, transportation and communications helped to coordinate interstate behaviour (Davies, 2013; Koskenniemi, 2001). There was thus a well-developed framework of international law and institutions in place decades before 1919, and it was fully understood that these

---

[1] It might be argued that the intellectual space into which IR moved during the late nineteenth century was created by the failure of the emergent discipline of Sociology to engage effectively with the issue of war (Tiryakian, 1999; Joas, 2003).

played a significant, if not determinant, role in how international relations was practised.

The prominence of racism in the formation of international thought has also largely been forgotten, at least in the West (Hobson, 2012). In its most extreme forms, racism advocated the replacement of the 'lower orders' of the human species (mainly 'brown' and 'black') by the 'higher orders' (mostly 'white', sometimes 'yellow'). Less extreme, if still potent, forms of racism raised questions about whether the 'lower orders' of humankind had the capacity to be 'uplifted' to the prevailing 'standard of civilization'. If 'lower orders' were so inherently inferior that they could not achieve modernity in their own right, or at least would take a very long time to do so, then this justified colonial stewardship and tutelage by the metropolitan powers. The echoes of colonialism and other forms of racialized social order can still be heard, for example in anti-immigrant rhetoric in many places around the world.

The 1919 start date for IR therefore omits the closeness of the links between IR, racism and colonial administration (Grant et al., 1916; Vitalis, 2005; Bell, 2007; Hobson, 2012). Questions about how metropolitan powers should relate to colonial peoples, whether native or settlers, preceded the nineteenth century. But the nineteenth century saw a major shift in how imperialism was practised. During this period, most European powers assumed direct responsibility for their colonies from the Chartered Companies that had often served as the vanguard of European imperialism. At the same time, white settler polities helped to construct racism as a primary institution of international society. Mass emigration from Britain to Australia, Canada, New Zealand and South Africa created states ruled by white elites who saw themselves as inherently superior to indigenous peoples. The scale of this enterprise is striking: white settlers in Australia increased from 12,000 in 1810 to 1.25 million in 1860; one million white British emigrated to Canada between 1815 and 1865, multiplying the country's population by a factor of seven; in 1831, the white population of New Zealand was little more than 1,000 – fifty years later, it was half a million; the white population of South Africa doubled during the 1890s alone and, by 1905, nearly half of the white miners working in the Rand were from Cornwall (Belich, 2009: 83; Schwarz, 2011: 60, 157). The cumulative effect of these repopulations was significant. Whereas at the beginning of the nineteenth century the Anglo-world was made up of 12 million (mostly poor) people, by 1930 it constituted 200 million (mostly rich) people (Belich, 2009: 555).

The racism fostered by white emigration forged what W. E. B. Du Bois (1994 [1903]: 61) called 'the new religion of whiteness'. Settler colonists became a racial caste united by both fear of rebellion by the indigenous population and by a sense of their own cultural and racial superiority (Abernathy, 2000: 286–99). Racialized 'paranoia' was an integrating force amongst settlers in the Greater Caribbean and impor- tant in fostering cross-colonial cooperation in both the Caribbean and West Africa (Mulich, 2013). Such racial fears were stoked by campaigns against indigenous peoples in Jamaica in 1865, New Zealand during the 1860s, and Sudan during the 1890s. They were also stoked by the publication of overtly racist tracts, some of which were highly influen- tial. Figures such as Charles Henry Pearson and Halford Mackinder combined anxieties about the relative decline of the Anglophone world with calls to reassert the 'bonds of blood' that conjoined white domin- ions (Schwarz, 2011: 63), while figures as diverse as Norman Angell and H. G. Wells argued that the English-speaking world provided a 'nucleus of authority' in a rapidly changing world (Bell, 2012: 47). As the British became a 'global people', white settlers helped to racialize international politics, making the colour bar a globally recognized tool of discrim- ination (Schwarz, 2011: 61; see also Lake and Reynolds, 2008).

A great deal of IR's early thinking was forged in this context. As a result, it was mediated by the politics of race (Schmidt, 1998; Vitalis, 2005 and 2010; Bell, 2012; Hobson, 2012). Figures such as Pearson and Mackinder, as well as Mahan, Kidd, Seeley and others, were deeply embroiled in debates about the appropriate task of colonial adminis- tration and the future of the Anglophone world. It is no surprise that one of the first IR journals was the *Journal of Race Development*; it was only in 1922 that the journal became known by its more familiar soubriquet: *Foreign Affairs*. At the first ever meeting of the American Political Science Association in 1904, 'Colonial Administration' was designated as one of the five fundamental branches of Politics (Vitalis, 2010). As we argue in Chapter 4, much of IR's intellectual history, and the historical developments that define many of its current concerns, are rooted in nineteenth-century concerns about the superiority – or otherwise – of white peoples and Western civilization.

Combined with these discussions of (white) racial and (Western) civi- lizational superiority was late nineteenth-century work on geopolitics by figures such as Ratzel, Mackinder, Mahan and Haushofer. Geopolitics emerged from the nineteenth-century complex of imperial competition, nationalism and racism. This combination was forged in the context of a world in which access to previously uncharted territories had become possible, if not straightforward. This was allied to a sense that, by the late nineteenth century, the international system was moving towards 'closure' (Lenin, 1975 [1916]; Mackinder, 1996 [1904]). Once all available territory was occupied and allocated, this pointed towards an intensification of imperial competition as European powers sought to re-divide existing territory. Geopolitics was influential in imperial thinking before 1919 and remained so until the end of the Second World War, and even longer in southern Europe and South America (Ashworth, 2013; Guzzini, 2013). Geopolitics also overlapped with the formalization of modern strategic thinking, most notably in Clausewitz's *On War* (1832), Jomini's *The Art of War* (1863) (see Gray, 2012: ch. 2) and Mahan's *The Influence of Sea Power Upon History, 1660–1783* (1890).

As with colonialism, IR has largely forgotten its geopolitical legacy, although strategic thinking remains respectable and some nineteenth-century authors, such as Clausewitz, are still influential. Geopolitics was delegitimized after the Second World War by its association with fascism, conveniently allowing the rest of the West to forget that they too were part of its heritage. So deep was this break that geopolitics (mainly in the form of critical geopolitics) only began to re-emerge in Anglo-American IR during the 1990s (Ó Tuathail, 1996; Ó Tuathail et al., 1998; Guzzini, 2013). The same sense of neglect was applied to the German origins of Realism in the works of Treitschke and Meinecke. Some Realists claim an alternative heritage in Thucydides, Hobbes and Machiavelli. But the German tradition of *machtpolitik* was a more potent source, particularly as this was carried via Treitschke to Nietzsche, Weber, Schmitt and Morgenthau (Williams, 2005).

The First World War, then, was neither a pristine starting point for contemporary international relations nor the beginning of IR as a mode of enquiry. It was more like the culmination of a number of strands of thought that had emerged, or been reworked, over the preceding century. Pearson, Mackinder, Ratzel, Mahan, Kidd, Seeley and Haushofer joined Angell, Hobson, Laski, Lenin, Zimmern and others as part of an increasingly systematic discourse about international relations. This discourse was concerned with fundamentally nineteenth-century concerns: the superiority (or not) of white peoples and the West; how to manage relations between more and less 'civilized' peoples; the role of geopolitics in shaping international order; the rights and wrongs of imperialism; the increasing hold of notions of popular sovereignty and self-determination; the relationship of free trade and protectionism to international conflict; the rising dangers and consequences of military technology; and the capacity of war to be mitigated by international law and intergovernmental institutions. IR did not spring into being in 1919 as a specific reaction to the horrors of the First World War. It has a longer genealogy, some of it dark, and much of it formed within the unprecedented environment of global modernity that unfolded during the long nineteenth century (Deudney, 2007: 61–88, 193–248).

Reconceptualizing IR along these lines would not only improve the discipline's theoretical utility; it would also give IR a more realistic sense of itself and its origins. Yet much of IR is indifferent to the nineteenth century and the global transformation, preferring the questionable 'turning points' of 1648 and 1919. The extent of the absence of the nineteenth century in IR is manifest in the range of textbooks used to introduce the discipline to students. We examined 89 books commonly listed as key readings for 'Introduction to IR' courses.[2] These included both volumes written as textbooks and monographs often employed as introductory readings, such as Waltz's *Theory of International Politics*. The books divided into three groups: IR texts (48), world history texts used for IR (21), and texts aimed more at International Political Economy (IPE) and Globalization studies (20). Of the 48 IR texts, only five contained significant coverage of the nineteenth century, and those were mostly restricted to post-1815 great power politics (Holsti, 1992; Olson and Groom, 1992; Knutsen, 1997; Ikenberry, 2001; Mearsheimer, 2001). Seven other texts had brief discussions of the nineteenth century along similar lines. The majority of IR texts either contained almost no history, or restricted their canvas to the twentieth century. The appearance of nineteenth-century thinkers was common in books focusing on international political theory, but their ideas were largely discussed *in abstracto* rather than related to the broader context of the nineteenth century and its impact on IR. The nineteenth century fared somewhat better amongst world history texts, although seven of

---

[2] We surveyed the reading lists for introductory IR courses at the following
    universities: Harvard, Princeton, Oxford, LSE, McMaster, Lund and
    Copenhagen. Reading lists were examined during summer 2011.

these discussed only the twentieth century and, of those, five only surveyed the world since 1945. Of the remaining fourteen volumes, ten either embedded discussion of the nineteenth century within a longer-term perspective or provided the century with sparse attention. Four books gave the nineteenth century a degree of prominence, especially the technological changes that affected military power. But these, once again, concentrated mainly on great power politics (Clark, 1989; Thomson, 1990; Keylor, 2001; Kissinger, 2003).

IPE/Globalization texts fared little better. Three books had no substantive historical coverage, while eight covered only post-1945 or twentieth-century history. Of the nine books that did mention the nineteenth century, only two gave it extensive attention (Frieden and Lake, 2000: 73–108, focusing on the rise of free trade; and O'Brien and Williams, 2007: 76–103, looking at how the industrial revolution reworked the distribution of power). Other IPE/Globalization texts tended to treat the nineteenth century simply as a prologue to more important twentieth-century developments or as a comparator for them (Hirst and Thompson, 1996). None of these volumes saw the long nineteenth century as the source of modern dynamics in international political economy.

It is quite possible, therefore, to be inducted into the discipline of IR without encountering any serious discussion of the nineteenth century. To the extent that the nineteenth century is discussed, it appears as a preamble to dynamics that take place in the twentieth century. Although mention is often made of the Concert of Europe and changes to the nineteenth-century balance of power, what mainstream IR misses are issues beyond the distribution of power – in other words the transformation in the *mode* of power that was fuelled by industrialization, the emergence of rational states, and the novel ideologies associated with historical progress.[3] Where the nineteenth century is present, it exists mostly as background material. It is almost entirely absent as a global transformation that put into place the configuration of conditions that to a great extent define modern international relations.

The Nineteenth Century as a Site of Data Accumulation

The second way that IR approaches the nineteenth century is as a source of data, particularly for those employing quantitative approaches.

---

[3] Pearton (1982) and Deudney (2007) are notable exceptions in this regard.

The Correlates of War project, for example, begins its coding of modern wars in 1816 (e.g. Singer and Small, 1972). Some Power Transition Theory also appropriates data from the nineteenth century (e.g. Organski and Kugler, 1980; Tammen et al., 2001). In both cases, there is little rationale for why these dates are chosen beyond the availability of data. Little attention is paid to *why* data became available during this period, which is rooted in the increasing capacity of the rational state to collect and store information, and its growing interest in doing so as part of the routine process of government. Nor does the transformation of warfare during the nineteenth century play a prominent role in these accounts, which are mainly concerned with accumulating data rather than examining their social content. A number of debates between advocates and critics of Democratic Peace Theory (DPT) are also played out over nineteenth-century events such as the War of 1812, the US Civil War, the Venezuelan boundary dispute of 1895, and the 1898 Fashoda crisis (see, for example, Brown, 1996). In comparable vein, high-profile debates over the efficacy of Realist understandings of the balance of power have been conducted over the nineteenth-century Concert of Europe (e.g. Schroeder, 1994; Elman and Elman, 1995) and, less prominently, over developments in the United States during the nineteenth century (e.g. Elman, 2004; Little, 2007).

What unites Correlates of War, Power Transition, DPT and Realist debates over the nineteenth century is a failure to read the period as anything other than a neutral site for the testing of theoretical claims. Not only are such enterprises flawed in and of themselves, erasing the context within which these events take place (Lawson, 2012), they also see the nineteenth century as 'just another' period, when it is actually a time of intense and compressed world historical transformation. The starting point for many of these approaches, the 1815 Congress of Vienna (also found in some liberal accounts of modern international order, e.g. Ikenberry, 2001), omits the most significant features of the Napoleonic Wars: the legal and administrative centralization ushered in by the Napoleonic Code; the French use of nationalism and mass conscription; the escalating costs of warfare; and the widespread employment of 'scientific' techniques such as cartography and statistics (Mann, 1993: 214–15, 435; Burbank and Cooper, 2010: 229–35). By failing to embed nineteenth-century events within the transformative configuration of global modernity, these accounts tell us little about the character of nineteenth-century international order. Nor do they give sufficient weight to the *generative* quality of nineteenth-century developments for international relations during the twentieth and twenty-first centuries.

The Nineteenth Century as a Fragment Within a Wider Theoretical Approach

The third way that IR approaches the nineteenth century is as a fragment within a wider theoretical approach. For example, both hegemonic stability theorists and neo-Gramscians use the nineteenth century as a means by which to illustrate their theoretical premises. Robert Cox (1987: 111–50) sees British hegemony during the nineteenth century as crucial to the formation of liberal world order. The breakdown of this order after 1870, Cox argues, generated a period of inter-imperialist rivalry and fragmentation that was only settled by the ascendance of the US to global hegemony after the Second World War.

Hegemonic stability theorists follow a similar line, although stressing a different causal determinant – a preponderance of material resources (particularly military power) rather than social relations of production. Robert Gilpin (1981: 130, 144, 185) pays considerable attention to how nineteenth-century British hegemony was premised on the fusion of military capabilities, domination of the world market and nationalism, highlighting the undercutting of this hegemony late in the century through processes of diffusion and 'the advantages of backwardness' possessed by 'late developers'. This analysis is not far removed from that provided by long cycle theorists, who see British hegemony as combining military (particularly naval) superiority and superior access to both fossil fuels and finance capital, before receding during the late nineteenth and early twentieth centuries because of imperial overstretch (Modelski and Thompson, 1996; Chase-Dunn, 2013).

For many members of the English School, the nineteenth century is seen as a period in which Western international society completed the expansion process begun during the sixteenth century (Bull, 1984a: 118). Traditional figures in the School tended to look upon the nineteenth century with nostalgia, seeing it as a period in which a relatively coherent Western international society flourished. They downplayed the role of imperialism in international society and contrasted its nineteenth-century cultural cohesion with the dilution of international society after decolonization (Bull, 1977: 38–40, 257–60, 315–17; Bull and Watson, 1984b: 425–35). Their account is based largely on the 'classical' institutions of international society (the balance of power, international law, diplomacy, great power management and war), with the addition of sovereignty (Bull, 1977). Only Mayall (1990) makes any systematic attempt to bring the impact of modernity into the framing of international society, exploring the disruptive impact of the rise of nationalism and the market on 'Westphalian' institutions.

More recently, some critically influenced English School scholarship has examined the ways in which major powers such as China and Japan responded to the coercive expansion of European international society. Both Keene (2002: 7, 97) and Suzuki (2009: 86–7) stress how international order during the nineteenth century was sustained by a 'standard of civilization' that bifurcated the world into 'civilized' (mainly European) orders and 'uncivilized' (mainly non-European) polities. Rule-based tolerance was reserved for the former, coercive imposition for the latter. These accounts not only effectively critique traditional English School interpretations in which the expansion of international society is seen as endogenous, progressive and linear, they also chime with scholarship that stresses the centrality of colonial encounters to the formation of modern international order (e.g. Anghie, 2004 and 2006; Shilliam, 2011; Zarakol, 2011). As such, they provide the basis for a more sustained engagement between IR and the nineteenth century.

A number of constructivists also trace contemporary concerns to the nineteenth century. Martha Finnemore (2003: 58–66, 68–73) argues that the origins of humanitarian intervention can be found in nineteenth-century concerns to protect Christians against Ottoman abuses and in the campaign to end the slave trade (also see Bass, 2008). Jeffrey Legro (2005: 122–42) highlights the Japanese move from seclusion to openness in the latter part of the century as an illustration of how the shock of external events combines with new ideas to generate shifts in grand strategy. Rodney Bruce Hall (1999: 6) argues that the emergence of nationalism during the nineteenth century was a major turning point in the legitimating principles of international society. Jordan Branch (2014) examines how a 'geometric cartographic transformation', beginning in the early modern period but taking off in the nineteenth century, led to new representations of political space as exclusive, linear and bounded. 'Mutually constitutive' changes in ideas and technologies produced stark points of demarcation between 'inside' and 'outside' that enabled the rationalization of state power 'inside' core states and their simultaneous expansion into 'outside' territories (Branch, 2014: 69–70, 135–41, 163–4; see also Neocleous, 2003; Strandsbjerg, 2008).

A number of critical IR theories have also examined aspects of the global transformation. Post-structural theorists have stressed the ways in which power–knowledge complexes served to harden inside–outside relations during the nineteenth century. Jens Bartleson (1995: 241), for example, sees modernity, which he examines through the discourse of late eighteenth- and early nineteenth-century European thinkers, as a 'profound reorganization' of sovereignty, marking the establishment of modern notions of 'inside' and 'outside'. Ayse Zarakol (2011) explores the ways in which the 'stigma' associated with the category of 'outsiders' carried by Russia, Japan and the Ottoman Empire influenced their reactions to global modernity.[4] In similar vein, post-colonial theorists have demonstrated how nineteenth-century rhetorical tropes, most notably narratives of 'civilization' and 'backwardness', were used to establish practices of dispossession, de-industrialization and colonialism (e.g. Grovogui, 1996; Inayatullah and Blaney, 2004; Shilliam, 2011). In this way, 'civilized' and 'barbarian/savage' serve as the nineteenth-century form of the 'inside/outside' demarcation that constitutes international society. This scholarship has also stressed the formative role played by resistance movements, ranging from slave uprisings to indigenous revolts, in subverting Western power and forging counter-hegemonic solidarities (Shilliam, 2011). Finally, some feminist scholarship has examined the ways in which nineteenth-century understandings of the status of women were entwined with novel distinctions between public and private in order to construct gendered divisions within Western orders and legitimate discriminatory policies towards 'primitive' peoples (e.g. McClintock, 1995; Towns, 2010).

Much of this scholarship serves as vanguard accounts of the importance of global modernity to IR; a great deal of our analysis in upcoming chapters builds on insights from these 'early adopters'. However, we move beyond such scholarship in three ways. First, by looking at parts

---

[4] For a parallel argument about the collective 'trauma' associated with experiences of imperialism in India and China, and an analysis of its contemporary resonance, see Miller (2013).

of the puzzle, existing accounts tend to miss the whole. Neo-Gramscian approaches stress relations of production, hegemonic stability theorists focus on power preponderance, constructivists on ideational changes, post-structuralists on discursive formations, and post-colonial theorists on the formative role of colonialism in constructing binaries of 'civilized' and 'barbarian/savage'. No account captures sufficiently the configurational character of the global transformation. Second, more often than not, nineteenth-century events and processes are used as secondary illustrations within broader theoretical arguments; as a result, the distinctiveness of the global transformation is lost. For example, it was not Britain but a particular configuration of social power relations that was hegemonic during the nineteenth century. For a time, Britain was situated at the leading edge of this configuration, but only as a specific articulation of a wider phenomenon (Mann, 1993: 264–5). Third, with the exception of post-colonialism, these explanations are often Eurocentric, failing to pay sufficient attention to the constitutive role played by non-Western actors in the development of nineteenth-century international order. The result is the reproduction of narratives of European mastery that omit the dynamics of empire-resistance and notions of inter-civilizational exchange that helped to generate global modernity.

Conclusion

A contents survey of ten leading IR journals from the 1920s to the present, and covering IR theory, IPE, Security Studies and Foreign Policy, broadly confirms our argument that IR does not treat the global transformation either as an important phenomenon in itself or as a period that is constitutive of how the discipline formulates its subject matter.[5] This survey uncovers no shortage of mentions of the nineteenth century, and many articles make use of nineteenth-century case studies or data. There even appears to have been something of a boom in the study of the nineteenth century during the 1990s, when aspects of the global transformation featured in a range of articles about hegemony

---

[5] We looked at the following ten journals: *European Journal of International Relations, Foreign Affairs, Foreign Policy, International Affairs, International Organization, International Security, International Studies Quarterly, Review of International Political Economy, Review of International Studies* and *World Politics*.

(e.g. Rupert, 1990; Lake, 1993; Layne, 1993). At times, articles look deeply into the nineteenth century. But even when they do so, there is a narrowness to their analysis that misses a sense of the whole (e.g. Pollard, 1923; Zimmern, 1928; Hoffmann, 1961; Palan, 2002; Towns, 2009). If there is often a sense that the nineteenth century was a time of dramatic change and a precursor to twentieth-century developments, these points are scattered across the literature without much sense that they form a profound and cohesive global transformation.

In general, therefore, and despite the existence of diverting fragments of relevant text, little IR scholarship assesses the overall impact of the nineteenth century on either the development of the discipline or the emergence of modern international order. If some scholarship in IR is aware of the trees that make up the nineteenth century, it remains predominantly blind to the overarching wood. When the nineteenth century is mentioned, it is usually seen as a site of data accumulation, as a case study within a broader theoretical argument, or as a staging post within a narrative of Western exceptionalism. Yet a great deal of both IR's intellectual history, and the historical developments that define most of its current concerns, are rooted in the global transformation.

We aim to build on the small body of work that does highlight aspects of the global transformation. These accounts join with the even smaller body of work in IR that sees modernity as the starting point for the discipline (e.g. Hinsley, 1982; Rosenberg, 1994; Knutsen, 1997: ch. 7; Halliday, 2002b). As the previous chapter outlined, our argument builds on these accounts by examining the ways in which global modernity, a historically specific configuration of industrialization, rational statehood and ideologies of progress, transformed the structure of international order during the long nineteenth century.

Why IR has Neglected the Nineteenth Century and Why this is a Problem

If the nineteenth century is so important, why has IR not engaged more effectively with it? The primary reason for this is, as noted above, that IR's foundational story emerges out of the First World War. While this point of origin could, in theory, have provided a gateway into problematizing the global transformation, in practice it did not. Instead, the

huge costs and casualties associated with the First World War, along
with its revolutions and breaking of empires, meant that fear of war
crowded out alternative agendas. The 1914–18 experience underlined
just how far humanity's powers of destruction had grown, establishing
an urgent *problématique* of war, peace and international order.
As Joll (1982) argues, the First World War devastated all three
nineteenth-century strands of thinking about how war could be
tamed: conservatives' trust in the balance of power; liberals' faith in
the mediating effects of free trade and constitutions; and socialists'
belief that class solidarity would trump nationalism. Even the hopes
of those, such as Ivan Bloch, who thought that the fear of using destructive new weapons would deter war were not met (Pearton, 1982:
137–9). The tripartite *problématique* of war–peace–order gave priority
to the volatile balance amongst the great powers and the prospects of
war between them.

The immediacy of the prospect of total wars between great powers in
the twentieth century meant that IR neglected the sources of these wars
in nineteenth-century processes. It also meant that the discipline failed
to examine fully the power gap between those that acquired the new
mode of power and those that did not: the problem of development/
underdevelopment was acknowledged, but its origin in the global
transformation was lost. These antecedents were pushed into the background, as were the precursors of IR thinking in colonial administration. Indeed, from the 1920s onwards, IR was almost obsessively
focused on the present and near future which were, in turn, largely
defined in terms of great power relations. This genesis launched IR as a
presentist discipline whose primary concerns were the (dis)order of the
great power system and how to understand the conditions that might
lead to war or promote peace. The unfolding of the twentieth century
with its profound ideological divisions and its unremitting improvements in powers of destruction reinforced the centrality of these
twin concerns. Under these conditions, it was easy to forget the world
before 1914 other than as material for debates about the causes and
possible alleviation of war. Colonial wars and imperial conquests
seemed extraneous next to the carnage of the First World War, just as
the economic crash of 1873 and the subsequent depression of 1873–96
paled next to the crash of 1929 and the great depression of the 1930s.
As early IR texts show, the administration of empires and the relations
between metropolitan and colonial peoples *were* a central concern for

IR thinkers during the first part of the twentieth century (e.g. Grant et al., 1916). But with great power rivalry and war as primary categories of enquiry, and the stakes of war raised by deep ideological differences and ever more destructive weapons of war, these topics lost their salience. In the twentieth-century world, what mattered most was how to contain war from breaking out between ideologically polarized great powers.

In this sense, the discipline of IR *is* a child of the twentieth century. It grew up under such extreme circumstances that most of its attention has been focused on narrow temporal and spatial terrains. If IR does not deal with 'one damned thing after another', it often comes close to that. The necessity of keeping up with rapidly changing capabilities makes IR vulnerable to what has been labelled 'hectic empiricism' (Buzan, 1981: 157). Technological and economic developments over the last century have made it easy to think that the contemporary period is both radically different from, and more sophisticated than, the past, and so has little to learn from it. This view flatters the white West, which has been ensconced as the zenith of development and 'civilization'. IR has internalized a Eurocentric narrative on the back of a Western-centric history that sees Western supremacy as a natural, even eternal, state of affairs. This is far from the mark. As this book shows, the Western-dominated international order of the past two centuries is a specific configuration belonging to a particular set of historical circumstances. In the contemporary world, the Western-led international order enabled by the early unevenness of global modernity is beginning to erode.

It is relatively easy, therefore, to explain *why* IR has not looked back effectively to the nineteenth century. But that is a long way from making the case that it *should* not do so. The obscuring, or at best marginalizing, of the nineteenth century is problematic because it sets the discipline on false foundations. The current benchmark dates (such as 1500, 1648, 1919, 1945 and 1989) around which IR organizes its research and teaching omit the configuration that established the modern international order. These benchmark dates are important for two reasons: first, because they stand as markers of the discipline's self-identity; and second, because they stand as markers for how IR is viewed by other disciplines. Benchmark dates matter as points of both internal and external demarcation. Benchmark dates also matter in another sense – they fix attention on specific events that, in turn, establish drivers of change

establish drivers of change. IR's habit of privileging major wars and
their settlements reproduces the sense that the discipline should be
oriented around the twin *problématiques* of war and great power
relations. A narrow set of benchmark dates means a narrow disciplinary
imagination. The result is that, much of the time, IR is looking in the
wrong places at the wrong things. It is worth thinking more carefully
about how IR constructs its benchmark dates and how it might do so
better, most notably, as we have argued elsewhere, by including landmark events from the long nineteenth century (Buzan and Lawson,
2014a). Doing so would open IR up to a richer and deeper set of
dynamics than it currently explores. We return to this point in
Chapter 10.

PART II

The Making of Modern International Relations

... of all our contemporary illusions, the most dangerous is the one that underpins and accounts for all the others. And that is the idea that we live in a time without precedent: that what is happening to us is new and irreversible and that the past has nothing to teach us. ... Neoclassical economics, liberalism, Marxism (and its Communist stepchild), 'revolution', the bourgeoisie and the proletariat, imperialism and 'industrialism' – in short the building blocks of the twentieth-century political world – were all nineteenth-century artefacts. (Judt, 2008: 193)

The configuration of global modernity transformed the polities within which it coalesced, and the international system that those polities came to dominate. The global transformation fostered radical change both domestically through linking industrialization with state capacity, infrastructural change, technological progress and scientific research, and internationally through coercive interventions in trade, production and financial regimes, and through the acquisition of new territories. This section of the book examines the emergence and institutionalization of the global transformation from the nineteenth century to the present day. The six chapters each take a particular line of development that defines a major theme of contemporary IR, and show: (a) how the basic disjuncture between modernity and what came before took place during the long nineteenth century; (b) what it was that changed, and how; and (c) how these changes impacted on international relations in the twentieth and twenty-first centuries. These six chapters provide the substance behind the book's two central claims: first, that the nineteenth century can be understood as the opening of a world historical transformation; and second, that this transformation established many of the main features of contemporary international order.

3 | *Shrinking the Planet*

Introduction

The shrinking of the planet is a celebrated feature of contemporary globalization (e.g. Giddens, 1985; Held et al., 1999). This chapter shows not only how the shrinking of the planet took off during the nineteenth century, but also how it is that these earlier developments, more than those that took place during the twentieth century, mark the major disjuncture from previous periods of world history. Using the analytic of *interaction capacity* (Buzan and Little, 2000: 80–4), we show how both physical and social infrastructures assumed their modern forms during the nineteenth century. In terms of physical infrastructures, the agrarian world of horsepower and sailing ships, with its limited speeds and small carrying capacities, gave way to the industrial world of fast, mass transportation over land and sea, and global high-speed communication. As Landes (1969: 41) puts it, albeit in somewhat over-simplified terms, the move was from technologies that relied on human skill and animal power, plus vegetable and animal materials, to those that relied on machines, plus heat engines and minerals. This formulation neglects both the metallurgy and the use of wind and water power that bridge earlier periods and the nineteenth century, but it does capture the core elements of this aspect of the global transformation. Access to new forms of energy shrank the planet by transforming both transportation and communication. In this chapter, we show how railways, steamships, inter-oceanic canals and the telegraph impacted on the dynamics of the international system. We then show how these developments were extended by radio, telephone, aircraft, motor vehicles, rockets and, most recently, the internet. We also give some space to global monitoring (which is an offshoot of these developments) and its impact on awareness of the planet as a single system, which can be traced to the emergence of global climate surveillance during the late nineteenth century.

In terms of physical interaction capacity and its impact on international relations, our argument is that nineteenth-century breakthroughs were at least as significant as, and probably more important than, subsequent extensions of them. Interaction capacity in the agrarian era was dominated by cost ratios for transportation of goods: if it cost £1 to move a given quantity of goods by sea, it cost £4.90 to do so by river and £28 by land (Meijer and van Nijf, 1992: 133). These cost ratios meant that overland spaces were a major barrier to interaction compared with forms of water transportation. During the eighteenth century, it took three years for a caravan to make the round trip from Moscow to Peking (Braudel, 1985: 454). The marriage of steam and steel during the nineteenth century greatly enhanced the capacity of transportation by water, not only on the oceans, but also by enabling navigation up rivers, which was fundamental to opening up China and Africa. In the form of railways, and later roads and automobiles, that same marriage also reduced age-old constraints on overland transport. Although a thin global trading system existed in the eighteenth century, it was only during the nineteenth century that a global market reaching deep into continental interiors came into being. And it was only during the nineteenth century that interaction capacity increased sufficiently to create a global international system in the military-political sense understood by Waltz (1979) and a global international society in the sense of primary institutions understood by Bull (1977).

In terms of social infrastructures, we focus on the rise of two novel types of organization. First are the permanent IGOs that emerged in the second half of the nineteenth century and which reflect the shift to multilateral diplomacy. These evolved into the well-known League of Nations and United Nations families of IGOs. Second is the expanding host of INGOs that also emerged in the nineteenth century and that blossomed during the twentieth century. This is the story of 'global civil society', which along with IGOs is fundamental to the creation of global governance. IGOs and INGOs together provided the social infrastructure that undergirded the more densely integrated international system that was, in turn, sustained by rapid increases in physical international capacity.

Physical Interaction Capacity

Globalization enthusiasts often talk about the compression of time and the death of distance in the increasing influence of the global over the local (Giddens, 1985: 173; Castells, 1996; Held et al., 1999; Cairncross, 2001). Our means of assessing these dynamics is through the term *interaction capacity*. Interaction capacity is the physical and organizational capability of a system to move ideas, goods, people, money and armed force across the system (Buzan and Little, 2000: 80–4). Interaction capacity is not just about a capability to move these things; it is also about the speed, volume and price at which such movements take place, which depends partly on technology, and partly on there being sufficient political order to support stable interactions. Some lightweight luxury goods (silk, porcelain, spices, precious metals and gems) have moved across Eurasia and other transnational circuits for millennia, though generally at a slow pace and a high price. There was a form of international economic system in Eurasia for many centuries preceding the global transformation, but it was defined by relatively low levels of interaction capacity, insufficient to support either bulk trade over long distances, or military-political contacts between the far ends of the system. Two thousand years ago, imperial Rome and Han China knew of each other, and had a significant trade in luxury goods and specie. But their armies never met, they had no diplomatic relations, and the trade between them was indirect rather than direct, taking the form of a relay through a range of intermediaries.

There is a big difference in the degree of integration between systems with low and high interaction capacity. A journey half way around the world would have taken a year or more in the sixteenth century, five months in 1812, one month in 1912, and less than a day in the contemporary world. The industrial and technological aspects of the global transformation vastly accelerated the speed and volume of both transportation and communication. It also lowered their price and made them both regular and predictable. The telegraph, and later the radio, separated communication from transportation, and made communication across the planet virtually instantaneous. This meant that the nineteenth century saw the emergence of an international order with a qualitatively different degree of interaction capacity from that of the eighteenth century and before. Increased interaction capacity created a more intensely connected global economy and enabled the projection of military power around the world. This shift in terms of physical infrastructures overthrew many of the geographical constraints that shaped the international relations of the agrarian order. By doing so it altered political imaginaries by generating a nineteenth-century discourse about the annihilation of space and time that is closely related to contemporary debates about globalization (Harvey, 1990: part III; Bell, 2007: 28, 83). It also created the political, economic and strategic content of the modern international system that IR tends to take for granted. But the international order constructed during the global trans-formation was radically different from that of earlier eras: the dominant units were different; the degree of economic, political, military and cultural contact and integration was much higher; gaps in both relative and absolute levels of power became much larger; and the degree of centralization around a handful of core states was much greater.

We look first at the nineteenth-century developments that consti-tuted the breakthrough from the agrarian era, and then at how this breakthrough has been extended during the twentieth and twenty-first centuries.

The Nineteenth-Century Breakthroughs

Three examples capture the impact of new technologies in shrinking time and space on a planetary scale during the nineteenth century: steamships and inter-oceanic canals, railways, and the telegraph and radio (see also Osterhammel, 2014: 712–33).[1]

Steamships and Inter-Oceanic Canals

During the fifteenth and sixteenth centuries, shipbuilding and naviga-tion techniques had improved sufficiently to enable European sailing ships to open the passages to the Americas and the Indian Ocean, and then to circumnavigate the world, establishing a thin global trading system. This technology allowed Europeans to dominate the maritime domain both commercially and militarily. By the early fifteenth century, the Chinese had also mastered ocean-going shipbuilding and navigation techniques that were in many respects more advanced than those of the Europeans (Hobson, 2004). But after some spectacular large-scale voyages mainly into the Indian Ocean between 1405 and 1433, the Chinese withdrew from long-distance navigation. This left the way clear

---

[1] It should also be noted that the global transformation did not just introduce new technologies, it also provided techniques by which to upgrade old technologies. The careful breeding of American draught horses, for example, meant that they were 50% bigger in 1890 than they had been in 1860 (Belich, 2009: 113).

for the Europeans a few decades later. This historical 'might have been' indicates that, by the fifteenth century, agrarian maritime technology was advancing in more than one place. The mobility and carrying capacity of such ships, and the high cost and low capacity of transport by land, meant that, until the coming of railways, it was 'easier to link distant capitals than country and city' (Hobsbawm, 1962: 22). Although wooden sailing ships enabled the making of a global trading system, their carrying capacity was small, their reliability low and their speed slow. It took the *Mayflower* more than two months to cross the Atlantic in 1620 (Woodruff, 1966: 237).

Steamships constituted a second revolution at sea by massively increasing interaction capacity. They greatly intensified the effects of earlier developments by increasing speeds, lowering costs and improving both reliability and carrying capacity. During the nineteenth century, as steam engines became smaller, more powerful and more fuel-efficient, they began to be installed in ships, initially driving paddle wheels, and later the more efficient screw propeller. Fuel efficiency increased by a factor of twelve between 1776 and 1850, making steam-powered freighters economical by the 1860s (Woodruff, 1966: 238). Boiler pressure, a measure of engine efficiency, increased from 5 pounds per square inch (psi) in the 1830s to 30 psi by the 1870s and 200 psi by the end of the century. As a result of these improvements, ocean freight rates dropped by 80% during the century as a whole, with a corresponding expansion in the volume of trade (Curtin, 1984: 251–2). One million tons of goods were shipped worldwide in 1800; by 1840, ships carried 20 million tons of tradable goods; by 1870, they carried 80 million tons (Belich, 2009: 107). Between 1896 and 1913, shipping costs fell by a third, acting as a further spur to global trade as it became possible, because of both cheaper shipping and freer trade, to purchase goods at some trading hubs at only modestly higher costs than could be found at source (Frieden, 2006: 19). The transportation costs of moving a given unit of mass from Britain to India in 1906 was just 2% of the cost it had been in 1793 (Osterhammel, 2014: 726–7).

The crucial change was from fairly small, wood-built, sail-powered vessels to larger iron and steel-built ships powered first by steam piston engines and, later, diesels and steam turbines. At first, steam power was a supplement to sail – only 9.8% of tonnage was carried through steam power by 1860. But, by 1913, steam tonnage accounted for 97.7% of shipping (Woodruff, 1966: 256). Iron and steel construction meant that ships could become much larger. By 1912, the steamships of the Canada to Britain Cunard Line weighed nearly 45,000 tons, ten times the size of the largest wooden ships (Belich, 2009: 107). Steam engines both freed ships from dependence on wind (although at the cost of dependence on coal or oil) and trebled their average speed. Because steamships were not dependent on weather or season, they provided predictable, regular services to replace sporadic and irregular links by sail. By the 1830s, the quality of metal had improved sufficiently, and its price had dropped sufficiently, that iron-hulled vessels like Brunel's transatlantic passenger ship *Great Britain* were becoming commonplace. In the years before the First World War, some two million passengers per year crossed the North Atlantic by sea. A journey that took between five and seven weeks under sail, and two weeks in the early steamers, could be made on a scheduled ocean liner in four or five days by the end of the century. Civilian steamships underpinned both the making of a global market and the mass migrations of Europeans to the Americas and elsewhere, a dynamic we return to in Chapter 6.

These new ships were able to take advantage of two new canals, Suez (1869) and Panama (1914). By eliminating protracted journeys around Africa and South America, these planetary geo-engineering projects slashed the length of many major shipping routes. Suez cut the length of journeys between London and Mumbai, Colombo and Singapore by 41%, 36% and 26% respectively (Ballantyne and Burton, 2012: 354). This reduced not only the time voyages took, but also the costs and risks of conveying goods across long distances. Refrigerated meat and fruit began to be exported in the last quarter of the nineteenth century, while a new 'system of ports' sustained the expansion in long-distance trade (Topik and Wells, 2012: 632). The rapid increase in maritime traffic during the late nineteenth century is indicated by the flow of ships through the Suez Canal: 186 in 1870; 2,026 in 1880; 3,389 in 1890 (Pearson, 2003: 206). The importance of canal building went beyond fostering inter-oceanic links. The Erie Canal in New York, built between 1817 and 1825, connected the Great Lakes to the Atlantic, playing a major role in extending the reach of US commerce. The Mississippi River System, also constructed during the nineteenth century, connected Minnesota with Louisiana, becoming one of the principal routes through which US agricultural and manufacturing products were exported around the world (Belich, 2009: 112).

Railways

During the eighteenth century, a first assault on the barrier of high transportation costs over land was made in the form of canal building in Europe and the US. But inland canals required suitable landscapes and so were limited in their penetration. The land barrier was only broken decisively in the nineteenth century by the same marriage of steam and steel that made the second revolution on the sea. Railways could be built across a much wider variety of terrain than canals, and it was their arrival that broke forever the characteristic of the agrarian world that interaction capacity was higher on water than on land, and much higher on the sea than on rivers. Railways opened up whole continents to the rapid, cheap movement of goods and people. Like ships, only more so because of their smaller size, trains required relatively compact and efficient steam engines. Stephenson's *Rocket* in 1814 was the first demonstration of a practical locomotive. Widespread railway building began in Britain during the 1820s, spreading to the United States, France and Germany during the 1830s. By 1840 there were 4,500 miles of track worldwide, expanding to 23,500 miles by 1850 and 130,000 miles by 1870; by the end of the century, there were half a million miles of track worldwide (Hobsbawm, 1962: 61). Imposing stations such as St Pancras in London, Gare D'Orsay in Paris and Grand Central in New York served both as 'monuments to progress' and as the 'nerve centres of global cities' (Topik and Wells, 2012: 651–2).

This expansion had a major effect on both trade and state administration. In 1850, it could take up to three weeks to cross the continental US by a combination of train and stagecoach; the coming of the transcontinental railways in 1869 reduced the journey to five days. By the 1880s the cost of transportation by rail in Britain was less than half that of canals and a sixth of that by road. The figures for the US are even more dramatic, with late nineteenth-century railways cutting the cost of transport by road compared to 1800 by a factor of between 30 and 70 (Woodruff, 1966: 225, 254). As one writer puts it (Mead, 1995/6: 16–17):

The rail networks that sprang up were the wonders of their age. They called forth all the political, engineering, manufacturing, financial and administrative genius of their times, and the mobility they offered their societies divided the humanity of the nineteenth century from all previous societies ... Long-distance travel became, for the first time in human history, a matter of routine.

Outside Europe, railways began to operate during the 1850s in India, where they reinforced colonial rule, and the Americas. By 1870, the United States had 50% more track than Britain, Germany and France combined, and by 1930, its network was four times more extensive than the three major European powers (Topik and Wells, 2012: 644). By this time, Canada also had more track than any European state. By the early part of the twentieth century, Latin America had constructed a fairly extensive rail network – its 61,000 miles of track was more than that laid in the whole of Asia and three times Africa's total (Topik and Wells, 2012: 645). Investment in railways served to internationalize capital – France invested heavily in Russian railways, while British investors provided the capital for railways in continental Europe, the Americas and Asia. By 1913, 41% of Britain's direct overseas investments were in railways (Topik and Wells, 2012: 644), while another 30% took the form of loans provided by Britain to foreign governments in order to finance railway construction (Schwartz, 2000: 138). Britain was not the only state in this position – in 1914, over half of US foreign debt was held in overseas railways securities (Topik and Wells, 2012: 644).

As the railways spread, they became pipelines from continental interiors to coastal ports, linking with steamships to provide a global transportation system. Railways linked Argentinian food producers to the port of Buenos Aires, Australian wool to Sydney, and South African diamonds and gold to the port of Cape Town. This allowed European states to import food and other primary products in a way that was not possible before, and they could establish mass production industries such as cotton that depended on raw materials grown in India, Egypt and the US. The combination of railways and steamships underpinned the division of labour between an industrial core and a commodity-producing periphery that first emerged as a defining feature of the global political economy during the nineteenth century.

Although railways opened up land transport as never before and tied it into maritime networks, in an important sense they worked in the reverse way to steamships. Instead of it being 'easier to link distant capitals than country and city', it was now possible to do both. While steamships linked distant capitals, railways linked cities to their sur-rounding countryside, and so became more important in integrating states than in connecting them to each other. In this sense, railways worked alongside new modes of transportation such as turnpikes, stagecoaches and canals in binding spheres of activity into tighter networks (Giddens, 1985: 173–4). Railways prompted the emergence of timetables and, in turn, pressed states to regularize time. 'World standard time' was pioneered at the Prime Meridian Conference in Washington in 1884 and the 'universal day' of twenty-four time zones was consolidated at the 1912 Paris International Conference on Time.[2] In this way, railways and other forms of nineteenth-century interaction capacity helped to generate modern notions of 'clock-time' (Giddens, 1985: 175). The improving infrastructure of overland transportation during the nineteenth century was an enabling factor not just in the development of a global market, but also in the development of the integrated, rational state.

The Telegraph and Radio

Until the coming of the telegraph, international communication was indistinguishable from light freight. Being light, it could take advantage of the fastest ships and pony express services. But it was still chained to the speed and range of existing agrarian technology. Even so, it had advantages over the movement of bulk goods. As Braudel notes (1985: 215), during the first half of the seventeenth century, 'news travelling overland always reached the Indian Ocean more quickly than the Dutch or English ships sailing towards it around Africa. The Portuguese authorities were always forewarned via Venice and the Levant of the Dutch expeditions on their way to attack them.' Not until the early years of the long nineteenth century did the real communication revolution occur, involving the separation of information from paper for the purposes of transporting it. The breakthrough technology was the telegraph. Optical telegraphs capable of sending messages 400 kilometres per day were available by the 1790s, albeit mainly for military purposes. During the nineteenth century, these were outpaced first by railways and then from the 1830s by the electromagnetic telegraph (van Creveld, 1991: 153–66).

The spread of the telegraph ran in parallel with that of railways and steamships. During the 1840s, telegraph networks spread throughout Europe and North America, increasing from 2,000 miles in 1849 to 111,000 miles by 1869 (Hobsbawm, 1975: 75–7). In 1851, the first

---

[2] 'Clock societies' were also fostered by the availability of personal timepieces: the world's output of pocket watches rose from around 400,000 units per year in 1800 to more than 2.75 million per year in 1875 (Osterhammel, 2014: 71).

underwater cable was laid across the Channel to connect Britain and France, and the first transatlantic cable opened in 1866. By 1870, a submarine telegraph system linked the UK and India; by 1887, over 200,000 kilometres of underwater cable connected (mainly imperial) nodes in the world economy; by 1903, there was a global network in place consisting of over 400,000 kilometres of submarine cabling (Held et al., 1999: 336; Osterhammel, 2014: 719). During this period, much of East Asia, including Japan and Australia, was linked by telegraph, although the trans-Pacific cable was not complete until 1902. Use of the telegraph was widespread, if uneven. At the end of the nineteenth century, two-thirds of the world's telegraph lines were British owned (Osterhammel, 2014: 722). In 1913, Europeans sent 329 million telegraphs, while Americans sent 150 million, Asians 60 million and Africans 17 million (Topik and Wells, 2012: 663).

The impact of the telegraph on the speed of communications was dramatic, far outpacing improvements in the speed of transportation. Communication times between Britain and India dropped from 5–8 months during the 1830s (sailing ship), to 35–40 days during the 1850s (rail and steamship), to the same day during the 1870s (telegraph) (Curtin, 1984: 251–2). Or to chart this shift another way, a letter sent from Paris to St Petersburg took 20 days in 1800, 30 hours in 1900 and 30 minutes in 1914 (Ferguson, 2001: 103). That kind of speed was not achieved in the realm of transportation for another 100 years. By the late nineteenth century, telephones were replacing the telegraph, still relying on wires, but replacing the cumbersome coding and decoding process with direct voice communication. At the same time radio (so-called 'wireless') technology made long-distance communication possible at the speed of light, and this also moved quickly from code to direct voice. The ability to broadcast by radio meant that communication became not only instantaneous, but also flexible. From 1901 onwards, radio extended the communication networks to ships, underlining just how new were the famous 'SOS' signals sent by the sinking *Titanic* in 1912. By 1907, there was a regular transatlantic radio link bringing Europe and North America into instantaneous contact with each other.

These developments impacted on many spheres of international relations, from war and diplomacy to trade and consumption. They greatly accelerated the movement of information and the range of people to whom it could be available. Governments could find out about political and military developments almost as they happened, and financiers and traders had faster access to information about supply, prices and market movements. One consequence of this was the enabling of concentrated command structures over long distances. With instant communication, neither ambassadors, nor admirals and generals, were granted as much independence of action, and firms kept tighter control over distant subsidiaries and partners. Radios also became a mass consumer good: half of all households in the United States owned a radio by 1930 and 90% did so by 1945 (Topik and Wells, 2012: 668). The boom in radio sales served as the forerunner to the post-war explosion in the manufacturing and consumption of domestic consumer goods.

Assessing Changes in Physical Interaction Capacity

By deepening and broadening interaction capacity, these three develop-ments created much of the infrastructure for the modern international system. They reduced the costs of transportation and communication, and increased both speed and carrying capacity. In combination, they made the world a single space in terms of political economy and political-military interactions. They also ratcheted up cultural encoun-ters, enabling (and often requiring) peoples to interact on a previously unprecedented scale.

It might be objected that the new modes of communication were too costly for most people in the nineteenth century to use them, and this is true. But the new modes of *transportation* were cheap enough for most people to use – the result was mass migration. At the same time, the development of global trade circuits impacted on the lives of most people around the world, for better or for worse. Although the telegraph and the radio were mainly tools of the commercial, political and military elites until the second quarter of the twentieth century, their impact filtered through to ordinary people via the real-time world news purveyed by the emergent mass media in the form of newspapers and magazines. Increasingly, the human population knew itself as a single entity for the first time (Armitage, 2013). From the eighteenth century back into antiquity, the world was composed of social orders that were only lightly and slowly connected to each other, and sometimes not connected at all. While interaction across Eurasia was historically significant, it was slow, remote and limited, as were other transnational circuits across the Pacific and the Atlantic. The nineteenth-century revolutions in interaction capacity shrank the world into the integrated modern international system in which we still live.

Subsequent Extensions

The technological revolutions that underpinned the global transformation have certainly not stood still since the nineteenth century. The many developments in transportation and communication technologies that mark the twentieth century are breakthroughs in their own right. Roads and automobiles have placed long-distance travel into the hands of publics around the world. Aircraft have added speed, and opened up a new dimension for mass travel and transportation. Television has made the world a more immediate, intimately connected place. Orbital satellites have provided planetary surveillance and enhanced electronic forms of communication. The internet has brought high volume, high speed, low cost communications to vast numbers of people around the world. As technological breakthroughs, these are just as impressive as steamships, railways and the telegraph.

At the same time, some older technologies have proved resilient, if requiring adaptation to contemporary conditions. Containers have greatly increased the scale and efficiency of freight movements that are possible by sea – in the contemporary world, the largest (mainly South Korean, Japanese and Chinese) container ships can carry over one million 29-inch televisions or more than 50 million mobile phones (Zeiler, 2014: 279). Whereas the largest tankers held 20,000 tons of oil in 1945, today's supertankers can carry 1 million tons (McNeill and Engelke, 2014: 383). China's breakneck construction of high speed rail networks both echoes nineteenth-century railway building in the West, and has similar consequences in terms of seeking to enhance the integration of the state.

Yet while such advances have continued to deepen levels of interaction capacity and interconnectedness, for the most part their effects are extensions of the nineteenth-century technological impacts noted above. They add quantity to these developments, but do not constitute a qualitatively new era in the way that the breakthroughs of the nineteenth-century global transformation delivered in relation to previous periods of world history.

Roads and Automobiles

Most of the empires of the ancient and classical era built roads in some form. China had a system of roads graded into five categories by the first millennium BC (Singer et al., 1954: 713–14). And by 200 AD, the Roman Empire boasted 300,000 kilometres of roads, just under one-third of which was paved (Forbes, 1955: 146; Singer et al., 1956: 500–15). But these roads were used mainly for communication and military movements, less so for commerce. European roads did not match Roman standards until the eighteenth century and initially could not compete with canals, or later railways, for the bulk movement of goods and peoples.

Roads did not come into their own until the invention of the internal combustion engine made automobiles practical during the late nineteenth century. In 1885, there were only 8,000 registered cars in the United States; by 1912, there were 902,000 registered cars in the US and, by 1920, the United States had 9.2 million registered cars, three-quarters of the world's total (Topik and Wells, 2012: 656). During the interwar years, four million cars were built each year in the US so that, by the onset of the Second World War, there was one car for every four people in the US, compared to a ratio of 1:12 in Britain, 1:98 in Germany and 1:1,195 in Japan (Topik and Wells, 2012: 656). The knock-on effects of the automobile industry were substantial: by the end of the 1920s, cars were responsible for 80% of US rubber production, 65% of leather production and 20% of steel production (Panitch and Gindin, 2012: 50). Automobile manufacturing also contributed significantly to aluminium, tin and nickel production.

Cars, along with radio, helped to forge the mass consumer societies that fuelled growth in the post-Second World War period, an issue we pick up in Chapter 5. For now it is worth noting the role that cars played in post-war development outside the United States. In Western Europe (particularly Germany) and East Asia (particularly Japan), car manufacturing played a major role in post-war reconstruction. Between 1945 and 2011, the number of cars in the world increased from 40 million to 800 million – and much of this growth took place outside the United States. Not only did such extensive growth boost the development of national markets in automobiles, it also served to globalize the industry. By the end of the 1980s, Japanese car manufacturers were building 695,000 cars per year *inside* the United States and they held nearly a third of the share of the US auto market (Zeiler, 2014: 316).

As a result of the global expansion in automobile production, roads became major trading routes, even if railways retained advantages in the movement of bulk goods. Yet while modern roads and road vehicles made transportation more personal and flexible, they augmented and refined the revolution in mass transportation accomplished by nineteenth-century railways.

Aircraft

Much the same can be said about the coming of aircraft. In its way, this was a spectacular achievement, adding a significant increment of speed to global transportation and communication, especially over long distances. Aircraft reinforced the elimination of the difference between land and sea that was pioneered by the steamship/railway revolution in the nineteenth century. They greatly facilitated the movement of people across long distances for purposes additional to migration, such as tourism and business. But again, this added to and refined the global transformation rather than constituting a transformation in its own right.

Starting in the late nineteenth century, the development of aircraft, like that of automobiles, stemmed from the availability of reliable internal combustion engines. The First World War saw not only great improvements in the size, range, speed and reliability of aircraft, but also the creation of a substantial manufacturing industry to produce them. The 1914–18 war established a link between military requirements for aircraft and civilian possibilities for their use that accelerated the deployment of aircraft for mass transportation. The military requirement for fighter aircraft emphasized the development of speed, while that for bombers emphasized range, carrying capacity and accurate navigation. The implications for the development of commercial airmail, freight and passenger services were obvious. At the end of the war, there was an abundance of redundant military aircraft, trained pilots and aircraft manufacturing capacity.

The first airmail services started immediately after the First World War. Early clients included banks, which used the service to carry cheques that would otherwise lose value during long-haul transit. During the 1920s, air passenger services began to link parts of Europe with parts of North Africa. By the 1930s, Britain, France, the Netherlands and Germany had developed imperial air services linking Europe to most of the Middle East, Africa, South and East Asia, and

Australia, while the US used flying boats to extend air services to South America, and by island-hopping across the Pacific, to New Zealand and the Philippines. Crossing the North Atlantic was a major technical hurdle, requiring not only long-range aircraft, but also planes capable of flying at night and that were reliable in all weathers. Zeppelins opened the Atlantic route in 1936–7, but airplanes were only just acquiring the necessary capabilities to cross the North Atlantic when the Second World War intervened.

The Second World War also saw a major surge in flight technology, especially in the development of jet engines and of the four-engine heavy bombers that pioneered the technology for long-haul mass air travel. During the war, airports were constructed in Newfoundland and Ireland that made it possible to fly the North Atlantic non-stop. After the war, this capacity was used to open commercial air services. With journey times cut from several days in even the fastest ship to just 15 hours by air, a boom in transatlantic air passenger travel followed, passing a million passengers a year by the mid-1950s, and surpassing sea trade in terms of passenger numbers during the latter part of the decade. The arrival of jet airliners extended the challenge presented by air travel, cutting the time for the transatlantic crossing in half, to not much more than seven hours. This stimulated further growth in North Atlantic air travel, reaching 8 million passengers by 1970, and nearing 40 million passengers by the early 1990s, by which time passenger traffic by sea had shrunk to negligible proportions (Davis, 1964; Hugill, 1993; Zeiler, 2014: 277).

Within the US, distance also continued to shrink. In 1929, the fastest passenger journey across the US could be done in two days by a combination of train (by night) and plane (by day), involving ten stops. By 1953 it could be done non-stop by air in just over seven hours (Woytinsky and Woytinsky, 1955: 529). The revolution in the air not only multiplied the speed of travel ten or twenty times over, it also hugely increased the volume of passenger traffic, making possible the worldwide rapid transportation system that developed during the 1960s and 1970s. On the basis of this fast maturing technology, by 2011 the airline industry worldwide was carrying 2.8 billion passengers and one-third of the value of all world trade (IATA, 2012: 14).

Space

The twentieth century also saw a technological revolution that opened up the domain beyond the atmosphere: space. This was based on the development of rockets, which took off when states assumed an interest in rocketry for military purposes during and after the Second World War. Rockets had no impact on mass transportation, but they had two specific, important impacts on interaction capacity as a whole. The first was in their role as fast, long-range, impossible-to-stop delivery systems for military payloads. This changed the face of strategic thinking, a point we come back to in Chapter 8. Second, from the 1960s onward, the same capability was used to put satellites into orbit, creating both an intense, real-time surveillance of the planet and a new, highly flexible global communications network. Fast global communications was an enhancement of the breakthrough made by the telegraph, and furthered by radio and telephone during the global transformation.

Planetary observation and surveillance might be thought of as a new capability. However, again, these are extensions of steps first taken during the nineteenth century. During the nineteenth century, most people were unaware of the ways in which the shrinking of distance enabled the emergence of planetary surveillance. Yet by 1876, the British Empire 'had the operational rudiments of a world climate observation system linked by telegraph and undersea cables' (Davis, 2002: 217). This 'observational revolution' combined scientific advances with economic motivations (the linking of climate to agricultural production, famine and trade) and empire (giving the requisite scale of interest and placement of observers), enabling the observation of the planet as a single system (Davis, 2002: 227). This was the antecedent of today's global planetary monitoring systems, which is best seen as an extension of the systems of observation from land, air and sea that developed during the nineteenth and twentieth centuries.

Electronic Media

As noted above, radio became a mass media after the First World War, with the BBC beginning broadcasting in Britain in 1922, and the BBC Empire Service (now World Service) being inaugurated a decade later. Since then, television, which became part of the mass media only after the Second World War, has added another layer to these developments, as has the advent of mobile phones. In the mid-1990s, there were around 55 million mobile phones in use around the world and these phones were mostly used for a single purpose – making and receiving calls. By 2010, there were 4.6 billion mobile phone subscriptions around the world with phones being used for an ever-expanding range of functions, from gaming to crowdsourcing, and from shopping to sending remittances (Zeiler, 2014: 279).

Many phones are also connected to the internet, which has added a further dimension to mass communication. Starting from military communication facilities in the 1960s, the internet became a network of networks during the 1980s, and took off into mass communications with the introduction of the World Wide Web format in 1993. Perhaps 150 million people were online by the late 1990s (Christensen, 1998); estimates suggest that well over 2 billion people were online by 2013, and that internet traffic was growing at a rate of 50% per year (Mulgan, 2013: 46). The internet does not increase the range or the speed of communication. In this sense it does not compare in terms of interaction capacity with the planet-shrinking breakthroughs of the nineteenth and early twentieth centuries. But by lowering costs, it has heightened both access to, and the volume of, communication, and in myriad and sometimes important ways to its content and purpose. In doing so, the internet has increased the reach, depth and impact of the communications revolution in ways that could be seen as transformative. One indication of this transformative capacity is the rise of a new agenda of cybersecurity (Hansen and Nissenbaum, 2009).

While the technological advances of the twentieth and twenty-first centuries have, therefore, been impressive in their own right, they have mainly enhanced the breakthroughs in interaction capacity that took place during the long nineteenth century. Roads, automobiles, aircraft, satellites and the internet have added speed, flexibility and/or access to the transportation and communication systems of the global transformation, while at the same time reducing its cost to users. It cost three weeks' wages for the average American worker to make a five-minute phone call from New York to London in the 1920s; it took them 15 minutes to earn enough to make the same call in 2000 (Frieden, 2006: 395). In the contemporary world, services such as Skype make such calls effectively free. Between 1930 and 2000, the price of air passage came down in real terms by 90%, while personal computers are now available for one-ten thousandth of the price of a top range computer from the 1970s (Frieden, 2006: 395). Yet for all these improvements in speed and price, only the internet seems to be opening up a dimension of physical interaction capacity that contains transformative properties. Space technology may eventually do so by extending the scale of human society into the solar system and beyond. But this is not yet in prospect.

Rockets still have cost and carrying capacity restrictions that limit their role as a mode of transport to a narrow band of functions largely still tied to near-Earth orbits.

Social Interaction Capacity

Social interaction capacity is about social technologies that, intentionally or otherwise, facilitate communication and other forms of interaction in human affairs. Such technologies include lingua francas, money, shared ideas and practices such as religion and diplomacy, more formal bodies of shared rules such as international law, and shared institutions, such as intergovernmental forums or organizations. They are part of the conditions that determine how international orders operate. Following Buzan and Little (2000: 266–7), we treat IGOs as the principal social technologies of interaction capacity in modern international society. Their existence deepens levels of political interactivity by providing not only pre-set pathways for diplomacy, but also common rules and practices, and obligations and opportunities to participate.

International orders before the nineteenth century were not without social technologies. Lingua francas have been a common feature of civilizations throughout history, and religions provided shared frameworks of norms, rules and institutions that could facilitate interactions across large distances. Agreement on the value of precious metals has long provided a cross-cultural medium for exchange – pre-nineteenth-century trading networks, for example, built long-distance networks of finance and commerce, including letters of credit (Curtin, 1984; Bentley, 1993). Diplomacy in the sense of established practices of communication between recognized political entities has also been around for a very long time (Cohen and Westbrook, 2000; Jönsson and Hall, 2005; Neumann and Leira, 2013). The ancient Greeks shared a lingua franca as well as shared institutions such as the Olympic Games and the Oracle at Delphi. Europe during the Middle Ages had Latin and later French as lingua francas, natural law as a frame of reference, and Christendom as a shared cultural resource. One remarkable example of how effective these social technologies were can be found in the 30-year travels of Ibn Battutah who, during the fourteenth century, was able to travel and work throughout the Islamic world, from southern Spain, through North Africa and the Middle East, to Central, South and East Asia, all the while staying within the basic conventions of Islamic society (Mackintosh-Smith, 2002).

Nineteenth-Century Breakthroughs

As with the shrinking of the planet by physical technologies, globalization enthusiasts place great store in the development of global governance in the form of IGOs and the rise of global civil society in the form of INGOs. They rightly see these developments as both novel and important. But they too easily give the impression that these breakthroughs in social interaction capacity are a twentieth-century phenomenon. Reus-Smit (1999: 127–49) is closer to the mark with his argument that, between 1776 and 1848, there was a fundamental change in the institutions of European international society. The dynastic principle of absolutism began to be replaced by nationalism and popular sovereignty. This, in turn, enabled a shift from natural to positive law (from law as given by God or nature, to law as made by the humans subject to it), and from dynastic to multilateral diplomacy. Reus-Smit sees these linked transformations as gathering pace during the second half of the nineteenth century and reaching full expression in modern form at the Hague Conference of 1899. As Bukovansky (2002: 64) argues, the general shift in the foundations of political legitimacy from dynasticism to popular sovereignty meant that 'the substance and meaning of *raison d'état* in the eighteenth century differed essentially from its articulation in the nineteenth and twentieth centuries'.

Here and in the rest of this book we distinguish *primary* from *secondary institutions* (Buzan, 2004). *Primary institutions* are constitutive of both states and international society in that they define the basic character and purpose of any such society. This type of institution is evolved rather than designed, constitutive rather than instrumental, and can be found as far back as one can trace the history of polities. The traditional set of primary institutions included: sovereignty, nonintervention, territoriality, diplomacy, international law, war, balance of power, and great power management. Nationalism and the market are more recent additions, while colonialism/imperialism and formal human inequality have lost legitimacy. Classical civilizations had some distinctive institutions such as suzerainty, or in China the tribute system (Zhang, 2001; Zhang, 2009). Tracking how primary institutions shift over time is fundamental to assessing changes in social structure

(Buzan, 2014a). *Secondary institutions*, such as the UN and the World Trade Organization (WTO), are consciously designed to serve the purposes of the entities that create them, and they are with very few exceptions not older than the mid-nineteenth century. Secondary institutions are in a fundamental sense derivative of the primary institutions that form the social infrastructure of international society.

With this in mind, we argue that there were three distinctive breakthroughs in social interaction capacity during the nineteenth century: the shift from natural to positive international law; the creation of permanent IGOs; and the emergence of INGOs. The shift from dynastic to multilateral diplomacy is largely captured by the first two of these developments. An important accompaniment to these dynamics, the partial shift to liberal understandings of trade, is discussed in Chapters 4–6. The emergence of IGOs as a central feature of international relations is therefore not a stand-alone development, but contingent on the radical changes in primary institutions generated by the revolutions of modernity.

International Law

While it is not disputed that positive international law became dominant over natural law during the nineteenth century, it is not the case that positive international law was invented during this period. The distinction between natural and positive law dates back to the Romans, but with the rise of sovereign states, the idea of a discrete 'international law' made by, and focused on, states gained ground. This was evident in the pre-nineteenth-century work of Hobbes, though in general a more Grotian mix of natural and positive law (in the form of interstate treaties), with the latter embedded in the former, held sway during the seventeenth and eighteenth centuries (Verosta, 2011). What was distinctive about the nineteenth century was a turn towards positive law and the relative decline of natural law. Positive law was less universalist in orientation than natural law, and its development tended to make sovereign states the arbiters of their own affairs (Neff, 2010: 4–17).

The shift towards the dominance of positive law is partly explained by the increasing alliance between sovereignty and the modern state. As Anghie (1999: 2) notes:

Positivist jurisprudence is premised on the notion of the primacy of the state. Despite subsequent attempts to reformulate the foundations of international law, the fundamental positivist position, that states are the principal actors of international law and that they are bound only by that to which they have consented, continues to operate as the basic premise of the international legal system.

The shift towards positive law is also partly attributable to the increase in interactions between states during the nineteenth century (Scupin, 2011). As we noted in the previous chapter, the global transformation saw a marked intensification in commerce and diplomacy, often linked to imperialism. The need to pursue coordination and inter-operability in far-reaching, complex systems of transportation, communication, trade and finance drove the expansion of positive international law as a way of dealing with an increasingly dense sphere of international interactions. The Hague Conferences of 1899 and 1907 even made some progress on highly sensitive issues of war, beginning to lay down rules and restrictions about how it was to be conducted. More generally, the shift towards formal sovereign equality as the norm among 'civilized' states in the 'family of nations' encouraged more contractual, legalistic relations between them. Indeed, the rise of positive international law reflected the increasing dominance of Europe, for positive law was European law. The inclination within the natural law tradition to treat (most) non-Europeans as equals was replaced by an association of positive law with the hierarchy provided by the 'standard of civilization' (Gong, 1984: 5–32).[3] In this sense, positive law contained a dual purpose: ordering conduct amongst sovereign equals in the core; and regulating 'difference' between core and periphery globally (Shilliam, 2013). We return to this point in Chapter 6.

Positive law was also promoted by liberals, who saw it as a means of coordinating relations between entities, whether these entities were persons or states or companies, and stipulated a range of issues that required adjudication through positive law (e.g. property rights, human rights, corporate rights, management of the market, etc.). The rise of positive international law thus went hand-in-hand with the development of IGOs – each fed into the other. This shift assumed modern form during the late nineteenth century; it remains the template for the legal

---

[3] For in-depth discussions of the concept of 'civilization', the 'standard of civilization' and their role in world politics, see Bowden (2009) and Linklater (2010).

and organizational structure of international society in the contemporary world.

Intergovernmental Organizations

The vast increases in physical interaction capacity discussed above, plus the move towards rational states and the global expansion of the market, created demands for coordination and standardization (Hobsbawm, 1975: 82–7). These demands, along with the shift to positive international law, resulted in the emergence of intergovernmental organizations as permanent features of interstate society. The link between physical and social interaction capacity is made clear by the functions of most early IGOs: the International Telecommunications Union (1865), the Universal Postal Union (UPU) (1874), the International Bureau of Weights and Measures (1875), and the International Conference for Promoting Technical Unification on the Railways (1882), as well as various river management commissions. The UPU, for example, responded to the need for inter-operability among state postal systems, and within empires, created by the new diasporas and the new transportation systems. By 1875, 6 million letters per year were being sent between Britain and the United States, a threefold increase from figures just 20 years earlier (Belich, 2009: 122). Constructing this kind of social interaction capacity was as important to the flow of information as the physical infrastructure of railways, steamships and the telegraph.

Regional organizations also began to develop during the last quarter of the nineteenth century. The world's first regional organization – the Pan-American Union (later the Organization of American States) – was founded in 1889–90 as the Commercial Bureau of the American Republics. Regional IGOs have a precursor in the series of conferences that go under the label 'The Concert of Europe'. These conferences were of a different order to permanent IGOs. The Concert provided an 'international public power' for governing European affairs (Mitzen, 2013: 5–11). But it did not generate permanent multilateral diplomatic institutions, one of the innovations associated with the rise of IGOs. Nor did the Concert focus on specific issue-areas, whether this was to do with communications or infrastructure. Rather than reflecting the general management of international political order, the new IGOs reflected the structural interdependence and functional differentiation characteristic of modernity. They were responses both to new technologies and to the greater interdependence of societies that were, by the late nineteenth century, transforming human societies on a global scale.

From the 1860s onwards, IGOs multiplied rapidly. By 1913, there were 45 (Wallace and Singer, 1970: 250–1), a modest start, but establishing the foundations for the more ambitious developments that followed the First World War. The Hague Peace Conferences of 1899 and 1907 founded the Permanent Court of Arbitration as a dispute settlement mechanism, and paved the way for the Permanent Court of International Justice (PCIJ) that was part of the Versailles Treaties in 1919. In this way, the founding of the League of Nations in 1919 was not the start of something new, but the culmination of developments in multilateral diplomacy, IGOs and positive international law that had been underway for more than half a century (Reus-Smit, 1999: 145–9). As with international law, the modern template of IGOs was established during the global transformation.

International Non-Governmental Organizations
The disruptive effects of the global transformation generated a space in which non-governmental organizations became increasingly vibrant sources of dissent and deliberation. These organizations were concerned with a wide variety of issue-areas, from religion and politics to sport and the environment. Some of these organizations linked up with similar bodies abroad; others expanded their membership and organization to different countries. In doing so they added weight to the category of non-economic INGOs previously occupied primarily by religious institutions, most notably those of the Roman Catholic Church and the Islamic ummah.

The growth of the mobilized middle classes and improvements in international communications during the nineteenth century provided a fillip to the formation of INGOs (Seary, 1996). So too did the spread of ideas across borders in the shape of transnational revolutionary movements, peace societies, anti-slavery associations, and more (Davies, 2013: 23–7). Alongside these groups were the religious lobbies that played into debates about the morality and practices of war, imperialism, intervention, public health, education, penal reform and market expansion. All in all, the period between the last quarter of the eighteenth century and the mid-years of the nineteenth century represented a long 'first wave' in the formation of modern INGOs (Davies, 2013: 36–44).

Boli and Thomas (1999: 7–10, 19) see these early INGOs as an integral feature of the modern world polity, having the function of 'enacting, codifying, modifying and propagating world cultural structures and principles', with states and IGOs as their targets. Various INGOs, perhaps most notably anti-slavery campaigners, petitioned the British government to raise their cause at the Congress of Vienna in 1815 (Davies, 2013: 28). By the 1830s, transnational associations were taking part in vigorous public debates around issues as varied as trade policy and population growth. Several prominent INGOs, including the Young Men's Christian Association (YMCA) and the International Red Cross, were formed in the 1850s and 1860s, as were issue-based groups such as those seeking to improve animal welfare, promote the arts, and formalize academic subjects ranging from botany to anthropology.

The latter half of the nineteenth century saw a further growth in INGO activity with the emergence of a number of groups formed in response to the inequities of industrialization and, in the last part of the century, the first industrial era depression. The organized labour movement formalized into the International Workingmen's Association (IWA, aka the First International) in 1864 and the Second International in 1889. Other groups, such as the International Association for Obtaining a Uniform Decimal System of Measures, Weights and Coins, sought to standardize the changes wrought by industrialization. A further tranche of INGOs put pressure on states to enact faster, deeper processes of democratization. A transnational movement for women's suffrage emerged in the last quarter of the nineteenth century; by the early years of the twentieth century, the membership of the International Council of Women counted up to 5 million women around the world (Offen, 2010a; Osterhammel, 2014: 507). The same period also saw the emergence of a range of groups, from 'patriotic alliances' to pan-regional movements, which sprang up in response to the resurgence of European imperialism (Davies, 2013: 55–6). And there were various attempts to unify languages, boost scientific cooperation and regulate cultural activities. The international organization of sports, many of which were codified during the late nineteenth century, took off around the turn of the century, including the formation of: the International Rugby Football Board (1887), the International Federation of Association Football (1904), the Imperial Cricket Conference (1909), and the International Lawn Tennis Association (1913). The International Olympic Committee was established in 1894 to revive the ancient Greek games in modern form.

At their pre-First World War high point, there were around 400 active INGOs around the world, some relatively temporary and limited in aspiration (such as the International Institute of Refrigeration), others more permanent and boasting a considerable portfolio of activities (such as the International Federation of Trade Unions) (Davies, 2013: 65–76; Osterhammel, 2014: 505–12). The global civil society that has been such a celebrated feature of the twentieth century has its origins in the long nineteenth century.

Subsequent Extensions

As is the case with physical interaction capacity, the basic story of social interaction capacity is one of nineteenth-century breakthroughs, with subsequent extensions and expansions occurring during the twentieth and twenty-first centuries.

International Law

International law has largely remained on the track laid down during the late nineteenth century. In line with the ongoing intensification and functional differentiation of the international system, positive international law has expanded into myriad domains and has remained the dominant framing for international legal regimes. Considerable progress has been made on the codification of international law and, particularly since 1945, positive law has been developed in areas ranging from the oceans and outer space, through to civil aviation, nuclear energy, monetary policy, the environment, human rights and policing (Neff, 2010: 25). This development remains tightly woven into multilateral diplomacy and the IGOs that have become regularized features of international relations.

The link between IGOs and positive international law is underlined by the development of a variety of legal IGOs that build on the foundations laid down at the end of the nineteenth century. The Permanent Court of Arbitration is still going, as is the International Court of Justice (ICJ). The League's Committee of Experts for the Progressive Codification of International Law morphed into the UN's International Law Commission. A variety of regional courts on both justice generally and human rights specifically have been set up by regional IGOs in Europe, Africa and the Americas, and a variety of tribunals have been formed to deal with war crimes emanating from the Second World War, the wars in the former Yugoslavia, and those in Rwanda and Cambodia. The International Criminal Court came into being in 2002; as of April 2014, it had been ratified by 122 states.

Intergovernmental Organizations

The twentieth-century story of IGOs involves a huge expansion along the lines laid down during the nineteenth century. The stories of the emergence of the League of Nations, the United Nations (UN) and their associated families of IGOs are well known and do not need repeating here (e.g. Boli and Thomas, 1999; Armstrong et al., 2004; Iriye, 2004; Kennedy, 2007; Mazower, 2009 and 2012). Suffice to say that the number of IGOs has risen (depending on the definition used) to around 250, becoming a central feature of political and economic life at both the global and regional levels. Many IGOs are forums, but a few, such as the WTO, the International Monetary Fund (IMF) and the European Union (EU), are international actors in their own right.

Perhaps the main innovation in this field is the grouping together of a number of IGOs within a single framework, a process begun with the League of Nations in 1919 and greatly extended by the UN after 1945. The League sought influence over a range of issue-areas. As well as having a Council and an Assembly, the League incorporated a Permanent Secretariat divided into a number of sections, including the Social Section, headed by the British feminist Rachel Crowdy, which led high-profile campaigns against slavery, the opium trade, and the trafficking of women and children. The League's sections were one aspect of a wider strain of internationalism that encompassed IGOs and INGOs, as well as treaties like the Kellogg-Briand Pact of 1928, which prohibited war as an instrument of policy and committed states to the peaceful resolution of disputes (Gorman, 2012).

The League handed over to the UN most of its associated bureaucracies, such as the PCIJ (which became the International Court of Justice), the International Labour Organization (ILO), the Health Organization (becoming the World Health Organization), and the International Commission on Intellectual Cooperation (becoming the United Nations Educational, Scientific and Cultural Organization – UNESCO). To these were added the IMF, the World Bank, the General Agreement on Tariffs and Trade (GATT, later the WTO), the International Atomic Energy Agency, the International Maritime Organization and many others, so that a whole family of IGOs, both functional and regional, is now linked through the UN system. This system rests on being seen as a solution to the problem of how to reconcile the imperatives of sovereign equality on the one hand, and those of great power privilege, managerial responsibility and legalized hegemony on the other. As Simpson (2004: 115–59) argues, this tension was first articulated at Versailles in 1919. The compromise reached was to construct two-tiered political arrangements with a general assembly embodying the principle of sovereign equality and an executive council embodying the principle of legalized great power hegemony (Morefield, 2004; Mazower, 2009). The tension between the latter and the former is a theme we pick up in Chapters 6 and 7.

International Non-Governmental Organizations

Alongside the expansion of IGOs has been a comparable spread of INGOs, which have become increasingly integrated within processes of law-making and multilateral diplomacy. In some ways, the increase in the number and function of INGOs is the most notable aspect of post-nineteenth-century developments in social interaction capacity – from the several hundred INGOs that existed before the First World War, the contemporary world has around 25,000 INGOs, the vast majority of which have been formed since 1970 (Mazower, 2012: 417; Davies, 2013: 6, 19). So great is the presence of INGOs that they now disburse more funds than the UN; two-thirds of the EU's relief budget is funnelled through INGOs (Mazower, 2012: 417).

Although the function of INGOs as pressure groups on governments and international law remains much the same as it was for nineteenth-century movements, the scale of issues covered by these organizations has expanded almost beyond recognition. The immediate post-First World War years saw the emergence of a large number of INGOs, from Save the Children to the International Chamber of Commerce. After a decline in the period leading up to the Second World War, there was a further expansion in INGO activity during and after the war, particularly around humanitarian issues (the Oxford Committee for Famine Relief (Oxfam) was a product of the war itself) and peace initiatives (such as the Federation of Atomic Scientists).

During the post-war period, the activities of INGOs became much more closely integrated with IGOs than was the case during the nineteenth century. In determining whether an INGO could be formally associated with an IGO, four essential criteria emerged: the INGO had to be non-profit-making; non-violent; eschew political action designed to damage the governments of the IGO's member states; and support the goals of the IGO (Willetts, 1996: 3–5). INGOs often favoured associations with IGOs because they hoped to act as pressure groups that played a formal role in international affairs. At the Rio Environmental Conference held in 1992, there were representatives from 178 countries and 650 INGOs. And the INGOs were not simply there as observers. The knowledge-based INGOs, such as the International Union for the Conservation of Nature and Natural Resources (IUCN) and the International Council of Scientific Unions (ICSU), helped to shape some of the agenda items and, equally importantly, had an input into some of the conventions that were established at the conference (Morphet, 1996). The intense involvement of INGOs in environmental negotiations has remained in place at subsequent conferences such as that in Copenhagen in 2009. In the same way, soon after Amnesty International was established in 1961, the organization was given consultative status at the United Nations, enabling it to attend relevant UN meetings, submit documents and make statements. Amnesty devotes a considerable amount of its time, expertise and resources to performing these tasks. It also lobbies a wide range of regional IGOs, from the Council of Europe to the League of Arab States (Cook, 1996).

In a number of instances, the link between IGOs and INGOs is institutionalized and the resulting organization consists of both governments and INGOs, as is the case with the Intergovernmental Panel on Climate Change (IPCC), the world's leading body for assessing climate change. The International Red Cross also incorporates both governmental and non-governmental members. The organization is governed by a Conference that meets every four years, with each state and each National Society having a representative and holding an equal vote. There is, however, a functional division of labour, with governments funding the International Committee of the Red Cross, which protects prisoners of war and acts as an intermediary in conflicts, and National Societies funding the Red Cross International Federation, which assists refugees and provides disaster relief. The International Labour Organization works along similar lines. Although its members are states, the representatives of the states come from government, trade unions and employer associations.

While the number, variety and influence of INGOs have increased dramatically since the nineteenth century, it remains the case that the organs of global civil society are principally based in the West and reflective of Western values (Clark, 2007: 183; Hurrell, 2007: 111–14; the influence of non-Western INGOs is examined in Davies, 2013). While the close entwining of IGOs and INGOs might seem like a distinctive feature of twentieth- and twenty-first-century international relations, the social order that engendered this move was manifest by the late nineteenth century. The Hague Conferences of 1899 and 1907, for instance, were to a great extent shaped by peace groups and the media, which were permitted access to both conferences (Clark, 2007: 61–82). A key theme of these conferences was the appeal to 'the public conscience' to constrain the conduct of war. Although global civil society matured during the twentieth century, it was born during the nineteenth century.

Conclusion

The density of connections established by the global transformation generated both deep and rapid levels of diffusion, whether of technological innovations or political ideologies, something central to periods of rapid social change (Diamond, 1998). During the nineteenth century, the shrinking of distance enabled the more or less instantaneous transmission of news, market information and military movements, and the crashing together of economic, political and cultural orders that were previously only sparsely connected. As noted in the last chapter, this transformation in interaction capacity opened up new imaginaries such as 'Greater Britain', which envisaged political communities taking advantage of the shrinkage of distance by cohering without being territorially contiguous (Bell, 2007). Such imaginaries, however, were not realized: maritime transport could not hold together these visions on its own and railways proved more effective at creating continental states such as the US and Russia (Deudney, 2007: 227–9, 232–9).

The planet also shrank in other ways during the nineteenth century. The disruption of the environment through deforestation, habitat destruction, soil erosion, overfishing and related processes began in earnest during this period. Vast forests, such as the Mata Atlântica in Brazil, were severely depleted, while millions of buffaloes were slaughtered in North America, as were great herds of elephants in Africa. These mutually reinforcing patterns of non-sustainable development originated in the nineteenth century, and have become a form of 'ecocide' in the twenty-first century (Diamond, 2005: 6). Indeed, the huge expansion of both the human population and industrial output (and its pollution) that took off during the global transformation makes it the central reference point for the time when human activity began to become a significant factor in climate change. The use of fossil fuels multiplied by a factor of five during the nineteenth century and by a factor of twenty during the twentieth century (Christian, 2004: 346–7). Although most people did not know it at the time, the global transformation marks the beginning of contemporary concerns about the environment. Likewise, and harking back to the long-standing integrative role of lingua francas, English began its rise to global dominance (Osterhammel, 2014: 780–3).

In most of the ways that count, therefore, the basic shrinking of the planet that marks modernity was established during the nineteenth century. Under conditions of global modernity, what Watson (1992: 14) calls *raison de système* (the belief that it pays to make the system work) became prominent, giving rise to the management of international society through various units of global governance, a point we return to in Chapter 9. Subsequent developments dramatically extended the range, speed and carrying capacity of both physical and social infrastructures, but they did not fundamentally transform them in the way that those of the nineteenth century had done. The key argument is that it is the breakthroughs of the nineteenth century, both technological and organizational, that mark the turning point to global modernity. The relative change between the pre-nineteenth-century world of horses and sailing ships without IGOs or INGOs on the one hand, and the nineteenth-century world of steamships, railways, telegraphs, radio, IGOs and global civil society on the other, is far bigger than that between the nineteenth-century world and the world of the twentieth and twenty-first centuries.

4 | *Ideologies of Progress*

Introduction

During the long nineteenth century, history became to be seen as directional, while social change began to be considered as normal rather than exceptional (Wallerstein, 2011a: 1). A European-wide movement, known as Enlightenment in Britain, *Lumières* in France, *Aufklärung* in Germany and *Ilustración* in Spain, sought to harness change through reason, experiment and the professionalization of scientific knowledge (Weiner, 2003a: 2–3; Israel, 2010: 5; also see Koselleck, 2000 [1959]). Statistical methods produced an 'avalanche of numbers' that were deployed in the hope of 'taming chance' and providing solutions to endemic social problems ranging from poverty to crime (Hacking, 1990: 5, 78; Porter, 1995). 'Radical enlightenment' figures, many of them associated with the Atlantic revolutionary movements of the late eighteenth and early nineteenth centuries, produced influential, widely circulated works on how society could be 'improved' (Drayton, 2000; Israel, 2012).[1] Condorcet's discipline of 'social mathematics' was renamed 'Sociology' by Auguste Comte, who argued that a 'science of the social' could uncover the 'laws of society' (Hacking, 1990: 39–40). Academic chairs in Sociology began to appear in France in the 1850s and in the United States during the 1860s. Other disciplines followed suit as the 'social movement' of social science sought to professionalize research in the cause of 'betterment' (Wallerstein, 2011a: 227). In 1856,

---

[1] Perhaps most famously, the Abbé Raynal led a team of researchers, including Denis Diderot, in the production of a multi-volume history of the Indian subcontinent and the Caribbean (*Histoire Philosophique des Deux Indes*). The widely circulated book went through 30 editions over a 17-year period. Interestingly, the authors of the *Histoire*, including Raynal and Diderot, were opposed to European imperialism, seeing it as fostering deprivation in both overseas territories and the metropole. For more on strains of Enlightenment anti-imperialism, see Muthu (2003).

the Association for the Promotion of Social Science was established in London; in 1865, an equivalent body was founded in the United States. Both bodies were explicitly aimed at improving public policy (Wallerstein, 2011a: 228). Major new universities such as Sciences Po (1871) and LSE (1895) were formed with overtly 'progressive' aims. The accumulation of data and the systematization of knowledge were intended to improve the human condition through concerted programmes of social engineering (Giddens, 1985: 181; Porter, 1995; Drayton, 2000; Weiner, 2003b; Israel, 2012; Osterhammel, 2014: 24–9).

These new techniques of professional research and knowledge collection were used both to enhance the power of states domestically (the collection and storage of information became routine tools of statecraft) and as tools for the extension of European power (where they helped to administer imperial rule) (Giddens, 1985: 181; Connell, 2007; Mignolo, 2011). During the long nineteenth century, European thinkers began to connect notions of progress to ideas of civilizational superiority, generating a linear trajectory from Ancient Greece to modern Europe in which 'progress' was considered to be self-generating through characteristics internal to the West (Bernal, 1987). Progress at home meant promoting scientific research, carrying out public health initiatives, improving education systems, fostering commercial exchange, and embracing technological change (Israel, 2010: 4). Progress abroad often meant a reinforcement of metropolitan superiority through a stark differentiation between Europeans and 'others'.

In this way, ideas of progress helped to constitute a tripartite distinction between 'civilized humanity' (Europeans, white settlers and (some) Latin Americans),[2] 'barbarous humanity' (the Ottoman and Persian empires, Central Asian states, China and Japan), and 'savage humanity' (everywhere else) (Hobson, 2012: 33; Ansorge, 2013: 19). By and large, Europeans respected sovereignty in the 'civilized' world, while 'barbarians'

---

[2] The position of Latin Americans in this classification was complex. On the one hand, Latin America was deeply racialized: indigenous peoples were serfs; blacks were slaves; mestizos had the status of non-noble Spaniards; Spaniards served as peasants, artisans, traders and independent producers; and colonial administrators stood at the apex of the social hierarchy. In this way, class and race were mutually reinforcing – colonialism and capitalism worked hand-in-hand (Quijano, 2000: 217; Osterhammel, 2014: 131–3). On the other hand, Latin American elites, both before and after independence, were sufficiently 'like' Europeans to be assimilated within colonial-Western international society, albeit as a relatively marginal and somewhat inferior constituency within it.

received partial political recognition. But, for 'savages', dispossession, colonial annexation and, at times, annihilation exposed the dark side of progress. A 'colonial matrix of power' rendered non-Europeans outside the scope of historical development – from this point on, these were 'peoples without history' (Quijano, 1992; Mignolo, 2011: xv), a point made bluntly by both Marx in one of his newspaper columns from the 1850s and Hegel in a lecture on world history from 1822:

> The whole of her [India's] past history, if it be anything, is the history of the successive conquests she has undergone. Indian society has no history at all, at least no known history. What we call its history is but the history of the successive intruders who founded their empires on the passive basis of that unresisting and unchanging society. (Marx, 1853)

> Anyone who wishes to study the most terrible manifestations of human nature will find them in Africa. The earliest reports concerning the continent tell us precisely the same, and it has no history in the true sense of the word. We shall therefore leave Africa at this point, and it need not be mentioned again. For it is an unhistorical continent, with no movement or development of its own . . . What we understand as Africa proper is that unhistorical and undeveloped land . . . which had to be mentioned before we cross the threshold of world history itself. (Hegel, cited in Magubane, 2005: 92)

Time and again, Western observers contrasted the progressive 'rational restlessness' of the West with the inert, passive nature of 'Oriental despotism' (Weber, 1978a [1922] and 1978b [1922]; Mann, 1988: 7–15; Aydin, 2007).

The notion of progress, therefore, had a dual function: it lay behind the 'improvement' of European societies through processes ranging from academic research to social engineering; and it served to distinguish peoples around the world on the basis of their 'civilizational' quotient (Drayton, 2000). These dual functions were underpinned by techniques that made populations 'legible' through practices ranging from censuses to mapping (Scott, 1999; Weiner, 2003b; Branch, 2014; Osterhammel, 2014: 24–9; see also Foucault, 2002 [1969]). They were also enabled by four new political ideologies: liberalism, socialism, nationalism and 'scientific' racism.[3]

---

[3] By political ideology we mean assemblages of beliefs, concepts and values that address how polities, economies and cultural orders relate to each other, how individuals and groups fit into these assemblages, and how human collectivities should be governed. Enduring ideologies, such as liberalism and conservatism, are

Each of these ideologies embodied a distinct vision of progress. Collectively they constituted an assault on dynasticism and religion, and the link between these two in the dynastic claim to rule by divine right. Liberalism was associated with a series of assumptions about progress as resulting from the freedom (founded on the idea of the purposive, autonomous, rights-bearing individual) generated by the rationality of market exchange (as embodied in the concept of private property) and government by consent (as represented by constitutional democracy). The association of liberalism with progress served as a major rationale for the expansion of international society both during and since the nineteenth century. For socialists, progress was linked to a materialist conception of historical development in which classes served as the primary agents of historical change. Some socialists favoured the forging of 'popular alliances' and 'united fronts' with other 'progressive' forces, seeing revolutions as two-stage processes in which a prior 'political' or 'bourgeois' revolution would ready the conditions for a more extensive, socialist uprising. Others favoured immediate social revolution in which the industrial proletariat, as the historical agents of progressive change, seized control of the primary organs of power. Nationalism was 'progressive' in the sense that it created new forms and scales of social order and political integration. More counter-intuitively, 'scientific' racism also had a 'progressive' element in its assertion that 'superior stock' should command historical development. There was a close, if often unacknowledged, relationship between liberal and socialist ideas of 'improvement', and racist proposals to use eugenics to 'upgrade' the biological quality of the human stock (Hannaford, 1996: 360, 370–1; Weiner, 2003a: 6; Bowden, 2009: locs. 755–848).

These ideologies expressed an important, novel feature of modernity – that progress was necessary for modern societies. Without this sense of forward momentum, it was politically difficult to justify the inequalities generated by industrial capitalism. During the nineteenth century, many social orders became more open and participatory. More people participated in economic, cultural and political life, many commanding significant skills and resources, and demanding a share of the prosperity associated with some aspects of the global

malleable – they adjust to different temporal and spatial contexts. On this issue, see Freeden (1996).

transformation. This sense of permanent upheaval is what gave fear of social revolution real bite. The easiest way for industrial societies to cope with this pressure was, and still is, to sustain levels of growth sufficient to provide for the effective management of disparities in wealth: so long as all boats rose, it mattered less if some rose higher than others. Staving off instability required economies that delivered sufficient employment and sustained reasonable standards of living. In this way, the nineteenth century established the addiction of industrial societies to permanent growth as a means of mediating the politics of inequality. Progress in the form of economic growth, allied to a degree of redistribution, was as important as nationalism in containing the class conflicts predicted by Marx, Engels and their successors.

Taken together, liberalism, nationalism, socialism and 'scientific' racism had three major effects: first, they challenged the basic framing for how societies were ordered; second, they rationalized vast programmes of social engineering, including industrialization; and third, they legitimized both rational state-building and the extension of Western power around the world. They also generated a complex set of tensions. In general terms, ideologies of progress had no single understanding of the role and extent of the market, making this a central point of contestation within global modernity. Liberals were torn over whether universal claims of rights, autonomy and self-determination could be applied, or forcibly extended, to 'uncivilized' peoples. For their part, socialists saw themselves in direct competition with liberals over the basic direction of modernity. Nationalist claims of self-reliance competed with liberal and socialist internationalism. 'Scientific' racism had connections to each of the other three ideologies, but fitted most easily with extreme forms of nationalism, most potently with the rise of fascism after the First World War. It is therefore no surprise that all of the great international conflicts and rivalries of the twentieth century were conducted in the names of these four ideologies. No additional ideologies of anything like the same weight or influence have taken hold since. Indeed, the four ideologies of progress that arose during the nineteenth century still retain a powerful hold on both IR as a discipline and international relations as a field of practice. This chapter charts their emergence, assesses their challenge, and examines their effects.

Liberalism

Liberalism is associated with a range of often conflicting value-commitments (individual autonomy and equality, pluralism and universalism), concept-practices (free markets, self-determination, human rights, representative government, collective security) and people (Smith and Paine, Mill and Wilson, Rawls and Nussbaum).[4] In IR, liberalism is often taken to mean cooperation via processes such as democratization, interdependence and the spread of international organizations (Rathbun, 2010). Sometimes the term is used to denote modernity itself (e.g. Deudney and Ikenberry, 2009).

Although many liberals claim a 'pre-history' dating back to Locke, the term 'liberalism' only emerged in self-conscious form during the early years of the nineteenth century, when it was used to refer to the curtailment of arbitrary monarchical power through a constitution (Bell, 2007: 8; also see Pocock, 1975; Freeden, 2005). It was not until the second half of the nineteenth century that liberalism became a 'living political tradition' – a composite of ideas concerned with the ways in which international law, commercial exchanges and republican constitutions could transform international morality (Bell, 2007: 8 and forthcoming: 9–15). During the early part of the twentieth century, some liberal texts became international bestsellers – Norman Angell's *The Great Illusion* (1910) was translated into 25 languages and sold 2 million copies. Prominent figures around the world appropriated liberal ideas as sources of both critique and mobilization (Bayly, 2011).

If there are many liberalisms, it is no surprise that there is an in-built ambivalence in terms of how liberal theory is realized in practice, captured, for example, by the ways in which self-declared liberals can simultaneously favour non-intervention (on the grounds of supporting self-determination) and intervention (on humanitarian grounds) (Lawson and Tardelli, 2013; Little, 2013). For some, liberalism is a 'plastic, changing thing' (Freeden, 2005: 20); for others, it is an 'all purpose word' representing 'a deep reservoir of ideological contradictions' (Bell, forthcoming: 2, 8).

---

[4] It is impossible to provide a concise guide to the modern literature on liberalism, but a selection of influential texts – both supportive and critical – would include: Rawls, 1971; Barry, 1973; Pocock, 1975; Nozick, 1984; Pogge, 1989; Young, 1990; Miller, 1997; Sandel, 1998; Walzer, 2004; Freeden, 2005; Losurdo, 2011; and Ryan, 2013.

Although liberalism comes in many forms, in general terms it is oriented around three core ideas: the individual as the primary site for the articulation of normative claims; the market as the primary site of economic exchange; and representative democracy as the primary site of political authority. In principle, these ideas are complementary: liberals favour republican polities in which free markets, sustained through private property regimes, provide the means for maximizing individual autonomy. Indeed, one of the central themes in liberal thought is the notion of the 'harmony of interests' – the idea that the world is, potentially, orderable (through relations of free market exchange and representative governance) in ways that serve the interests of all.

In practice, the relationship between these principles is often deeply contested. First, as Gilpin (1987) argues, there is an ongoing tension between the redistributive demands of liberal states domestically and the liberalization of trade, production and finance internationally. He calls this 'Keynes at home and Smith abroad' (Gilpin, 1987: 355; see also Ruggie, 1982). The emergence of industrial capitalism, with the accompanying hopes and fears of revolutions, was an ongoing expression of this tension. Second, most societies combine liberal and illiberal elements: liberal markets are often embedded within authoritarian political structures (a point we return to in Chapters 5 and 9) and all liberal states experience competing claims between individuals and collectivities over how to arbitrate claims of autonomy, the distribution of wealth, and security. Third, there are tensions between ideas of 'negative liberty' (a 'liberty of restraint' premised on external non-interference in order to maximize individual autonomy, protect private property and foster human rights) and 'positive liberty' (a 'liberty of imposition' geared at direct intervention in order to generate the 'right' conditions for liberty to arise) (Berlin, 1969; Sørensen, 2006). Because the latter tends towards a universalizing project, liberal states are often expansive in terms of their international conduct – liberalism has been used to justify both military intervention and imperialism (Armitage, 2000; Pitts, 2005; Bell, 2007). The result has been a series of extensive debates over the rights and wrongs of extending the liberal project around the world (for a positive assessment, see Ikenberry, 2011; for a critique, see Jahn, 2005).

There are four main points to note about the relationship between liberalism and the global transformation. First, following the Atlantic

Revolutions of the late eighteenth and early nineteenth centuries, liberalism became closely associated with principles of individual rights, popular sovereignty and self-determination. From this point on, liberalism (and, in particular, republicanism) was seen as a major threat to dynastic order – the 'Rights of Man' were deeply corrosive to notions of aristocratic privilege, while events like the Haitian Revolution presented a challenge to the place of slavery and the institution of racism as core components of international society.[5] In the early part of the century, liberals and nationalists in Latin America threw off Spanish rule. European liberals were less successful in 1848 when a series of uprisings was crushed by absolutist regimes defending conservative principles.[6] Yet liberal movements in Europe and elsewhere grew in strength during the latter part of the century, achieving a suite of political gains ranging from the recognition of civil freedoms to constitutional reforms. Constitutionalism was central to the wave of revolutions that took place in the early part of the twentieth century in Russia, Iran, Turkey, China and Mexico (Sohrabi, 1995; Kurzman, 2008; Osterhammel, 2014: 559–71). Pro-democratic movements unseated imperial regimes, held competitive elections (albeit in franchises limited to propertied men), convened parliaments and instituted civil freedoms. As with the revolutionaries of 1848, the constitutionalists were defeated. However, even if the revolutions of 1848 and 1905–12 failed in the short run, their main rationale (political liberalization) was more successful in the long run. Anti-imperial struggles during the twentieth century were, to some extent, the successors of these earlier struggles for autonomy and rights (Reus-Smit, 2013), as were the 'democratic revolutions' in Eastern and Central Europe in 1989 (Thompson, 2004) and, it could be argued, the 2011 Arab uprisings (Lawson, forthcoming).

---

[5] This challenge was not wholly successful. For example, although the slave trade was formally banned, it remained an important component of the Atlantic economy until the latter part of the nineteenth century. During the nineteenth century as a whole, an estimated 3.3 million African slaves were transported from Africa to the Americas (Bayly, 2004: 403).

[6] A companion event to the 1848 revolutions is worth noting – the first women's rights convention, which took place at Seneca Falls in the United States in mid-July of the same year. Like those who instigated the 1848 revolutions, participants in the Seneca Falls Convention had to wait a considerable time for the realization of their goals. On how the 1848 revolutions and the Seneca Falls Convention formed part of a transnational field of contentious politics, see Hewitt (2010).

Second is the association of liberalism with the extension of the market. Although liberal arguments for free trade predate the global transformation (Hirschman, 1977; Neal, 1990; Carruthers, 1996; Allen, 2009; Pincus, 2009), free market policies – including the reduction of tariffs, the removal of state subsidies, and the free flow of finance – only became mainstream state practices during the nineteenth century (Latham, 1997). This aspect of the liberal corpus was held most strongly in Britain, where virulent debates took place over legislation such as the Navigation Acts, which protected trade between Britain and its colonies, and the Corn Laws, which provided protection for cereal producers in Britain and Ireland (often aristocratic landowners). During the middle part of the nineteenth century, financial reforms in Britain stripped the power of guilds, abolished local tolls and duties, removed restrictions on interest rates, and created a national currency. The result was the construction of a national market for the first time (Latham, 1997: 435–7; also see Weber, 1978a [1922]: 353–4). Free trade enthusiasts in Britain and France lobbied successfully for bilateral free trade treaties, signing the Cobden Chevalier Treaty in 1860, and sought to internationalize tariff reductions. British policy-makers led the way – between 1848 and 1860, Britain reduced its number of dutiable goods from 1,146 to 48 (Clark, 2011: 107). At the same time, joint-stock companies 'opened the globe' to capitalist expansion, extending both the range and depth of market interactions (Hobsbawm, 1975). The marketization of social relations, in which 'generalized money' served as a unifying form of exchange, became a core component of international relations, a position it retains today. We return to this issue in the next chapter.

Third, beyond the challenge presented by liberal ideas of political representation and market exchange, the idea of individuals as the primary site of normative articulation challenged the basis of aristocratic orders. This prompted the rise of humanitarianism in general, and the human rights regime in particular (Barnett, 2011; Moyn, 2010 takes a different view). The development of humanitarian concerns was apparent in British campaigns against both the slave trade and the Indian practice of *sati*. Such campaigns were linked to developments within Britain (including parliamentary reform, Catholic emancipation, and the Chartist movement) and outside it (including the emergence of transnational advocacy groups and INGOs, most notably the International Committee of the Red Cross) (Onuf, 2004; Bass, 2008).

As we discuss in Chapter 7, the relationship between liberalism and humanitarianism became even more pronounced, and even more influential, during the twentieth and twenty-first centuries, playing a central role in embedding nineteenth-century ideas of individual autonomy within the governance structures of modern international relations. Formal sites of global governance, not least the UN, are founded on these ideals, as are a number of INGOs.

Fourth, liberalism was a central strand in the expansion of European imperialism. Although the relationship between liberalism and imperialism was complex (Mehta, 1999; Pitts, 2005; Hobson, 2012), many liberals favoured an extension of imperial practices on the grounds that they 'uplifted' the peoples of Asia and Africa (Bell, 2010). Cultural points of differentiation were used to justify imperialism both as a legitimate solution to 'backwardness' and as a means of realizing the responsibilities of the civilized to those considered to be lower down the civilizational ladder. In France, Paul Leroy-Beaulieu's *De La Colonisation chez les Peuples Modernes* was a highly influential account of the mutually beneficial progress that could be generated between colonizer and colonized through the cultivation of indigenous elites. In Britain, J. S. Mill (1859; also see Bell, 2010) argued that peoples outside the civilized world could not be subject to international law, as this required a level of reciprocity that 'barbarians' were incapable of achieving. It was in the interests of these peoples to be conquered and, thereby, 'uplifted' by a higher civilization. Such reasoning fostered an extension of liberal 'goods' beyond settler colonies (Jahn, 2005). Liberals could offer 'tutelage' to peoples facing barriers of political, economic and cultural 'backwardness' that hindered their 'maturity' (Bell, 2007). It does not require a great stretch to see the ways in which these liberal 'civilizing missions' have been reinforced either implicitly (e.g. Ikenberry, 2011), or explicitly (e.g. Cooper, 2002; Ferguson, 2004), in contemporary debates about the duties of liberal peoples to those suffering under the yoke of 'backward' social orders, whether this is understood as a deficient (i.e. non-market) economy, a regressive (i.e. authoritarian) form of governance, or a backward (i.e. explicitly religious) culture.

In sum, liberalism was intimately involved with the 'progressive' agenda of the global transformation. During the long nineteenth century, liberalism corroded the legitimacy of absolutism and aristocratic rule, and helped to justify the expansion of the market and imperial projects. Many of its main ideas stand as central strands of contemporary international order. As noted in Chapter 3, liberal IGOs and INGOs have become core components of multilateral diplomacy. The world is more democratic and more open to trade than at any other time in human history. Such gains were not achieved easily. Even the most liberal regime of the nineteenth century – Britain – took the entire century to extend its franchise to non-propertied men. Women were not granted the vote until the early part of the twentieth century.[7] And, for the most part, liberal states restricted, or denied, the franchise for citizens and subjects who inhabited their overseas territories.

Nevertheless, the 'liberal ascendancy' has been one of the principal vectors of world historical development over the past two centuries (Ikenberry, 2011). The First World War indirectly promoted socialism and fascism as alternatives to liberalism. The Second World War marginalized fascism and promoted both socialism and liberalism. The outcome of the Cold War marginalized socialism, leaving liberalism as modernity's principal ideological current. If liberalism has outlasted socialism and found ways of coming to terms with nationalism, ideological struggles have not ceased with the end of the Cold War. While the market side of liberalism has triumphed quite widely, its political and cultural agendas have not. As we discuss in Chapter 9, authoritarian strains of capitalist governance are alive and well in the contemporary world. How best to embed market relations in wider social and political orders remains an open question.

Socialism

Nineteenth-century socialism shared a number of synergies with liberalism, most notably a commitment to progress and reason, and an opposition to dynasticism and aristocratic rule. However, socialism also provided a multifaceted challenge to liberalism. First, socialists were opposed to the ontological and normative individualism celebrated by liberals, seeing these as harmful consequences of a schema premised on private property. Because private property was seen as a

---

[7] While women virtually everywhere were treated unequally during the nineteenth century, the particular needs of evangelical missionary work to access family structures in non-Western societies gave women a prominent role in that field (Darwin, 2012: 279–91).

form of exploitation rather than as a means of empowerment, socialists favoured the collectivization of ownership rather than the liberalization of production. Second, socialists saw the basis of social order not as a harmony of interests, but as rooted in class antagonisms. As such, progress was likely to require radical rupture rather than gradual reform. Third, socialists saw the industrial proletariat rather than the bourgeoisie as the principal agents of progressive social change. Given this, socialists favoured universal franchise and the empowerment of trade unions and labour organizations rather than a supposedly meritocratic franchise limited by property, education or gender.

Socialism was drawn from a number of sources: British political economy, German philosophy and French radical politics (Hobsbawm, 2011: 34). During the early part of the century, the promise of radical change was carried by insurrectionary 'brotherhoods' such as the Russian Decembrists, the 'League of the Just' (later the Communist League) and Gracchus Babeuf's 'Conspiracy of Equals'. Beyond these groups were friendly societies, anarchists, syndicalists, mass movements such as the Chartists and, from the 1840s, self-declared communists (Calhoun, 2012). Like liberalism, socialism came in multiple modes rather than singular form. 'Utopian' socialists (such as Saint-Simon, Robert Owen and Charles Fourier) favoured the establishment of small-scale enclaves, such as Owen's 'New Lanark', as bulwarks against the inequities of market society. 'Scientific' socialists (such as Marx and Engels) sought the construction of mass political parties and unions that could confront and transform industrial capitalism as a system (Eley, 2002: 27–9). The emergence of industrialization, the rational state and ideologies of progress saw a shift within many radical movements away from a strategy of secret societies aimed at seizing power through an elite putsch to the notion of mass revolution carried through by the industrial proletariat. However, it was only in the latter part of the nineteenth century, mostly *after* Marx's death in 1883, that the 'scientific' strand of socialism became pre-eminent.[8]

The socialist prognosis of modern society was sharp – society was bifurcated between haves and have nots, a division premised on

[8] The role of Engels in this regard is difficult to overestimate. As Marx's literary executor, Engels edited Volume 2 and Volume 3 of Marx's *Capital*, publishing them posthumously in 1885 and 1894 respectively. Volume 4 was later edited and published by Karl Kautsky as *Theories of Surplus Value*.

differential access to the means of production. In short, bourgeois society was divided between those who controlled the means of production and those who provided its labour power. Over time, the socialist argument ran, this system of both direct and indirect exploitation would generate the development of a distinct class-consciousness amongst the industrial proletariat. Indeed, the emergence of industrial society meant that, for the first time, classes were not just *de facto* 'classes-in-themselves' but self-conscious political actors – 'classes-for-themselves' (Thompson, 1968: 9). These classes-for-themselves could express political consciousness in both reformist and revolutionary forms. The former was expressed in agitation for an extension of the franchise, workplace reforms, welfare regimes, public education programmes, and the like. The latter was a more comprehensive doctrine aimed at 'expropriating the expropriators' through social revolution. This revolutionary strand of socialism promised a far greater threat to absolutism than that provided by liberalism; it also posed a considerable threat to liberalism.

As noted above, the most powerful, if by no means only, strand of socialism was associated with Marx and Engels. Their 'Communist Manifesto', written during the tumult of the 1848 uprisings in Europe, became the principal statement of socialist intent. However, it was not until the 1870s that the Manifesto became widely circulated internationally. Most notably, the 1872 trial of the leadership of the German Social Democratic Party had the unintended consequence of legitimizing the Manifesto. Used by the prosecution in an attempt to establish the guilt of the accused, the recording of the Manifesto as an official court document made it difficult to suppress thereafter. Between 1871 and 1873, the Manifesto was published in six different European languages. By the end of the nineteenth century, hundreds of editions had been produced in over 30 languages, including Japanese and Chinese (Hobsbawm, 2011: 104).

The spread of the Manifesto matched the spread of the socialist movement more generally. Trade union confederations emerged in Britain in 1868 and spread to a number of other countries over the next half century. International trade secretariats (federations of national trade unions) covering printers, shoemakers, miners, tailors, transport workers, public sector workers, and more emerged in parallel. British and German union membership alone increased by well over 3 million members each between the mid-1880s and 1914 (Eley, 2002: 75). Large-scale socialist parties, such as the German Social Democratic Party, an officially Marxist organ after 1891, had hundreds of thousands of members and millions of voters. More dramatically, socialist-inspired communards seized power in Paris in 1871. This realization of the socialist challenge may not have had the impact anticipated by the British liberal William Harcourt, who claimed in 1888 that 'we are all socialists now'. But both in practice and in inspiration, socialist movements played a major role in raising awareness of the inequalities of industrialization and in generating support for programmes intended to alleviate these inequities.

However, even as socialism grew, so splits within the movement appeared. The 'First International' (International Workingmen's Association) of socialist-inspired parties split in the aftermath of the Paris Commune over the desirability (or otherwise) of leading a United Front against bourgeois power and the requirement (or otherwise) of seizing state power as a lever of social control and transformation. Reformist governments defanged the socialist challenge by introducing welfare reforms, public health and education programmes, and opening up the franchise, albeit slowly. During and after the First World War, most of the revolutionary factions within the socialist movement were defeated either by those who prioritized nationalism over class solidarity or who preferred parliamentary roads to socialism. Even the first great success of socialism, the Bolshevik Revolution in Russia, was offset by the failure of socialists to seize power in Germany during and after the First World War, itself a reflection of strategic differences within leftist parties. These differences sometimes prompted bloody fallouts, such as the 1921 Kronstadt Mutiny, in which Lenin ordered the Soviet state to crush a rebellion of leftist-inspired sailors.

The basic components of socialism as a system of thought were in place by the end of the nineteenth century. What was added during the twentieth and twenty-first centuries was the experience of socialism in practice. Initially, despite the failure in Germany, things went quite well. The First World War, in which governments directed economies to meet the requirements of total war, seemed to demonstrate that, given the amplified powers of the rational state, the command economy could work. Humane, efficient practices of social democracy developed in Scandinavia.[9] Stalin's much less humane and much less efficient regime

---

[9] Scandinavian social democracies were not always humane. Between 1935 and 1975, the Swedish state sterilized nearly 63,000 people (mostly women) on the basis that they were 'racially or socially inferior' (Weiner, 2003: 6). This serves to

in the Soviet Union also managed to industrialize quickly, in stark contrast to the depression-ravaged West. On the eve of the Second World War, the Soviet Union was responsible for 19% of the world's industrial production (up from 4% in 1913), while the USSR had more doctors per capita than either Germany or Britain (Halperin, 2013: 174).

The Second World War further burnished socialism's progressive credentials. The Soviet Union emerged victorious from the war, sharing in the enhanced legitimacy that victory provided. In the elections that followed the war, socialist parties around Europe averaged around a third of the popular vote. During the post-war period, many socialist states in Central and Eastern Europe grew faster than their Western European counterparts (Frieden, 2006: 337). Outside Europe, post-war decolonization was deeply infused with socialism. For many post-colonial states, the Soviet model was an attractive one. Between 1928 and 1970, the Soviet Union grew at an average rate of 5.6% per year (Lane, 1996: 153–4). Even when this rate slowed in the 1970s, many states in the global South preferred the 'virtues of communism': 'relatively incorrupt political elites committed to relatively egalitarian development', including high rates of literacy, full employment and strong public health systems (Mann, 2013: 221, 363). Socialist-inspired revolutionaries took power in China, Vietnam, Cuba, Ethiopia, Afghanistan and elsewhere. Tanzania, Algeria and Nicaragua were showcases for leftist progressivism and there was a general, much-lauded, drive towards 'Afrocommunism'. In 1982, at the time of the death of Soviet leader Leonid Brezhnev, the Soviet network stretched to 31 component states: states run by Soviet clients (e.g. Cuba and Vietnam); states oriented towards socialism (e.g. Ethiopia and Nicaragua); two independent communist states (China and the Democratic People's Republic of Korea); a group of what the Soviets considered to be 'less advanced states of socialist orientation' (e.g. Algeria and Iraq); and several more marginal cases (e.g. Ghana and Surinam) (Halliday, 2010: 118–19).

However, socialism in practice suffered from the limitations of excessive state bureaucracy, particularly when this was combined with repression. Stalin's purges were exposed during the 1950s and restiveness

illustrate just how mainstream ideas of eugenics were amongst those on both the left and right, even after the Second World War.

about Soviet control in Central and Eastern Europe was apparent in periodic uprisings against Soviet rule: East Germany in 1953, Hungary in 1956, and Czechoslovakia in 1968. The scale of the bloodshed unleashed by Mao's purges in China and Pol Pot's 'year zero' in Cambodia became manifest during the 1970s.[10] North Korea developed into an oxymoronic form of dynastic communism. And many other socialist-inspired post-colonial regimes became acutely repressive. At the same time, the command economy proved to be no match for the creative destruction of market societies, particularly following the shift towards services, information and finance in the 1970s and 1980s. By the mid-1980s, the Soviet economic model was visibly failing, while China had begun the process of 'reform and opening up' to the market. This was followed by the implosion of the Soviet Union between 1989 and 1991. Along with China's reorientation towards the market, the Soviet collapse appeared to spell the end of the socialist challenge as a political programme, if less so as a body of thought and mode of critique.

When assessing the overall impact of socialism, it is possible to discern both successes and failures. The main success is socialism's contribution to a general sense of 'sinistrism' – a shift to the left in terms of how issues of representation, equality and social justice have been, and continue to be, framed (Tombs, 2000; Eley, 2002). Ideas of equality and social justice are now embedded in most social orders, as are socialist-inspired policies such as universal suffrage and the eight-hour working day. One ongoing example of this is the experience of Cuba, one of the few remaining self-declared socialist states in the contemporary world. Whatever its shortcomings in terms of respecting its political opponents and managing its economy, Cuba's socialist regime has performed well on a range of social indicators: Cuba has the highest levels of literacy and the lowest infant mortality rates in Latin America (Sassoon, 2010: 756). Cuba's experience speaks to the wider way in which socialist concerns about equality, development and redistribution have become central currents of contemporary political debates around the world, just as a previous generation of socialist

[10] Mao's purges are not as well known as those carried out by Stalin; most commentators tend to focus on the bloody events of the Cultural Revolution instead. However, after the 1949 revolution, Mao's regime killed between 4 and 5 million people, at least half of whom were executed. For more on this, see Westad (2012: 322).

thinkers inspired debate around land reform, anti-colonialism and anti-racism (Sassoon, 2010). Both in Cuba and further afield, socialist-inspired thinking is alive and well; indeed, the aftermath of the 2008 financial crisis has seen a revival of interest in Marxian thought (e.g. Harvey, 2011).

Socialism has also made an impact on the development of modern international order through its encouragement of revolution, a point we return to in Chapter 5. No continent bar Antarctica has been spared a revolution conducted in the name of socialism (Halliday, 1999). Indeed, one of the principal orienting strands of international relations over the past two centuries has been the challenge presented by revolutionary socialist states such as Russia, China and Cuba. Although the systemic challenge offered by these states disappeared with the collapse of the Soviet Union, China's rising power still operates under the banner of socialism, even if this label obscures more than it reveals. We discuss China's experiment in fusing party control with a market economy in Chapter 9.

In terms of socialist failures, three are worth particular attention. First, as noted above, is the tendency of the left to splinter. Not only have socialist movements frequently been hindered by factionalism, any hope of inspiring global revolution was undercut by differences over tactics: whether efforts to inspire revolution should be centred in the city or the countryside; the Cuban preference for *foco* vs. the Maoist notion of a 'people's war'; debates over whether revolutions would be successful only when conditions were organically 'ripe' or whether they could be actively 'ripened' by a vanguard party, and more. There were also considerable differences in the interpretations of Marxist thought fostered by socialist theorists and revolutionaries, from Lenin, Trotsky and Gramsci to Mao, Castro and Cabral. Such differences were reinforced by Soviet attempts to lead the socialist movement, something that rubbed up against diverse ideas of how 'progressive' ideals should be realized. In the 1880s, socialist sectarianism manifested in disputes over the need, or otherwise, of seizing state power; in the post-First World War period, a schism opened between those who favoured accommodating socialism within parliamentary systems and those who wanted to supersede capitalist society; in the 1930s, the split came over the Spanish Civil War; in the 1960s, it arose over the invasion of Czechoslovakia and the 1968 uprisings in Western Europe; in the early years of the twenty-first century, the war on terror split the left once again. History repeats itself, wrote Marx in the *18th Brumaire*, 'the first time as tragedy, the second time as farce'. It is only too easy to imagine what Marx would have made of history repeating itself five, six or seven times over.

The second failure is the poor experience of 'actual existing socialism'. The Soviet Union succumbed to the inefficiencies of excessive bureaucratization, failing as much because of its internal weaknesses as it did through international competition (Armbruster, 2010). In this sense, socialism was hoisted on the petard of liberal success. Over the long run, the 'possessive individualism' (Macpherson, 1962) that lay at the heart of liberal capitalist orders appeared, to many people around the world, more attractive than the collectivization promoted by socialism. Finally, the internationalist current of socialism was undercut by the capacity of nationalism to serve as the principal form of affective solidarity within modern international society.

Nationalism

The central idea of nationalism is that the nation should be the basis of the state. The definition of 'nation', and the precise criteria for a group of people to be counted as a nation, are contested. But the basic idea is simple: 'nations', being self-identifying groups sharing some combination of culture, language, ethnicity and history sufficient to produce a strong sense of 'we', should have the right to claim their own polity. Within this logic, ideally all states should be nation-states, with the state becoming the container and protector of its particular national identity. There is considerable debate within the field of nationalism studies over whether the nation pre-exists the state (nation-state) or is mainly constructed by the state (state-nation) (Rejai and Enloe, 1969; Smith, 1991; Breuilly, 1993; Sewell, 2004; Buzan, 2007 [1991]: 74–83). In practice, even in the case of what are thought to be pre-existing nations, such as France and Japan, the state has played a major role in making the nation. But while nations are modern constructions, this does not mean that they can easily overcome the hold of pre-existing affective sentiments, whether of place, kinship or faith. Despite this, national sentiments have generally come to dominate rival affective affinities.[11]

---

[11] For more on debates around the emergence and development of nationalism, see: Kedourie, 1960; Anderson, 1983; Gellner, 1983 and 1992; Bhabha, 1990;

Nationalism shifts the foundations of political legitimacy from the dynastic claims of aristocratic genealogies to the people constituted as a nation (Mayall, 1990: 26–8). Nationalism in this sense is a nineteenth-century product. Yet, as Gellner (1992: 289) notes, nationalism has the paradoxical quality of being deeply rooted in modernity on the one hand, while appealing to older understandings of community and identity on the other. Unlike agrarian polities, which did little to promote linkages amongst their constituent communities, modern industrial states had to find ways of integrating their citizens into a coherent whole (Gellner, 1983: 8–38). This tension existed both where a unified state already existed but needed to be consolidated (France, Britain) and where a new state had to be created out of previously disparate entities (Germany, Italy). It also existed in settler colonies where diverse immigrant populations had to be forged into nation-states (the US, Australia). During the early years of the republic, the US faced particular difficulties in this regard not just because of widespread resistance to centralizing government, but also because it was not obvious how to distinguish American from British on ethnic, cultural or linguistic grounds (Hobsbawm, 1990: 18–20).

The modern idea of nationalism had its first major expression in the French Revolution, where, among other things, it revealed its potential as a source of military mobilization. The 'nation in arms', notions of 'universal service' and the '*levée en masse*' enabled the mobilization of over a million troops and imbued these troops with a strong motivation to fight (Giddens, 1985: 224–5). The French Revolution, the rebellions in Spain, Naples and Greece, and the Latin American wars of independence during the early part of the nineteenth century further expanded the scope of nationalism. The nationalist idea spread, somewhat ironically, through transnational networks. It also spread through print (Anderson, 1983) and, in later incarnations, through cinema. In many parts of the world, an emerging bourgeoisie pressured regimes for political representation. These forms of representation were often legitimized by nationalism and through accompanying sentiments such as popular sovereignty. In 1848, these movements reached their apogee in the European 'Springtime of Nations', in which much of Western and Central Europe became embroiled in uprisings against dynastic rule.

Hobsbawm, 1990; Mayall, 1990; Smith, 1991 and 1998; Breuilly, 1993; Connor, 1994; Hall, 1999; Gorski, 2000; Calhoun, 2007; and Özkirimli, 2010.

Although, as noted in the previous section, most of these rebellions failed, they were not without effect, at times tangible (as in the abolition of serfdom in the Habsburg Empire) and, at other times, less tangible (as in the fear they generated in absolutist regimes). From this point on, many absolutist regimes sought to ally gradual democratization with a form of elite nationalism, seeing these concessions as a prophylactic against more radical uprisings. For both absolutist regimes and their bourgeois challengers, nationalism proved to be a powerful vehicle of mobilization.

Despite its partial co-optation by absolutist regimes, nationalism was usually corrosive of dynastic rule. It transformed people from being subjects of their ruler to being citizens of their state, in the process relocating sovereignty from the ruler (*l'état c'est moi*) to the people (*volonté générale*), an idea encoded in the French Revolution's *Declaration of the Rights of Man and Citizens*. The Atlantic Revolutions of the late eighteenth and early nineteenth centuries transformed the moral purpose of the state (Bukovansky, 2002: 211). Thereafter, nationalism became closely associated with rational state-building. The conflation of people and state constituted a radical reworking of the sovereign territorial state. Not only did sovereignty shift from ruler to people, but the territory of the state became identified with the history and location of the people rather than being determined by hereditary rights or dynastic nuptials. Often this resulted in the forcible 'unmixing of peoples' – ethnic 'weeds' were removed through resettlement programmes, deportations and population transfers, as was the case in the Caucasus during the early 1860s, Alsace-Lorraine in 1870–1, and in parts of the Balkans during the late 1870s (Weiner, 2003a: 9; Osterhammel, 2014: 139–43). The mass movements of refugees, and the expulsions, massacres and ethnic cleansing that often accompanied these movements, became depressingly familiar features of international relations during the twentieth century. When the absolutist state became the nation-state, territory became sacralized as the historic homeland of the people (Mayall, 1990: 84).

Since dynastic rule was closely correlated with imperialism, in principle undermining one undermined the other. In practice, however, the nineteenth-century picture was mixed. Dynastic rule and the great diversity of status that was possible within imperial administration were powerful tools for constructing conglomerate empires containing many nations – or rather, before the rise of nationalism, many peoples with different languages, cultures and ethnicities (Osterhammel, 2014: 463). As nationalism took root and spread, particularly after 1870, it challenged the three conglomerate empires of Eastern and Southern Europe: Habsburg, Romanov and Ottoman. During the early part of the twentieth century, the spread of nationalism (and liberal ideas about human rights and equality), along with the upheaval of the First World War, corroded first the Austro-Hungarian and Ottoman Empires, and, after the further upheaval of the Second World War, the colonial empires of Britain, France and other Western states. Bulgaria, Greece, Montenegro and Serbia went to war with the Ottoman Empire in 1912. And after the First World War, nationalism played a major role in uprisings in Ireland, Palestine, Syria and Iraq, also helping to ferment revolution in the Ottoman territories, Mexico, Persia, Indochina and China. During the twentieth and twenty-first centuries, nationalism, sometimes reinforced by religion, prompted the partition of a number of states (such as Palestine/Israel, Yugoslavia, and India/Pakistan/Bangladesh) and the emergence of bloody, if unsuccessful, separatist wars in others (such as Nigeria, Indonesia and parts of the Caucuses).

While nationalism was usually destabilizing of relations within empires (Barkey, 2008), it often had stabilizing effects within core states. The new class politics generated by industrialization, particularly the structural tension identified by Marx and Engels between the bourgeoisie and the proletariat, threatened to destabilize industrial societies. Nationalism provided the adhesive to override class divisions. A shared sense of nation bound people together and facilitated the internal mobility required by industrial economies (Gellner, 1983: 137–43). At the same time, nationalism facilitated the overcoming of local identities, so increasing the social cohesion of the state through the cultivation of distinctly national cultures. As nationalism took root, people who would not formerly have thought of themselves primarily, or at all, as French, Italian, Spanish, British or German increasingly began to do so, helped by the formation of national currencies, national languages, national education systems and, in many places, national military service. Nationalism was strong enough to contain the cosmopolitan impulses of revolutionary internationalism (Halliday, 1999: 146), most notably in 1914 when appeals to it trumped rival appeals to class solidarity.

Nationalism also transformed international order by establishing the nation-state rather than empires as the principal unit of international politics (Mayall, 1990; Hall, 1999; Reus-Smit, 2013), so much so that the term 'nation-state' has become an aspirational synonym for 'state'. The tightening of the link between state and territory raised the prominence of territoriality in interstate disputes. The seizure of Alsace-Lorraine by Germany from France in 1870 is perhaps the best-known example of this effect, poisoning relations between the two and playing its part in the road to the First World War. The problem was that the nationalist idea, although clear in principle, was much less so on the ground. Different nations were not coterminous with clearly bounded territories, but often blended into each other through intermarriage and the territorial intermingling of different peoples. This blending has caused difficulties in the Balkans since the dissolution of the Austro-Hungarian Empire. It is also what has made the application of the national principle so problematic in post-colonial states (e.g. Afghanistan, Indonesia, Sri Lanka, Nigeria, Pakistan) and racially divided states (South Africa up to 1994, the US up to the 1960s). Some early versions of nationalism assumed that smaller ethno-cultural identities would have to be assimilated into larger units (Hobsbawm, 1990: 23–32). In practice, though, the nationalist impulse has remained troublesome in many places, including China, Nigeria, India, the Balkans and Russia. Nationalism has thus given rise to numerous disputes over territory and identity – irredentism and secessionism – that continue to resonate in the contemporary world (Mayall, 1990: 57–63).

To some extent, the success of nationalism is evident in the number, range, depth and significance of the disputes it provokes. From Kosovo to Korea and from Sri Lanka to Sudan, the international agenda is home to apparently intractable disputes that have their roots in nationalism. Such problems were much less of an issue in a world of empires. That they have not noticeably dented the legitimacy of nationalism is itself testimony to the success of this idea in shaping human affairs. Despite being inherently a foreign import, nationalism has gone global with the same ease as football. It is a naturalized discourse that plays a central role in defining the terms of political identity and legitimacy around the world.

'Scientific' Racism

As noted above, nationalism is closely associated with the idea of popular sovereignty. Together, these ideas pointed towards the replacement of elite politics by some form of mass politics. This might be democracy, in which case nationalism was central to providing a *demos* sufficiently coherent to sustain the polity. But nationalism could also support more extreme visions of mass society, not least when it was fused with notions of *demos* to generate chauvinistic understandings of political community (Mann, 2004). One of the most pronounced of these expressions was 'scientific' racism.

'Scientific' racism is the idea that one can and should establish a social hierarchy based on biological markers, either visible (as in skin colour) or in the bloodline (as in who counts as Jewish, black or Chinese). Even if claims based on biological and cultural superiority were often mixed, the emphasis on colour and blood made by nineteenth-century 'scientific racists' distinguished their views from the construction of 'civilized' and 'barbarian' found in many agrarian empires, which was premised mainly on cultural, political and/or religious grounds (Hannaford, 1996: 1–126).[12] In its 'scientific' form, racism grew partly out of Enlightenment tendencies towards classification and partly from European colonial encounters (Keal, 2003: 56–83). Having 'scientific' standing based on classification schemes and empirical observation of differences in levels of development gave racist views both legitimacy and respectability, something reinforced by two developments: first, the growing technological and military superiority of Western societies during the latter half of the nineteenth century (Ferguson, 2004: 196–203, 262–4); and second, the popularity of Darwin's theory of evolution, which was used to support the idea that different races represented distinct steps on the evolutionary ladder. The superficial synergy of an enormous power gap between core and periphery, the predominant whiteness of the core, and social Darwinist thinking created a toxic brew (Osterhammel, 2014: 494–5). Fears that the 'tropical races' would swamp those in 'temperate zones' became pronounced at the end of the nineteenth century (Darwin, 2009: 66–7). Well-known figures in Britain, including James Bryce, Halford Mackinder, Benjamin Kidd and Charles Pearson, favoured a hardening of imperial strategies that could guard against racial miscegenation (Hobson, 2012).

---

[12] It is worth noting that there were often racial overtones to these forms of differentiation. Aristocratic ideas about 'good breeding', for example, were close kin to formalized racism (Hobsbawm, 1975: 312).

For 'scientific' racists, the condition of society depended on the quality of its racial stock (Hannaford, 1996: 272–6). On this basis, 'scientific' racism generated a hierarchy in which, broadly speaking, lighter skinned peoples inhabited the highest rung on the ladder and darker skinned peoples were situated at the bottom. The social Darwinist view that the gradual extinction of the 'lesser races' would benefit humankind was commonly expressed as part of this discourse (Bell, 2007: 115). However, biology was the key to unlocking 'scientific' racism. Prejudices against people of different ethnicity, culture and/or religion are as old as human history. Cultures were often compared and ranked by their ability to deliver economic growth or sustain a sufficiently 'high' culture. But this was generally done without reference to race. The main difference between cultural and 'scientific' racism was that the former allowed for those classified as inferior to become more 'civilized' by assimilating the 'higher' cultural or religious form. In classical Confucian society in China, for example, a non-Han barbarian could become 'Chinese' by acquiring the requisite culture, and a civilized Han could lose this status by abandoning it. When discrimination was based on biology, however, its effect was to fix hierarchical rankings permanently – in short, difference became 'ascribed' rather than 'achieved'. Cultural differentiation, therefore, pointed towards a civilizing mission in which higher cultures should help lower cultures to 'improve'. Biological differentiation, in contrast, pointed towards displacement through direct occupation, selective breeding (eugenics) or outright extermination.[13]

In basic form, 'scientific' racism stood in opposition to both the liberal view that all people (or, more commonly, all men) were equal, and to the view that differences among people were essentially cultural, and therefore in principle remediable. 'Scientific' racism was not incompatible with democracy because the two could be combined if the franchise was restricted by race, as it was (formally) in apartheid South Africa and (usually more informally) in parts of the United States. Indeed, the simultaneity of the rise of racism and the rise of liberal ideas about

---

[13] In post-Holocaust times, it is difficult to appreciate just how normal racism was across nineteenth-century Western society. Anyone wanting to taste the flavour of it should look at Taylor (1840: 17, 19), with its talk of the Caucasian as the 'highest variety of the human species' and the possibility of 'breeding out the taint' of inferior types by interbreeding with Caucasian stock.

human equality is an apparently contradictory feature of the nineteenth-century ideational landscape (Smaje, 2000: 8–12).

'Scientific' racism shared two important synergies with other nineteenth-century ideologies of progress. First, racism overlapped with the liberal emphasis on meritocracy. In its more ruthless form, liberal meritocracy allowed those with superior talent, energy and entrepreneurial skills to dominate those who were less able, and to see this as progressive (Hobsbawm, 1962: 224–62). This attitude chimed well with a racist logic that saw 'superior races' as dominating their 'inferiors' on grounds of 'merit', arguing that doing so would 'improve' the human species as a whole. Second, racism overlapped with nationalism, especially ethno-nationalism. From the late nineteenth century to the end of the Second World War, nations were increasingly differentiated on the basis of their success in war, empire-building, colonization, industrialization, population growth, science and 'high culture'. It was a short step to see these rankings as reflecting biological determinants (Hannaford, 1996: 229–30; Wallerstein, 2011a: 264). An essentializing racial language emerged within the West of Anglo-Saxons, Aryans, Latins and Slavs, and also the racist (as opposed to religious) variant of anti-Semitism, exemplified by high-profile events such as the Dreyfus affair in France and the election of the prominent anti-Semite Karl Lueger as Mayor of Vienna at the end of the century (Hobsbawm, 1990: 107–8; Hannaford, 1996: 277–368; Tombs, 2000: 15). Such thinking was prominent throughout the West in the later nineteenth century. Its ghastly apex was the racist nationalisms that engulfed many parts of the world during the interwar years.

If 'scientific' racism was particularly prominent from the last quarter of the nineteenth century to the mid-point of the twentieth century, older associations between race and culture were influential both before and after this period. Indeed, during the nineteenth century, race and culture were often fused to construct the hierarchies that later came to be labelled 'Orientalism' (Said, 1978 and 1994). Christendom was no exception to the long-standing rule that each belief system considers itself to represent the highest form of human development. But with the exception of the conquest of the Americas, Europe's principal cultural encounter before the nineteenth century was its long engagement with the Islamic world. Although most Christians believed in the superiority of their faith, their engagement with Islam gave them no reason to think that their culture, technology or mode of social organization were superior to that of the Muslim world. Indeed, for many centuries the reverse was the case, providing one reason why 'the Turk' was so feared in Europe.

As the power gap between Western states and other parts of the world opened up, so too did the idea that the inherent superiority of Atlantic culture must be the explanation for this gap. As we discussed in Chapter 2, Anglo-American epistemic communities imagined variously a 'Greater Britain' spanning large parts of the world, a transnational league of liberal democracies that could serve as the 'nucleus' of global order, and even a world state, all of which were to be buttressed by a 'stratified geo-racial identity' in which race served as the main point of demarcation (Bell, 2012: 34).[14] Figures such as Andrew Carnegie and Cecil Rhodes fostered the notion of a 'racial peace' sustained through 'Anglo-Saxon Brotherhood' (Bell, 2013: 3). Such ideas remained prominent during the interwar years, when transnational epistemic communities established a number of forums intended to bolster Anglosphere leadership, including the Council on Foreign Relations and the Royal Institute of International Affairs (Bell, 2012: 47).[15] US foundations such as Carnegie, Ford and Rockefeller served as forums through which to globalize the worldview of Anglo-American elites (Parmar, 2012). It is not difficult to see the connective tissue between these interwar epistemic communities and contemporary figures such as Niall Ferguson (2004), Andrew Roberts (2006) and others who celebrate the pioneering role in modern history played by the 'English-speaking peoples'. These ideas, though shorn of overt racism, are the contemporary manifestations of earlier notions of Western cultural superiority (Vucetic, 2011).

Overall, therefore, although forms of social differentiation have been used as modes of inclusion/exclusion throughout history, the deployment of 'scientific' racism, and the relationship between culture and race as the principal point of differentiation within the modern world, were products of the long nineteenth century. Since imperial relations

---

[14] It was not just a sense of superiority that fuelled such plans. As noted earlier in this chapter, around the turn of the twentieth century, British elites became concerned about both domestic unrest and the rising power of Germany and Japan. This anxiety played a major role in the formulation of ideas that could sustain British, and Anglosphere, influence (Bell, 2012: 35).

[15] Although not completed until the 1950s, Winston Churchill's four-volume *The History of the English-Speaking Peoples* was begun during the 1930s.

dominated the interaction between polities during the interwar years and into the Cold War period, this cocktail provided the basis for post-war discourse about 'modernization' and 'development' (Inayatullah and Blaney, 2004; Zarakol, 2011). Such a discourse represents both a basic continuity with older strands of thought (based on the superiority of the West) and a reworking of this assumption (without the overt racism that marked earlier strands of thought). To a great extent, IR has occluded this thematic, whether conceived as a twentieth-century discourse or as one shaped by the global transformation.

At the same time, nineteenth-century processes contained the seeds for the contemporary turn to post-racism. By moving so many people around the world, European imperialism made race a central issue not just in the colonies, but also in metropolitan regions – nineteenth-century dynamics served as the forerunners for contemporary interest in inter-cultural flows (Gilroy, 1993: 2; Abernathy, 2000: 364–6). Mass migrations during the nineteenth century fostered transnational networks based on shared political identity, economic exchange and cultural expression. Gilroy (1993) provides two micro-narratives of such experiences. During the 1870s, the Fisk University Jubilee Singers, an African-American group who sang mainly spirituals, toured Europe. In Britain, the Singers appeared before a number of elite audiences, including Queen Victoria, becoming celebrated advocates for a new form of cultural circulation. In quite different vein, William Davidson, the illegitimate son of the Attorney-General of Jamaica, was hanged for his role in the Cato Street Conspiracy, a failed attempt to murder the British cabinet in 1820.

These 'impure lineages' were a consequence of the intensified con-nections that marked the global transformation (Gilroy, 1993: 2). At times, they acted as the discursive component of structural inequalities, helping to constitute and sustain uneven experience of global modern-ity. At other times, they became sites for the articulation of resistance to such inequalities. In this way, José Martí used his mestizo identity as a means of galvanizing support for Cuban independence, just as Haitian slaves rearticulated notions of freedom by connecting them to broader themes of racial equality (Shilliam, 2009: 71–2). Movements such as négritude were complex entanglements of anti-colonialism, Marxism and nationalism, tying together metropoles and colonies within shared communities of fate (Goedde, 2014: 554–7; Shilliam, forthcoming). Decolonization was one component of this process, as was the mobilization of social movements associated with civil rights and anti-racism, and the emergence of diasporas as distinct international actors. During the twentieth and twenty-first centuries, such interactions between peoples deepened, becoming an increasingly regularized feature of social life around the world.

Overall, 'scientific' racism is the most clearly unsuccessful of the four ideologies of progress inherited from the nineteenth century. The doctrine reached its peak during the 1930s and 1940s when its unification with ethno-nationalism produced fascism. Fascism is thus not so much a twentieth-century contribution to the ideational landscape of international relations as it is a combination of the extreme ends of two ideologies inherited from the nineteenth century. The defeat of the fascist powers, added to the struggles against colonialism both before and after the Second World War, jettisoned 'scientific' racism as a core component of world politics. Its defeat contributed to the delegitimation of empire and to the success of anti-colonial movements. Interestingly, nationalism was not much tainted by its association with 'scientific' racism. Nationalism emerged from the Second World War stronger than ever, proving malleable enough to be used by advocates of both universal human rights and decolonization (Reus-Smit, 2013).

The occlusion of the major role played by 'scientific' racism in international relations is one of the most alarming features of an IR divorced from its nineteenth-century roots. As Bell (2013: 1) notes: 'for the opening few decades of the [twentieth] century, race was widely and explicitly considered a fundamental ontological unit of politics, perhaps the most fundamental unit of all'. It has been too easy, not just in IR, but in Western society generally, to blame racism on the Nazis and the Japanese, and to forget that until less than half a century ago it was part of *mainstream* Western thinking about world politics. The victors, of course, write the history, and Nazi Germany and Imperial Japan took racist practices to extremes. But racism was not something exclusive to their societies. It was part of a wider set of experiences and attitudes that underpinned *Western-colonial* international society.[16] The neglect of racism by IR scholarship makes it difficult to comprehend the resentment felt by those peoples who were victims of it (Miller, 2013). As we

---

[16] *Western-colonial* international society is the term we use to denote the first phase of global modernity. We define this term and discuss its transformation into *Western-global* international society in Chapter 6.

discuss in Chapter 9, an evening-out of the global distribution of power will require far greater engagement with this issue.

Conclusion

If the previous chapter argued that the revolutions of modernity remade the physical landscape of international relations with a scale and depth that marked a decisive break from the agrarian world, this chapter has argued that these same revolutions also remade the global ideational landscape. They established a package of ideologies that marked a radical change of both individual and collective identities. In the process, they set economic, political and cultural relations onto quite different tracks from those of earlier periods. They may have challenged each other, and they have varied in their success, but they are still, along with the Axial Age religions and various strands of conservatism, the main ideational framing for world politics. Of the four 'ideologies of progress' that underpinned the global transformation, liberalism and nationalism have had the greatest influence on contemporary international society. Socialism remains influential as an idea, but has been undermined by the shortcomings of its application in practice. 'Scientific' racism is the clearest loser, even if many racist legacies linger on.

More generally, the idea of progress continues to underpin contemporary societies. Ideologies of progress have sustained the sense of cumulative growth, both economically and cognitively, that stand as the signal feature of the modern world (Gellner, 1988: 177). They have fuelled (mainly liberal) projects of 'modernization' and development as well as (mainly socialist) revolutionary movements intended to accelerate the path of modernity itself. However, by the end of the nineteenth century, there were increasing concerns about the limits of progress. Freud, Nietzsche, Sorel, Du Bois, Schmitt and Pareto all, in their different ways, highlighted the uncertainties and dislocations of modern society. Concern with 'unreason', which later became a central point of reference for both post-structuralist thought and revolutionary figures such as Frantz Fanon, reignited interest in affective sentiments that lay outside the modern notion of linear, directional progress. These concerns fed into strands of modern thought that were concerned with the 'ambivalences' of global modernity. First captured in the work of nineteenth-century theorists such as Marx, Durkheim and Weber, these ideas were rooted in concern for the limits of 'progress'. Whether rendered as alienation, anomie or disenchantment, these theorists argued that modernity served to fracture subjectivities and reduce the cohesion of modern societies. Frankfurt School theorists and, more recently, 'late-modern' thinkers also highlighted the ways in which the material aspects of progress were not matched by normative or cognitive progress.[17] The global transformation introduced debates around 'progress and its discontents' that still serve as a central feature of the ideational landscape of contemporary international relations.

Given this, it is not surprising that all four of the ideologies of progress we highlight in this chapter are being questioned. Liberalism has been critiqued by communitarians for its universalism and commitment to individualism, by post-colonial scholarship for its connections to 'civilizing missions', and by those on the left for its adherence to market regimes that are premised on dispossession and serve to foster inequality. Socialism, as noted above, has been weakened by the practices of self-declared socialist states, which have been unable to demonstrate that a combination of command economies and party states can deliver better outcomes than liberal and social democratic forms of political economy. Nationalism has come under pressure because of its association with ethno-chauvinism, the emergence of 'post-national' projects such as the European Union, and from various currents of internationalism, ranging from the Muslim notion of ummah to the human rights regime. And 'scientific' racism has been delegitimized as a constitutive trope, even as it is often reproduced in subliminal form (Hobson, 2012). Nevertheless, as we made clear at the beginning of this chapter, no ideologies of anything like the force of these four have come into being in the contemporary world. In the twenty-first century, liberalism, nationalism, socialism and racism still serve as the basic reference point for much of the theory and practice of international relations.

---

[17] As with the ideologies of progress discussed above, it is impossible to do justice to the diversity of thinking associated with this orientation. A selective sample includes: Adorno and Horkheimer, 1979 [1944]; Spivak, 1988; Žižek, 1989; Butler, 1990; Connolly, 1991; Deleuze, 1994; Agamben, 1995; Chakrabarty, 2000; Badiou, 2001; Derrida, 2001 [1967]; Foucault, 2002 [1969]; Rancière, 2006; and Mignolo, 2011.

5 | *The Transformation of Political Units*

Introduction

This chapter, along with Chapters 6 and 7, represents a division of labour in terms of how to discuss the emergence and expansion of the global transformation. In this chapter we focus on the transformation of political units. In the next chapter we focus on the ways in which rational states, industrialization and ideologies of progress bifurcated international order into a core–periphery structure that was global in nature and centred in the West. Chapter 7 charts the partial erosion of this core–periphery structure, concentrating mainly on developments since the Second World War. Together, these three chapters track the transformation of political, legal, economic, military and cultural relations from the nineteenth century to the present day. As all three chapters make clear, the processes of transformation in what became the core, and the restructuring of international order into a core–periphery form, were deeply intertwined. What happened in the emergent core both drew from and impacted on the emergent periphery, and what happened in the periphery both fed into and was shaped by what happened in the core. It is the two together that constitute the global transformation.

In earlier chapters, we noted the ways in which, during the nineteenth century, polities in the core were transformed by a shift in their 'moral purpose' from absolutism to popular sovereignty. The ideologies of progress redefined the identities of both states and peoples, thereby altering the foundations of political legitimacy. Nationalism sacralized borders and represented those outside these borders as alien, while liberalism, racism and, on occasion, socialism legitimized expansion into these alien spaces. The result was the rearticulation of imperialism as a progressive practice. In Chapter 1, we examined the ways in which imperial techniques from fingerprinting to administrative systems were imported from imperial territories to the core, helping to augment the bureaucratic capacities of rational states. We also examined the ways in which notions of progress underpinned civic reforms, grand cultural projects, scientific research programmes, and the birth of both IGOs and INGOs. In Chapter 3, we linked the emergence of the rational state to improvements in infrastructure, from railways to the telegraph. In Chapter 8, we will examine the transformation of warfare and its impact on the development of states in the core, as well as relations between them. Taken together, these developments stimulated a 'caging' of competences within nation-states as polities assumed the functions previously undertaken by private actors. Newly empowered state bureaucracies encroached on areas previously the preserve of guilds, municipal corporations, provincial estates, charities, religious orders and other such bodies (Tilly, 1990: 23). As Marx put it, such bureaucracies acted as a 'gigantic broom' that 'swept away all manner of medieval rubbish, seigneurial rights, local privileges, municipal and guild monopolies and provincial constitutions' (cited in Phillips and Sharman, forthcoming: 220). During the second half of the century, state personnel grew from 67,000 to 535,000 in Britain and from 55,000 to over a million in Prussia/Germany; during the same period, state-military personnel tripled in Britain and quadrupled in Prussia/Germany (Mann, 1986: 804–10). The nineteenth century saw the emergence of 'rational states'.

This account presents a challenge to the widely held view in IR (if only in IR) that 'modern' states emerged during the seventeenth century, an account we critiqued in Chapter 2. It presents an even greater challenge to those IR theories, particularly neo-realism, that see states as 'like-units' differentiated by capability, but not by function (Waltz, 1979). As this chapter explores, the polities that emerged in the nineteenth century were quite distinct from their pre-nineteenth-century counterparts, whether understood in terms of their capabilities, functions or identities. This chapter concentrates on the different types of political unit that emerged from global modernity, both those that harnessed the new mode of power and those that resisted its expansionary impulses.

The first section examines the role of imperialism in the transformation of political units. In the core, imperialism was sustained by three rationales: profit, power and progress (Darwin, 2012: 26–9). The search for imperial profits extended the revenue raising capacities of Western states; the quest for power acted as a spur to imperial expansion; and ideologies of progress provided the rationale for imperialism, connecting it to notions of 'betterment' and 'tutelage' – what today we understand as the agenda of 'development'. In the periphery, imperialism provided an extended challenge to existing modes of governance. Frequently, this challenge was met by 'modernizing missions' (Chibber, 2013), successfully so in the case of Japan, less so in the cases of China, Egypt, Brazil, the Ottoman Empire, Siam and Mexico. Both at home and abroad, imperialism transformed the capabilities and identities of political units. However, although the bifurcation between imperial and non-imperial was sometimes stark, it was not monolithic. Empires were institutionally heterodox, as were the political units they sought to control. As such, the imperial encounter fostered different types of political unit.

If imperialism was the 'top-down' dynamic that lay behind the transformation of political units, the pressure of revolution provides its 'bottom-up' dynamic. Imperial powers were required to repress regular uprisings in order to maintain and extend their overseas interests. We discuss these anti-imperial struggles in Chapters 6 and 7. In this chapter, we concentrate on the challenge presented by revolution. Revolutionary states sought to mobilize the new mode of power through projects of rapid state transformation. They also sought to extend their transformative projects to other societies, sometimes successfully, at other times less so. At home, core states met this challenge through a combination of reform and repression. Abroad, they took part in counter-revolutionary campaigns, both in the form of civil, interstate and proxy wars, and through the development of rival spheres of influence sustained through aid, training, trade and security alliances. Both revolutionary and non-revolutionary states sought to enhance their *infrastructural* and *despotic* power (Mann, 1988). Infrastructural power is 'power through', i.e. the capacity to diffuse the exercise of power throughout a social order, most commonly through bureaucracies. Despotic power is 'power over', i.e. the capacity to command without consultation, most commonly associated with the deployment of coercive force. Both of these dimensions of state power were augmented by the revolutionary challenge – revolution and the fear of revolution were fundamental to the transformation of polities during the global transformation.

The third dynamic that transformed modern polities was the relationship between states and markets. As the last chapter explored, the conceptual distinction between states and markets was the cornerstone of liberal political economy. However, throughout the modern era, it has been the embedding of markets within forms of governance that has fostered the extension of capitalism around the world. During the nineteenth century, even those states considered to be quintessentially 'liberal' – Britain and the United States – relied on the state to open up markets, protect private property, secure contracts and regulate trade. A close relationship between states and markets was also crucial to 'developmental states' such as Germany and Japan during the last quarter of the nineteenth century, the Asian Tigers during the Cold War, and contemporary China (Beeson, 2009). However, if states and markets have had a closer relationship than that envisioned by liberal political economists, there has not been a singular form of state-led development. The third section of the chapter unpacks the varying relationship between states and markets in the development of global capitalism.

Imperialism and the Transformation of Political Units

Until the global transformation, nearly three-quarters of the world's population lived in large, fragmented, ethnically mixed agrarian empires (Bayly, 2004: 27–8). In Asia, such entities included the Javanese empire, Qing China, Mughal India and Tokugawa Japan. In the Middle East, there was the Ottoman Empire and Qajar Iran. In Europe, the Habsburg and Russian dynasties presided over large continental empires. And in the Americas, inter-imperial conflict marked the expansion of the Spanish, Portuguese, French and British into territories occupied by the Inca and Aztec empires, and the many 'nations' of indigenous peoples. During the long nineteenth century, these agrarian empires were challenged by the new mode of power that underpinned the global transformation. Bastions of the classical world, most notably the Ottoman Empire, China and Japan, underwent prolonged, often humiliating, encounters with Western powers (Gong, 1984; Hodgson, 1993; Suzuki, 2009; Yurdusev, 2009; Zarakol, 2011). Defeat was particularly hard to swallow in China. As Paine (2003: 336) rather unkindly puts it: 'Only in the late nineteenth century did the Chinese learn that civilization had a plural.' When the Chinese imperial order fell, it did so from a great height.

Although many Western states were imperial powers well before the nineteenth century, the mode of power that generated the global transformation greatly extended the range and scope of Western imperialism. Indeed, nineteenth-century imperialism was the starkest possible expression of the uneven and combined character of global modernity. Because imperialism was the outward expression of the new mode of power vested in industrialization, rational statehood and ideologies of progress, it exemplified the unevenness between the haves and have-nots of global modernity. At the same time, imperialism was one of the principal means through which polities and peoples were combined on a global scale. As noted in Chapter 1, during the long nineteenth century, European powers sought to exert control, both directly and indirectly, over most of the globe. If the bulk of European imperialism took place during the 'Scramble for Africa', which saw European powers assume direct control of large parts of Africa, the extension of imperialism went well beyond the 'Scramble'. Between 1810 and 1870, the US carried out 71 territorial annexations and military interventions (Go, 2011: 39). The US first became a continental empire, seizing territory from Native Americans, the Spanish and the Mexicans. It then built an overseas empire, extending its authority over Cuba, Nicaragua, the Dominican Republic, Haiti, Hawaii, Puerto Rico, Guam, the Philippines, Samoa and the Virgin Islands. Other settler states also became colonial powers in their own right, including Australia and New Zealand in the Pacific. As noted in Chapter 1, Japan constructed an empire in East Asia, while Russian expansionism accelerated during this period, both southwards to Uzbekistan, Kazakhstan and Turkmenistan, and eastwards to Sakhalin and Vladivostok. Imperialism, therefore, was a central vector within the uneven and combined character of global modernity and an equally central tool of the core–periphery international order that arose from it.

If there was a sharp bifurcation between imperial powers and those subjected to imperialism during the global transformation, empires were not monolithic spaces governed through centralized facilities of command and control. Rather, imperialism fostered a 'chaotic pluralism' of institutional design (Ballantyne and Burton, 2012: 301). Empires were complex networks of 'micro-regions', consisting of trading posts, garrisons and settlements, which parcelled out decision-making to a range of local intermediaries: trading officials, garrison commanders, colonial administrators, ships' captains, and more (Benton, 2010: 31; Blumi, 2012; Benton and Mulich, forthcoming). In the case of the British, their 'imperial web' included direct-rule colonies (e.g. India after 1857), settlement colonies (e.g. Australia), protectorates (e.g. Brunei), condominiums (e.g. Sudan), bases (e.g. Gibraltar), treaty ports (e.g. Shanghai), and spheres of influence (e.g. Argentina). The variety of forms that imperial rule took meant that empires had to be adaptable: their governance was less a case of one-size-fits-all than it was the result of 'institutional bricolage' (Barkey, 2008: 7). The British, for example, ran their empire from three different bureaucratic homes: the Colonial Office, which was responsible for settler colonies and direct acquisitions; the Foreign Office, which looked after Britain's African protectorates and the Chinese treaty ports; and the India Office, which not only took charge of the Raj (through the Viceroy), but also managed Afghanistan, Tibet, Burma, Aden and territories in the Gulf. Other fragments of empire were parcelled out to the War Office and the Admiralty, while the Treasury maintained a general interest in the financing of overseas territories (Darwin, 2012: 192–3). These 'overlapping spheres of influence' meant that the experience of imperial subjects in different parts of the empire was not uniform; Britain ran a 'ramshackle empire' rather than a well-oiled machine (Darwin, 2012: 8, 194).

The image of a late nineteenth-century map of the world in which imperial territories are represented by a single colour is, therefore, highly misleading. Empires were fragmented, 'irregularly shaped corridors and enclaves' that had porous borders and fluid sovereignty regimes (Benton, 2010: xii, 3; Benton and Mulich, forthcoming). British India included several hundred 'Princely States' that retained a degree of 'quasi-sovereignty', as did nearly 300 'native states' in Dutch East Asia (Phillips and Sharman, forthcoming: 48–9). In British (if not French) Africa, such arrangements were the norm. Some places, such as the 'uplands' of South-East Asia, managed to elude imperial control altogether (Scott, 2012). This meant that elites in imperial territories had to be either cultivated or created in order to govern empires effectively (Newbury, 2003). Where imperialism was successful, it relied on establishing partnerships with local power brokers: the Straits Chinese, the Krio of West Africa, the 'teak-wallahs' of Burma, the Chettiar of South India, and others (Darwin, 2012: 178, 299). Two hundred Dutch officials and a much larger number of Indonesian intermediaries ran a cultivation system that incorporated two million agricultural workers (Burbank and Cooper, 2010: 301). In India, the ratio of British citizens to locals in the Princely States established by the crown was 1:250,000 (Burbank and Cooper, 2010: 307). A little over 1,000 civil servants were responsible for all 15 of Britain's African colonies (Mann, 2012: 47). And 76,900

French administrators were responsible for 60 million colonial subjects (Hoerder, 2012: 511). The legitimacy of empire, requiring the maintenance of authority over culturally and politically diverse populations, depended on extensive collaboration between metropolitan and indigenous elites (Barkey, 2008: 277).

If empires were sites of 'customization' rather than 'standardization' (Phillips, 2013; also see Motyl, 1999; Nexon and Wright, 2007), they were not benign spaces of heterodox cooperation. To the contrary, empires were deeply oppressive. We have already noted the dispossession and de-industrialization that undergirded the expansion of the market to imperial spaces. Such policies went hand-in-hand with other modes of coercive extraction. For example, the abolition of the slave trade during the early years of the nineteenth century, and slavery more generally during the middle part of the century, was accompanied by a marked increase in the numbers of both bonded labourers and transported convicts (Tinker, 1974). Britain's Asian convicts were transported to penal colonies in the Indian Ocean (such as the Andaman Islands, Penang and Singapore) where they were put to work felling timber and draining swamps in brutal conditions (Anderson, 2000). Empires were also deeply destructive of the natural habitats they occupied: Manchuria was deforested by the Japanese in the interests of its mining and lumber companies, while 'wild lands' in India were cleared by the British so that nomadic pastoralists could be turned into tax-paying cultivators (Ballantyne and Burton, 2012: 314–19).

Even starker was the brutality visited on indigenous peoples by the coercive apparatus of imperialism: empires were killing machines, whether by war, famine, disease or exploitation. The Belgians were responsible for the deaths of up to ten million Congolese during the late nineteenth and early twentieth centuries (Rosenberg, 2012: 12). In the opening years of the twentieth century, Germany carried out a systematic genocide against the Nama and Herero peoples in its South West African territories, reducing their population by 80% and 50% respectively (Steinmetz, 2007; Rosenberg, 2012: 12). Germany also pursued a 'scorched earth' policy in its East African colonies following the 1905 Maji Maji Rising – 250,000 Africans died in the ensuing famine (Black, 2009: 167). Kenya and Algeria both witnessed mass campaigns of slaughter by, respectively, British and French imperial forces. Similar stories could be told about the conduct of the Americans in the Philippines, the Spanish in Cuba, and the Japanese in China. In some parts of the world, such as Tasmania, Tahiti and Southwest Africa, the result was the extermination or massive reduction of the indigenous population – the 'loss rate' of indigenous peoples in some white settler colonies reached as high as 95% (Mann, 2012: 38–9). Overall, the casualty list of empire numbered tens of millions (Osterhammel, 2014: 124–7).

Imperialism, therefore, both constructed and sustained the development of a core–periphery international order. Indeed, imperialism was the principal means through which Western states exerted their power around the world. As discussed in Chapter 4, empire was intricately bound up with ideas of 'betterment' and 'tutelage' – as Europeans saw themselves at the apex of world civilization, imperial projects were legitimated by a duty to 'uplift' uncivilized peoples. Aesthetic 'contact zones' such as Paul Gauguin's use of Tahitian motifs romanticized 'primitive societies', as did the collections of ethnographic trophies and colonial 'specimens' displayed in Western museums. The 1889 Exposition Universelle in Paris included a 'village nègre' in which 400 Africans took part in a 'live display' of indigenous expression (Rosenberg, 2012: 886–902). In 1931, an International Colonial Exposition at Vincennes near Paris acted as a showcase for the apparently peaceful, prosperous imperial societies that were seen as benefiting from European tutelage. The exhibition received 3.5 million visitors in its first month (Abernathy, 2000: 116).

At the heart of imperialism, therefore, was a claim about the material, cultural and moral superiority of the white West. Western powers expressed the new mode of power that underpinned global modernity by exacting vastly unequal terms of exchange with peripheral polities, even if these polities had once been great empires themselves, as was the case with China and India. Indeed, the decline of China during the global transformation helps to illustrate the ways in which imperialism served to transform political units during the long nineteenth century.

Imperialism with Chinese Characteristics

Between 1820 and 1950, Chinese per capita income dropped from 90% to 20% of the world average, while the country's share of global GDP fell from around a third to 5% (Maddison, 2007a: 43). During this period, China lost wars with Japan, Britain and France. It saw large parts of its territory handed over to foreign powers and suffered the ignominy of having to sign a number of unequal treaties, as well as accommodating foreign consuls, officials and merchants, all of whom enjoyed extensive extraterritorial rights. China went through two major rebellions, including one (the Taiping Rebellion) that produced more casualties than any other conflict during the nineteenth century. During the twentieth century, the country underwent bloody revolutions in 1911 and 1949 before embracing market reforms in the late 1970s. No wonder that this period is known in China as the 'Century of Humiliation'.

Before the global transformation, the Chinese imperial state restricted trade to a handful of entrepôts: Macao (for trade with Portugal), Canton (for trade with other Western states), Xiamen (for trade with the Philippines), Ningbo (for trade with Japan and Korea), and Kyakhta (for trade with Russia). There was a short trading season, after which foreign traders were obliged to leave the country.[1] Many Western powers pressed China to open up to higher levels of trade, particularly the British, for whom the (illegal) opium trade was extremely lucrative: by the 1830s, the British were exporting 30,000 chests of opium from India to China each year, each of which carried 150 pounds of opium extract (Mann, 2012: 101). It was, therefore, little surprise when, in 1840, Britain used the pretext of a minor incident involving the arrest of two British sailors to instigate conflict (the so-called 'First Opium War') with China, which it won easily.

The Treaty of Nanjing that followed the war required China to cede Hong Kong to the British, pay an indemnity for starting the conflict and open up five new treaty ports. The treaty also legalized the opium trade, forced China to accept British consuls and guaranteed extraterritorial rights for British nationals. Following its defeat, the Chinese state began to examine European practices, translating European texts on international law and diplomacy for the first time (Suzuki, 2009). However, it was not until defeat in the Second Opium War of 1856–60, which included the Anglo-French sacking of the Summer Palace in Peking, that the Chinese government initiated a full 'modernization mission' – the 'self-strengthening movement' – aimed at accelerating industrialization and rationalizing the state apparatus. China also established a new

---

[1] This was not unusual. Japan was closed to foreign trade (except for a handful of Dutch traders) until the late 1850s, while trade in the Niger Delta was restricted until the 1880s (Darwin, 2012: 153).

office (*Zongli Yamen*) to entreaty with European powers, posting ambassadors to a number of European states and dispatching fact-finding expeditions to Japan, Europe and the United States.

These steps did little to halt Chinese decline. Following the Second Opium War, China was obliged to sign a range of unequal treaties, including some that guaranteed low tariffs on European imports. These disadvantages were augmented by a weakening of the infrastructural power of the Chinese state through domestic unrest. During the 1850s, a rebellion originating amongst the Hakka minority in Guangxi spread to the Yangzi region and the imperial capital of Nanjing. The rebellion was oriented around a strain of apocalyptic Christianity, blended with elements of Manchu and Confucian thought (Spence, 1996; Phillips, 2011: 184–5).[2] Over the next decade, the 'Taiping Rebellion' mobilized over one million combatants and spread to an area the size of France and Germany combined (Meier, 2012: 89). The conflict severely diminished imperial control. It also destroyed both land and livelihoods: between 1850 and 1873, over 20 million people were killed and China's population as a whole dropped from 410 million to 350 million (Phillips, 2011: 185; Osterhammel, 2014: 120–1, 547–51).

The Taiping Rebellion was not the only uprising experienced by China during its Century of Humiliation. In 1898, a series of 'modernizing' reforms by the 17-year-old Emperor Guangxu prompted a 'palace coup' by the Empress Dowager Cixi (Phillips, 2011: 197). Cixi fanned a wave of assertive nationalism, including a movement – the Boxer Rebellion – that sought to overturn the unequal rights held by Westerners. The defeat of the Boxers by a coalition of Western forces led to the permanent stationing of foreign troops in China, as well as a range of new concessions. Key aspects of public finances were handed over to outsiders, most notably the Maritime Customs Services, which was used to collect taxes, regulate tariffs and finance the substantial indemnity owed to the Western powers. In 1911, a republican revolution overthrew the 'last emperor', Puyi, and installed the nationalist-inspired constitutionalist Sun Yat-Sen as President. However, the result of the revolution was not a recentralization of state authority, but a

---

[2] The Taiping strain of vernacularized Christianity was far from being the only example of its kind. In New Zealand, a Maori prophetic movement tried to establish a 'City of God' on the North Island, while various forms of evangelicalism were combined with indigenous belief systems in the Americas, Africa, and elsewhere.

further fracturing of authority into regional warlordism. The following decades saw China lose parts of its territory in wars with Japan and, from 1927, descend into full-scale civil war, a conflict that was only resolved by the victory of the communists in 1949. All in all, the period between the First Opium War to the 1949 revolution was a time of considerable regression in China. In 1952, China's GDP per capita was lower than it had been in 1820 (Maddison, 2007a: 164).

China's experience of the global transformation was more the norm than the exception for formerly powerful, now peripheral, polities. Even when states carried out extensive 'modernizing missions', as in the Tanzimât period in the Ottoman Empire, King Chulalongkorn's Siam, Porfiriato Mexico, or the post-1891 Brazilian Republic, they remained vulnerable to European predation (Rosenberg, 2012: 920; Chibber, 2013: 266). Western powers, from Britain to Belgium, used the new mode of power associated with global modernity to enhance both their power and their wealth. As was the case in China, imperialism did not require direct colonization. Except for those obsessed with having their 'place in the sun', imperial powers were often conscious of the costs of taking on full colonial administration and reluctant to do so unless they had to. For much of the long nineteenth century, Britain favoured 'free trade imperialism', using free trade, backed up by gunboat diplomacy, as a vanguard by which to open up territories for capitalist accumulation (Gallagher and Robinson, 1953). This meant that Britain often resisted formal territorial control when its main aims were met, as was the case in China, Egypt, Siam and much of Latin America.[3]

The influence of imperialism as a transformative dynamic is especially clear in such cases. As noted above, settler colonies assumed the brunt of the transformative project – they were usually home to the fiercest violence and most extensive plunder. But even those polities that escaped formal annexation were radically transformed by their encounter with core states. Imperialism promoted Western power with an intensity and scale that was unprecedented in human history. One of its effects was a condition of virtually constant war between core and peripheral polities. Between 1803 and 1901, Britain alone was involved

---

[3] It is important to note that profit was not always the main aim of imperial powers. Britain chose to keep Canada rather than (sugar-rich) Guadalupe for strategic rather than commercial reasons – to keep British North America out of the hands of the French. And safeguarding the route to India and East Asia meant maintaining a number of unprofitable, but strategically important, territories.

in 50 major colonial wars (Giddens, 1985: 223). The result of these wars was a major increase in the *despotic* capacities of imperial states, a point we return to in the following chapter. It was also a dynamic that strengthened the *infrastructural* capacities of imperial states. Imperial wars required states to raise revenue, which they often achieved through increased taxation. The rise of the rational state was intimately bound up with the intensification of European imperialism.

To some extent, therefore, the story of imperialism during the global transformation is one of stark bifurcation between imperial powers and those subjected to their control. But such analysis occludes the variety of modes of imperial rule that sustained relations between core and periphery. Just as there were many imperial powers, so too were there many types of imperial governance. Although some aspects of the encounter between core and peripheral powers were consistent, not least the huge power gap that existed between them, this did not lead to the development of homogeneous political entities. On the contrary, the experiences of China, Argentina, Fiji, Australia, Afghanistan, India, Egypt, Nigeria, Cyprus and Ireland could scarcely have been more different – and these were just territories within the British imperial web. Although imperialism intensified combined development, it also intensified the unevenness of global modernity. At the same time, although imperialism played a leading role in fostering the development of a core–periphery international order, it also cultivated the struggles against imperialism that did much to erode this order. We return to these dynamics in Chapters 6 and 7, where it will become clear that the spread and intensification of imperialism during the global transformation was a central feature in the construction of many features of contemporary international society from the emergence of a global economy to issues of inequality and (under)development.

The Revolutionary Challenge

If imperialism was a potent expression of the ways in which rational states imposed their authority on political units around the world, few states underwent imperialism without a fight. As the previous section outlined, China's response to Western imposition was one of resistance as well as subjugation. Such dynamics were also present within core states, where publics faced incursions by the state on ever-increasing spheres of social life. Global modernity witnessed the emergence of what Michael Mann (1993: 597) calls 'popular modernity'. Millions of Britons joined the Chartist movement and the campaign against the slave trade during the first half of the century, and many millions more around the world joined trade unions, left-wing political parties, improvement societies, benevolent associations, movements for suffrage, and campaigns for education and health reforms, during the second half of the century. The global transformation saw the birth of mass politics. As Osterhammel (2014: 604) notes, the context for this was a situation in which, while popular sovereignty was an increasingly widespread idea, democracy as a practice remained limited: 'The state was much more widespread as an agency of rule than as an arena of participation.'

One of the most potent expressions of mass politics was the strike. The development of the strike was closely linked to the spread of the market. The depression of the 1870s and 1880s, for example, prompted a transnational wave of strikes. Miners took part in strikes from Silesia to Mexico, as did transport workers from Cardiff to Cairo. This period also saw a general strike in Argentina, a labour strike in the Dutch Indies and a strike amongst dockers in Japan. Strikes and associated practices were often met by state oppression. In 1886, seven anarchists were sentenced to death after a bomb was thrown at police during a demonstration in Haymarket Square in Chicago. States routinely suppressed the activities of labour movements. Yet labour militancy persisted. This first transnational wave was followed by a second, bigger wave of labour unrest both during and after the First World War. In Germany, an average of 10,000 workers were on strike each month in 1916; the following year, Germany experienced 562 strikes involving 651,000 workers (Halperin, 2013: 163). By 1920, there were 34 million trade unionists in Europe (Halperin, 2013: 166). Britain saw its first Labour government in 1923, while the left came to power in France the following year.

The militancy of mass publics was felt most keenly when it came to the threat of revolution. The 1848 revolutions and the experience of the Paris Commune, allied to the capacity of anarchist groups to carry out high-profile assassinations (including that of a Russian Tsar, an Austrian Empress, a Spanish Prime Minister, an Italian King and an American President), meant that fear of 'the social problem' was keenly felt. States responded to the revolutionary challenge by carrying out concerted 'invasions of social life', ranging from the advent of policing as a formal institution to regular censuses of their populations (Tilly, 1990: 23). The infrastructural and despotic capabilities of states grew commensurately with these encroachments as elites sought to stabilize the disruptive effects of global modernity through dual programmes of reform and repression (Lacher and German, 2012: 108).

On the reform side, pressures for absolutism to become more 'enlightened' and for parliamentary systems to become more republican fostered demands for political representation (met by successive British Reform Acts), the provision of welfare (as in Bismarck's pioneering 'social insurance' scheme) and mass education (which helped to increase rates of literacy and, in turn, fuelled the rise of the mass media).[4] As Bismarck put it (in Freedland, 2012: 141): 'it is better to lead revolutions than to be conquered by them'. In many places, serfdom was abolished. All male subjects became citizens of the Habsburg Empire in 1867 and the Ottoman Empire in 1869. Parliaments were introduced by the Habsburgs (1861), the Ottomans (1876–7) and the Romanovs (1906). On the repression side, parliaments were routinely suspended, opposition parties banned and the media suppressed. In Britain, those out of work were forced into workhouses, where they were kept in abject conditions and paid a pittance for their labour. Orphanages and prisons became additional sources of bonded labour (Halperin, 2013). Further afield, leftist groups were purged (as in most of the Middle East) and anti-colonial movements crushed (as in Malaya, India and Jamaica). All around the world, there was an expansion in both the infrastructural and despotic powers of the state.

These strategies could not always hold back the revolutionary tide: during the modern era, revolutions were conducted by socialists in Russia, slaves and *gens de couleur* in Haiti, nationalists in Algeria, radical military groups in Ethiopia, peasants in Mexico, and Islamists in Iran. These revolutions were underpinned by a fundamental shift in the concept of revolution. Until the French Revolution, revolutions tended to be seen as recurrent or circular processes, the turning of wheels rather than fundamental ruptures (Arendt, 1963: 42–3; Davidson, 2012: chs. 2 and 3).

---

[4] The emergence of the mass media was not just a national phenomenon, it also had an international dimension. For example, international press agencies appeared during the nineteenth century for the first time, including Associated Press (founded in 1848) and Reuters (founded in 1851).

During the last quarter of the eighteenth century, the meaning of revolution changed in association with broader ideational shifts.[5] As charted in the previous chapter, concepts of popular sovereignty and the general will (*la volonté générale*) became influential. From this point on, most revolutionaries claimed to be restarting history from a 'year zero'. 'We have it in our power,' wrote Thomas Paine (2004 [1776]: ix), 'to begin the world over again. A situation, similar to the present, hath not happened since the days of Noah until now. The birthday of a new world is at hand.' After the French Revolution, the concept of revolution was universalized, naturalized and, ultimately, mythologized around the French experience (Kumar, 2001). The French model of revolution – as the inevitable, final reckoning of historical progress itself (*la révolution en permanence* as Proudhon put it) – came to stand as the principal understanding of revolution in the modern era. Revolutions symbolized the march of progress, standing for irresistible and irreversible change.

The concept of revolution-as-rupture spread around the world over the next two centuries. Leon Trotsky (1997 [1932]) spoke of the need for 'permanent revolution' that could stoke the fires of global insurrection, while Ayatollah Khomeini, Iran's Supreme Leader following the 1979 revolution, invoked the potential of revolutions to change the world: 'state boundaries are the product of a deficient human mind ... The revolution does not recognize borders and frontiers, it will go through them' (in Abrahamian, 1993: 49). To some extent, Paine, Trotsky and Khomeini kept their promises. The revolutions in France, Russia, Iran and elsewhere had major effects both on their home societies and the wider world. The French Revolution introduced modern notions of nationalism and popular sovereignty, concepts of 'left' and 'right', the metric system, and a conflict between absolutism and republicanism that dominated European international society during the nineteenth century. The Russian Revolution pioneered a model of state-socialist development that was a powerful draw for states around the world during the twentieth century. Although the short-term success of the Bolsheviks in fostering revolution was slight, by 1950 a third of humanity

---

[5] Some scholarship (e.g. Pincus, 2009) traces the modern conception of revolution back to the late seventeenth century, with particular reference to the Glorious Revolution in England. Some (e.g. Wilson, 1968) go even further, seeing the late sixteenth-century Dutch Republic as the forerunner to modern revolutions.

lived under regimes that took their inspiration from the Russian Revolution. Other revolutions claimed a comparable impact, including the Chinese Revolution of 1949 with its demonstration of the radical potential of the peasantry, and the Iranian Revolution, which unleashed a militant form of Shi'ism onto the world stage. Revolutions were attempts by both core and peripheral polities to harness the new mode of power and employ it for state-led projects of radical transformation.

Revolutions, however, were more than 'progressive' projects of radical transformation. They could also be defensive projects aimed at protecting a way of life (Calhoun, 2012). Peasants, weavers and artisans often took part in revolutions not in order to rebuild society from scratch, but in the hope of containing the dislocating effects of global modernity. Some revolutionary uprisings, like the one that seized power in Iran in 1979, rested on belief systems that legitimated this sense of return rather than rupture. Such movements represented profound challenges to existing conditions. Yet they were rooted in ideals of tradition, order and community (Calhoun, 2012; see also Hobsbawm, 1959; Thompson, 1969; Hill, 1975). In this way, it is possible to discern a 'conservative' strand of revolution, the most striking example of which is fascism.

Interwar fascism sought to forge novel social orders through programmes of intense social transformation that combined 'organic nationalism, radical statism, and paramilitarism' (Mann, 2004). Fascism was a revolutionary project in that it sought the simultaneous transformation of political relations (through the development of a militarized, expansionist police-state premised on a stark division between 'inside' and 'outside'), economic relations (through the construction of a command economy that could sustain total war), and symbolic relations (via sets of rituals and movements that realigned the emotional commitment of the *ethnos* to the *demos*) (Mann, 2004; Tooze, 2007). Fascism sought to solve the 'crisis' provoked by the global transformation through a toxic blend of 'transcendent ideology', despotism and permanent armament (Mann, 2004).

The sources of social power and sanctioning ideology of fascism were quite distinct from its 'progressive' contemporaries, most notably Bolshevism. Whereas fascism relied on 'the cooperation of the throne [the monarchy], the altar [the church], and the sword [the military]', Bolshevism sought to subvert and overthrow these forms of traditional order (Mayer, 1971: 21–2). Whereas fascism safeguarded private property and maintained capitalist order (Tooze, 2007), Bolshevism attempted to eradicate the power of the bourgeoisie through collective ownership and central planning. And whereas fascism depicted a society of anxiety and *ressentiment*, which it promised to remedy through a reinstatement of hierarchy and privilege, Bolshevism sought to foster a new society resting on the power of the working class. In this way, fascism stood for social transformation premised on the continuity, or return, of traditional order, whereas Bolshevism promised social transformation through a radical rupture with existing conditions. Both offered models for how to radically transform polities through harnessing the mode of power that underpinned global modernity.

If fascism provided one alternative to the 'progressive' agenda of socialist and republican revolutions, 'revolutions from above' offered a second. In some peripheral states, either the lack of a consolidated landed class (as in Japan and Turkey) or the decline of a landed oligarchy that failed to modernize sufficiently (as in Egypt and Peru) provided the opening for an 'independent force' of high-ranking military officials and civilian bureaucrats to seize power (Trimberger, 1978: 4–5). These officials were well placed to carry out 'revolutions from above' in which charismatic leaders (such as Ataturk and Nasser) used the state as a means of enacting 'modernizing missions'. In most cases, the result was a personalistic regime based on autocratic paternalism (McDaniel, 1991: 70). As they developed, these autocratic-paternalist regimes proved as vulnerable to revolution from below as the regimes they had replaced were vulnerable to revolution from above. Personality cults and the arbitrary use of despotic power failed to substitute for the lack of institutional buffers between exclusionary states and civil societies. The slight infrastructural reach of these polities meant that elites were insulated from publics. There were few effective channels by which to meet grievances, institutionalize contestation and decompress protest movements. It was just these weaknesses that enabled revolutionary pressures to erupt in North Africa and the Middle East in 2011 (Lawson, forthcoming: ch. 7).

A third conservative variant of the revolutionary challenge arose from what Antonio Gramsci (1971 [1929–35] and 1988 [1929–33]) termed 'passive revolutions'. For Gramsci, 'passive revolutions' occurred when a revolutionary crisis yielded not radical rupture, but a form of 'revolution-restoration' in which dominant classes and state elites combined to deploy crisis for their own ends. In these instances, Gramsci argued, social relations were reorganized, but in a way that was geared at sustaining rather than overturning existing power relations. 'Passive revolutions' of this kind have been a major form of state development in the modern world, tying together processes as apparently diverse as the Italian Risorgimento (Gramsci, 1971 [1929–35] and 1988 [1929–33]), Mexican development after the 1910 revolution (Morton, 2010), and Indian party politics in the post-war era (Riley and Desai, 2007). Such dynamics can also be seen in the projects of authoritarian modernization associated with contemporary Gulf states, Singapore and, perhaps, China (Lawson, forthcoming: ch. 1).

The modern revolutionary challenge has therefore assumed multiple forms, from the 'progressive' revolutions of France, Russia, China and Cuba to the 'defensive' projects associated with interwar fascism, 'revolutions from above' and authoritarian modernization. Whichever form revolutions have taken, they have acted as projects of state transformation, seeking to institute a 'new framework for historical development' (Hobsbawm, 1986: 24). Such frameworks ranged from programmes of redistribution to the advent of land reform, and from the introduction of new constitutions to the development of novel legislative environments. In Cuba, for example, over 1,500 new laws were enacted in the first year of the revolution alone (Paige, 2003: 24). Material transformations of this kind were reinforced by symbolic transformations, embracing spheres as apparently humdrum as the transformation of holidays. In Cuba, the revolutionary regime replaced Santa Claus, who was considered to be an 'undesirable alien', with the 'authentic' Cuban figure of Don Feliciano (Paige, 2003: 24). More often than not, revolutions led to the formation of stronger states, both infrastructurally and despotically. In Iran, nearly 3,000 people were executed and over 12,000 dissidents were killed in clashes between the *ulama* and its opponents between 1979 and 1983. The aftermath of the French Revolution – the 1793–4 'Terror' and the civil war in the Vendée region – claimed at least a quarter of a million lives (Osterhammel, 2014: 540). If no revolutionary movement succeeded in implementing its full aims, most states around the world took their challenge seriously, whether as something to be emulated or feared.

Revolutions and International Order

As well as offering a *specific* challenge to states everywhere, revolutions also presented a *general* challenge to international order. Revolutionary movements ran counter to many of the ground-rules of international order (including sovereignty, the sanctity of international law and diplomacy), proclaiming ideals of 'universal society' and world revolution. The 1917 Bolshevik Revolution, for example, provided a short-term challenge in the form of the withdrawal of Russian forces from the First World War, a medium-term challenge in the provision of support for like-minded movements (the Soviet Union invaded Poland in 1920, provided aid for German revolutionaries in 1923, supported the republicans during the Spanish Civil War from 1936–9, and helped to install socialist regimes in Europe and Asia during the late 1940s), and a long-term challenge in the establishment of a systemic alternative to market democracy.

If the Bolshevik Revolution challenged the credibility of the existing international order, it simultaneously challenged the credibility of this order's great powers. In order to justify their position at the apex of international society, great powers must act decisively in the face of revolutionary challenges (Bisley, 2004: 56). Occasionally, this action takes place in support of a revolutionary movement, as with the 1989 revolutions in Central and Eastern Europe and, to a lesser extent, the 2011 Arab Uprisings. More frequently, great powers act to suppress revolutions, seeing them as threats to the status quo. As Andrew Scott (1982) observes, intervention by counter-revolutionary states is both informal, covering covert practices and cultural ties, and formal, taking in propaganda, training, aid and the provision of arms. These two forms of aid can be distilled into five sets of activities (Bisley, 2004: 52–3): first, direct military intervention, as in US intervention alongside white armies during the Russian Civil War; second, financial aid, whether open or clandestine, for counter-revolutionary forces, as with US support for Nicaraguan Contras or Mujahedeen groups in Afghanistan and Pakistan during the 1980s; third, low-scale harassment, such as propaganda campaigns, public diplomacy and the jamming of radio signals common to Western strategies in Eastern and Central Europe during the Cold War; fourth, deprivation, such as sanctions, of the kind that the US has sustained against Iranian and Cuban revolutionary regimes; and fifth, disruption, through the non-recognition of revolutionary states and associated practices. Often, counter-revolutionary policies combine two or more of these activities. US involvement in the Russian Civil War included direct military intervention (9,000 American troops were sent to Siberia and nearly 5,000 to North Russia), financial aid ($450 million for the post-Tsarist government and almost $200 million for use against the Bolsheviks after the October Revolution), and wider assistance in the form of food relief, medical aid, and the like – in 1921 alone, around $20 million was earmarked for such aid in opposition-held Siberia (Tardelli, 2013).

On occasion, counter-revolutionary forces have succeeded in rolling back revolutions, perhaps most notably during the Springtime of Nations in Europe in 1848–9. More frequently, these campaigns have been unsuccessful, as in Haiti, Cuba, Vietnam and Algeria, leading to protracted struggles between revolutionary regimes and counter-revolutionary forces. If counter-revolution has a mixed record, so too does the experience of revolutionary states in changing the contours of international order. While the Bolshevik Revolution ushered in over 80 years of conflict between state socialism and market democracy, it is difficult to see many large-scale ramifications that emerged from the Mexican or Ethiopian revolutions. Indeed, there is a paradox at the heart of the relationship between revolutionary states and international society – revolutionary states must establish relations with other states and coexist with the system's rules, laws and institutions, even while professing to reject these practices. Although the Declaration of the Rights of Man claimed that 'the sovereignty of peoples is not bound by the treaties of tyrants', the French revolutionary regime signed a resolution on non-intervention in 1793, stating that 'the invasion of one state by another state tends to threaten the liberty and security of all' (in Armstrong, 1993: 217–18, 227). For their part, the Soviet revolutionary regime enjoyed a selective approach to international law, arguing through the principle of 'socialist legality' that promises must be kept (*pacta sunt servanda*) and that new circumstances invalidated previous treaties (*rebus sic stantibus*). In this way, the Bolsheviks annulled foreign loans, but upheld the treatment of prisoners of war. In general, pressures to conform have provided a counter-weight to claims of self-reliance and international revolution. On the one hand, revolutionary states have exhibited a particular form of 'revolutionary sovereignty', one that simultaneously legitimizes domestic autarchy and international intervention. On the other hand, in order to function as states, revolutionary states have been forced to give up many of their revolutionary aims (Calvert, 1984: 120–2).

Revolutions, therefore, are intimately connected to the development of both political units and international order. Revolutions have prompted a range of state-led modernization programmes, from Bolshevism to fascism. Fear of revolutions has prompted major reform programmes, partly out of elite concerns over the prospects of revolution, partly because of the militancy of mass publics. During global modernity, the revolutionary challenge has transformed the infrastructural and despotic capacities of political units, whether by following through a revolutionary programme, as in China, or in response to the challenge of revolutionary states, as in the US. As well as augmenting state capacities, revolutions have played a central role in constructing and challenging international order. Over the past two centuries, revolutions have been at the heart of global modernity's most pressing debates: the extension of capitalism around the world and the development of movements intended to counter its inequities; the expansion of European imperialism and the forms of resistance that rose up against it; and the circulation of radical ideas, particularly around rights, autonomy and equality, which served as the 'world cultural scripts' for projects of state transformation in Europe, South Asia, the Americas, Indochina and Africa (Beck, 2011). Whether as ideas or in practice, revolutions have played a major role in the development of systems of governance everywhere.

States and Markets

Beyond experiences of imperialism and the multiple challenges presented by revolutions, the third force that transformed political units during global modernity was capitalism. Crucial here was the conceptual and legal separation of politics and economics that is central to liberal ideas of political economy. As this section makes clear, this separation is as much ideal as real. It is ideal in that state and market remain tightly intertwined: just as the market requires the state to recognize private property and provide a legal apparatus that can sustain accumulation and enforce contracts, so the state requires the revenues that accrue from property, accumulation and contracts. But it is also real inasmuch as market logics are given a significant degree of autonomy, representing a substantial difference from the tightly integrated political economy of state socialism. We first chart the basic contours of the shift from agrarian to industrial economies before examining the variable forms that the relationship between states and markets has taken since the nineteenth century.

As we discussed in the Introduction, the shift from agrarian to industrial economies that enabled the global transformation was not a 'big bang'. Small-scale factories, mines, mills and foundries served as micronodes of industrial development. Many breakthroughs that were crucial to the industrial revolution took place either before the long nineteenth century or during its incipient years. The Spinning Jenny, Water Frame and Spinning Mule, all of which were central to the transformation of the cotton industry, were invented in 1770, 1775 and 1778 respectively. The early forms of steam engine were also an eighteenth-century technology, as was gas lighting.

However, even if some industrial technologies emerged before the nineteenth century, this did not mark the flowering of either the factory system or industrial society, which belong to the nineteenth century. The first step in this transformation was the commercialization of agriculture. Legislation such as the 1801 Great Enclosures Act in Britain codified practices that had built up over preceding centuries, privatizing the commons and turning land into a productive commodity. Mechanization and the adoption of 'cash cropping' (producing a crop for sale rather than for livestock feed) restructured the landlord–peasant relationship as a commercial relation between landowners, tenant farmers and landless labourers (Brenner, 1976 and 1985). From this point on, labour power was bought and sold as a commodity (Wolf, 1997: 78). Accompanying processes such as crop rotation increased both profitability and productivity (Christian, 2004: 411).

As Table 5.1 shows, agriculture remained an important component of core economies throughout the long nineteenth century. In some parts of Europe, such as Italy, two-thirds of the population continued to work on the land at the beginning of the twentieth century (Blanning, 2000: 3, 97). However, in general terms, the structural shift prompted by the commercialization of agriculture was well underway by this time: the percentage of Americans working in agriculture halved during the nineteenth century while, by 1913, virtually every country in Northern and Western Europe was industrialized, even if, in some instances, this industrialization was concentrated in regional 'islands' (Frieden, 2006: 59; Osterhammel, 2014: 638).

Core states not only carried out structural adjustment programmes on their own societies, they also did so in their overseas territories. The Dutch cultivation system (*cultuurstelsel*) in Indonesia was based

Table 5.1: *Structural employment in the core (%)*

		UK	US	Netherlands
1820	Agriculture	37	70	42
	Services	30	15	30
	Industry	33	15	28
1890	Agriculture	18	38	36
	Services	41	38	22
	Industry	43	24	22
1950	Agriculture	5	13	14
	Services	48	54	46
	Industry	47	33	40
2003	Agriculture	1	2	3
	Services	75	78	77
	Industry	24	20	20

Source: Maddison (2007b: 76).

on bonded labour (the Dutch operated a 'pass law' system to prevent evasion or flight) and the forced delivery of crops. Around half of the revenue collected by the Indonesian government under the cultivation system was remitted to the metropole, constituting 20% of the net revenue of the Netherlands treasury (Osterhammel, 2014: 443). From the 1870s until the early part of the nineteenth century, the Dutch shifted to a plantation system that fuelled a boom in commodity exports. But the local population experienced few of the gains: Dutch settlers enjoyed 50 times the level of per capita income as indigenous Indonesians (Maddison, 2007b: 137).

The commercialization of agriculture was, therefore, a process repeated, if in varying forms, around the world. As profits could only be achieved through higher productivity, lower wages or the establishment of new markets, expansion of the system was constant, leading to the development of both new areas of production (such as south-eastern Russia and central parts of the United States) and new products (such as potatoes). Arable land in Europe, Russia and the settler colonies increased from 225 million hectares in 1860 to 439 million hectares in 1910: 'a rate of growth without precedent in history' (Osterhammel, 2014: 211). In 1900, Malaya had around 5,000 acres of rubber production; by 1913, it contained 1.25 million acres (Wolf, 1997: 325). Between 1890 and 1913, more than 10 million acres of land in Argentina and an equal amount in Canada were planted for wheat production (Frieden, 2006: 22). De-industrialization was equally rapid. As we discussed in Chapter 1, after 1800, the British government ensured that British products undercut Indian goods and charged prohibitive tariffs on Indian textiles. By 1820, British products were being exported in bulk to the subcontinent. By 1850, Lancashire was the centre of a global textile industry, reversing centuries of subcontinental pre-eminence in this area (Parthasarathi, 2011: 151–3; Riello, 2013). Within a generation or two, the de-industrialization of India meant that centuries-old skills in 'strategic industries' such as cloth dyeing, shipbuilding, metallurgy and gun making had been lost (Arnold, 2000: 100–1; Parthasarathi, 2011: 259).

Both the commercialization of agriculture and the coercive de-industrialization of rival sites of competition were significant stepping-stones in the development of industrial capitalism, providing a logic by which sectors from textiles to armaments were restructured. Industrialization emerged in two main waves. The first (mainly British) wave centred on cotton, coal and iron. The crucial advance was the capture of inanimate sources of energy, particularly the advent of steam power, a process that enabled the biggest increase in the availability of power sources for several millennia (McNeill, 1991: 729; Christian, 2004: 421; Morris, 2010: 500). Britain's lead in this field presented a major advantage – by 1850, 18 million Britons used as much fuel energy as 300 million inhabitants of Qing China (Goldstone, 2002: 364). Also crucial was the application of engineering to blockages in production, such as the development of machinery to pump water efficiently out of mineshafts (Morris, 2010: 503; Parthasarathi, 2011: 151–2). Engineering and technology combined to generate substantial gains in productivity: whereas a British spinner at the end of the eighteenth century took 300 hours to produce 100 pounds of cotton, by 1830 the same task took only 135 hours (Christian, 2004: 346). Machines and fertilizers raised productive standards even as they forced people off the land. The introduction of fertilizer doubled grain production in Germany between 1880 and 1913 without there being an increase in available land; the time it took to produce a hectare of wheat in Germany dropped from 150 hours to nine hours during the same period (Belich, 2009: 3).

Towards the end of the nineteenth century, a second (mainly German and American) wave of industrialization took place, centring on advances in chemicals, pharmaceuticals and electronics. Once again, new sources of energy were critical, with oil and electricity emerging alongside coal, and internal combustion engines and turbines replacing steam piston engines. The oil industry took off in Russia, Canada and the US from the middle of the nineteenth century, initially to provide kerosene for lighting. Before the century's end, pipelines and tankers were bringing oil to a global market, and further advances in distillation and mechanical engineering were opening up its use as a fuel. During the 1880s, electricity began to be generated and distributed from hydro-electric and steam-powered stations. A number of new techniques and products were developed, such as the distillation of coal into tar for use in products ranging from explosives to dyes, and the application of chemicals to the manufacture of steel and other alloys. Perhaps most notably, advances in light metals and electrics, allied to the use of oil products for fuel, provided an impetus to the development of cars, planes and ships (Woodruff, 1966: 181–2; McNeill, 1991: 737), a process discussed in Chapter 3.

Modes of Capitalist Governance

The commercialization of agriculture and the two stages of the industrial revolution represent the main landmarks in the development of modern capitalism. Lying behind these landmarks was a fundamental shift in how economies operated. During global modernity, economic interactions that had previously required personal, often intimate, connections became carried out through 'faceless' transactions via the 'symbolic token' of 'generalized money' (Simmel, 1978 [1900]: 332–3; Giddens, 1990: 19). The arrival of the all-purpose price mechanism was a crucial feature in the emergence of modern capitalism. Under these conditions, every product was exchangeable, including labour. Hence, for the first time, 'free labour' could be sold (as wages) according to market logics. The bracketing of a private ('free') sphere of market exchange had the simultaneous effect of generating a public sphere of political regulation. The economy became seen as the realm of civil society mediated by logics of market exchange ('the self-regulating market' organized through 'the invisible hand'), while politics became seen as the realm of the state governed by the national interest ('*raison d'état*'). The separation of states and markets that, from a contemporary viewpoint, appears natural is, in fact, specific to modernity (see also Giddens, 1985: 135–6; Rosenberg, 1994: 126; North et al., 2009: 72).

The view of markets as self-regulating and autonomous obscured the fact that states and markets were mutually constituted. In fact, such a view rested on a 'sleight of hand' in which markets became conceptualized as natural forces rather than policy practices, and as realms of depoliticized technical expertise rather than sites of political contestation (Krippner, 2011: 145–6). This occluded the ways in which the 'free market' itself was a political condition, an ideal that could be extended or reversed. Since the nineteenth century, one of the main tasks of states has been to establish regulatory orders that enable capitalist accumulation on the one hand and protect publics from the dislocations arising from this accumulation on the other. In this respect, there have been four main phases in the development of global capitalism: the first, running from the third quarter of the nineteenth century to the First World War, was marked by high flows of capital and finance; the second, during the interwar years, was marked by capital controls and, as a result, a reduction in global transactions; the third, from 1945–73, saw a gradual relaxation of capital controls and the partial recovery of financial and capital flows; the fourth, from the early 1970s until the present day, has been one of relatively unconstrained controls and, therefore, high capital mobility (Eichengreen, 1996: 3). As we discuss in Chapter 10, the process that became known as 'globalization' in the last quarter of the twentieth century is the contemporary manifestation of dynamics that first appeared in the last quarter of the nineteenth century.

If globalization was born in the last quarter of the nineteenth century, so too was capitalist crisis. The deepening of transnational trading circuits, enabled by the commercialization of agriculture, the two industrial revolutions, imperial expansion and the increasingly widespread adoption of the gold standard, meant that far-off places became intimately connected. In 1889, the British bank Barings, one of the largest investment houses in the world, failed to sell a large issue of Argentinian bonds. When, the following year, the Argentinian government defaulted, Barings' holdings became worthless. The subsequent 'panic' meant that capital flows to Argentina all but ceased for five years (Schwartz, 2000: 140). Such crises were regular features of the first stage of globalization (Reinhart and Rogoff, 2009). Even more destructive was the world's first global-scale depression, which took place between 1873 and 1896. The depression had three major impacts on economies around the world. First, it induced deflationary pressures that pushed the prices of commodities down to, and sometimes below, the cost of production – between 1871 and 1895, the price of grain fell by a third, the price of textiles by 40%, and the price of sugar, tea and coffee by nearly 50% (Schwartz, 2000: 140). Second, as prices fell, there was a decline in metropolitan demands for peripheral products. Because of the dependence of the periphery on the core, the results of such a drop-off were extreme, as in the South Asian famines we highlight in the following chapter (Davis, 2002: 63). Third, depression was met by capital flight from peripheral polities (Eichengreen, 1996: 46), a process that, again, prompted major turmoil. These dynamics were to be repeated on a number of occasions over the ensuing century. The depression of 1873–96 was the precursor to twentieth-century industrial and trade cycles (Hobsbawm, 1975: 85–7), just as the Barings crisis was the portend for later financial 'panics' (Darwin, 2009: 121). Both illustrated the ways in which the expansion of the market to a global scale could result in dramatic price fluctuations and commodity speculations, with cascading effects for economies and polities around the world.

The two decades following the depression were generally marked by growth, in part because of the increasing number of countries that adopted the gold standard, in part because of falling tariffs.[6] During this period, US GDP grew by an average of 4.9% per annum, while Germany grew by an average of 3.9% and Britain by 2.6% (Schwartz, 2000: 153). Some countries surpassed these levels: between 1893 and 1913, the GDPs of Canada and Argentina tripled and their output per person doubled (Frieden, 2006: 16). High levels of growth were fuelled by two main types of relationship between states and markets. A minority of states, led by Britain and the United States, were self-declared liberal capitalist states. Liberal capitalist states sought to provide the maximum possible space for the 'self-regulating' market, for

---

[6] It should be noted that, in many places, tariffs remained high during this period. Russia operated a tariff on manufactured goods that ran to as much as 84%, roughly double the level found in the Americas and Oceania, and triple the rates of continental Europe. For more on this issue, see Frieden (2006: 42–3, 65).

example through accepting the strictures of a 'neutral' mechanism such as the gold standard.

A majority of polities combined liberal economies with political illiberalism (Lacher and Germain, 2012: 115–19). This liberal–illiberal combination was in keeping with prevailing views that capitalism did not easily align with democracy. For many of both its detractors and advocates, capitalism prompted tendencies towards oligopoly (Mann, 2013: 132–3; also see O'Donnell, 1973; Evans, 1979). As noted in the previous section, during the nineteenth century, most industrializing states (gradually) extended the franchise to (some) propertied men. But any further extensions were circumscribed by concerns that the working class would limit private property and favour radical redistribution. More often than not, industrialization took place under the guise of interventionary, often authoritarian, 'developmental states'.

Exemplifying this trend was Japan. Japan's rise was enabled by a series of state-directed policies. First, the Meiji state carried out an extensive programme of land reform, taxing land rather than yields, thereby incentivizing productivity gains and stabilizing revenues. Second, taking advantage of burgeoning regional trade (intra-Asian trade grew by 5.4% per annum between 1883 and 1913), the state used revenues from trade and land reform to support the development of light industry, particularly textiles (Schwartz, 2000: 98, 253–4). Third, the state purchased capital goods that could be used in the production of higher-value, heavy industrial goods, such as steel. Finally, the state protected domestic firms that moved into the manufacture of cars and electronics. Germany's state-led modernization followed a broadly similar trajectory to that undertaken by Japan. Both Japanese and German elites stressed the importance of industrialization as a means of overcoming their 'backwardness'. In the case of Germany, industrial production multiplied by a factor of five between 1870 and 1913; by 1920, Germany produced 20% more electricity than Britain, France and Italy combined (Topik and Wells, 2012: 669).

In many ways, Germany and Japan were the original 'developmental states' (Blyth, 2013: 134), with Japan serving as a particular source of inspiration for peripheral modernizers (Osterhammel, 2014: 560, 563). All 'late' developers require considerable capital if they are to catch up with early movers. Often, the scale of the capital required, and the need to underwrite the risks involved, is beyond the capacities of the private sector (Blyth, 2013). As more states have become capitalist and as global competition has increased, so the need for states to foster capitalist development has increased. In this sense, Japanese and German models of state-led development were pioneers of the 'catch-up' policies implemented, not always successfully, by a range of polities over the past century. We come back to this point both below and in the following two chapters.

Beyond Japanese and German 'late' development, the most striking feature of the late nineteenth-century global economy was the rise of the United States. The ascent of the US was rapid: its share of global production climbed from 23% in 1870 to 30% in 1900 and 36% in 1913 (Panitch and Gindin, 2012: 28). US growth was predicated on the emergence of a new type of firm that took over the whole productive process, from the supply of raw materials, to manufacturing, wholesale, research and development, and retailing. Housing the entire productive process within single firms prompted gains in economies of scale that, in turn, prompted advances in productivity: from 1870–1913, US productivity went from being 14% lower than Britain's to being 20% higher (Panitch and Gindin, 2012: 28). Also crucial to this advance was the introduction of the moving assembly line, which helped to reduce the cost of labour, shorten production time and, as a result, lower prices. Beyond growth and productivity gains, the consequence of these innovations was the arrival of mega-firms: by the end of the nineteenth century, the largest company in the world was US Steel, which produced 40% of the world's supply (Topik and Wells, 2012: 615–16). In 1904, 318 American companies produced 40% of US manufacturing output (Panitch and Gindin, 2012: 30). One of the biggest companies of them all, Ford, employed 120,000 workers on a 2,000 acre site in Illinois, while sourcing its own wood and rubber directly from plantations it owned in Latin America.

The emergence of giant transnational corporations like Ford was a significant step in the development of modern capitalism.[7] In Britain, the Companies Act of 1862 was a turning point, reducing the costs of forming a company, removing the need to receive legislative approval for one, and limiting the liability of shareholders. Comparable acts were

---

[7] The essential quality of a transnational corporation (TNC) is that its activities, whether these entail the extraction of resources, manufacturing or the provision of services, take place in more than one territory, and that there is an organizational hierarchy crossing national borders.

signed in France (*Loi Sur les Sociétés Commerciales*) in 1867 and Germany (*Aktienrechtsnovelle*) in 1870. From this point on, there was a major increase in portfolio investment as companies pooled investments into high-interest, often long-distance, infrastructural and public works projects. Transnational companies invested in mining, plantations, railways and ports, often with the backing of states, which supported firms through a range of practices, such as the subsidies provided by the British government to shipping companies for the carriage of mail. The rise of such companies went hand-in-hand with the growing power of core states (Stavrianos, 1990: 95–111).

The period between the third quarter of the nineteenth century and the First World War was, therefore, marked by two basic patterns of state–market relationship: first, the rise of liberal capitalist states, which rose on the back of transnational entities (such as TNCs) and portfolio investment projects (particularly in infrastructure); and second, the emergence of illiberal state-capitalist development projects, exemplified by Japan and Germany. The First World War brought this first era of global capitalism to an end, opening a period of economic nationalism and regionalism. In the immediate aftermath of the war, a number of states, most notably Germany, experienced hyperinflation, a process that virtually wiped out savings and assets. Many states also experienced high levels of unemployment. The result was a tightening of the relationship between states and markets. The pre-1939 Polish state, for example, owned 100% of the country's munitions and armaments, 80% of its chemicals, 50% of its metals, and 90% of its air and road transportation (Schwartz, 2000: 249–50). Such figures were not uncommon.

As well as upping their management of national economies, core states split into three main blocs: the US and the Americas, which retained the gold standard; the UK-backed sterling area, which increasingly moved towards a system of imperial preferences; and a Central European zone, centred around Germany, which operated tight currency controls. Japan and France ran smaller blocs in East Asia and the Francophone sphere respectively. To some extent, these zones marked a perpetuation of pre-First World War trends. Even during the high water mark of the first global era, one-third of Britain's trade took place within its empire (Frieden, 2006: 47). But the fragmentation of the interwar years was deeply constituted, particularly after the Great Depression, which saw international trade drop by two-thirds. This drop-off hurt both core and peripheral states alike. In the core, there was a major retraction in economic output, as well as wide-ranging bank failures, foreclosures and a surge in unemployment. In the periphery, there was a collapse in commodity prices and a near collapse in exports as core states raised tariffs and devalued their currencies. The geopolitical consequences of the Great Depression were also significant. During the 1930s, fascism, socialism and various forms of populism sought to embed productive activities within authoritarian political orders. The result was 'economic warfare' as rival visions of political economy competed through trade wars, competitive devaluations, debt repayments and exchange controls. By 1936, all Eastern, Southern and Central European states were authoritarian. Increasingly, it was liberal ideas of political economy that were marginal.

The period after the Second World War marked the third stage in the development of global capitalism. After 1945, there was a concerted effort to move away from the economic autarchy and protectionism of the interwar years. Most core states adopted a Keynesian approach, using state stimulation to produce mild inflation that was, in turn, linked to stable rates of growth (Mann, 2013). Keynesian ideas also lay at the heart of a host of new international financial institutions (IFIs), most notably the Bretton Woods Institutions: the IMF, which was intended to act as global lender of last resort, and the World Bank, which was to provide loans and investment. Although the agreement to create a permanent International Trade Organization was not enacted, states did establish the GATT, which began the process of reducing tariffs. GATT (later the WTO) did its job, albeit in fits and starts. Via a number of multilateral trade rounds, states reduced tariffs on manufacturing products from an average of 40% in the 1940s to an average of 5% by the end of the century.[8]

For a generation after the Second World War, the turn to Keynesian stimulus and management helped to reinvigorate both growth and trade. This was the 'golden age' of 'embedded liberalism' (Ruggie, 1982; Maddison, 2001). Between 1950 and 1973, per capita GDP around the world rose by an average of 3% per year (equivalent to a doubling every 25 years), while trade increased by 8% per year (Ruggie,

---

[8] Agriculture, of much greater significance to states in the periphery, proved to be a stickier issue, as exemplified by the ups and downs of the Doha Trade Round, which began in 2001 and concluded with a compromise settlement in Bali in 2013.

1982; Maddison, 2001: 24). At the heart of the 'embedded liberal' order was the United States. The war had devastated European states, both winners and losers alike: by the end of the war, German GDP had returned to its 1890 level, while living standards in Britain had fallen by a third (Frieden, 2006: 261). In 1946–7, an estimated 100 million Europeans lived on rations of just 1,500 calories per day (Loth, 2014: 13). The United States, by contrast, had seen its economy grow by 50% during the war. In the five years after the Second World War, this boom continued, fuelled by a 60% rise in personal consumption (Panitch and Gindin, 2012: 83). The US used its wealth to provide aid (including the Marshall Plan, which we discuss in Chapter 7) and foreign direct investment (FDI) to Europe, and encouraged the development of the European Coal and Steel Community (1951) and the Treaty of Rome (1957). It also provided substantial aid and investment to Japan. This turn towards Europe and Japan formed part of a general reorientation away from investment in peripheral states towards investment in core states: in the quarter century after the Second World War, the US invested three times as much in Europe and Japan as it did in Latin America (Frieden, 2006: 293).[9] High value-added industries, such as cars, oil and chemicals, became deeply embedded features of trade and investment between industrialized states. During the 1960s, FDI increased by twice the level of global GDP, while international trade grew 40% faster than global GDP (Panitch and Gindin, 2012: 114).

If Keynesianism endorsed an activist state in terms of developing and managing markets in the core, states in the periphery went even further in establishing a leading role for the state in development projects. Such projects split into two basic models: 'import substitution industrialization' (ISI) and 'export-led industrialization'. Most peripheral states, including India and virtually every Latin American state, followed a strategy of ISI. Advocates of ISI, such as Raúl Prebisch (1950), argued that south–south

---

[9] To some extent, the gap in US investment in peripheral states was filled by the Soviet Union, which began to provide substantial aid, investment, loans and 'technical assistance' to the Third World in the 1950s. By 1954, Soviet aid to the Third World amounted to $1.44 billion per year; in 1960, just before the Sino-Soviet split, aid to China alone took up 7% of Soviet national income (Zeiler, 2014: 245). The globalization of Soviet aid prompted a renewal of US programmes, perhaps most notably Kennedy's 'Alliance for Progress', which provided billions of dollars in loans, food aid and investment to Latin American states. These programmes were intended both to counter Soviet influence and to generate the 'take off' promised by Rostow's (1960) modernization theory.

investment and regional integration, allied to restrictions on foreign capital and the introduction of quotas on northern imports, would foster domestic growth and jobs (Zeiler, 2014: 258). States subsidized domestic producers, offering them tax breaks, cheap credit and preferential access to raw materials and parts. They also sought to diversify economies away from primary goods towards infant industries and services, while manipulating currencies so that firms could buy foreign equipment and technologies. High tariffs were placed on manufacturing imports: 74% in Mexico, 84% in Argentina and 184% in Brazil (Frieden, 2006: 304).

In some respects, ISI was successful. Mexican industrial production increased by a factor of four and Brazil's by a factor of eight between 1945 and 1973. By the late 1970s, Brazil produced almost all of its consumer goods and had become a major car manufacturer: from making 50,000 cars per year in the 1950s, Brazil produced one million cars per year by 1978 (Schwartz, 2000: 244). Such turnarounds were not uncommon. By the early 1970s, India produced 90% of its textiles, 98% of its aluminium, and 99% of its iron and steel, all of which had been predominantly imported at the time of independence. Nigeria's industrial production grew at 11% per year during the 1950s and 1960s, while Thailand's output per person doubled from 1948–73 (Frieden, 2006: 317). Despite these successes, there were four big problems with ISI: first, a lack of competitiveness tended to distort the market, raising the possibility of rent seeking and generating monopoly companies that were often inefficient; second, the lack of foreign competition meant that little was gained by way of technology transfer and transnational learning; third, ISI prompted balance of payment deficits in that states had to borrow heavily in order to establish and protect nascent industries, yet received little back as levels of FDI were low and domestic companies were effectively excluded from international markets; and fourth, ISI foundered because of weak domestic consumption as a result of the inequalities that tended to characterize post-colonial economies (Haggard, 1990; Halperin, 2013; Mann, 2013). If few peripheral economies had a big enough consumer base to sustain growth, even fewer could compete with the quantity and quality of goods manufactured in core states and by Western-based multinational corporations (Zeiler, 2014: 259).

In contrast to the ISI majority, the 'Asian Tigers' (South Korea, Taiwan, Hong Kong and Singapore) followed 'export-led industrialization'. On the one hand, this meant adopting many of the same state-led strategies found in ISI countries: protecting manufacturers, undervaluing currencies (and thereby distorting prices), and subsidizing nascent industries through tax breaks and cheap credit (Kohli, 2004). State institutions, such as Economic Planning Boards and State Development Banks, ensured that the interests of state and capital were mutually aligned (Haggard, 1990; Schwartz, 2000; Chibber, 2003). On the other hand, as with Japan before them, the state-led development of the Asian Tigers was oriented towards exports. In the case of South Korea, foreign investment, mainly from the US and Japan, acted as the impetus for the state to subsidize a move into low-quality, low-price goods (particularly consumer non-durables such as cheap clothes and plastic toys), which were mostly overlooked by industrialized economies. Once this bridgehead had been established, profits were reinvested in capital equipment and advanced technologies, which were directed towards new export products, most notably consumer durables (such as household goods), heavy industry and, later, electronics. Crucially, and unlike ISI states, capital was only allocated to firms that met export targets. This made competition tough.

Export-led industrialization proved to be as successful for the Asian Tigers as it had been for Japan. Enabled both by astute state-led policies and by extensive aid and investment from foreign backers, the Asian Tigers tripled their GDP per capita in a little over two decades – by 1988, they accounted for 8.1% of world trade, almost double the share held by the whole of Latin America (Frieden, 2006: 317; Loth, 2014: 134). In South Korea, exports increased at an average rate of 8% per year between 1962 and 1989; per capita income rose by a factor of 52 during the same period (Zeiler, 2014: 312). The success of the Asian Tigers' 'strategic development' influenced Chinese leaders to 'open up' through a combination of export-led industrialization and 'labour-intensive development' in the late 1970s (Wong, 1997; Sugihara, 2013). China also followed the Asian Tigers in using authoritarianism to maintain a system of low wages, while keeping both labour organizations and dissent in check.[10] We discuss the prospects of China's blend of 'state-bureaucratic capitalism' in Chapter 9.

[10] Over the medium term, this system of low wages is a potentially major problem for China. The vast majority of Chinese workers earn less than $10 per day. Yet the country needs to increase levels of consumer spending if it is to maintain growth. The paradox is that, as with other states before it, substantial wage increases in China will cause some businesses to relocate to cheaper alternatives. For more on this point, see Duncan (2012).

The third stage of global capitalism, captured by ISI development projects and the rise of the Asian Tigers in the periphery, and the upturn in growth and trade that represented the golden age of embedded liberalism in the core, lasted broadly until the early 1970s. As with other stages of capitalist development, it was brought to an end by crisis. The crisis of the early 1970s arose because of three main dynamics: first, a fiscal crisis in a number of Western states prompted by high inflation (partly brought about by the fourfold increase in oil prices by the Organization of the Petroleum Exporting Countries – OPEC – in the aftermath of the Yom Kippur War) and increasing international competition (not least from the Asian Tigers); second, the collapse of the Bretton Woods system of semi-fixed exchange rates due to contradictions between the needs of the international monetary system and domestic politics, particularly in the US (Frieden, 2006: 339–60); and third, the emergence of deregulated Euromarkets that acted as 'slush funds' for speculations against the dollar (Eichengreen, 1996; Blyth, 2002; Cerny, 2010; Ferguson, 2010; Zeiler, 2014). During the 1970s, the United States experienced its first trade deficit since the late nineteenth century as investment flowed overseas, both to Europe and to the Asian Tigers. Industrial output in core states fell by 10% in 1974, while the same year saw the inflation rate in the ten largest non-communist countries average 13% (Zeiler, 2014: 285). Over the decade as a whole, around two-thirds of the world's states grew more slowly than they had during the 1960s (Ferguson, 2010: 8). In a number of core polities, some business elites began to favour an alternative to Keynesianism – neoliberalism (Blyth, 2002: 138).

The contrast between neoliberalism and Keynesianism was striking. Keynesianism favoured capital controls and fixed exchange rates, and its stated objectives were full employment and stable growth, guaranteed by an interventionist state. Neoliberalism saw deregulated markets rather than interventionist states as the basic source of a vibrant economy. Neoliberals argued that governments distorted the market by seeking short-term fixes to market disequilibrium (such as printing money). In contrast, neoliberals assumed that capital flowed naturally to the most productive sectors of the economy. As such, they favoured deregulation, whether in the financial sector or manufacturing, so that market forces could stimulate entrepreneurial activities. The primary policy emphasis for neoliberals was the control of inflation that, it was assumed, would stabilize prices and avoid wage–price spirals that, in turn, led to unsustainable levels of public spending. For neoliberals, lower taxes allowed individuals greater freedom, while also translating into higher levels of both consumer spending and private sector investment. Neoliberals were relatively sanguine about the impact on state finances of this move – a rolling back of the public sector in order to stimulate entrepreneurial activities was a central component of the neoliberal framework. As one of the architects of neoliberalism put it, the heart of capitalism was 'the separation of economic power from political power' (Friedman, 1962: 9).

The neoliberal era marked the fourth stage of modern capitalism. Although early experiments in neoliberalism took place in Chile under the Pinochet regime, it was only with the elections of Margaret Thatcher in Britain and Ronald Reagan in the US that neoliberalism became instituted in core states. Thatcher and Reagan were the vanguard of a broader neoliberal movement made up of state elites, entrepreneurial networks, think-tanks, financial journalists, academics and IFI officials (Cockett, 1995: 4; Stedman Jones, 2012: 134–5). This vanguard exported neoliberal policies – competitive exchange rates, control of the money supply, inflation targets, the reduction of capital and currency controls, lower rates of taxation, and so on – around the world. Structural adjustment programmes, liberalization and floating currencies became conditions of international investment and, more importantly, marks of 'good' conduct. The Washington Consensus provided a list of ten 'must do' policies, an 'instruction sheet' of neoliberal 'fundamentals' that diffused widely (Blyth, 2013: 162). This diffusion took place despite periodic crisis, including the Latin American sovereign debt crisis of the early 1980s, the Nordic banking crash of the early 1990s, the 1997 financial crisis in emerging markets, and the bursting of the dot-com bubble at the turn of the century. By 2000, virtually all member states of the Organisation for Economic Co-operation and Development (OECD) had abandoned capital controls (Mann, 2013: 144). States, regional organizations and IGOs had become carriers of neoliberal orthodoxy. Keynesianism, ISI and export-led industrialization alike were engulfed by the emergence of neoliberalism as a kind of 'global common sense' (Cerny, 2010: 140).

In many ways, neoliberalism represented the reconvening of dynamics begun in the first era of globalization. As with the last quarter of the nineteenth century, a lack of capital controls fostered the rise of financialization. Financialization was not so much about the dominance of the financial sector as it was about the dominance of financial activities (Krippner, 2011: 2). Whereas in 1970 the financial sector provided 4% of US GDP and 10% of its profits, by 2010 it was worth 8% and contributed 40% of total profits (Turner, 2011: 18). This period saw financial services become far more profitable than productive activities. In 2009, oil futures trading was worth ten times the value of physical oil production and consumption, while foreign exchange trading ran at 73 times the value of global trade (Mulgan, 2013: 19). Major manufacturers, such as Ford, began to generate more profits through financial instruments, such as the financing of loans to buy cars, than from selling cars (Krippner, 2011: 3–4). In a return to the portfolio investments pioneered by British companies in the late nineteenth century, late twentieth-century firms became 'bundles of assets' through which investors sought to collect interest, dividends and capital gains rather than generate profits through productive growth (Fligstein, 2001). This shift was enabled by 'neoliberal statecraft', which opened up the regulatory environment in global finance,[11] spawning the emergence of a 'shadow economy' of off-balance sheet derivatives (Krippner, 2011: 149). In 2010, the value of contracts taken out on these derivatives amounted to $700 trillion, a sum that equated to the world's total GDP over the preceding two decades (Duncan, 2012: 30). As these innovations spread around the financial system, banks raised leverage to unprecedented levels – in 2011, the operational leverage of Deutsche Bank was 40:1 and its asset footprint was worth 800% of German GDP (Blyth, 2013: 83).

In this way, financialization, dependent on the accumulation and recycling of debt in the form of derivatives, and increasingly reliant on short-term trades between interlocking institutions, ran well ahead of productive capital, producing a chronically leveraged – and, therefore, highly volatile – system. This volatility was laid bare by the volume of financial 'panics' that took place in 'emerging states' during the 1990s. In part, these crises emerged from the mobility of capital that arose after the lifting of capital controls (Panitch and Gindin, 2012: 248). During the decade as a whole, $1.3 trillion of private sector capital was invested in developing states (compared to $170 billion during the 1980s). These

---

[11] At the heart of this 'statecraft' was lobbying. Between 2006 and 2010, the IMF estimates that US firms spent $4.2 billion on political activities, of which the financial sector was the most prominent (in Crouch, 2011: 68).

were often speculative investments that departed soon after arriving. In 1996, the inflow of private capital to Thailand amounted to 9.3% of GDP. The following year, as the Asian financial crisis picked up pace, this capital headed for the exit – the outflow of private capital from Thailand in 1997 was worth 10.9% of GDP (Panitch and Gindin, 2012: 255). Such crises were the forerunners to the global financial crisis of 2008. Although the causes of the global crisis were less to do with capital mobility than the systemic risk prompted by financial interdependence and an over-reliance on property markets, their basic package of excessive leverage and debt was common to many previous crises (Reinhart and Rogoff, 2009). The scale of the crash was, however, more severe than almost all of its predecessors. Between 2008 and 2011, OECD countries lost an average of 8% of their GDPs; the cost of the crisis in the US alone is estimated at $13 trillion (Blyth, 2013: 45–6).

Neoliberalism is, therefore, the most recent act in a longer-term dynamic fuelled by the relationship between states and markets during the global transformation. As this section has chronicled, global modernity has seen the emergence and institutionalization of various forms of relationship between states and markets. The first stage saw liberal capitalist states forge transnational entities and extend both investment and trade, while illiberal capitalist states initiated state-led development programmes. In the second stage, capitalism retreated behind national and regional blocs. The third stage was marked by 'embedded liberalism' in the core, best captured by the line attributed to the German Finance Minister Karl Schiller: 'as much market as possible, as much state as necessary' ('*so viel Markt wie möglich, so viel Staat wie nötig*'). In the periphery, most states followed a strategy of ISI, while a minority followed the export-led development pioneered by Japan. In the fourth stage, neoliberalism promised a return to the liberal concept of the autonomous, self-regulating market – the result was a major increase in financialization and capital flows. Yet, as the discussion above makes clear, neoliberalism spread through a global political apparatus made up of IFIs, states, lobbying groups, and more. This most recent stage of global capitalism provides further support for the claim made by Fernand Braudel (1977: 64) that 'capitalism only triumphs when it becomes identified with the state'.

Despite the prevalence of liberal conceptions of political economy, this section has illustrated the interdependence of states and markets. As we have discussed, during the nineteenth century, with very few exceptions, the expansion of capitalism took place in and through states – China's state-led development is the latest act in a long-running saga. This does not mean that each state fosters capitalist development in the same way, still less that global capitalism has fostered convergence around a single logic of capitalist governance. To the contrary, the contemporary world is divided into four main types of capitalist state: 'liberal capitalism', centred on the US, Britain and other Anglophone countries; 'social democratic capitalism', exemplified by much of continental Europe, South America, India, Japan and South Korea; 'competitive authoritarian capitalism', characterized by Russia, a number of states in the Middle East, sub-Saharan Africa, Central America and South-East Asia; and 'state bureaucratic capitalism', highlighted by China, Vietnam, most of the Gulf monarchies (including Saudi Arabia) and some Central Asian states. The strengths, weaknesses and interactions between these different forms of capitalist state are the subject of Chapter 9.

Conclusion

This chapter has analysed the transformation of political units through their enmeshing in dynamics of imperialism, revolution and capitalism. All three of these dynamics transformed polities. Imperialism spread and intensified the power gap between core and periphery, while prompting 'modernizing missions' in many of the polities it encountered. The revolutionary challenge transformed those states where revolutions took place and demanded a response elsewhere, whether in the form of reform or repression. Capitalism was embedded in a host of governance structures, developing in a series of stages oriented around the changing relationship between states and markets (on which more in Chapter 9). Taken together, these three dynamics, added to those generated by the deepening of interaction capacity and the ideologies of progress discussed in earlier chapters, produced a wholesale transformation of political units around the world.

In core states, the revolutions of modernity prompted the rise of rational states that were defined by: increasingly fixed 'national' boundaries, even if these states were expansionist in their interactions with other polities; a commitment to 'progress' via 'development' and 'modernization', both at home and abroad; the reform of political institutions as mass publics contested sites of legitimacy and authority;

and a much denser suite of institutional connections between state and society. However, as this chapter has made clear, this was only one amongst many types of political unit that emerged in and through global modernity. Often, the mediation point between these polities was 'the standard of civilization'. Yet even this was a moving target. As we explore in Chapter 6, the standard of civilization was defined variously through race, religion and power capability. As such, the transformation of polities during the global transformation produced a huge variety of political units.

This variety eludes straightforward classification. As we pointed out in the introduction to this chapter, IR theories such as neo-realism simplify polities into 'like-units', thereby ironing out their divergent forms. At the other end of the spectrum, Rosenau (1966) provides a complex, multi-variable matrix of state types. In between these extremes lies a range of attempts at constructing workable typologies. North et al. (2009) differentiate between 'natural states' and 'open access orders', placing emphasis on the degree of separation between state and market. Buzan (2007 [1991]: 92–100) differentiates between 'weak' and 'strong' states in terms of their degree of socio-political cohesion. A moment's reflection adds a further host of ways that states are often differentiated: by degrees of 'development' ('developed' to 'developing'; 'advanced' to 'emerging'; 'successful' to 'failed'; 'post-modern' to 'pre-modern'); by forms of government (democratic or authoritarian); by modes of political economy (liberal, social demo-cratic, competitive authoritarian, state bureaucratic); by relationship to the colonial process (core/periphery, colonial/post-colonial); and by power capability (superpower, great power, regional and/or middle power, small power). Into this mix can be thrown typologies based on culture, religion and 'civilization'. Jacques (2010: 194ff.), for example, thinks of China as a 'civilizational state'. Other nation-states (such as Iran, Egypt, India or Japan) could make a similar claim. And if the civilization in reference is 'Confucian', then China is just one, albeit very big, state within that wider cultural sphere.

The array of ways in which states are differentiated is seldom prob-lematized and its origins rarely questioned. But the range of political units that exists in the contemporary world owes much of its variety to the ways in which imperialism, capitalism and revolution, along with the processes we highlight in other chapters, transformed political units during global modernity. At risk of oversimplification, we can highlight four main trajectories taken by polities during the global transformation (Buzan, 2012). First, leading-edge states in Europe were the primary agents of imperialism and market expansion, and also the frontline, at least initially, of the revolutionary challenge. Their development was not significantly mediated by intrusive encounters by non-European powers into their region. Although modernity was, as we have argued, a global process, most European states experienced the new mode of power as a temporal rather than spatial disjuncture. In other words, modernity represented a new era, but not subjugation to external rule. This was not the case for most other polities, which experienced a dual disjuncture of both time and space. For these polities, modernity not only marked a new era, it also represented a spatial shift in that external powers sought – and often assumed – control over their governance, economy and culture.

If most core states in Europe experienced a single (temporal) disjuncture, polities that were extensively repeopled represent the clearest example of a dual (temporal and spatial) disjuncture. Paradigmatic here was the experience of white settler states, particularly in the Americas and Australia, where the native populations were violently displaced by European settler populations and, in some places, by African slaves. In these polities, relatively little by way of indigenous governance or culture survived. Since the settlers who repopulated these lands were mostly European, they shared a sense of cultural compatibility with core states. These polities also tended to trade extensively, and on relatively egalitarian terms, with core states. The consequence was that, over time, these polities became part of the core. The white settler colonies were founded early in the process of European colonialism and they also constituted the first round of decolonization in the late eighteenth and early nineteenth centuries. Despite the closeness between these states and their progenitors, many of these states (with the notable exceptions of Canada, Australia and New Zealand) had to rebel against their European metropoles to win their independence. Some of these societies (mainly those colonized by Britain) moved into the core. Others, particularly in Latin America, became part of the periphery.

A less extreme, if still substantial, disjuncture was experienced by those polities that lost their independence to imperial powers, but not their existence as peoples occupying their ancestral lands. This was the case for most polities in Africa, South and South-East Asia, the Pacific

Islands, and (briefly) much of the Middle East. These polities were subject to various modes of imperial rule in which their forms of governance, and often their borders, were restructured along Western lines in order to reflect Western interests. As discussed earlier in this chapter, such states often resisted Western domination – in most places, decolonization was the result of a concerted challenge from below. But, as we show in Chapter 7, the price of decolonization was acceptance of Western notions of rational statehood and market exchange, the principles of Western international society and, for the most part, the boundaries created by Western imperial powers.

While the outcome of the colonization/decolonization process was to create a set of states superficially compatible with Western conceptions of rational statehood, the degree to which pre-imperial ties were retained varied greatly. At one end of the spectrum were post-colonial states whose boundaries and people retained clear connections to pre-colonial formations. This was true for most of the states in mainland South-East Asia, for several in the Middle East (e.g. Oman, Iran, Egypt, Morocco), and for a few in sub-Saharan Africa (e.g. Swaziland, Lesotho). In the middle of the spectrum, one finds states like most of those in the Indian subcontinent, where there was a mix of arbitrary boundaries and links to pre-colonial forms. At the other end of the spectrum were post-colonial states that were little more than arbitrary assemblages of people finding themselves corralled by boundaries drawn with little or no reference to local history, culture or geography. There were many of these in sub-Saharan Africa, and some in the Middle East and the offshore archipelagos of South-East Asia. Many ethnic groups found themselves on both sides of the new borders, and most states contained anything from a handful to hundreds of such groups. For these states, nationalism was a double-edged sword. One edge was useful for mobilizing opposition to colonialism, and therefore had integrating potential. The other edge tended towards internal fragmentation or conflict with neighbours by legitimizing 'ethnic' claims for self-government against 'national' identities, whether these were Nigerian, Congolese or Indonesian.

A fourth trajectory was undertaken by polities that maintained the greatest ties to their previous social orders. These polities were not colonized, but underwent a coercive encounter with the West and a prolonged process, mediated by the 'standard of civilization', to gain independence and recognition as full members of international society.

As we surveyed briefly in this chapter, and come back to in chapters to come, China and Japan are cases in point. Comparable experiences took place in Ottoman Empire/Turkey, Iran, Siam, Egypt and Ethiopia.[12] For North-East Asia and the Middle East (Ottoman Empire), these encounters saw classical great powers succeed in keeping the West largely at bay until imperial powers broke down their doors in the nineteenth century. At that point, the Middle East experience became largely one of colonization, whereas North-East Asia was more associated with 'modernizing missions'. China and Japan quite rightly saw international society as based on a double standard, with recognition as equals reserved for those deemed to be 'civilized' and varying degrees of subordination accorded to those seen as 'barbarian' or 'savage'. As will be unfolded in subsequent chapters, these two polities took very different paths in response to Western intrusion. Both retained something close to their original boundaries and population. Yet the depth of the disjuncture caused by their remaking as rational states should not be underestimated. The classical social order in East Asia was overthrown both within and between states, and traditional patterns of culture, power and identity were transformed.

These four trajectories, however stylized, go some way towards explaining how global modernity generated such a diverse population of political units. Ironically, the most extreme form of temporal/spatial disjuncture (repopulation, often via extermination) resulted in the least tension with international society, while, arguably, the least extreme disjuncture ('modernizing missions') triggered huge transformations and left a legacy of major tensions between core and peripheral states within a starkly bifurcated international order.

These processes of imperialism, revolution and capitalism, and the many forms of encounter they fostered between a dominating core and a subordinated periphery, established both the main actors and the central dynamics that constituted modern international society. By the end of the nineteenth century, the principal actors that characterize the modern international system were in place: the rational state in

---

[12] This is not to say that the experience of these polities was the same or that their encounters with the 'standard of civilization' did not change over time. For example, during much of the reign of Sultan Abdulhamid II, the Ottomans emphasized the 'otherness' – and power – of 'Islamic Civilization'. It was only during the early Republican period that Western civilization became seen as *the* civilization in Turkey. For more on this point, see Bilgin (2012).

both its liberal democratic and authoritarian developmental form, intergovernmental organizations, global civil society, and transnational corporations. Dynamics of capitalism, revolution and imperialism – and reactions to them – tied these actors together. These ties were massively strengthened by the shrinking of the planet discussed in Chapter 3 and deeply infused by the ideologies of progress discussed in Chapter 4. The next chapter focuses on how the revolutions of modernity established a core–periphery order that rested on a deep, enduring power gap between those in possession of the new mode of power and those who were subjected to it. Chapter 7 carries that story forward by showing how the core–periphery structure has been eroded by the embedding of the new mode of power within an increasing number of polities.

6 | *Establishing a Core–Periphery International Order*

Introduction

During the nineteenth century, the core of the global transformation rested with European states and their settler colonies, with the addition during the latter part of the century of Japan. As discussed in the previous chapter, these states conducted a multiple assault on peoples around the world, undermining their institutions of governance, their modes of production and their legitimating ideologies (Abernathy, 2000: 1–12). The core states of the global transformation created an international 'society of empires' that subordinated indigenous people, sanctioning their dispossession and, on occasion, their genocide (Keal, 2003: 21, 35). The power inequality at the heart of this emergent core-periphery relationship was unprecedented in world history.

This chapter and the next augment the analysis of the previous chapter by charting the main components that underlay: (a) the emergence of a core–periphery international order; and (b) its partial erosion. In this chapter, we focus on the ways in which the gap between core and periphery was opened during the nineteenth century and more or less maintained until the middle of the twentieth century. Chapter 7 examines how this gap began to be reduced, mainly in the period after the Second World War, but sometimes earlier. If this chapter is about how modernity intensified both the uneven and combined aspects of historical development, the next chapter is about the ways in which the combined character of development has been enhanced even as its uneven aspect, particularly in relation to the distribution of power, has diminished. These two dynamics are closely intertwined – this is *not* a transformation in which a change arose autonomously in one place and was then exported to the rest of the system. The changes discussed here, as with those in the previous chapters, were constituted by interactions between the core and the periphery – the transformation to modernity was global from the beginning and remains so today. Analysing the global dimensions of modernity is what IR has to contribute to debates about modernity in Sociology and World History. But our concern here is somewhat different – to establish the implications of the global transformation for how IR understands itself and its subject matter.

The establishing of a core–periphery order built on developments in physical interaction capacity discussed in Chapter 3, the four ideologies of progress discussed in Chapter 4, and the transformation of political units discussed in Chapter 5. During the nineteenth century, development became both more intensely uneven (because of the gap opened up by the new mode of power) and more intensely combined (because imperialism, the extension of the market and improvements in physical interaction capacity saw the core establish its social order around the world). While uneven and combined development has been a long-standing feature in human history (Rosenberg, 2010 and 2013), the revolutions of modernity both intensified unevenness between polities and, for the first time, tied the world into a single structure. The small size of the core, combined with the extent of the gap between it and the periphery, underline just how extreme and narrow the new international hierarchy was.

In the sections that follow we divide the imposition of a core–periphery international order into four sectors: political-legal, military, economic and demographic. There is no chronological or rank order amongst these sectors. All are interlinked, with none obviously assuming the role of 'ultimate primacy'. Rather, the extension of global modernity was gradual, uneven, complex and multifaceted.

Political and Legal Inequality

In order to grasp the political inequality that was constructed between core and periphery during the nineteenth century, one has to start from the practice of relative equality that preceded it. From the beginning of European overseas expansion during the fifteenth century through to the late eighteenth century, Europeans dealt with other parts of the world more or less in the way they dealt with each other: as a mixture of egalitarian and hierarchical. This is not particularly surprising given that, during these centuries, much of the world shared core aspects of agrarian civilization, including dynastic politics and agrarian notions of status and role. The gap that yawned during the nineteenth century had scarcely begun to open.

We have already noted the provinciality of IR's view of modernity as hinged to 1648 and the Treaty of Westphalia. As Reus-Smit (1999: 87–121) points out, Westphalia did not establish modern states practising sovereign equality. Rather, it reinforced dynastic, absolutist states that, while sovereign, were not equal. The dynastic diplomacy amongst such states reflected the different degrees of aristocratic status amongst their rulers (dukes, princes, kings, emperors and suchlike). This mix of sovereignty and hierarchy was a comfortable fit with the practice in much of Asia (Alexandrowicz, 1967: 14–40). Indeed, in their interactions with European polities, the Ottomans and Chinese thought of themselves as the culturally and politically superior party. In Africa and the Americas, Europeans engaged in diplomacy and made treaties with local peoples, chiefdoms and kingdoms. When they moved into the Indian Ocean, the Europeans found a well-developed international society in place (Phillips and Sharman, forthcoming). Grotius' seventeenth-century argument that Europeans should accept the principle that the high seas constituted international territory was based on the precedent provided by the Indian Ocean international society (Alexandrowicz, 1967; Krishna, 2006). From the European side, the ability to deal with alien peoples and civilizations on equal terms was rooted in natural law, which predominated in Western thought.

The idea of relative equality between peoples broke down during the nineteenth century, to be replaced by hierarchical relations that favoured Europeans. Partly this came about because of the shift in the balance of power in favour of the emerging Western core. But there were also two significant political-legal developments in nineteenth-century Europe that underpinned a new understanding of hierarchy. The first of these was the formalization of a privileged role for great powers within European international society, an issue we come back to in the subsequent section on intervention. For now, it is worth noting that, after the Treaty of Vienna in 1815, there was a shift towards 'legalized hegemony' for the great powers in which they saw themselves as having, and were recognized by others to have, managerial responsibility for international order (Simpson, 2004: 3–131). Legalized hegemony was most clearly expressed in the Concert of Europe in which great powers collectively and explicitly managed the European balance of power (Mitzen, 2013). In effect this meant managing global affairs, since the expansion of European empires increasingly linked the European and global spheres. This hierarchical order was asserted by the great powers. But it was also accepted, often consensually, by 'lesser' ones (Simpson, 2004). During the nineteenth century, therefore, a form of hierarchy emerged based around a distinction between greater and lesser powers. Since this coincided with the global expansion of Western power, this hierarchy operated not just in Europe, but also around the world. As noted in Chapter 3, this mix of sovereign equality and legalized hegemony remains embedded in the structure of many contemporary IGOs.

The second development was the opening of a conceptual gap between 'civilized' and 'uncivilized' ('barbarian' or 'savage'), and the claim by the former of higher political and legal standing over the latter. This was the so-called 'standard of civilization'. The formalization of the 'standard of civilization' reflected the increasing dominance of positive over natural law in Western thinking and practice. Natural law made all humans equal under the sight of God, offering some kind of basis for inter-cultural encounters. Positive law linked the civil arrangements of states to their standing in international society (Shilliam, 2013). Those that were considered to be 'deficient' in some way became 'quasi-sovereign' – part or all of their governance was transferred to the 'wardship' of a colonial power (Grovogui, 1996: 79–81). In this way, positive international law was explicitly the law of 'civilized' European states (Koskenniemi, 2001: 73–5, 99–116; Kayaoğlu, 2010). For example, the nineteenth-century codification of the laws of war distinguished between 'privileged belligerents' (inhabitants of the 'civilized' world) and 'unprivileged belligerents' (those who lived outside this zone) (Ansorge, 2013). During the nineteenth century, privileged belligerents became subject to rules that determined the scope of legitimate violence, not least that it should be discriminate and proportional. Unprivileged combatants were considered to be outside such rules – violence in uncivilized spaces took place without legal restrictions (Anghie, 2004: 241–2; Sylvest, 2005).[1] The effect of this stratification was to privilege Western states and peoples, and to downgrade other parts of the world (Alexandrowicz, 1967: 2, 156, 236–7).

---

[1] The lack of legal restrictions did not mean that colonial practices were not subject to occasional public critique. For example, the brutal suppression of the Morant Bay Rebellion in Jamaica in 1865 prompted considerable public disquiet in Britain, leading to suggestions that the official responsible, Governor John Eyre, be tried for atrocities committed by his troops.

As a consequence, non-European polities that had previously been acknowledged as sovereign were now viewed, at best, as potential candidates for admission into a European-dominated international society.

There is, therefore, a close link between the turn to positive law and the expansion of Western power through the 'standard of civilization' (Kayaoğlu, 2010). European positive law did not completely override indigenous legal codes. The legal structure of imperial rule was usually a layered, 'lumpy' amalgam of imperial and indigenous (Benton, 2010: 8). The Indian penal code, for example, blended British and Indian jurisprudence, and it was this blend that was exported to many of Britain's imperial territories in South-East Asia and East Africa (Metcalf, 2007: 19, 32). But there was still a basic shift in that, before the nineteenth century, European international law was one amongst several regional legal systems that had universalist pretensions (Onuma, 2000). The establishing of positive law during the nineteenth century was a double shock to those on its receiving end, not just in the challenge it posed to their legal systems, but also in the imposition of a legal code that actively discriminated against them. The reason behind the periphery's depth of resentment against colonialism, both then and now, has to be understood against the impact of this double shock.

It is not possible to understand today's politico-legal order without appreciating its colonial genealogy. The expansion of European international society required stark changes of identity, starting with 'Christendom' in the emergence phase, then during the nineteenth century to 'Western' in order to integrate the Americas and other European offshoots, and finally to the 'standard of civilization' in the late nineteenth century (Gong, 1984: 4–6; Watson, 1984; Clark, 2005: 35–50, 48). In some ways, the shift from Christian to Western to 'civilization' marked a shift from highly exclusive to less exclusive points of differentiation (Aydin, 2007: 20; Phillips, 2012: 13–14). When international society was considered to be exclusively Christian, majority Muslim polities such as the Ottoman Empire fell axiomatically outside its ambit. However, the shift to an idea of 'civilization' based on the 'modern' capacities of a polity meant that, in theory, international society was universal (Aydin, 2007: 21). This is one reason why the Ottomans, the Egyptians, the Japanese and others embraced modernizing projects during the long nineteenth century – the implementation of legal, administrative and fiscal reforms held out the promise of equality of status. In theory, if rather less so in practice, 'civilization' was a 'ladder that could be climbed' (Aydin, 2007: 29).

The first major expansion of modern international society at the beginning of the nineteenth century turned what was essentially a European international society into a Western international society through incorporation of the new states of the Americas. This was not considered to be overly problematic because the Americas had been substantially repeopled by European migrants, so ensuring a degree of cultural homogeneity. Indeed, the rapid rise of the United States after the end of its civil war in 1865 began to move the centre of gravity of this order across the Atlantic. As the global transformation enforced an ever-larger power gap between Western states and other parts of the world, this Western international society became global in scale and more explicitly hierarchical in structure. Much of Africa and Asia was colonized, and internalized within the sovereignty of the Western (and later Japanese) metropolitan powers. These colonized countries became subordinate subjects of metropolitan law and politics, and were often seen, and treated, as culturally and racially inferior.

The hierarchical form of centred globalist international society created during the nineteenth century is best labelled *Western-colonial*. This international society was global in scale, but extremely unequal. Its core comprised most European states and their now independent former settler colonies in the Americas. Its periphery was a mixture of colonies, largely absorbed into the sovereignty of their metropoles (most of Africa, South Asia and South-East Asia), and a handful of classical agrarian powers still strong enough to avoid colonization, but weak enough to be treated as unequal (China, Iran, Egypt, the Ottoman Empire, Japan). Although there was a trickle of erosions of inequality between core and periphery before 1945 (discussed in Chapter 7), this Western-colonial international society broadly endured until the end of the Second World War. At that point, the delegitimation of imperialism and widespread decolonization offered a more concerted assault on the structural bases of international inequality.

Yet in many respects, international society after 1945 remained significantly hierarchical. What had been a *Western-colonial* international society became a *Western-global* one. By adopting the term *Western-global*, we take a position on how to understand contemporary international society and how to deal with the legacy of its colonial origins. The idea that there is a global international society rests on the view that it emerged from the expansion of Western international society to planetary scale, with decolonization producing states that were homogeneous, if only in the sense of being sovereign equals. The price of independence, or for those not colonized the price of being accepted as equals by the West, was the adoption of Western political forms and the acceptance of the primary institutions of Western international society: the market, the legalized hegemony of great power management, positive international law, and suchlike. 'Modernization theory' held out the prospect of the 'Third World' becoming more like the 'First World' (Rostow, 1960), while, as argued in Chapter 5, polities around the world were categorized as 'developed' and 'developing', or 'advanced' and 'emerging'. In each of these classifications, the Western mode of economic, political and cultural organization was taken to be both natural and pre-eminent.

In significant respects, therefore, the post-1945 era saw the maintenance of a hegemonic, core–periphery structure in which a Western core was surrounded by regional international societies that existed in varying degrees of differentiation from, and subordination to, that core. This allowed for a thin global international society to operate, based on a number of shared primary institutions. But there were significant variations in terms of how these institutions were practised (most notably, sovereignty and non-intervention), plus the continued projection of contested Western values (most notably human rights, the market and democracy). These created considerable differentiation between Western states and many non-Western states. Although the term 'standard of civilization' fell out of use after 1945, the practice continued (Buzan and Gonzalez-Pelaez, 2009; Buzan and Zhang, 2014), morphing into the politer terminology of human rights and conditionality, albeit now *within* a universal international society rather than constituted through relations between insiders and outsiders (Gong, 1984: 90–3 and 2002; Donnelly, 1998; Jackson, 2000: 287–93; Keene, 2002: 122–3, 147–8; Clark, 2007: 183; Bowden, 2009). The practices associated with the promotion of the Washington Consensus before the 2008 financial crisis also reflect 'standard of civilization' attitudes, as does the idea that a 'league' or 'concert' of democracies should assert managerial responsibility over international society (Ikenberry and Slaughter, 2006; Geis, 2013).

The degree to which hierarchy remains a powerful current within international society is evidenced in numerous ways. The idea of legal inequality defined by different degrees of 'civilization' can be fast-forwarded from the nineteenth century to the present in terms of how 'outlaw' or 'rogue' states such as Iran and North Korea are treated (Simpson, 2004: 3–22, 278–316). Even though all states hold formal *de jure* sovereignty, some are *de facto* more equal than others in terms of having more formal rights, as in the 'Permanent 5' members of the UN Security Council. The core also retains its own collection of IGOs, which can be used not only to conduct its own business, but also to bypass UN bodies in which peripheral states wield voting majorities, including the OECD and the G7/8. More generally, hierarchy within today's international society is reproduced in the extensive demands for states to measure up to contemporary notions of civilization.

Core states are also *primus inter pares* in global civil society. As noted in Chapter 3, many INGOs have achieved official standing within IGOs (Clark, 1995; Clark, 2007: 189–93), playing significant roles in the promotion of values ranging from environmental stewardship to restraints on war. But these non-state actors still mainly serve to enhance Western power by projecting Western values (Hurrell, 2007: 111–14; see also Armstrong, 1998). The starkly unequal political and legal order of nineteenth-century Western-colonial international society is no longer in force, but many of its legacies and practices remain in place. Post-imperial residues remain symbolically powerful in the periphery, keeping alive resentments from earlier times (Miller, 2013). The West ignores these sentiments at its peril, too easily constructing itself and its privileges as a benign, neutral, universal, even natural standard. A useful window on this aspect of inequality is provided by the issue of (non-)intervention, which is a corollary of the principle of sovereign equality.

Intervention

Analysis of the development of practices of intervention helps to clarify the ways in which international order over the past two centuries has been premised on a bifurcation between core and periphery.

During the initial phase of global modernity, practices of intervention were linked to changing ideas about hierarchy that, in turn, constituted a change in how international order was imagined. Rather than associating international order with a 'ranking of powers' based on precedence, title and position, the late eighteenth and early nineteenth centuries witnessed a shift towards the 'grading of powers' based on power capabilities (Keene, 2013). The 'grading of powers' led to the formal recognition of 'great powers'. Great powers possessed special rights (for example, over intervention) and responsibilities (such as a duty to maintain international order). They also agreed to recognize sovereignty among themselves. It was only with such mutual recognition, and a concomitant hardening of notions of inside and outside, that intervention as a discrete social practice could emerge. The mutual recognition of territorial sovereignty acted as a brake on territorial transgressions. In turn, intervention became a specific right afforded *to* the great powers *by* the great powers. Intervention relied on a notion of 'dual authority' that tied together great powers horizontally, while constructing a vertical point of demarcation between them and other states (Clark, 2011: 96–7).

To associate intervention with global modernity does not mean giving it a single tenor. To the contrary, intervention has been deployed in two different ways in the modern world: as a means of 'order maintenance' and as a tool of 'order transformation' (Lawson and Tardelli, 2013). In the first instance, intervention was a means through which absolutist regimes sought to contain the challenges of insurgent ideologies such as nationalism and republicanism. The best-known example of this is the early nineteenth-century Concert of Europe system (Holbraad, 1970; Schroeder, 1994; Jarrett, 2013). The Concert of Europe explicitly linked domestic and international security – instability at home threatened instability abroad. As a result, the *internal* organization of states became seen as a potential threat to *international* order (Finnemore, 2003: 117–18). This permitted counter-revolutionary interventions in situations when domestic unrest was seen as unsettling to international order, such as the reinstating of Ottoman authority in Lebanon/Syria in 1839–40. Far from being a neutral tool of statecraft, intervention during this period sought to maintain a form of state sovereignty that limited types of political expression considered threatening to incumbent elites, whether this took the form of alternative religious beliefs, republicanism, socialism, nationalism or anti-colonialism.

In part, the right to intervene held by great powers rested on superior power capabilities; in part, it rested on status. The link between intervention and status was important in that it pressed great powers to commit funds and military provisions to interventions even at significant cost to themselves (Taliaferro, 2004). The 60-year campaign to end the slave trade cost Britain more than 5,000 lives, as well as an average of nearly 2% of national income per year (Kaufmann and Pape, 1999: 631).

The second component of the modern conception of intervention was 'order transformation'. During the nineteenth century, intervention became associated with a family of practices, including blockades, sanctions and gunboat diplomacy, which were responsible for the coercive restructuring of 'other' societies. Intervention was a means by which to transform 'backward' places. Even during the early years of the global transformation, some interventions contained a radical purpose – the opening up and transformation of foreign spaces. Groups such as the French *parti du mouvement* favoured intervention in defence of oppressed 'nationalities' in Poland, Italy and Belgium, while Britain carried out self-declared 'liberal' interventions against the slave trade, in Greece and in the Iberian Peninsula during the early part of the nineteenth century. The rising power of Britain – and later the United States – accompanied a shift away from the use of intervention as a duty to support other great powers towards the recognition of a right to self-determination, exemplified by the emergence of the legal category of 'belligerency' within civil wars (Little, 2013). The United States (in 1815) and Britain (in 1819) used this category to proclaim their neutrality in the Latin American wars of independence rather than affirm their support for Spain and Portugal. What lay behind such practices were understandings of *who* could intervene and *when* they could intervene; intervention was an illustration that states were not *de facto* equal, even if they were *de jure* sovereign (Lingelbach, 1900: 4).

Military Inequality

Military developments during the nineteenth century changed the strategic landscape in ways that are characteristic of global modernity and are still strongly present in the contemporary world. We examine the systemic effect of these developments in Chapter 8. In this section, we focus on the impact of modern military power on the making of a core–periphery structure, and the relations within it.

The kind of military inequality that marked relations between the West and most other parts of the world during the nineteenth century was largely absent from the agrarian era. Ever since they intruded into the Indian Ocean trading system in the late fifteenth century, Europeans had held an advantage in sea power. Their ships were better gun platforms than those of the Indian Ocean civilizations, and the major powers of Asia (China, Japan, the Mughals) were land powers that spent relatively little time on maritime affairs (Lach, 1993: 1891–2; Pearson, 2003: 114–26; Darwin, 2007: 53–4, 95–9). This was why Europeans were able to dominate maritime trade and establish 'maritime highways' through coastal trading cities such as Cape Town, Singapore and Aden (Darwin, 2007: 16). By the middle of the eighteenth century, Britain had become the dominant sea power in the Indian Ocean and was beginning to extend its control inland. Despite this advantage, Europeans were generally unable to penetrate much into the land masses of Eurasia until late in the eighteenth century. The interaction capacity of the agrarian era was too low to support a fully fledged international system.

Technological and organizational developments in the nineteenth century massively accelerated these advantages. The links between industrial production, technological innovation and equipment, along with shifts in military organization, training and doctrine, were one of the foundations of the core–periphery order that developed during the nineteenth century. In the front line, the main military technologies were quick-firing breech-loading rifles, machine guns, modern shell-firing artillery and steam-powered iron warships. These were backed up both by the deep logistical capabilities of railways, steamships and industrial production, and by the rapid communications enabled by the telegraph (Giddens, 1985: 224–5; Osterhammel, 2014: 483–93). Medical advances against diseases, perhaps most notably the use of quinine as a prophylactic against malaria, also played a major role in opening Africa to European intervention from the mid-nineteenth century. Such techniques helped to give the whip hand to the core over the periphery (Headrick, 2010: 117–20, 139–70).

Two examples illustrate the extent of the military power gap between core and periphery. During the First Opium War against China, a minor East India Company warship (the appropriately named steam sloop *Nemesis*) had no difficulty using her superior firepower and manoeuvrability to destroy a fleet of Chinese war junks and wreak havoc on China's coastal defences. The *Nemesis* simply represented a different order of warfare to anything the Chinese had experienced before (Lovell, 2011). Similarly, at the Battle of Omdurman in 1898, a force of approximately 8,000 British troops and 17,000 colonial troops equipped with modern artillery and machine guns took on a rebel army of some 50,000 followers of the Mahdi. In a day's fighting, the

British and colonial troops lost 47 men, the rebels around 10,000. Military superiority, allied to broader advances in political economy, organization and strategy, allowed European states to intimidate, coerce, defeat and, if they wished, occupy territories in the periphery. The arrogance generated by this gulf in military capabilities is well captured in Hilaire Belloc's famous lines about nineteenth-century colonial wars:[2]

> Whatever happens
> we have got
> the Maxim gun,
> and they have not.

Western powers maintained their advantage by trying to restrict the access of colonial peoples under their rule to advanced weapons like the Maxim (an early form of machine gun). This posed an enduring problem, because as well as wanting to restrict the access of non-European colonial peoples to modern arms, Western powers used colonial troops to administer and extend their empires. The general solution to this dilemma was to deny colonial troops access to the most advanced weapons, and to restrict officer ranks mainly to white Europeans. Using this formula, Britain made extensive use of India as an imperial hub, not least by using large numbers of Indian troops to take and hold India itself. The sepoy components of the British army in India numbered 200,000 men (Darwin, 2012: 131–2). India's 'martial races', particularly Punjabi Sikhs, were put to work all over the empire (Metcalf, 2007: 72).[3] Britain deployed Indian police officers, bureaucrats and orderlies in China, Africa and the Middle East, while Indian troops fought in 15 British colonial wars, including those in China, Malaya, Egypt, Sudan, Burma, East Africa and Tibet (Metcalf, 2007: xii, 1–15; Black, 2009: 151–71; Darwin, 2009: 183). Other European

---

[2] This arrogance was, at times, tempered by respect for the non-white forces that European powers came up against. Rudyard Kipling's poem 'Fuzzy Wuzzy' serves as a useful illustration of this point. Assuming the voice of a British rank-and-file soldier, Kipling praises the prowess of the Beja warriors who formed the bulk of the Mahdist forces during the 1890s, closing with the lines: 'An' 'ere's to you, Fuzzy-Wuzzy, with your 'avrick 'ead of 'air – You big black boundin' beggar – for you broke a British square!'

[3] The discourse of 'martial races' was infused by patriarchy – Sikhs, Zulus and Masai were imbued with heroic, masculinist qualities, while Malays and Tamils were considered 'soft', 'effeminate' and 'emotional'. On this, see Streets (2010).

states also made extensive use of colonial forces: 70% of the Dutch army deployed in the Dutch East Indies were indigenous forces, while 80% of the French expeditionary forces that fought in North and East Africa were colonial conscripts (MacDonald, 2014: 39–40).

Despite nineteenth-century legislation that sought to nationalize militaries, 'foreign forces' continued to play a leading role in colonial armies during the twentieth century (Barkawi, 2011b: 39–44). Over one million members of the Indian army fought for Britain in the First World War, as did a similar number of troops from the white dominions and nearly 150,000 troops from other colonies (Abernathy, 2000: 112).[4] Two million members of the Indian army fought for Britain in the Second World War (Mann, 2012: 55), while nearly 10% of the French army in 1940 was from West Africa alone (Barkawi, 2011a: 51). During the First Indochina War in the early 1950s, France's 74,000 European troops were outnumbered by 47,000 West African troops and 53,000 Indochinese who were deployed from the French colonial service (Barkawi, 2011a: 605).

While some colonials joined the ranks of the metropolitan armed forces, others fought against the occupiers. 'Low intensity' resistance to empires was virtually constant, taking the form of local skirmishes and raids that were met by 'grimly banal' police actions by imperial powers (Darwin, 2012: 119, 148). There was more formalized resistance to imperialism in Latin America, the North-West Frontier, Central Asia, Indochina, the African interior and in white settler colonies, most notably North America (where various alliances of Native Americans fought, and occasionally defeated, settler forces), South Africa (the site of regular frontier wars with Xhosa and Zulu armies, as well as a full-scale war with the Boers), and New Zealand (in the form of the Maori Wars), which meant that these regions were never fully pacified (Black, 2009). At the same time, superior Western military technology and tactics did not always lead to predetermined outcomes (MacDonald, 2014). Colonial powers could be, and were, defeated in battle. In Haiti, a successful revolt by slaves and *gens de couleur* threw off French colonialism, while the French were also defeated during their intervention in

---

[4] Despite playing a prominent role in the First World War, the Indian government was forced to pay £100 million per year in order to pay off the British war debt, plus an annual fee of £20–£30 million for 'war related expenses' (Abernathy, 2000: 112).

Mexico during the 1860s. The British suffered notable defeats during the Afghan Wars, particularly in the 1880 Battle of Maiwand in the Helmand Valley. In South Africa, both the Boers and the Zulus gave the British a bloody nose before being defeated. The Italians were defeated by the Ethiopians at both Dogali (1887) and Adwa (1896), as were the Spanish by Rif Berbers at Melilla (1893).

Despite these defeats, imperial powers tended to win longer wars. By the end of the nineteenth century, there were only three sovereign polities in Africa: Ethiopia, Liberia and the Boer Republic, and of these only Ethiopia was a non-Western creation. This was a pattern common to most continents – short-term victories were usually followed by long-term defeat, as testified by the outcomes of the Indian Revolt (1857), the Boxer Rebellion (1898–1901) in China, and the Tonghak Rebellion in Korea (1894–5). Although usually unsuccessful in the long run, these movements did challenge both the ideas and practices of empire, whether in specific form such as the ceding of formal political rights to *gens de couleur* within the French Empire after the Haitian Revolution, or the preliminary unbundling of empires as the pre-eminent form of political authority (Burbank and Cooper, 2010: 225–9).

In this way, the focus by IR scholarship on the 'long peace' enjoyed by European powers during the long nineteenth century misses two crucial points. First, because it refers only to Western great powers, it sits at odds with the experience of those at the wrong end of the global transformation – there was no 'long peace' in the periphery, but something more like a continuous war. The bifurcation between war abroad and peace at home had major significance for the development of international order, reinforcing a sense of European cultural and racial superiority, which in turn facilitated its coercive expansions around the world (Anghie, 2004: 310–20; Darwin, 2007: 180–5, 222–9). Second, it misses the extensive transformation in organized violence that took place during this period. We return to this issue in Chapter 8.

With a few exceptions to be discussed in the next chapter, this basic story of a militarily dominant core repressing a subordinated, but often resistant, periphery more or less holds until the end of the Second World War. Thereafter, this highly unequal pattern of military relations began to change, as we show in Chapter 7. Until then, ongoing and rapid military innovation in the core, and the practice of keeping advanced weapons out of the hands of peripheral peoples, maintained the gap. Even victories won by the periphery were much begrudged. France, for example, recognized Haiti only in 1825, two decades after its defeat. And even then, this recognition was conditional on the provision of compensation for losses stemming from the revolution. Haiti was not recognized by the United States until 1862.

Vestiges of the nineteenth-century period of high military inequality between core and periphery can still be observed today. The nineteenth-century use of colonial troops has some resonances with current practices. The French Foreign Legion has forces from 136 countries, while 10% of the Spanish army is composed of South Americans (Barkawi, 2011b: 48). Familiar too is the West's contemporary preference for intervention by drones and air power rather than boots on the ground, with its echoes of gunboat diplomacy and aerial bombing for colonial 'policing' during the interwar years. The nineteenth-century pattern of peace at home and war abroad, and its accompanying sense of 'civilized' at home and 'barbaric' abroad, are alive and well in concepts such as 'two worlds' or the 'zone of peace and the zone of conflict' (Goldgeier and McFaul, 1992; Singer and Wildavsky, 1993). Western wars and interventions from Korea and Vietnam to Afghanistan and Iraq serve to reinforce this dualism. The colonial policy of trying to keep advanced weapons out of the hands of peripheral peoples is not so different in rationale from contemporary attempts to curb the spread to the periphery of nuclear weapon and missile technology, advanced avionics and weapons packages for aircraft, and advanced electronics for military applications. The West still strives to keep its military edge not just over rival great powers, but also over the periphery.

Economic Inequality

The economic dimensions of core–periphery relations were even starker and more dramatic than the political-legal and military dynamics discussed above. Indeed, it was nineteenth-century changes in the economic sector that largely define the modern meaning of core and periphery in terms of an industrial core organizing key components of the world economy, and an underdeveloped periphery mainly providing its raw materials, and often suffering disadvantageous terms of trade and finance.

The economic aspect of the global transformation was deeply intertwined with politico-legal and military changes. Where one was positioned in the global division of economic labour was both shaped by, and helped to shape, governance structures and military capabilities.

As Chapter 1 highlighted, before the global transformation, economic discrepancies between Europe and Asia were slight, and the balance of trade often favoured Asian producers. Towards the end of the eighteenth century, nodal points of production and consumption such as Hokkaido, Malacca, Hangzhou and Samarkand enjoyed relative parity with their European counterparts across a range of economic indicators, and were technologically equal or superior in many areas of production. Long-distance commodity chains linking Seville, Amsterdam, Acapulco, Manila, Edo, Guangdong, Beijing and other cities had long been established for silver, porcelain and other goods (Goldstone, 2002: 331). India stood as a key point of intersection – its huge coastline, skilled artisans and plentiful traders made it a central node in the transnational exchange of goods, ideas and institutions (Roy, 2012: 1).

During the nineteenth century, the relative parity that marked these networks was replaced by stark inequality between a core of central sites of accumulation, industrial production and consumption, and a periphery producing mainly raw materials. The industrializing vanguard tilted the balance of trade firmly in Europe's favour. As noted in the previous chapter, the industrial core established a global political economy through the same two major processes that it used to transform itself: first, the commercialization of agriculture; and second, the industrial revolution. Both of these processes drew significantly on the emulation and fusion of non-European ideas and technologies – what John Hobson (2004: 2) calls 'resource portfolios' of ideas, institutions and technologies. Western industrial powers used these transnational connections to establish a global economy in which the trade and finance of the industrial world forced their way into the periphery, eroding local and regional economic systems, and imposing global price and production structures (Darwin, 2007: 180–5, 237–45). Dispossession and de-industrialization enabled European states to turn an age-old and more or less balanced system of trade in elite goods into a global order of mass trade marked by inequality (Goody, 1996; Wolf, 1997; Goldstone, 2002).[5]

Although other periods of world history have seen periods of extensive economic growth, the mixture of quantitative take-off and

---

[5] As with other elements of the global transformation, dispossession was unevenly carried out. Within the British Empire, for example, dispossession was extremely high in North America, Australia, Malaya and South, Central and East Africa, plus parts of India and Sri Lanka. However, it was relatively low in the Asian dependencies and West Africa. For more on this, see Darwin (2012: 79–86).

qualitative change during the global transformation was unprecedented. As discussed in Chapter 5, the proximity of coal and water in Britain produced major advances in energy production (Morris, 2010: 500). Improvements in energy power eased pressures on labour, something further enabled by the arrival of new world crops such as potatoes, which produced far more calories per acre than traditional crops. New institutional innovations, such as limited liability companies, took advantage of these developments by investing capital in long-term, often long-distance, projects. Previously constrained by limits to energy usage and resource availability, European powers stumbled upon a new economic configuration of industrial production and finance that dramatically shifted power relations both within their own societies and further afield. At the same time, resources from colonial possessions, the plantation system and other transnational networks flowed back into Britain and other European capitals. Banks, shops, hotels and insurance companies provided a 'battering ram' for the extension of European capital (Darwin, 2007: 16).

During the nineteenth century, state-issued paper money and instruments of credit increasingly came to replace bimetallic systems based on the relationship of gold and silver. Currencies like the French Assignat, which began as a bond before evolving into a currency, got around the problem of constraints on money supply in a specie economy (Gilpin, 1987: 119–23). They also served to unite the multitude of weights and measures that had previously been used in commercial transactions: ruttees, mashas and tolas in India; catties, piculs and taels in China (Darwin, 2012: 173). Until 1862, cowrie shells were used as currency in Calcutta while, until 1852, Burma had no coinage at all (Darwin, 2012: 155). Monetized economies, sustained by an interlocking web of commercial lending organizations, banks and insurance companies, enabled the extensive circulation of goods (Braudel, 1985: 581). The intensity of economic globalization during this period is indicated by the fact that in two decades between 1850 and 1870, iron trade increased by a volume of six, grain by a volume of five, and coal by a volume of 25 (Hobsbawm, 1975: 49, 66). After several centuries in which the volume of world trade had increased by an annual average of less than 1%, trade rose by over 4% in the half century after 1820 (Osterhammel, 2014: 726). Between 1870 and 1913, trade in wheat, coffee, tea and cotton doubled, mining output tripled, and the production of cocoa and rubber increased by a factor of four (Frieden, 2006: 22); by the early years of the twentieth century, world trade was increasing at a rate of 10% per year (Hirst and Thompson, 1996: 20; Held et al., 1999: 155). And it was not just the volume of trade that was increasing at such a rapid rate – its value was also soaring. Between 1850 and 1913, the value of world trade (at constant prices) increased tenfold (Osterhammel, 2014: 726).

As the first, and for a time only, industrial power, it was British industrial and financial muscle that led the way in establishing a core–periphery global economy. In 1890, Britain alone was responsible for 20% of the world's industrial output; a decade later, its share of the world market for manufactured goods was 40%, while the country produced a quarter of the world's fuel energy output (Goldstone, 2002: 364; Clark, 2011: 107). As noted in Chapter 1, the 'bill on London' meant that sterling became the world's principal trading currency. By 1913, Britain's overseas investments were worth £4 billion, amounting to 44% of the world's total (Kennedy, 1989: 156; Darwin, 2009: 274; Clark, 2011: 107). Around 10% of national income stemmed from interest on these foreign investments (Silver and Arrighi, 2003: 337). Exchanges in wool, metal and grain served alongside merchant banks, the stock exchange and other purveyors of high finance. London was the central node within a vast transnational network of credit, capital, goods, information and people (Darwin, 2009: 144). As Keynes opined (in Eichengreen, 1996: 33), the Bank of England was 'the conductor of the financial orchestra'.

The development of transnational networks in production and finance often had deeply destructive effects. The extension of the market was tied to the extension of forms of coercive labour such as debt peonage, while whole territories were turned over to the export of commodities on unequal terms, including the 'sugar colonies' of Fiji, Formosa and Hawaii (Topik and Wells, 2012: 762). In India, land and water were privatized under British direction so that they could be used as a taxable resource. At the same time, communal food stores were forcibly removed from villages so that basic foodstuffs could be sold commercially. Whereas in 1870 all forests in India were communally managed, by 1880 all had been expropriated by the Raj (Davis, 2002: 327). Dispossession meant that, when droughts hit in 1877, many Indians could afford neither food nor water. The resultant famine and associated epidemics, followed by a second in the 1890s, killed 15 million Indians (Davis, 2002: 6–7; Osterhammel, 2014: 206–9). Between 1888 and 1891, one-third of the population of Sudan and Ethiopia also died from starvation and related epidemics caused by a combination of drought and the exposure of their food supply to the market (Davis, 2002: 6). As these examples illustrate, the core ruthlessly adapted production and trade in the periphery to its needs, creating what Kenneth Pomeranz (2000: 207) describes as a seemingly 'permanent periphery'. This structure of inequality proved to be remarkably durable, mainly surviving even after decolonization. Outside the West, only Japan joined the economic core during the nineteenth century; it remained an exception until well after the Second World War, a point we return to in the next chapter.

The core–periphery structure of the global economy did not, therefore, change much during the first half of the twentieth century, particularly while colonialism was still largely in place. As discussed in the previous chapter, decolonization provided scope for the implementation of state-led development projects. But the narrowing of political inequality after 1945 did not bring the expected economic gains to much of the periphery. The production and finance structures inherited from the colonial era proved durable, leading *dependencia* theorists to argue that the colonial-era division between a low-profit, primary-producing periphery and a high-profit, capital-intensive, secondary-producing core was being reconstituted (Prebisch, 1950; Frank, 1966; Cardoso and Faletto, 1979; Evans, 1979). Galtung (1971) noted how the global core–periphery structure reproduced itself within Third World states, many of whose elites shared the interests and ideologies of the core. Indeed, the fostering of comprador elites within peripheral states appeared to foster a relationship of sustained peripheral 'underdevelopment'. Chapter 5 examined the strategies developed to address this inequality, most notably ISI and export-led industrialization. If some attempts to 'catch up' succeeded, others produced disastrous results, as with China's 'Great Leap Forward'. In many peripheral economies, there was stagnation, as in India's 'Hindu rate of growth'.

Thus, although the *political* inequality of colonial international society gave way after 1945 to the formal sovereign equality of Western-global international society, the *economic* inequality between core and periphery largely remained in place. Many new states were poor, locked into a Western-made global economy over which they had little influence and from which they could not easily extricate themselves. There was a rhetorical shift from imperialism to development, capturing the ways in which the inequality gap was narrowed politically, but remained wide economically. The distinction between developed and aid-giving countries on the one hand, and underdeveloped/developing and aid-receiving on the other, was an indication of the ongoing structural inequalities of the post-colonial world. It was only in the last quarter of the twentieth century that robust signs emerged to suggest that this most durable of inequalities was beginning to narrow. We come back to this issue in the next chapter.

Demographic Inequality

As noted in Chapter 1, population increases resulting from the availability of new resources are a standard feature of macro-historical transformations. This was spectacularly true for the global transformation, which generated new agricultural resources and new industrial technologies, better diets and better healthcare. As discussed in Chapter 4, global modernity also saw the development of new modes of transportation. Taken together, these changes produced two linked dynamics concerning demography and core–periphery inequality. The first concerns changes in the rate and distribution of population growth, and is underpinned by industrialization and the increased resources it made available to sustain larger populations, initially in the core and later in the periphery. The second concerns migration, particularly the movement and, oftentimes, resettlement of unprecedented numbers of people from their homelands to other parts of the planet. This second dynamic was underpinned by the new modes of transportation made available by the industrial revolution and the opportunities opened up by both the expanding global economy and imperialism. It also rested on the expropriation of land from the peasantry and the dispossession of indigenous populations. Taken together, these demographic changes are seen by some as 'perhaps the most important single phenomenon of the nineteenth century' (Hobsbawm, 1962: 170).

The Growth Rate and Distribution of Population

The basic picture of the demographic inequality created by the global transformation can be seen in Tables 6.1 and 6.2. Table 6.1 shows that the global population nearly doubled from just over 1 billion in 1820 to 1.8 billion in 1913. This was the beginning of the geometric curve of human population growth, which in the 200 years between 1800 and

Table 6.1: *World population, regional totals (thousands)*

	Europe	Western offshoots	Latin America	Asia	Africa	World
1600	111,428	2,300	8,600	378,500	55,000	555,828
1700	126,810	1,750	12,050	401,800	61,000	603,410
1820	224,068	11,230	21,220	710,366	74,208	1,041,092
1913	496,803	111,401	80,515	977,604	124,697	1,791,020

Source: Maddison (2001: 241).

Table 6.2: *Share of world population (% of total)*

	1600	1700	1820	1913
Europe	20.0	21.0	21.6	27.7
Western offshoots	0.4	0.3	1.1	6.2
Latin America	1.5	2.0	2.0	4.5
Asia	68.1	66.6	68.3	54.6
Africa	9.9	10.1	7.1	7.0

Source: Maddison (2001: 243).

2000 increased by a factor of six (Christian, 2004: 342; also see McNeill and Engelke, 2014: 400–4). Within this curve lie major inequalities. Population in the West (Europe plus settler colonies ('offshoots') plus Latin America) increased from just over 250 million to nearly 670 million, a multiple of well over 2.5. As Table 6.2 shows, examined in terms of relative percentages of the global population, the population of the West increased from 24.7% to 38.4% between 1820 and 1913.

During the same period, the population of Asia increased from 710 to 978 million, a major increase in absolute numbers, but not proportionately. In fact, the relative population of Asia dropped from 68.3% of the global total to 54.6%, a decline that mirrored the relative increase in the West (see also Potts, 1990: 220; Blanning, 2000: 1; Osterhammel, 2014: 117–24). During this period, the population of the West increased six times faster than that of Asia, and also began to live significantly longer, with the exception of Japan. In the first instance, the new resources unleashed by global modernity worked to significantly increase the

West's share of the global population. This rising population was not the main factor in the making of a core–periphery international order. It was the change in the mode of power that enabled a moderately sized power like Britain, with a population of around 30 million at the end of the nineteenth century, to dominate a quarter of the world's population. But the rapid increase of population in the core was a key driver of mass migration.

Migration

Migration as an issue in international relations did not originate during the nineteenth century. To the contrary, voluntary and involuntary migrations have been a long-standing influence on historical development. One important example is the role played by nomadic barbarians in assailing agrarian empires from China to Rome during the classical era. Rome famously dispersed the Jews, and during the sixteenth and eighteenth centuries, nearly 10 million Africans were shipped to the Americas in the slave trade (Maddison, 2001: 35). An even older slave trade run by Arabs moved perhaps as many Africans to the Middle East (Bairoch, 1993: 146–8; Osterhammel, 2014: 150–4).

During the nineteenth century, new modes of transportation, economic incentives, and the political and ideological framework of colonialism provided the means for unprecedented numbers of people to move around the world. There were two principal migration circuits in operation during the long nineteenth century. The first was to the Americas and mainly involved Europeans. In the century before 1914, 50–55 million Europeans, amounting to roughly one-sixth of the population of the continent, emigrated to the Americas (Maddison, 2001: 231). These were mostly peasants fleeing 'land hunger' due to the commercialization of agriculture and the expansion of trade (Rosenberg, 1994: 163; Hatton and Williamson, 1998: 3). For many of these emigrants, the United States was the preferred destination. Of the 20% or so who settled in Latin America rather than North America, most went to Brazil, Argentina and Uruguay: nearly 1 million Europeans settled in Brazil between 1850 and 1870; around 800,000 settled in Argentina and Uruguay during the same period (Hobsbawm, 1975: 63). Europeans also moved in as elite populations in South Asia and several parts of Africa. As Ferguson (2004: 54, 112) states in bald terms: 'the indispensable foundation of Empire was mass migration . . . It turned whole continents white.'

The second mass migration circuit was in Asia. Here, around 50 million Indian and Chinese labourers and merchants repopulated parts of South-East Asia, the Indian Ocean Rim and the South Pacific (Hoerder, 2012: 435). This migration circuit took place under considerably less favourable conditions than those attended by white Europeans. As we noted in Chapter 1, up to 37 million labourers left India, China, Malaya and Java during the nineteenth and early twentieth centuries, many of them to work in near servitude as 'coolies', chattels and other forms of bonded labour (Davis, 2002: 208). Added to this were substantial numbers of voluntary migrants from the Indian and Chinese commercial classes, as well as those who came to administer imperial territories. Asian migrations were more circular in form than European migrations, with more people returning to their point of origin. One exception to this was the Qing Empire's movement of 8 million Han settlers into Manchuria (Osterhammel, 2014: 146, 154–64). As with the influx of Europeans into the Americas, the scale of the Asian migration circuit reshaped whole societies – in 1921, the population of Malaya and Singapore was made up of 1.6 million Malays, 1.2 million Chinese, 500,000 Indians and 60,000 'others' (Hoerder, 2012: 519). Today, (mostly Southern) Chinese constitute 30% of the population of Malaysia, along with 10% of the population of the Philippines (Westad, 2012: 217).

Beyond these two mega-migration circuits, migrants flocked to new areas of production, most spectacularly during events such as the mid-nineteenth-century Gold Rush in California. Six million Russians moved to Siberia to work its mines, helping to boost its population from 4.3 million in 1885 to 12.8 million in 1915 (Belich, 2009: 482). Another 4 million Russians migrated to Central Asia, many of them to work on oil plants around Baku (Osterhammel, 2014: 148). The result of these migrations was a complex shuffling of peoples. Over 100,000 Chinese settled in Cuba between 1847 and 1874; 2,000 of them fought in the Cuban War of Independence during the 1870s (Westad, 2012: 27). Frequently, when migrations took the form of non-white settlement into predominantly white countries, the result was anti-immigrant legislation. Chinese immigration to the US was banned in 1882, followed by comparable legislation against Japanese labourers in 1907. The 1901 Immigration Restriction Act in Australia was the legislative corollary of the government's 'white Australia' policy. The British Empire also tried to disrupt the movement of its subjects from non-white to settler colonies. Such sentiments prompted the introduction of passports as an institutionalized feature of international travel during the early part of the twentieth century – from this point on, it was legally possible to exclude 'aliens' (Mann, 2012: 316). The familiar tension between economic imperatives favouring migration, and social and political reactions against it, was thus established during the nineteenth century. The flavour of the resultant tensions is captured in this passage from a very early IR textbook (Kerr, 1916: 175), which except for the unrestrained frankness of the language could express much contemporary anti-immigrant sentiment in the West.

The immigrant labourer was accustomed to living on a lower scale of living. He was willing to accept far lower wages than the white labourer. He was outside the trade unions. He was usually of the labouring class, which is the most backward of all, and the one least susceptible of being assimilated into a civilization on European lines. He became, therefore, a grave menace to the white labouring class which saw their prospects of stable employment flitted away by strangers, for no other reason than they could live at a far lower standard, and could afford to accept a far lower wage. Further, the coolie labourer was accompanied or followed by the trader, and the Asiatic trader not only usually worked for longer hours, but was satisfied with smaller profits than the white trader. He therefore tended to get the custom not only of his own fellows, but of the white customer also. Thus the white trader as well as the white labourer suffered.

One spin-off from these migrations was the creation of the modern tourism industry: by 1911, 1 million Britons were visiting continental Europe each year and 250,000 Americans were travelling to Europe as tourists (Rosenberg, 2012: 983). Travel guides by Thomas Cook and Karl Baedeker served these tourists, while the Ottoman writer Ahmed Midhat provided an 'Occidentalist' guide to Western society. These guides sat alongside Jules Verne's *Around the World in Eighty Days* (1873), a swashbuckling account of the adventures that could be gained through foreign travel. Explorers such as Stanley, Shackleton, Scott, Amundsen and Mallory were wildly popular, while the 1857 book by the British explorer David Livingstone, *Missionary Travels and Researches in South Africa*, was a bestseller. Luxury cruises and even floating universities toured the world, providing opportunities for a wealthy elite to experience the distant 'exotica' opened up by foreign travel (Pietsch, 2013).

A second spin-off was the creation of modern cities. Those forced off the land by the commercialization of agriculture usually moved to cities, which expanded rapidly as a result: between 1800 and 1900, London grew from just over 1 million to 6.5 million inhabitants; the population of Berlin rose by 1000% and that of New York by 500% (Bayly, 2004: 189). By 1851, over half of the British population lived in cities (Hobsbawm, 1975: 205); by the 1890s, so did a third of Western Europeans (Maddison, 2001: 248). Some cities emerged almost out of nowhere. The population of Chicago grew from a little under 100 inhabitants in 1830 to 1.1 million in 1890, making the city twice the size of Rome or Cairo (Belich, 2009: 339). In 1891, Melbourne, a city that was only 55 years old, had a population 15% bigger than Buenos Aires and 550% bigger than São Paolo (Belich, 2009: 356). These cities were transformed by the development of overland and underground railways, street lighting, steamship ports, and often vast sewerage systems, technologies that were deployed in cities from Calcutta to Dakar, and from Hanoi to Manila (McNeill and Engelke, 2014: 455; Osterhammel, 2014: 241–321).

The nineteenth century, therefore, witnessed an unprecedented movement of peoples around the world. This process was driven largely by economic motives, linking mass migration to the development of a global economy. The outcomes of these migrations, from the creation of a new superpower in North America, through the establishment of migration circuits along imperial pathways, the seeding of minority populations all around the planet, the representation of these peoples as 'exotic others', and the drive towards urbanization, played a major role in the generation of twentieth- and twenty-first-century international order. Such migrations made English the pre-eminent global language and created durable, if unequal, cultural connections between former colonies and their metropoles. In the contemporary world, the economic motivation for migration remains, as do many of the imperial pathways and cultural connections that emerged during the nineteenth century. But the colonial aspect of migration has gone and, as we show in the next chapter, recent years have seen the demographic shoe move to the other foot.

Conclusion

This chapter has traced the establishment of a global core–periphery order during the long nineteenth century. Politically, legally, militarily, economically and demographically, a relatively small group of polities created a Western-colonial international society that privileged their people, their economies and their interests. They subordinated other parts of the world while, at the same time, coercively and unevenly extending to planetary scale the configuration that underpinned global modernity. This highly unequal order endured more or less until the Second World War; many features of it, both large and small, remain in evidence today. These features are not just residual legacies. They are in many respects the foundations of contemporary world politics. The nineteenth-century colonial order serves as the origins of both the contemporary global economy and the contemporary Western-global international society. A remarkable amount of the contemporary agenda of international relations has its roots in this time, including issues of aid, intervention, inequality, migration and identity.

Perhaps most obviously, the whole issue of development in its modern form arose because of the power gap that opened up between core and periphery during the nineteenth century. This was not just the long-standing matter of acquiring a prevailing high culture that differentiated 'civilized' and 'barbarian'. Rather, wholesale transformations were required to close the gap between core and periphery. Those roots remain very much alive politically, especially so in the periphery. They are forgotten, or occluded, in the core. This disjuncture is becoming increasingly important as the gap between core and periphery narrows. That narrowing, sometimes from a surprisingly early stage, is the focus of the next chapter, which looks at how the local embedding of modernity is extending beyond a handful of Western states.

7 | *Eroding the Core–Periphery International Order*

Introduction

In this chapter we stay within the general framing of a core–periphery, Western-global international society. But rather than focusing on how inequality was established and maintained, we turn to the closing of the gap between core and periphery. Again, the underpinning logic is that of the unfolding revolutions of modernity within a framework of uneven and combined development. But, in this chapter, the main driver is not a story of expansion in which a core imposes its mode of power on the periphery. Rather, it is a story of how the revolutions of modernity begin to increase the relative wealth and power of parts of the periphery, narrowly at first, but widening out significantly more recently. At the same time, elements of global modernity changed attitudes within the core, thereby undermining the legitimacy of colonialism. The Second World War was a watershed in this development, with several changes in primary institutions significant enough to mark a transition from Western-colonial to Western-global international society. Much of the chapter is, therefore, devoted to developments after 1945. However, we also find notable elements of the eroding of the power gap in earlier periods.

The logic of uneven and combined development remains strongly evident during this period. Global modernity emerged in a context in which peoples lived in a variety of political, economic and cultural formations, from nomadic bands to city-states and empires. In terms of size, these social orders varied from groups of a few dozen to empires consisting of tens of millions. Some were able to resist or adapt to the assault of modernity; others were consumed by it. At one end of the spectrum were indigenous peoples in settler colonies who were all but obliterated; at the other were those like the Japanese who adapted the modern mode of power to indigenous social formations. In between were a great variety of struggles to come to terms with the challenge presented by the new mode of power, some successful, others less so. This variety meant that the power gap between core and periphery, and the challenge posed by the global transformation to those in the periphery, prompted quite different experiences of modernity.

As in the previous chapter, we divide the chapter into four sections: political-legal, military, economic and demographic. Our main purpose is to connect the dynamics that enabled the establishment of a core–periphery international order in the nineteenth century to the current shape of international relations.

Political and Legal Catch-Up

The political and legal core–periphery structure established during the nineteenth century was, in effect, a three-tier international society. In the core, Western states largely recognized each other's sovereign equality and, under the terms of the 'standard of civilization', could admit to this inner circle polities such as Japan, and more arguably the Ottoman Empire, that were deemed to have met the required standard. The periphery was defined by the many peoples, mainly in Africa, Asia and the Pacific, who were colonized and taken into both the 'tutelage' and the sovereignty of their metropole. By definition these peoples had no independent standing in international society. In between these two categories was a semi-periphery of states such as China, Siam, Argentina, Egypt and Iran.[1] These polities were not formal colonies – as such, they retained a degree of sovereign independence. However, they were not deemed to be fully 'civilized' either, and were subject to (often significant) degrees of tutelage, as well as unequal treaties that granted extraterritorial rights to Westerners.

Although Western-colonial international society was deeply unequal, it was not a closed shop. For all of its invidious inequalities and cultural prejudices, the 'standard of civilization' did provide a pathway, albeit a narrow one strewn with obstructions, by which states and peoples in the periphery could move towards political and legal equality (Aydin, 2007; Phillips, 2012). Just as colonization and the 'standard of civilization'

---

[1] We use the term 'semi-periphery' broadly along the lines of world systems analysts, i.e. as representing the 'core of the periphery' and the 'periphery of the core' (Wallerstein, 2011b; also see Galtung, 1971).

were the keys to political and legal inequality, so decolonization and sovereign equality were the keys to closing these gaps. Paradoxically, positive international law, which was one of the foundations of the 'standard of civilization' and thus the imposition of inequality, also provided the foundations for claims to sovereign equality.

Given the European cultural and racial bias that lay behind the 'standard of civilization', it is no surprise that before 1945 new countries formed from areas repeopled by Europeans found the political path from periphery to core easiest to travel. Most of these countries had been European colonies since the sixteenth and seventeenth centuries, and many of those in the Americas provided the first great wave of decolonization between the last decades of the eighteenth century and the early part of the nineteenth century. When they achieved independence, they were given recognition as sovereign equals. The independence of the US was accepted in 1783, and most of Latin America followed between 1811 and 1824, with a few laggards coming later, most notably the Dominican Republic (1865) and Cuba (1902). Canada gained partial independence from Britain in 1867, and in 1931 the Statute of Westminster established legislative equality for the (mainly white) dominions of the British Empire. Decolonization within Europe also took place relatively early: Greece (1829), Bulgaria (1878), Montenegro (1878), Romania (1878), Serbia (1878) and Albania (1913) broke from the Ottoman Empire; Poland (1916) and Finland (1918) broke away from Russia; and the Republic of Ireland (1922) broke away from Britain. The dissolution of the unions between Sweden and Norway (1905) and Denmark and Iceland (1944), as well as the break-up of Austria-Hungary in 1918, resulted in several new countries being admitted into the core of Western-colonial international society, even if this did not amount to decolonization in the standard sense.

Somewhat more surprising is the early progress towards sovereign equality made by a handful of non-Western countries. Liberia gained independence in 1847, while Egypt was functionally independent from the Ottoman Empire after 1801, following a complex route of degrees of subordination by France and Britain before reattaining independence in 1922. Iraq achieved partial independence in 1932 and Lebanon pulled free from France in 1941. In these movements and others, the spread of the ideologies of progress, often combined with indigenous cosmologies, ate away at the notion of Western political and legal superiority. Meiji Japan combined nationalism and imperialism with local forms of identity-construction. Sun Yat-Sen incorporated notions of Han distinctiveness with modern ideas of nationalism. And Bengali insurgents mobilized around the 'heroic history' of Hinduism (Darwin, 2007: 348–52). The 'awakening' prompted by Japan's defeat of Russia was realized in nationalist revolutions against 'backwardness' in Iran, China and the Ottoman Empire, as well as in the emergence of a 'pan-Asian' strand of thought whose leading voices, such as the Bengali poet Rabindranath Tagore, commanded large audiences (Collins, 2011). The Young Turks sought to make the Ottoman state the 'Japan of the Near East', praising its assertiveness and fashioning of a distinctly 'Asian modernity' (Aydin, 2007: 78). The many failures of the League of Nations, particularly over Manchuria, added to the sense that Asia needed to be freed from Western 'double standards'. In many places, nationalism and the right of self-determination were deployed as tools of mobilization against Western imperialism (Zarakol, 2011).

The closing of the political and legal gap by some states in the years before 1945 was reinforced by the success of some non-Western states in gaining membership to the array of IGOs that emerged after the 1860s. Membership of these groups constituted a significant form of diplomatic recognition. If the leading group within these IGOs was Western hemisphere states, during the second half of the nineteenth century, membership was expanded to include significant numbers of non-Western countries, including some still under colonial rule. Consider the following examples of non-Western states gaining membership up to and including the League of Nations:

- *International Telecommunications Union* (founded 1865): Turkey 1866, India 1869, Iran 1869, Egypt 1876, Japan 1879, Thailand 1883, and Sri Lanka 1897.[2]
- *Universal Postal Union* (founded 1874): Egypt 1875, Turkey 1875, India 1876, Indonesia 1877, Iran 1877, Japan 1877, Liberia 1879, Thailand 1885, Tunisia 1888, Korea 1900, Algeria 1907, Ethiopia 1908, and China 1914.[3]
- *Permanent Court of Arbitration* (founded 1889): Iran 1900, Japan 1900, Thailand 1900, China 1904, and Turkey 1907.[4]

---

[2] www.itu.int/cgi-bin/htsh/mm/scripts/mm.list?_search=ITUstates&_languageid=1 (accessed 20 January 2013).
[3] www.upu.int/en/the-upu/member-countries.html (accessed 20 January 2013).
[4] www.pca-cpa.org/showpage.asp?pag_id=1038 (accessed 20 January 2013).

- *League of Nations* (founded 1919): amongst the founding members were China, India, Liberia, Persia/Iran and Siam/Thailand; and joining later were Abyssinia/Ethiopia (1924), Iraq (1932), Turkey (1932), Afghanistan (1934) and Egypt (1937).

The Hague conferences of 1899 and 1907 were turning points in the widening of international society, bringing the states of the Americas into the core of interstate diplomacy (Simpson, 2004: 135). But the entry of peripheral states into the realm of diplomatic practices began much earlier than this. Particularly noteworthy is how some non-Western countries that were still colonial and/or semi-colonial, most obviously India, Sri Lanka, Indonesia and Iraq, nonetheless achieved diplomatic recognition as actors within international society at a time when Western-colonial international society was at its height. By providing early entry points for peripheral states into international society, IGOs foreshadowed the shift from Western-colonial to Western-global international society.

The most spectacular early move towards closing the political and legal status gap between core and periphery was made by Japan. Following the shock caused by the appearance of American gunboats in Tokyo Bay in 1853 and the subsequent signing of unequal treaties, Japan sent over 100 representatives on a mission to 11 European countries and the United States in order to negotiate revisions to the unequal treaties and learn from the West's institutions and infrastructures. The Iwakura Mission subsequently borrowed extensively from the bureaucratic structures and industrial production techniques of Western states (Kunitake, 2009). A number of bestselling texts promoted the blending of traditional Japanese culture with modern Western ideas. Some of these texts, such as Fukuzawa Yukichi's 'Conditions in the West' (*Seiyō Jijō*) and 'An Encouragement of Learning' (*Gakumon no Susume*), were highly influential.

In 1867, the Japanese state instituted a radical reform programme: the Meiji Restoration. The Charter Oath of the Meiji Restoration made frequent references to Confucianism. However, it did so in the context of the need to revive Japanese thought and practices within a new, 'modern' context (Aydin, 2007: 26). Under the slogan *fukoku kyōhe* (rich country, strong military), the Meiji oligarchy sought to erode feudal forms of governance, abolish the Shogunate and replace the Samurai (who numbered over 5% of the population) with a conscript army. The Meiji pioneered the Asian version of the developmental state.

They imported industrial technologies (often through 'international experts'), increased military spending (which climbed from 15% of government spending in the 1880s to around 30% in the 1890s and nearly 50% in the 1900s) and mobilized the population through an ideology of (sometimes chauvinistic) nationalism (Suzuki, 2009: 116–17; Mann, 2012: 111). This domestic reconfiguration embraced social relations ranging from clothing to penal codes. Many thousands of students were sent to Europe, especially Germany, while the eminent 'philosophy ceremony' at Tokyo University (renamed as Tokyo Imperial University in 1886) was reoriented around the 'Four Sages of Universal Philosophy': Buddha, Confucius, Socrates and Kant (Aydin, 2007: 27–8). At the same time, a regime of private property was introduced along with new systems of taxation, banking and insurance. The Meiji state built cotton mills, cement works, glass factories and mines, and maintained a leading interest in armaments; between 1873 and 1913, Japan constructed the sixth largest merchant marine in the world (Maddison, 2007b: 150). During the Meiji period as a whole, the state was responsible for 40% of the capital investment in the country: this was state-led development with a vengeance.

Domestic reforms went hand-in-hand with efforts to achieve equal diplomatic and political status. Japan initially had to accept extraterritorial treaties and tariff controls. However, it campaigned vigorously, and successfully, against them – extraterritoriality was revoked in the late 1890s and tariff controls were removed in 1911 (Gong, 1984: 164–96). As discussed in Chapter 1, Japanese leaders also understood that, to be treated as an equal in international affairs, it was necessary to become an imperial actor (Zarakol, 2011: 160–6). Japan therefore practised 'dual emulation', overhauling both its domestic social order and foreign policies with the aim of becoming recognized as a 'civilized' member of international society (Suzuki, 2005: 143). Okakura Kakuzō, a prominent Japanese scholar, wrote powerfully of this dual emulation, and its success in raising Japan's status, in his *Book of Tea*, first published in 1906 (cited in Suzuki, 2005: 137):

In the days when Japan was engaging in peaceful acts, the West used to think of it as an uncivilized country. Since Japan started massacring thousands of people in the battlefields of Manchuria, the West has called it a civilized country.

Japan's rise added a novel dimension to the hierarchical structure of international order. After its surprise defeat of China in 1894–5 and its even more surprising defeat of Russia in 1904–5, Japan became accepted within Western-global international society as the first non-white, non-Western great power. For all this, Japan failed to achieve full equality. During the latter part of the nineteenth century and the early part of the twentieth century, ideas of 'civilization' were narrowed, becoming re-affirmed around 'eternal' hierarchies of religion (e.g. Christian vs. Muslim) and race (e.g. 'white' vs. 'yellow') (Aydin, 2007: 40–1). Civilization was no longer achievable through modernizing projects; rather, it was inscribed through permanent differences. In this sense, while Japan foreshadowed the rise of other peripheral polities in terms of gaining sovereign equality and great power status, it failed to overcome the racism that underpinned Western-colonial order. The continuing hold of racism was made explicit at the 1919 Versailles Conference, when a Japanese attempt to be accepted as racial equals was rejected by Western powers (Clark, 2007: 83–106). This humiliation resulted in an anti-Western turn in Japanese policy that laid the basis for geopolitical contestation during the interwar years (Zarakol, 2011: 166–73). Only after the Second World War did the West abandon official racism.

Up to the Second World War, the advances in political and legal status we have charted were exceptions to the rule rather than serving as shifts in the basic ordering principles of Western-colonial international society. Indeed, the interwar years maintained many of the practices of the colonial era, classifying territories on the basis of their 'primitive' (for which read racial) quotient (Mazower, 2012: 166–7). Of the 48 states that sent delegates to the first assembly meeting of the League of Nations, only four were from Asia (including the Raj) (Mazower, 2012: 254). There were several significant changes in the primary institutions of international society after the Second World War. Some of these (war, territoriality, the market) are discussed in subsequent sections. The most important for closing the political-legal gap were sovereignty, colonialism and human inequality/racism. As the previous chapter showed, Western-colonial international society rested on the idea that sovereignty was divisible and that people could be ranked, culturally and/or racially, in terms of their place within the 'standard of civiliza-tion'. This stratification worked partly on the basis of relative power and, more frequently, on classifications of the superiority/inferiority of cultures and races (Hannaford, 1996; Keene, 2002; Salter, 2002; Anghie, 2004; Hobson, 2004 and 2012; Shilliam, 2011; Bell, 2012). Divisible sovereignty enabled core states to treat each other as sovereign equals while according the periphery either partial sovereignty (unequal treaties, extraterritoriality, protectorate or dominion status) or none at all (colonization).

After 1945, the legitimacy of this package collapsed in one of the most important developments in twentieth-century international relations – decolonization (Holsti, 2004: 274). The precursors to decolonization were apparent in the interwar years when the formal language of empire was, to some extent, replaced by the principle of trusteeship, the introduction of the mandate system and modifications to the notion of dominion. The trusteeship principle embodied the idea that 'political power should be exercised for the benefit of those persons who are subject to it' (Bain, 2003: 50–2). The mandate system, which was first applied to the colonies of the defeated Central Powers, Germany and the Ottoman Empire, was a formula for replacing empires without either annexing their colonies or granting them independence (Mayall, 2000: 17–25; Bain, 2003: 90–1). It formalized and legitimized two ideas: first, that imperial powers had obligations to provide for the welfare of indigenous populations; and second, reflecting the increasing scope of nationalism, that if a people could demonstrate a capacity for self-government, they had a right to claim it. Dominions occupied a legal space that was neither fully colonized nor fully sovereign. Mostly a term reserved for white settler states, dominions assumed increasing powers of self-governance, including playing active roles within the British Empire delegation at the League of Nations (Gorman, 2012).

Despite the emergence of these new forms of hierarchical management between core and periphery, imperialism remained central to core–periphery relations both between the wars and after the Second World War. Britain's empire encompassed more than 33 million square miles of territory during the 1930s and the French fought a bloody campaign during the 1950s to 'keep Algeria French' (Go, forthcoming). As noted in the previous chapter, during the first half of the twentieth century, Japan built an empire in East Asia, as did the US in the Americas and Asia, and white settler states such as Australia and New Zealand in the Pacific (Ballantyne and Burton, 2012: 286). When it came, the shift from an international society ordered through formal structures of inequality to one of formal sovereign equality was a radical change.

Several reasons lay behind decolonization. First, there was a change in the power structure in the core from a multipolar system of seven great powers to a bipolar world of two superpowers. European colonial powers were now in the second tier of a system dominated by the US and the Soviet Union, both of which were explicitly anti-imperialist. At the same time, the major imperial powers had been seriously weakened by the war. France and the Netherlands had been defeated and occupied, while, as discussed in Chapter 5, Britain had been financially drained. For their part, the Japanese, despite being defeated, had broken the myth of white power in Asia through their conquests of American, British, French and Dutch territories early in the war. Second, public opposition to colonialism within metropolitan states heightened, partly because of the contradiction between the pursuit of democracy at home and colonialism abroad (Mayall, 2000: 64–5; Bain, 2003: 134–9; Holsti, 2004: 262–74; Phillips, 2012: 13–14). This was reinforced by the experience of fascism, which discredited both racism and any pretence that Europe represented a superior 'standard of civilization'. Nationalism and the right of self-determination provided powerful weapons against claims of imperial legitimacy. Colonialism thus came under pronounced attack at a time when its principal exponents were themselves weakened.

The third reason was resistance in the periphery. In this regard, post-Second World War developments had their precursors in earlier movements. The Indian National Congress was formed in 1885 and the African National Congress in 1912. In 1920, Marcus Garvey's Universal Negro Improvement Association issued its *Declaration of the Rights of the Negro Peoples of the World*, which called for a general 'awakening of race consciousness' (Mazower, 2012: 165). A Congress of Oppressed Nationalities met in Brussels in 1927, while anti-colonial movements from Syria to Ethiopia fought sustained insurgencies against imperial powers. 'First peoples' such as the Maori, Kikuyu and Nisga'a petitioned the British crown to end the unequal privileges afforded to white settlers, while Indians living in southern and eastern Africa lobbied international organizations for equal treatment within imperial spaces (Crawford, 2002; Gorman, 2012). In the aftermath of the Second World War, the Philippines achieved independence from the US (1946) and Britain pulled out of the Indian subcontinent (1947). Despite pressure from some core states to maintain the existing order, most notably France (unsuccessfully in Vietnam and Algeria) and Portugal (more successfully in Angola and Mozambique), by the late 1960s most of Africa, the Middle East and Asia was free from formal colonialism. Following the successful revolutions carried out by Mao, Castro, Cabral and others, resistance movements were better equipped to conduct insurgencies, both in terms of their weaponry and their tactics. With the exception of a few scattered islands and territories, by the mid-1970s formal Western colonialism was over.

After 1945, therefore, Western-colonial international society morphed into a Western-global international order. Rather than being a three-tier colonial society regulated by divided sovereignty, international order became a global-scale society grounded on sovereign equality (Reus-Smit, 2013). Many status inequalities lingered on, and some of these were both significant and formal. But the changes in how international society was ordered, in terms of both primary and secondary institutions, were profound. Most notably, the package of colonialism, human inequality/racism, the 'standard of civilization' and divided sovereignty unravelled. It was replaced by a package of universal sovereign equality, self-determination and human equality/anti-racism. Underpinning this new set of primary institutions was self-determination, now to be applied almost unconditionally. Accompanying self-determination was a strength-ened liberal notion of universal human rights, which gave practical form to human equality and anti-racism (Clark, 2007: 131–51). The new norm of human equality was embedded in the Charter of the United Nations and most visibly expressed in the 1948 Universal Declaration of Human Rights (UDHR), which made individual human beings 'rights holders on their own behalf' (Mayall, 2000: 33). Human rights were also embodied in many UN Conventions and Committees, as they were in a number of regional bodies. All in all, the shift from Western-colonial to Western-global international society involved substantial changes to the institutional structure of international society, establish-ing a 'sovereign state monoculture' that eroded claims of Western superiority (Phillips, 2013: 28).

Accompanying the new package of primary institutions was an important carry-over from colonialism and the mandate system: the right of the periphery to 'development'. Although the overt arrogance of the 'standard of civilization' was gone, the colonial construction of non-Europeans as being at a lower stage of development within a single model of development was sustained during the post-colonial period (Bain, 2003: 13–21). The colonial obligation of the metropolitan powers to 'uplift' the natives morphed into an obligation on the part of the rich world to 'assist' in the 'development' and 'modernization' of the 'Third World' (the landmark text is Rostow, 1960; for critiques, see: Inayatullah and Blaney, 2004; Zarakol, 2011; Halperin, 2013). Development thus became the successor primary institution to colonialism. Development drew legitimacy from both a sense of obligation by the former colonial powers (now 'developed' states) and a sense of prerogative by post-colonial ('developing' or 'underdeveloped') states. It also drew legitimacy from its synergies with the redistributive dimensions of the human rights and human security regimes with their emphasis on rights to adequate nutrition, clean water, shelter, education, and more. For Western policy-makers, development also had the benefit of preserving market advantages by providing investment opportunities for firms, shoring up compliant elites and, perhaps most importantly, helping to curtail the spread of communism (Rostow, 1960; Mann, 2013). After 1945, the 'development project' became a universal goal, albeit one attended by considerable uncertainties and disagreements over how it was to be realized.

This shift in the primary institutions of international society was supplemented by associated transformations in secondary institutions, particularly in the family of IGOs gathered within the newly minted UN. After the Second World War, Western countries sought to maintain their formal advantages within international organizations. Indeed, 'legalized hegemony' formed the backdrop to a range of debates that took place during the early years of the UN: the make-up of the Security Council; the formation of a Trusteeship Council to monitor readiness for self-determination; and the adjudication of responsibility between metropolitan powers and local authorities over human rights provisions (Reus-Smit, 2013). However, as noted above, the war had weakened European states and heightened demands for autonomy. Post-1945 decolonization strengthened demands by peripheral states and peoples for plenipotentiary status within international society. During the 1950s and 1960s, membership of Western-global international society tripled as the General Assembly filled with new states from Africa, the Middle East and Asia. Between 1940 and 1980, 81 colonies and four quasi-colonies became independent states (Abernathy, 2000: 133). By 2000, two-thirds of the non-European member states of the United Nations had once been governed by European powers: 37 of these states had experienced more than 250 years of European rule and 60 of them at least 100 years of imperial rule (Abernathy, 2000: 12). The General Assembly became the expression of the now universal institution of sovereign equality.

The influx of peripheral states into the UN reaffirmed the sentiments expressed by earlier anti-colonial movements. In 1946, the UN passed a motion condemning racial discrimination in South Africa; thereafter, this vote became an annual event. The 1947 Asian Relations Conference in Delhi formed part of a broader pan-Asian movement that both built on earlier developments (such as the interwar Pan-Asian People's Conferences in Nagasaki and Shanghai) and acted as the forerunner to the ambitious agenda initiated at the Bandung conference in April 1955, in which 29 African and Asian states met to condemn colonialism and seek a diminution of great power influence in favour of universal, egalitarian principles of self-determination (Pasha, 2013). In 1960, the UN General Assembly passed Resolution 1514 – 'Declaration on the Granting of Independence to Colonial Countries and People' – advocating a more or less unconditional right of self-determination. In 1965, the General Assembly backed the Convention on the Elimination of all Forms of Racial Discrimination. The force of positive international law was now being wielded to rectify the political and racial inequalities that it had facilitated during the nineteenth century.

Such changes also affected issues of political economy, leading to the development of the World Food Programme (1961), the G77 group of 'underdeveloped' states (1967),[5] the UN Conference on Trade and Development (1964) and the related proposals for a New International Economic Order (1974) (Gareis and Varwick, 2005: 11). This South–South cooperation was the forerunner to a range of contemporary developments, not least the emergence of the G20 and BRIC group of states as influential forums of global governance. States in these bodies are employing precisely the same tools as those previously used by Western states to extend their influence. China is now the world's second largest bilateral aid donor, providing 'development assistance' to over 100 states in the global South, including those that are off-limits to Western donors (Chin and

---

[5] The demands of the G77 group for tariff preferences, development aid and special IMF drawing rights were made explicit following a conference in Algiers in October 1967, but this programme was first articulated at the 1966 Solidarity Conference of the Peoples of Asia, Africa and Latin America in Havana, which included representatives from 82 countries. The Havana conference outlined a range of inequalities fostered by the legacies of imperialism and colonialism, prompting the G77 programme endorsed a year later in Algiers. Thereafter, the G77 'established itself as the economic lobby for the Third World' (Loth, 2014: 129).

Quadir, 2012: 499). The Export-Import Bank of China provides a greater volume of loans than the G7 states combined. Indeed, all BRIC states are now net donors rather than net recipients. And all BRIC states are using state-led financial institutions, such as National Development Banks and Export-Import Banks, in projects intended to drive growth and magnify their influence.[6]

Intervention

As in the previous chapter, the issue of intervention provides a useful window on the erosion of political/legal inequality. We noted in Chapter 6 that, over the past two hundred years, practices of intervention had been conducted through two basic rationales: 'order maintenance' (usually in the core) and 'order transformation' (usually in the periphery). During the long nineteenth century, the emergence of great powers, whose very definition was that they were able to carry out interventions, but were themselves secure from interventions (Bull, 1984b: 1), helped to construct a bifurcated international sphere, one that largely respected non-intervention within the core, but which intervened frequently in the periphery. During the Cold War, both superpowers pursued intervention as a means of extending their sphere of influence and maintaining the balance between them. In practice, this entailed 'intervention within the blocs, non-intervention between them, and a tenuous non-intervention outside them' (Vincent, 1974: 353).

In the post-Cold War world, the practice of intervention has changed. The rise of China and other formerly peripheral states sits alongside, and to some extent in challenge to, the right of core states to intervene militarily. Yet, as contemporary debates around Libya, Syria, Mali and Côte d'Ivoire illustrate, military intervention remains a prominent tool of statecraft for Western states and, increasingly, IGOs. At the same time, intervention is becoming associated with a full-spectrum suite of practices that coercively reorders societies without recourse to direct military action. As the practice of intervention has evolved over the past two centuries, it has become more expansive, shifting from a discrete

---

[6] Such policies are not restricted to the BRICs. States in the Gulf, for example, are also using aid as a means of generating influence and developing alliances: Saudi foreign aid is worth $5 billion per year (4–5% of GDP), two-thirds of which goes to Arab countries and other Muslim states.

practice reserved for the great powers to one that is permanent in form and universal in aspiration. This, in turn, mirrors the shift from Western-colonial to Western-global international order, with hints towards the emergence of a new global structure: 'decentred globalism'.

In Chapter 6 we argued that colonial great powers intervened regularly, even if this sometimes came at considerable costs to themselves. This dynamic was equally strong during the Cold War when interventions by both superpowers had the potential to turn into costly and damaging wars, most notably for the US in Vietnam and the Soviet Union in Afghanistan. The 'blowback' of intervention has also been pronounced in the post-Cold War world as repeated failures have taken their toll on intervening as well as target states: the US has spent over $200 billion on relief and reconstruction in Iraq alone (Dodge, 2013: 1206). If superior power capabilities made intervention something great powers *could* do, their concern for status made intervention something great powers *had* to do, even at considerable cost to their treasuries.

Aspects of the great power 'right to intervene' as a tool of 'order maintenance' remain central to the governance of the contemporary world, most notably in the obligations of the UN Security Council to uphold international order and, following the agreement on the Responsibility to Protect, to intervene in order to halt genocide, ethnic cleansing, war crimes and crimes against humanity (Bellamy, 2010). This amounts to a prolongation of the inequality of the core–periphery order. However, both challenges to, and evolutions of, these practices illustrate the ways in which international order is being reshaped by the rise of formerly peripheral states. The emergence of new units of global governance is placing considerable strain on traditional practices of great power intervention. Of the five states that abstained on the Security Council vote to authorize force against Libya in 2011, four (Brazil, Russia, India and China) are BRIC states. The great powers that first claimed the right to intervene were closely tied to Western ideas and practices. In a world in which Western power no longer serves as the fulcrum of international order, it is not axiomatic that great powers will take a comparable view of intervention, particularly when emerging powers have spent many years struggling for non-intervention to be recognized in *de facto* as well as *de jure* terms. It is only with post-Second World War decolonization and the emergence of a fully global sovereign order that intervention became a practice mainly constituted between sovereign states. In previous iterations, it is better seen either as an inter-imperial practice or as one carried out within imperial domains.

At first, the extension of the sovereign state system after the Second World War expanded the possibilities of intervention as the emerging post-colonial 'Third World' became caught up in superpower competition. Hans Morgenthau (1967), amongst others, stressed the need for the superpowers to prop up newly decolonized states given the weakness of indigenous governance structures. The provision of military and economic aid created ties of inequality that the provider could exploit by either supplying or withdrawing aid, thus dramatically influencing local political developments. At the same time, local elites often invited external aid as a means by which to counter domestic rivals and implement development projects. The US justified its frequent interventions in the interests of preserving the global correlation of forces, as, for example, in the 'domino' metaphor used to legitimize its intervention in Vietnam: if the Vietnam 'domino' fell, it would knock over others in sequence and so change the balance between the Soviets and the West. For their part, the Soviets limited the sovereignty of satellite states and intervened to maintain the homogeneity of their bloc, while intervening in a range of polities in the Third World, from Afghanistan to Ethiopia. Given the frequency of interventions by both superpowers, the Cold War in the Third World was sometimes akin to a clash between two 'regimes of global intervention' (Westad, 2005: 407).

Over the past 30–40 years, the suspension of formal sovereignty rights for states in the global South has become less straightforward. As noted above, post-colonial states, aided by the increasing clout of the BRICs and other international collectivities, have re-emphasized their right to non-intervention. Intervention is, at least to some extent, shifting from overt methods of coercive restructuring towards 'everyday' forms of 'interventionism' (Duffield, 2007; Hameiri, 2010; Williams, 2013). Both public and private actors, it is argued, are now 'intervening' in polities around the world to such an extent as to coercively reshape state–society relations without resorting to military force. At the same time, if intervention was a central tool through which the nineteenth-century 'standard of civilization' was regulated (Shilliam, 2013), there are a number of challenges to the continued construction of hierarchy through difference. Most notably, racism is no longer a viable mode of differentiation for political purposes. Indeed, advocates of intervention in the contemporary world tend to deny any fundamental source of difference between peoples around the world. Rather, inequality is the result of supposedly temporary, fixable conditions: deficient institutions, weak governance, a corrupt ruling elite, and so on. This means that there are no longer formal barriers to intervention. Rather, the claims of present-day advocates of intervention are universal. As the former Secretary General of the UN, Kofi Annan (2012: 13), puts it: 'if the UN truly was to reflect a humanity that cared more, not less, for the suffering in its midst, and would do more, and not less, to end it, the organization has to be an agent of intervention in every sphere of human security'.

Kofi Annan's remarks speak to a world in which boundaries of inside–outside, no longer resting on racial differentiation or constrained by norms of sovereign territoriality, are dissolved. Rather, the bundling of territoriality with rights of reciprocal sovereignty is to be replaced by a fluid notion of sovereignty that is contingent on meeting standards of human protection. This is an important reformulation of the sovereignty norm. Rather than sovereignty being associated with the *control* of a territory, it is now seen as a *responsibility* that comes into force when states pass a certain yardstick (Orford, 2011). Forms of international administration, including international courts, territorial mandates and peacekeeping forces, are the 'neutral' mechanisms through which an international political apparatus is assuming the functions of nation-states, particularly in the global South. The UN is now the second largest deployer of troops in the world (after the US); in 2013, the organization was responsible for 100,000 peacekeepers in 15 operations. All of these operations are taking place in the global South, the vast majority of them in Africa. At the same time, peacekeeping operations are assuming increasingly expansive roles – of the 49 UN-mandated peacekeeping operations undertaken between 1989 and 2011, 34 contained a commitment to state-building (Dodge, 2013: 1192). In this sense, the line of 'civilizational apartheid' that separated core from periphery and which made the sovereignty of the latter contingent on the caprice of the former has not disappeared, but is being reinscribed through the functions of international organizations, even as such differences are denied through claims of universality.

The shift in intervention as a tool of great power privilege to one mediated by IGOs represents a major change in intervention as a social practice. First, interventions carried out by the UN are claimed to represent not just the views of some members of international society, but international society as a whole. Second, such interventions are no longer only structured in a global-to-local way. Rather, South–South interventions are also increasing in importance, both those under the auspices of regional IGOs and those conducted by states in their region. During the Cold War, Egypt intervened in the Yemeni Civil War (1962); China and Cuba intervened in the Angolan Civil War (1970s); India intervened in Bangladesh/East Pakistan (1971) and in the Maldives (1988); Syria intervened in the Lebanese Civil War (1976–present); Vietnam intervened in Cambodia (1978); Tanzania intervened in Uganda (1979); and Pakistan intervened indirectly in Afghanistan (1979–present). Since the end of the Cold War, the African Union (AU) has intervened in Darfur (2003, 2008), Burundi (2003–4) and Somalia (2007–present); the Economic Community of West African States (ECOWAS) has intervened in Liberia (1990), Sierra Leone (1997), Guinea-Bissau (1999), Ivory Coast (2003) and Mali (2013); and the GCC has intervened in Bahrain (2011). Since 2011, several Middle Eastern states have intervened in the Libyan and Syrian civil wars. As the relative balance of global power continues to even out, such South–South interventions are likely to become increasingly regular features of international affairs.

Military Catch-Up

There are two aspects to the military dimensions of the closing gap between core and periphery: first, the changing function and legitimacy of war as a primary institution of international society; and second, changes in the balance of military capability between core and periphery.

In terms of the institutions of international society, up until the end of the First World War states were free to go to war for a variety of purposes, from extending their home territory and preventing a rival from rising, to empire-building abroad and the pursuit of economic gain (Holsti, 1991). This broad legitimacy for war was an intrinsic feature of Western-colonial international society. The two Hague Conferences before the First World War sought to impose some limits on war, but only those conflicts fought between 'civilized' nations (Ansorge, 2013). The League of Nations attempted to restrict the right of war, but without much success. Except for the widespread, but not total, non-use of chemical weapons, the Second World War was a relatively unrestrained affair in terms of both motives and means: total war fought between mutually exclusive ideologies in pursuit of unconditional surrender. In this context, territorial rights were subject to the right of conquest restrained only by the correlation of forces.

In terms of the balance of military capabilities, the last chapter pointed to a number of victories won by peripheral polities over core forces during the long nineteenth century. However, as we also pointed out in Chapter 6, even when peripheral peoples won the battle, they usually lost the war. Indeed, only two cases stand out as major examples before 1945 of a significant narrowing of the gap between core and periphery: Ethiopia's defeat of Italy at the Battle of Adwa in 1896, and Japan's defeat of Russia in 1904–5. The Ethiopian victory over the Italians at the end of the nineteenth century presaged a wider victory that saw Ethiopia become one of only three independent states in Africa and, later, the only African member of the League of Nations. Defeat by the Ethiopians at Adwa prompted a crisis in Italy: the Italian commander, General Oreste Baratieri, was court martialled, while the ignominy of defeat saw riots erupt in Italy's major cities, a series of events that caused the government itself to collapse (Jones, 2011). The defeat also unsettled geopolitical relations in the region, prompting the British to fight a protracted campaign against Mahdist forces in Sudan (to shore up Italian rule in Eritrea) and coming close to war with France over claims to the Upper Nile (the 1898 'Fashoda Crisis'). More generally, the Ethiopian victory posed a difficulty for European international society in that its members were forced formally to admit a non-white, albeit Christian, power. This was put to the test in the aftermath of Mussolini's invasion of Ethiopia in 1935, one explicitly intended to right the wrongs of Italy's humiliation at Adwa. The failure of the League of Nations to condemn Italy exposed the contradictions that lay at the heart of Western-colonial international society.

Ethiopia's victory was won in a conventional military battle using Western-manufactured weapons. As such, it did not foreshadow the ways in which later anti-colonial movements, making extensive use of terrain, locally embedded networks and guerrilla tactics (what would now be called 'asymmetric' warfare), helped to unravel Western empires in the twentieth century. But even successes like Adwa did not prevent the formation of a core–periphery international order. Rather, as its repercussions show, it is better to see metropole and colony as part of a 'single analytical field' – core and periphery are co-constitutive features of the modern international order (Cooper and Stoler, 1997: 4; Barkawi, 2011b: 53; see also McClintock, 1995; Short, 2012).

If the Ethiopian defeat of Italy marked an important victory for a non-Western, non-white people against a European great power, Japan's victory over Russia was more significant still.[7] First, unlike Ethiopia's defensive war, which was geared around ensuring its survival, Japan's was an offensive, expansionary war, which elevated Japan into the ranks of the great powers. Second, while, like Ethiopia, Japan won the war in face-to-face conventional battles, it did so with cutting-edge naval and land forces fully equipped and organized in the modern way. Third, Japan's defeat of a major European power was carried around the world via new technologies and medias, contributing to a sense of pan-Asian, 'Eastern' solidarity in India, China, Persia and elsewhere (Aydin, 2007: 73). As we noted in the previous section, although Japan lost the Second World War, its initial victories over the US, Britain and France awakened both Western and colonial publics to the apparent superiority of a non-white power, unsettling the former and offering hope to the latter (Bayly and Harper, 2005). But the impact on the power gap between core and periphery of Japan's military modernity was subsumed within the country's move into the core. So successful was Japan's modernizing mission that the country took an active role in core dynamics, such as great power balancing and empire-building. Japan thus became part of the great power aspect of the revolutions of modernity, a path that China and India are now seeking to follow – we take up their attempt to do so in the following chapter.

The landmark cases of Ethiopia and Japan were part of a wider process in which military technologies spread from the core to the periphery, not just Ethiopia and Japan, but also China, the Ottoman Empire and a number of states in Latin America. Here the main mechanism was capitalism, with companies such as Armstrong and Krupp eager to sell their wares internationally, and peripheral states eager to acquire the power and status of military modernity. Some peripheral states, most notably Japan, made extensive use of this mechanism to develop cutting-edge military power. Others, most notably China,

---

[7] The importance of Japan's victory is captured well by Alfred Zimmern's reaction to it. Zimmern (in Vitalis, 2005: 168), due to give a lecture to students at Oxford about Greek history, began his talk by announcing, 'I feel I must speak to you about the most important historical event that has happened, or is likely to happen, in our lifetime: the victory of a non-white people over a white people.'

acquired some of the trappings of military modernity, but little of the organizational, strategic and training capabilities to make them effective in battle (Osterhammel, 2014: 482–93).

Just as in the political-legal sector, 1945 was a watershed year in the military sector. This was true in terms of changes in both the relevant institutions of international society, and the balance of military capabilities between core and periphery. As part of the package of changes in primary institutions associated with the shift from Western-colonial to Western-global international society, after 1945 there were significant transformations in the practices associated with war and territoriality. War remained an institution of international society, but its legitimate use was narrowed to the right of self-defence, plus uses authorized by the UN Security Council, while the right of anti-colonial war was legitimized by decolonization (Pejcinovic, 2013). The restraints on war were accompanied by a firming up of the norm that delegitimized transfers of territory by force (Holsti, 2004: 103–11). Reinforcing the now universalized legitimacy of self-determination and sovereign equality, transfers of territory became legitimate only by consent. As a consequence, between the major rounds of decolonization following the end of the Second World War and the end of the Cold War, the political-territorial map of the world began to assume an almost frozen character.

Both of these developments were reactions to the events of the Second World War, in which great powers battled for control over large swathes of territory. Decolonization removed the legitimacy of conquest as a rightful basis for territorial claims and embedded constraints on territorial disputes within post-colonial states. The rise of the market as a primary institution, on which more in the next section, also downgraded or removed economic motivations for war by delinking wealth and the possession of territory (Bull, 1977: 195). As shown above, one exception to this norm was the practice of intervention in which transnational solidarities in the form of human rights superseded sovereignty claims, thereby extending the right of war beyond self-defence (Mayall, 2000: 95–6, 102–4; see also Hurrell, 2007: 63–5).

In terms of the balance of military capabilities, at least initially the Western powers remained overwhelmingly strong in comparison to what after 1945 became 'the Third World'. Yet the onset of the Cold War, which ran in parallel with decolonization, changed this condition. In a reversal of the colonial policy of denying modern weaponry to the periphery, the pursuit of rival political agendas by the two superpowers, abetted by some former colonial powers and, after 1949, by the state socialist regime in China, pumped modern weapons and, up to a point, training to both client regimes and opposition movements throughout the Third World. There were both political and economic motives behind the enthusiasm in the core for arming the periphery. When complex weapon systems such as jet fighters were transferred to the Third World they often rotted because of a lack of expertise to maintain them and a lack of opportunity to use them. But light infantry weapons such as the AK-47 assault rifle, mortars and rocket-propelled grenades transformed the military balance between core and periphery. These weapons were simple to maintain and use. Their widespread availability, along with the spread of tactics and training for deploying them, increased the difficulty for outside powers of holding territory against determined local opposition. The basic condition for Western military superiority in Belloc's lines quoted in Chapter 6 was that 'they' (the periphery) did not have machine guns. Increasingly after 1945, they did. Although the core retained a considerable superiority in its command of sophisticated military technology, it lost ground, literally, in its capacity to occupy foreign territory and impose systems of governance.

The British exit from India, and the French defeats in Vietnam and Algeria, were harbingers of this change in the military balance, as, up to a point, was the inability of the US to achieve more than a stalemate in Korea in the early 1950s. It was not that Third World states could emulate Japan's achievement and set themselves up as military peers to core powers, or defeat them in head-on wars. But they could and did conduct sustained territorial defence and guerrilla wars long enough to raise the economic and political costs of foreign occupation to an intolerable level. The defeat of the US in Vietnam during the 1970s and of the Soviet Union in Afghanistan during the 1980s underlined the effectiveness of these territorial defence strategies, as did earlier revolutionary wars in China and Cuba, and later campaigns in Iraq and Afghanistan. In the Cold War cases, the key to the victory of the periphery was arms supply and support by core powers from the opposing side of the Cold War. In this sense it was, at least up until 1989, largely divisions in the core that empowered the Third World (Halliday, 2010). Nevertheless, this still marked a significant shift in military relations between core and periphery, because it was the core's

ability to take and hold foreign territory that had underpinned colonialism. That capability dwindled after 1945 because of changes in
behaviour in the core as much as because of Japanese-like modernization projects in the periphery.

Despite these changes, the core retains significant military advantages
in the contemporary world, particularly in its capacity to inflict destruction from the air. Spectacular examples of this include the smashing of
Saddam Hussein's armies in the Iraq wars of 1991 and 2003, and the
opening phases of the US-led invasion of Afghanistan in 2001. Less
spectacular but nonetheless significant demonstrations of the ongoing
military superiority of the core were provided by Western interventions
in the former Yugoslavia in 1995 and 1999, and in Libya in 2011.
Britain's defeat of Argentina in the 1982 Falklands/Malvinas war, its
intervention in Sierra Leone in 2000 and France's intervention in Mali
in 2013 also register in this regard. So too do Israel's defeats of its Arab
neighbours in various wars, most notably 1956, 1967, 1973 and 1982,
and its bombings of nuclear reactors in Iraq in 1981 and Syria in 2007.
The extensive use of armed drones by the US in the global war on terror
since 2001 continues to demonstrate both the ongoing military technological superiority of the core and its hesitation in becoming engaged on
the ground in the Third World. In a way, this shallow form of military
superiority echoes that of the early European position in the Indian
Ocean where, from much of the sixteenth century until the eighteenth
century, they enjoyed superiority at sea, but relatively slight military
influence on land.

The military superiority of the core in terms of technological edge
and powers of destruction thus remains formidable, particularly that of
the US with its enormous leads in military technology, expenditure and
research and development (R&D).[8] But the conditions in which it can
apply that superiority have narrowed. And even this residual superiority is now beginning to be questioned. A number of peripheral
countries have powerful armed forces with good training and equipment, including South Korea, Turkey, Singapore and Taiwan. Many of

---

[8] Reliable comparative figures on military R&D are notoriously hard to come by.
The total US defence R&D spending for 2010 was over $77 billion (in constant
fiscal year 2005 prices) (National Science Foundation, 2012: Table 4-28). That
was more than the total military expenditure of Japan ($59 billion), France
($62 billion) or Britain ($63 billion), and about the same as Russia ($78 billion) for
the same year (SIPRI, 2013).

these states are dependent on core arms producers (mainly the US, Russia, Britain, France and Germany) for their equipment. But some big states, most notably China, India and Brazil, are also acquiring the ability to build, maintain and use advanced weapons systems of their own. Both North and South Korea have put satellites into orbit on their own rockets. In 2013, China landed a rover on the moon and India sent an orbital probe to Mars. It is, perhaps, a significant marker of this military power shift between periphery and core that both India and China are acquiring aircraft carriers at the same time as Britain has (albeit temporarily) decommissioned them.

The process of nuclear proliferation is also eroding the advantage of the core in powers of mass destruction. China (1960), followed by India (1974), Pakistan (1989) and North Korea (2006), conducted test nuclear explosions before going on to develop nuclear weapons. South Africa built and then dismantled several nuclear weapons during the 1980s. And it is widely assumed that Israel has had nuclear weapons since the 1970s. Iraq under Saddam Hussein was probably trying to acquire nuclear weapons, and Iran is widely suspected of trying to acquire the necessary technology and materials to shorten its lead-time towards them. One motive for many such peripheral states to acquire nuclear weapons, or a short option on them, is to deter interventions by Western powers (Smith, 2006). Concerns over peripheral states gaining control over nuclear weapons, and other weapons of mass destruction, lay behind a number of early twenty-first-century interventions, including those in Iraq and Libya.

These developments in conventional and nuclear military capability have not completely displaced the military power gap that emerged during the nineteenth century. Although the acquisition of the capacity for effective territorial defence was an important shift in the military balance between core and periphery, it did not match the closing of the gap in the political-legal sector. The very terms 'asymmetric war' and 'weapons of the weak' serve as illustrations of enduring inequalities in this regard. However, recent developments suggest that the military gap is now beginning to close in a more general way. With the autonomous command of nuclear warheads, rockets ranging from short to intercontinental range, aircraft carriers, nuclear submarines, satellites, stealth aircraft, drones and other advanced military technologies, China and India are beginning to look like new Japans.

Economic Catch-Up

The economic dimension of peripheral catch-up is both a simple and a complicated story. It is simple because this sphere is the one in which inequality between core and periphery has been most durable. It is complicated because of the way in which industrial capitalism works simultaneously as both a system of exploitation and as a system of development. At the same time, as already hinted in the discussions of colonialism and development above, changes in the structure of primary institutions affected how the market and industrial capitalism operated before and after 1945.[9]

Before 1945, the story is the largely one-sided one laid out in Chapters 1 and 6, in which the industrializing core deployed the configuration of power associated with global modernity to dominate the economies of the periphery. During the nineteenth century and the first half of the twentieth century, industrial capitalism and the market worked within the institutional framing of Western-colonial international society. Because Britain controlled India, it could manipulate trade and tariffs to its advantage. And because it had defeated China, it could use gunboats, opium and extraterritoriality to position itself favourably in the Chinese market. A wide collection of territories, from Argentina to Singapore, served as conduits of British financial muscle.

So long as imperialism was in place, therefore, metropolitan powers could construct terms of trade as they wished. Yet even under these skewed conditions, the inbuilt tendency of industrial capitalism to spread through trade and investment continued to operate (Abernathy, 2000: 387–407). Development was certainly uneven, but it was also combined in significant ways. On the one hand, as previous chapters showed, capital and manufactured goods flowed from the core into the periphery. On the other hand, commodities increasingly flowed from the periphery into the core: by 1900, Britain was importing 60% of its total calories, and the average distance travelled by the fruit, vegetables and animals it

---

[9] One issue we do not have the space to explore is the substantial dimension of the contemporary global political economy that is formed out of the illegal and/or informal trade in drugs, commodities and people. This trade not only 'employs' large numbers of people and generates vast revenues, it is usually organized through transnational criminal networks that play an influential role in the economic and political life of many countries around the world. See Berdal and Serrano (2002) and Glenny (2009).

imported was 1,800 miles (Schwartz, 2000: 105); at the outbreak of the First World War, Britain imported 87% of its food and a similar proportion of its raw materials (Ruggie, 1982: 401, fn. 69). These two-directional flows, however unequally constituted, could increase both trade and growth. West African trade, for example, centred on palm oil, groundnuts, timber and cocoa, increased by a factor of four between 1897 and 1913 (Frieden, 2006: 74). In Latin America, economies grew at four times the rate of Asian states and at six times the rate of Central and Eastern European states between 1870 and 1913 (Frieden, 2006: 73). In some sectors, peripheral states led the world: by 1900, Brazil produced 80% of the world's coffee exports; by 1913, Chile provided half of the world's copper and Malaya produced half of the world's tin (Frieden, 2006: 73–5).

As noted in the previous chapter, before 1945, the most successful cases of economic development outside the core were Japan and the white settler colonies. Between 1860 and 1928, GNP per capita in Japan more than doubled (from $175 to $410), growing slightly faster than both Western Europe ($379–$784) and Eastern Europe ($231–$426) during the same period (Bairoch, 1981: 12). For their part, the white settler colonies closely associated with Britain (the US, Canada, Australia, New Zealand and, up to a point, South Africa) broadly followed Western rates of growth. North America did spectacularly well, rising from a GNP per capita of $536 in 1860 (already higher than Western Europe) to $1,657 in 1928 (Bairoch, 1981: 12). Between 1870 and 1913, the US share of global GDP doubled (from 9% to 19%) and, by 1914, the United States enjoyed the highest levels of GDP per capita in the world. By the end of the Second World War, the US was globally pre-eminent: the country produced nearly half of the world's energy supplies, and held 60% of its oil reserves and around half of its currency and gold reserves; its national income was worth twice that of Britain, France, Germany, Italy and the Benelux countries combined; and its workers earned twice as much as their equivalent in Britain, five times as much as Germans, and seven times the salary of the equivalent Russian (Arrighi, 2010: 284; Go, 2011: 103; Zeiler, 2014: 208).

As discussed in Chapter 5, the US presided over a system of 'embedded liberalism' that represented a 'golden age' of capitalist development. Key to this was the aid and investment provided by the US, exemplified by the Marshall Plan. Under the terms of the Marshall Plan, the US provided

$13 billion (around $150 billion in 2013 money) in economic and technical aid to 16 European states, equivalent to around 4% of US GDP for three years (Schwartz, 2000: 138; Zeiler, 2014: 219). Although the exact outcomes of the Marshall Plan are difficult to pinpoint, it clearly played a major role in European recovery: between 1948 and 1963, per capita GDP in Western Europe doubled (Frieden, 2006: 278). The Marshall Plan was part of a broader development strategy that saw the US provide credits and grants to 14 'frontline states' seen as buffers against communism: Japan, South Korea, Taiwan, India, Iran, Pakistan, Vietnam, the Philippines, Greece, Yugoslavia, Austria, Turkey, West Germany and Italy. These frontline states received a disproportionate amount of US aid: between 1946 and 1978, South Korea and Taiwan each received more aid (nearly $6 billion) than the whole of Africa ($5.6 billion) (Halperin, 2013: 190). Whereas previous US aid regimes had prioritized Latin America, the immediate post-war period saw only 2% of US aid go to the region (Escobar, 1995: 33). Patterns of investment ran along similar lines. American investment in European and Japanese firms rose from $2 billion in 1945 to $41 billion in 1973 (Frieden, 2006), reversing a long period in which US investment was primarily oriented towards the Americas.

As discussed in Chapter 5, US aid and investment was one reason for the emergence of new capitalist powers in the periphery, most notably the Asian Tigers. Japan also recovered well from the Second World War. Its output increased by a factor of eight between 1945 and 1970, partly because of a major programme of investment and procurement by the US, partly through a continuation of the state-led development strategy employed by previous governments, and partly on the back of a consumer boom. From a baseline of virtually nil in 1945, by 1970 90% of Japanese households owned a television, washing machine and refrigerator (Frieden, 2006: 279). By 1970, Japan's GDP per capita was equivalent to states in Western Europe. In 1980, it overtook the Soviet Union to become the world's second largest economy. During this period, Japanese car manufacturers and electronics companies became major global players, while Japanese investors financed purchases ranging from the Rockefeller Center to Universal Studios, and bought heavily into government securities. In a portent of similar Chinese purchases a generation later, Japanese investors bought 40% of all US Treasury bonds sold between 1985 and 1990 – around $170 billion worth of securities (Zeiler, 2014: 317–18).

China's move towards 'reform and opening up' began in the late 1970s, initiating a period of rapid growth and industrialization that saw it surpass Japan's GDP in 2010, and put it on course to be the world's largest economy by 2030 (Lin, 2012: 2), or possibly even earlier. Since 1979, China has averaged around 9% growth per year, while trade has grown a hundredfold. The result of this growth has been, for many, a substantial improvement in living standards: between 1980 and 2010, average incomes in China rose from $200 to $5,400, a rate of change that has seen over half a billion people lifted out of poverty (Freedland, 2012: 206; Zeiler, 2014: 323). To put this into perspective, during the nineteenth century, it took states an average of 70 years to double their per capita income; during the twentieth century, the average figure was 35 years. China doubled its per capita income in just ten years, between 1979 and 1989 (Lin, 2012: 15). This rise in living standards has seen a concomitant rise in quality of life indicators: since 1978, infant mortality has halved and life expectancy has risen to a level not far off that found in much wealthier countries (Mann, 2013: 221).

Although no other country has come close to matching the scale, depth and intensity of China's development over the past generation, India's economic reforms of the early 1990s have triggered a period of sustained economic growth, as have more recent reforms in countries such as Brazil, Turkey, Mexico, Malaysia and Nigeria. Even in these apparent success stories, however, development has taken place in piecemeal fashion. Liberalization has hollowed out state capacities, empowering private militias and large corporations who inhabit 'resource extracting economic enclaves' throughout the global South (Ferguson, 2006: 13; also see Bayart, 1993; Reno, 1999; Hibou, 2004; Sassen, 2014). These enclaves are less embedded in national economies than they are part of transnational circuits of production, exchange and finance (Robinson, 2004; Carroll, 2010; Sassen, 2014). Transnational retail chains, agribusinesses and sites of commodity extraction realize capital that often 'hops' and 'skips' to a range of (usually offshore) locations, after a share of the rents has been extracted by local elites (Shaxson, 2011). The result is 'socially thin development' in which oil, diamonds, gold and other commodities serve as a means of elite empowerment – and formal GDP growth – while generating few jobs and raising few taxes (Ferguson, 2006: 203). Over a billion people in the global South live on less than a dollar a day in countries that the global development apparatus largely ignores (Collier, 2007). At the same time, tendencies towards oligarchy and rent seeking are highest amongst resource sectors, particularly oil and mining, which are often found in the global South (Mulgan, 2013: 64–5). Such developments have their precursors in the *vendepatrias* (country sellers) and comprador elites who worked with imperial powers to set up enclaves of plantations, mines and commercial concessions during the nineteenth century (Frieden, 2006: 87–8). This comparison does not bode well for the prospects of developing a more sustainable, equitable form of growth over the long term.

The West, therefore, remains extremely powerful when it comes to the economic sector. Indeed, in some respects, the world economy is *more* unequal than it was a century ago. In 1913–14, 42% of global foreign investment went to Latin America, Africa and Asia; the corresponding rate for these three continents in 2001 was 18%. While the 2001 proportion of global foreign investment in Asia was the same as it had been in 1913–14 (12%), investment in both Latin America and Africa declined sharply during this period, from 20% to 5% in the former and from 10% to 1% in the latter (Osterhammel, 2014: 740). Western capital, institutions, corporations and personnel still dominate much of the global economy (Carroll, 2010). By the close of the twentieth century, the global North held 90% of the world's financial assets and 65% of global GDP; core states also provided 85% of global FDI and were recipients of two-thirds of it (Panitch and Gindin, 2012: 211). Much of the maintenance of Western economic power is vested in the United States: two-thirds of the world's biggest telecommunications firms are American, as are four-fifths of the world's largest media firms, five-sixths of the world's principal retailers, and 14 of the 16 biggest global healthcare firms (Panitch and Gildin, 2012: 289). Western companies also conduct most of the world's R&D, and are responsible for most of the value-added components of contemporary knowledge economies: US firms sell 75% of the world's computers and 91% of its computer software (Panitch and Gindin, 2012: 190–1).

Despite the unevenness that such dynamics exhibit, the rise of the Asian Tigers and China is a sign that the gap between core and periphery is closing in a more systematic fashion. First, the global distribution of capabilities is beginning to even out: per capita growth in East Asia since the late 1970s is the fastest in history, occurring at ten times the pace of that experienced by Western states during the late nineteenth and early twentieth centuries (Maddison, 2005: 11). Second, to some extent there is a 'spatial fix' underway in contemporary capitalism as manufacturing (to a considerable extent) and services (to a lesser extent) relocate from core to peripheral states. In the global South, manufacturing is now worth a higher proportion of GDP than is the case for states in the North. Mexican manufacturing is worth 90% of its total exports, up from 55% in 1980; the comparative figures for Malaysia are 87% and 25%, and for Turkey 81% and 29%, respectively (Panitch and Gildin, 2012). Not only are former peripheral states becoming prominent manufacturers, they are also competing, albeit from a low starting point, over the 'commanding heights' of contemporary capitalism. Apple products are made mainly in East Asia, even if the higher value aspects of the productive process are retained in the US, while India and China are home to IT giants in their own right, such as Tata and Huawei. A number of cities in former peripheral spaces have become hubs of finance capitalism, including Singapore and Hong Kong.

A general sense of this evening-out can be seen in Figure 7.1, which shows the average GDP of the four largest core states measured in terms of their total 2012 output (US, Japan, Germany, France), the four BRIC states (Brazil, Russia, India, China), and the largest four non-core states

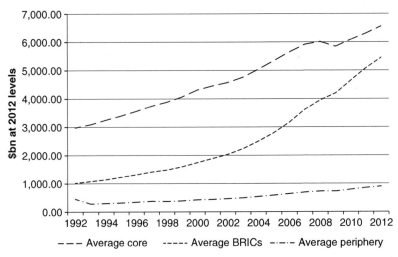

Figure 7.1: Average GDP of core, BRICs and peripheral states (2012 US$ billion)

Source: IMF (2013) World Economic Outlook Database: www.imf.org/ external/pubs/ft/weo/2013/02/weodata/index.aspx (accessed 26 January 2014).

in terms of their total 2012 output (Mexico, South Korea, Indonesia, Turkey – labelled as 'periphery' in the figure). In absolute terms, it is clear that core states remain ahead, but that the BRICs are catching up fast. This is less the case in relative terms – BRIC states remain well behind core states in terms of GDP per capita. However, a number of (usually small) non-BRIC, non-Western states, such as Qatar and Singapore, now have some of the highest levels of GDP per capita in the world. And many other former peripheral states are also rapidly increasing their per capita output (IMF, 2013).

Another way of observing these dynamics is through the share of global GDP held by members of the OECD. As shown in Figure 7.2, this is projected to fall below 50% in 2017. What makes this especially noteworthy is that OECD membership already includes some of the wealthiest former peripheral states, including South Korea, Turkey, Mexico and Chile. The OECD forecasts that, because of the speed of their respective growth rates, the combined GDP of China and India will exceed the combined GDP of the G7 by around 2025. This rise is all the more notable given that, in 2010, China and India accounted for less than one half of the G7's GDP (OECD, 2012: 22).

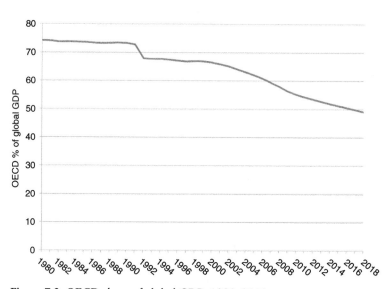

Figure 7.2: OECD share of global GDP, 1980–2018
Source: IMF (2013) World Economic Outlook Database: www.imf.org/external/pubs/ft/weo/2013/02/weodata/index.aspx (accessed 26 January 2014).

Economic catch-up is even becoming apparent in the field of R&D. In 2009, the US was still the global R&D leader, spending 31% of the world's total. But this represented a decline of 7% from 1999. During the same period, the R&D spend of East/South-East Asia and South Asia rose from 24% to 32% of the global total (National Science Foundation, 2012). The economic gap that opened during the long nineteenth century is decisively, if somewhat selectively, beginning to close.

Demographic Catch-Up

Demographic catch-up worked in the same two ways that established demographic inequality during the nineteenth century: growth rates and migration. As the revolutions of modernity deepened in intensity, the growth in the availability of resources, plus the spreading of both better diets and improved medical care, meant that life spans and population growth rates in the periphery increased. And with decolonization, the migratory flow from core to periphery went into reverse. Migrations from periphery to core were driven mainly by large differences in wealth between states. Migrants used the improving logistics of global transportation opened up in the nineteenth century and often followed former colonial pathways. People from Asia, Africa and Latin America began to flow into Europe and North America, and many of the Europeans that had settled in Africa and Asia returned home. Flows of people across borders within the periphery also increased.

The Growth Rate and Distribution of Population

As we showed in Chapter 6, global modernity triggered a spurt in population growth that favoured the West. Increased supplies of food and improved medical care, not to mention the many opportunities for migration and settlement in 'new worlds', meant that European populations increased at a faster rate than other peoples, becoming a significantly larger proportion of the world's population. This demographic factor reinforced Western power.

During the twentieth century this trend went into reverse. As shown in Figure 7.3, over the last century, the population of Europe has gone into relative decline, while populations in the Third World have seen a relative increase. There are two mechanisms at work here. One is the

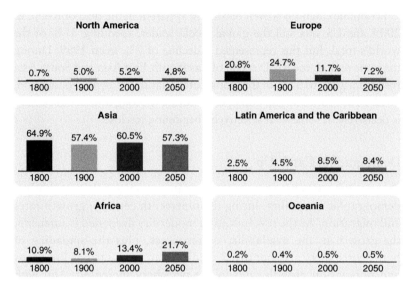

Figure 7.3: World population distribution by region, 1800–2050
Sources: United Nations Population, *Briefing Packet: 1998 Revision of World Population Prospects*; and *World Population Prospects: The 2006 Revision*.

spreading of at least some medical and nutritional benefits to the Third World, accelerating population growth. The other is the effect of rising prosperity and gender equality in the core, where contraceptive effects have slowed growth rates significantly, often to below the replacement rate. By 2000, Europe accounted for just under 12% of the world's population, less than half the proportion it had constituted a century earlier. Asia more or less held its place, albeit with large local variations: Japan declined, China stabilized, and India and Pakistan continued to grow. North America also held its place. However, the big gainers in terms of relative population size were states in Africa and Latin America. By the late twentieth century, rates of population growth were falling in most places, though they remained three times higher in low-income countries than in rich ones.

The global transformation has therefore had a dual impact on demography, first increasing population growth rates, and then decreasing them. As with everything else contained within the global transformation, these effects have occurred unevenly. And that unevenness has shaped the shift in the relative weight of different populations over the past two centuries. These demographic changes do not seem to have much impact on people's ability to become and stay rich. But demographics are certainly making a comeback in relation to raw power. As we have noted before, in the early stages of the global transformation, the power generated by modernity enabled countries with relatively small populations to dominate countries with relatively large ones, the exemplary cases being Britain and India, and the Netherlands and Indonesia. As global modernity spreads more widely and, in part, more equitably, differences in population size have started to matter again. China, India, Brazil, Indonesia and others are seen as rising powers both because they have made qualitative changes to accommodate the modern mode of power and because they have large populations and territories that amplify their qualitative capabilities. Older great powers such as Britain, Germany, France, Russia and Japan are hard pressed to compete with these emerging giants as the power differential associated with the global transformation is closed. The US does not have this problem. It still has a large and growing population, partly fuelled by migration, and is better placed to keep pace with the new giants.

Migration

As noted in Chapter 6, there were two dominant patterns of migration during the long nineteenth century: first, from Europe to the Americas and the other white settler colonies; and second, the movement of people within the periphery, particularly Indians and Chinese to South-East Asia, Africa, the Pacific and the Caribbean. There was some movement from the periphery to the Americas, such as Chinese settlements in the US, Hawaii, Canada, Peru and Cuba. But many of these movements were restricted through anti-immigration legislation, as we discussed in Chapter 6. There was little migration from the periphery to Europe, though there were some exceptions to this rule: for example, between 1914 and 1954, more than 2 million Algerians settled in France (Alba and Silberman, 2002: 1174). Some elite figures from the periphery also lived in the core, but usually only temporarily: Mahatma Gandhi studied Law in London in the late 1880s and Ho Chi Minh lived in the US, Britain and France between 1911 and 1923. Other members of the peripheral elite, including a number of Indian princes, took part in 'grand tours' to Europe, partly to raise the status of their positions and territories, and partly to be 'made modern' through

Table 7.1: *Bilateral migrations from periphery to core, 1970–2010*

	1970	1980	1990	2000	2010
	Migration per decade				
India–UK	336,567	401,255	429,885	524,796	756,471
Pakistan–UK	143,669	192,672	243,379	350,867	476,144
Algeria–France	1,493,990	1,424,707	1,375,771	1,057,135	1,455,780
Turkey–Germany	442,229	1,653,805	1,460,465	2,008,979	1,526,349
Mexico–US	936,424	2,408,502	4,662,233	9,367,910	12,497,843

Sources: For 1970–2000: World Bank, *Global Bilateral Migration Database*: http://data. worldbank.org/data-catalog/global-bilateral-migration-database. For 2010: United Nations, Department of Economic and Social Affairs, Population Division (2013) *Trends in International Migrant Stock: The 2013 Revision – Migrants by Destination and Origin.* N.B. the UN calculates migrant stock at mid-year.

becoming more accustomed to European ways of life. The success of Japan's modernizing programme meant that a range of figures, including Chiang Kai-shek, Zhou Enlai and Sun Yat-Sen, travelled there to learn from the Japanese experience.

These instances aside, the major reversal in mass migration, with periphery to core becoming its dominant direction, took place in the post-war period. The extent of such migrations is evident from Table 7.1.

In part, the reversal in migration flows arose because of the need for peripheral labour in core states. West Germany, for example, recruited 2.6 million migrant labourers between 1945 and 1973 in order to staff manufacturing production lines, including many from the Middle East (especially Turkey) (Castles et al., 2014: 107). West Germany's experience was not unusual – between 1965 and 2000, the foreign-born population of Western Europe rose from 2.2% to 10.3% (Goedde, 2014: 561). The movement from periphery to core was also bound up with the experience of decolonization, involving the 'return' of former colonizing populations and economic migration by former colonial subjects (Alba and Silberman, 2002: 1169–70). Some of the South Asian and Afro-Caribbean troops who had fought for Britain during the Second World War stayed on in the UK. Others were recruited to help rebuild the country after the war, beginning in a regularized way with the arrival of the *Empire Windrush* ship in June 1948. By the early 1950s, there were over 200,000 South Asian and Afro-Caribbean immigrants in the UK; this number reached 541,000 in 1961, 1.2 million in 1971 and 1.5 million in 1981 (Anwar, 1995: 274; Castles et al., 2014: 108–9). As Massey et al. (1998: 2) put it:

> Whereas migration during the industrial era [i.e. up to 1945] brought people from densely settled, rapidly industrializing areas to sparsely settled, rapidly industrializing regions, migration in the post-industrial era brought people from densely settled countries in the earliest stages of industrialization to densely settled post-industrial societies.

By 2010, over 200 million people were migrating each year, an increase of 58 million since 1990 (UN Department of Economic and Social Affairs, 2011: xviii–xxii).[10] Most moved to Europe (70 million), followed by Asia (61 million) and North America (50 million). Over the past generation, many former countries of emigration, such as Italy and Spain, have become destinations for immigrants from other parts of Europe, as well as from developing countries (Castles et al., 2014: 14, 124). Such dynamics have resulted in a net loss of populations in the developing world – Asia loses 1.3 million people per year and the Caribbean 1.1 million people per year. The general periphery-to-core pattern of this migration, and its extent and proportion, are set out in Tables 7.2 and 7.3.

The mass movements from periphery to core were not just economically important to the migrants themselves, they were also important to wider dynamics within the global economy. In 2010, recorded remittances from migrants to their homelands amounted to $310 billion, several times the amount received through official development assistance (United Nations Department of Economic and Social Affairs, 2011: xviii–xxii). Unrecorded flows may add another 50% to these figures (Castles et al., 2014: 73). These remittances are often from professionals rather than low-paid workers. The three largest recipients of remittances – India ($21.7 billion per year), China ($21.3 billion) and Mexico ($18.1 billion) – all receive money mainly from high-income workers (Sassen, 2008: 7). In some countries, remittances constitute a major proportion of GDP: in 2009, the ratio of remittances to GDP in Tajikistan was 50%, followed by Tonga (38%), Moldova (31%), Lesotho (27%), Samoa (26%) and Lebanon (25%) (Castles et al., 2014: 74).

---

[10] This does not include the often vast numbers of refugees and other displaced peoples generated by conflicts and natural disasters. According to the UN, there were over 50 million refugees, asylum seekers and 'internally displaced people' around the world in 2013.

Table 7.2: *Countries with the highest numbers of international migrants, 2010*

Rank	Country	Migrants (thousands)	International migration as: % of country's population	% of world migration
1	US	42,813	13.5	20.0
2	Russia	12,270	8.7	5.7
3	Germany	10,758	13.1	5.0
4	Saudi Arabia	7,289	27.8	3.4
5	Canada	7,202	21.3	3.4
6	France	6,685	10.7	3.1
7	UK	6,452	10.4	3.0
8	Spain	6,378	14.1	3.0
9	India	5,436	0.4	2.5
10	Ukraine	5,258	11.6	2.5

Source: United Nations Department of Economic and Social Affairs, Population Division (2009).

Table 7.3: *International migrants by region, 1990–2010*

	Numbers of international migrants (millions)		Distribution of international migrants (%)		International migrants (% of population)	
	1990	2010	1990	2010	1990	2010
World	155.5	213.9	100.0	100.0	2.9	3.1
More developed regions	82.4	127.7	53.0	59.7	7.2	10.3
Less developed regions	73.2	86.2	47.0	40.3	1.8	1.5
Least developed countries	11.1	11.5	7.1	5.4	2.1	1.3
Africa	16.0	19.3	10.3	9.0	2.5	1.9
Asia	50.9	61.3	32.7	28.7	1.6	1.5
Europe	49.4	69.8	31.8	32.6	6.9	9.5
Latin America and Caribbean	7.1	7.5	4.6	3.5	1.6	1.3
North America	27.8	50.0	17.9	23.4	9.8	14.2
Oceania	4.4	6.0	2.8	2.8	16.2	16.8

Source: United Nations, Department of Economic and Social Affairs, Population Division (2009).

If periphery-to-core movements represent one major reorientation of migration flows, a second trend is characterized by increasing migration within regions. In Europe, migration circuits have become much more deeply integrated, particularly following the 1985 Schengen Agreement, which abolished border controls between signatories – by 2013, the Schengen area incorporated 26 member states. Most contemporary African migration also takes place within the continent, with South Africa its principal destination. In Asia, the expansion in migration over the past 25–30 years has been propelled by high levels of growth in parts of the Gulf, East Asia and South-East Asia. In the Americas, the pattern of migration is primarily regional and northwards (to the US and Canada) (Goedde, 2014: 563). However, following the 2008 financial crisis, Latin America also began to receive a steady stream of immigrants from Southern Europe – a partial return to the core–periphery pattern of migration that marked the first phase of the global transformation (Castles et al., 2014).

One important continuity between contemporary migrations and previous circuits is represented by the movement from countryside to city that, as we noted in the previous chapter, was a central feature of migration during the long nineteenth century. This trend accelerated during the twentieth and twenty-first centuries. In 1890, only two cities (London and New York) had a population of more than 2.5 million; by 1990, there were 74 such cities (Belich, 2009: 2). In 2012, there were 75 cities with populations of at least 5 million people and approximately 500 cities with populations of over a million; over half of the world's population now lives in cities (McNeill and Engelke, 2014: 449). As with the industrializing states of the core during the nineteenth century, industrializing states of the periphery in the twentieth and twenty-first centuries are also undergoing mass urbanization. In Africa and Asia, the percentage of the population residing in urban areas rose from 14.5% and 16.4% in 1950 to 40.7% and 42.7% in 2000 respectively. Latin America urbanized earlier: 41.5% of the continent lived in cities in 1950, rising to 76.4% by 2000. The result of these trends is the emergence of mega-cities such as Shanghai, Mexico City, Jakarta, Karachi, Mumbai and São Paulo: 12 out of the 16 largest cities in the world are located in the global South (Halperin, 2013: 220).

These global cities act as a spur to migration, both for the wealthy global elite who work in finance and the professions, and for poorer migrants who build their office blocks, and who work as their cleaners and carers (Sassen, 2001 and 2010; Taylor, 2004; Carroll, 2010: ch. 3). In this sense, contemporary global cities are the continuation of dynamics unleashed by the global transformation. As noted in Chapter 5, in the early phases of global modernity, the commercialization of agriculture, new production techniques, and the development of global markets in agricultural products forced people off the land and into cities. These cities became entrepôts of modern capitalism; the most successful became nodes within global financial, commercial and productive circuits. The emergence of twenty-first-century mega-cities represents an intensification of these dynamics, with many of the same consequences: the concentration of capital and the formation of inequality. Around 1 billion people live in the slums that fester in these global cities (Davis, 2006), often in conditions reminiscent of the nineteenth-century industrial city captured evocatively by Alexis de Tocqueville in his depiction of Victorian Manchester (in Hobsbawm, 1962: 42):

From this foul drain the greatest stream of human industry flows out to fertilize the whole world. From this filthy sewer pure gold flows. Here humanity attains its most complete development and its most brutish; here civilization works its miracles and civilized man is turned almost into a savage.

During the long nineteenth century, therefore, patterns of migration were established by power differences, surplus population in the core, labour shortages in settler colonies, an expanding global economy, and racism. After decolonization, drivers of migration shifted to employment shortages in the core, income disparities between core and periphery, and an increasingly globalized economy in terms of production and finance. Urbanization has been a constant of both early and recent stages of the global transformation, although its principal locus has shifted from core to peripheral states. In the contemporary world, the old core has become less attractive due to slower growth, increasing unemployment and tougher barriers to entry. Some Europeans continue to migrate to the US and the former settler colonies, while there is still some movement from core to periphery. What is most striking are both the movement from periphery to core and, increasingly, movements within the periphery, as in migrations from South Asia to the Gulf, a route that sees many migrants serve as the contemporary equivalent of nineteenth-century indentured labourers. The story of migration post-1945 has become both complex and multidimensional.

Conclusion

Slowly and unevenly, but at an accelerating pace, the massive inequality across the planet that was established during the nineteenth century is being eroded. The mechanism behind this closing of the power gap is the same one that created it in the first place: the revolutions of modernity. Politically, legally and demographically, the gap has narrowed significantly. Economically and militarily it has narrowed less, but still appreciably. This is both changing the composition of the core (making it larger, more diverse and less white/Western) and changing its relationship to the periphery (as the core and semi-periphery get bigger, and the periphery smaller). The revolutions of modernity began by producing an unprecedented degree of inequality in a context of highly uneven and combined development. Development remains highly combined and that is likely to increase rather than decrease. It is still uneven, but that unevenness is diminishing. Some parts of the former periphery have either caught up with and joined the old core, or are on their way to doing so. We can now see the pattern that runs from the initial phase of the global transformation, with its huge intensification of both unevenness and combination, to the current phase in which combination continues to intensify, but the unevenness in the global distribution of the mode of power has begun to diminish significantly. Western-centred global modernity is giving way to 'decentred globalism', a structure we explore in Chapter 9.

This chapter highlighted the importance of the period around the Second World War as a significant watershed in international relations. As noted in the Introduction and Chapter 2, 1945 is already seen as a major turning point in IR, a view we largely concur with (Buzan and Lawson, 2014a). However, it is a mistake to take 1945 (or 1919) as starting points for thinking about contemporary international relations. Without the foundations of the nineteenth century, neither the significance of the changes around 1945, nor the force of the continuities in the core–periphery structure, can be fully understood. The period around 1945 is certainly a key development in the unfolding of the global transformation, marking the first systematic weakening of the core–periphery structure established during the long nineteenth century. But as we show in the next chapter, it is not the only such development.

One addendum to this story of an eroding core–periphery order is offered by the handful of states that buck the dynamics we have traced.

They provide an interesting perspective not only on the continuing legacies that the nineteenth century has bequeathed to contemporary international relations, but also on the significance both of the nineteenth-century power gap and its erosion. As noted in Chapter 5, in most of the world, European colonization either repeopled continents, overwhelming the indigenous peoples and making new states (Americas, Australia, New Zealand), or else involved relatively light settlement that was withdrawn or absorbed when decolonization took place (Asia, most of the Middle East and Africa). But there were a few places where European settlement was not big enough to displace or overwhelm the indigenous population, but too big and too deeply rooted to be easily withdrawn or absorbed. The main cases of this sort were Kenya, Rhodesia/Zimbabwe, South Africa and Israel. In the face of widespread decolonization, these states tried to sustain themselves in nineteenth-century style while all around them trends pointed in quite different directions.

The three African cases were eventually resolved by majority rule. In Kenya the white population was relatively small and never took control of the post-colonial state, although the Mau Mau Rebellion in the 1950s stands as one of the more vicious episodes in British imperial history. Rhodesia/Zimbabwe and South Africa both went through protracted struggles between minority white-ruled regimes clinging to nineteenth-century colonial and racial attitudes, and majority black liberation movements. The white minority regimes in both places benefited from the fact that their neighbours, Mozambique and Angola, remained under Portuguese control until 1975. Anti-racism and anti-apartheid sentiments commanded wide and deep support in both the Third World (where they were important sources of mobilization for post-colonial states and peoples), and in the West (where they fuelled both liberal and socialist sentiments). Both white minority regimes were eventually forced to give way to majority rule: Rhodesia/Zimbabwe in 1980 and South Africa in 1994.

Although Israel is sometimes lumped together with apartheid South Africa, it is a quite different story, and one that remains an unresolved remnant from the era of European colonialism. In some ways, the story of the Jewish people has parallels with those of the Armenians and Kurds: these are peoples who, for much of their history, have been striving to achieve statehood. However, the story of modern Israel has other parallels, not least with the histories of European settler colonies.

The Zionist movement can in some ways be seen as a typical nineteenth-century European colonial project, successfully promoting the emigration of mainly European Jews to Israel/Palestine. This was not, however, a standard nineteenth-century story of Europeans settling foreign territory as part of the rights of 'superior races'. Israel/Palestine was the erstwhile homeland of the Jews from which they had been expelled by the Roman Empire in AD 135 after several revolts and wars. And in Europe, a millennium of persecutions and anti-Semitism, culminating in the horrors of the Holocaust, provided a powerful motivation for Jews to make a claim of their own to a state, and to have this claim accepted as legitimate. Although rejected by Arab states, a partition of Palestine ending the British mandate was approved by the UN in 1947. Jewish emigration to Israel/Palestine during the first half of the twentieth century had increased the number and proportion of Jews in the territory, and Israel declared independence in 1948. The Arab–Israel war that accompanied independence resulted in large population movements, with the bulk of the Arab Palestinian population becoming a diaspora, and many Jews from Arab countries moving to Israel. Jews consequently became, and remain, the dominant population of Israel, currently constituting around 75% of the populace.

The problem was that the Zionist project achieved its goal at exactly the moment that the colonial ethos collapsed. Few non-Jews gave much credence to the Zionist homeland claim in itself. To accept a 2,000-year-old territorial claim as legitimate cause for a current reoccupation would mean that the Greeks (or Turks) could claim much of the Eastern Mediterranean, the Iranians much of the Middle East, the Arabs much of Spain, the Italians much of Western Europe, and the Mongols most of China, Russia and Central Asia. There was much sympathy for the Jewish people after the Holocaust, but the background importance of the colonial ethos for legitimizing Zionism should not be underestimated. The relevance of the colonial ethos to Israel's case is captured in the following passage from Darwin (2012: 258), written about settler colonies in New Zealand, Australia, South Africa and the Americas, but whose relevance to Israel's contemporary settler movement is easily apparent.

Settlers had much stronger motives to impose total defeat and demand total subjection. They had less need to rely upon local power brokers and make the concessions they sought – or so they believed. And once their settler bridgehead had reached a critical size, the settler mentality crossed a psychological threshold. The land they had occupied now became home (if not Home). It now was, or should be, a white man's country, whose indigenous people were at best a resource to exploit, at worst a menace to crush. The result was a shift in moral awareness of enormous importance. What might once have been thought of as the rights of original inhabitants were re-imagined instead as the barbaric hangovers of a redundant society. It is easy at this distance to deplore this transition; easier still to suppose that we would not have succumbed to the same moral temptation.

As a consequence, Israel has had a very hard life. It is not going too far to say that Israel lives in a permanent existential crisis. Its legitimacy and diplomatic standing are under constant question. It is in an unending state of serious tension, and frequently serious conflict, with its neighbours. And it remains a focus for widespread and strongly felt anti-colonial, anti-racist and, often, anti-Semitic sentiments.[11] Given the history of anti-Semitism in the West, the international politics around Israel remain highly charged and often poisonous. The issue of Israel embarrasses Europe and makes life difficult for the US, Israel's principal backer, throughout the Islamic world. The West's tolerance of, or support for, Israel complicates the politics of a wide range of issues from the control of nuclear proliferation (the West does not complain about Israel's nuclear arsenal), through human rights (the poor treatment of Palestinians both within Israel and in Gaza and the West Bank by Israeli 'settlers' – the very name invoking colonialism), to the war on terror (where Israel tries to certify its security problems through reference to a global conflict).

Given these conditions, Israel's security depends on being able to maintain a local version of the military and economic power gap that opened up between the core and the periphery during the nineteenth century. Close US, and at times French, support for Israel since the 1960s has so far helped it to do this successfully, as has the generally sluggish development and fractious politics of its Arab neighbours. But as the revolutions of modernity spread, maintaining this gap will become more difficult. The military pressures on Israel from both the spread of missiles and the nuclear programmes of some of its

---

[11] Opposition to Israel and/or its policies is in principle distinct from anti-Semitism, but in practice the two are often conflated, both by opponents and supporters of Israel.

neighbours are harbingers of a more general dynamic. Given the intensity of enmity in the Middle East, whether Israel can learn to live with rising Arab and Islamic powers, or they with it, is an open question. For the time being, Israel appears confident in its ability to maintain the regional power gap, so much so that it does not need to reach a settlement with its neighbours. But just like the West in relation to rising non-Western powers, it is unlikely to be able to keep that gap open in the long run, and will not for ever be able to pursue security without coming to terms with its neighbours.

The political potency of Israel in contemporary international relations, and earlier of the three African states discussed above, can only be understood fully when one sees how they fit into the broader history of the nineteenth-century global transformation, with its huge power gaps and accompanying resentments about inequality and racism. Israel has the misfortune to be the most prominent ongoing expression of this legacy and the profound ways in which it continues to shape world politics. Its military dilemma also points towards the subject of the next chapter, which moves away from core–periphery questions to focus on great power relations within the core.

8 | The Transformation of Great Powers, Great Power Relations and War

The Impact of the Global Transformation

During the nineteenth century, the character of military relations amongst the great powers changed markedly (Pearton, 1982; Giddens, 1985: 223–6; Gray, 2012: chs. 3–5), so much so as to change the qualifications for having status as a great power. Key to this was that from the 1830s and 1840s onwards, continuous and rapid technological innovation underpinned what has become a permanent 'revolution in military affairs' (RMA). We have already argued in Chapter 6 that new weapons, new logistics and new modes of military organization and training gave the West a decisive power advantage over other peoples during the first stages of the global transformation. This advantage was one of the main factors enabling the extension of Western control over large territories and populations in Africa and Asia. It also featured in the eastward and southward expansion of Russia, as well as the westward expansion of the US after independence.

In this chapter, we focus on the core, where the other major consequence of this new mode of military power unfolded: the transformation of great power war and the criteria by which states could establish themselves as, and be accepted as, great powers. Changes in military organization and technology underlie both core and core–periphery dynamics. Another link between them is that, up until the Second World War, the acquisition (or loss) of colonies was an important marker of great power standing: Britain and France had their 'place in the sun' and the second round of industrializing powers, Germany, Japan and the US, wanted theirs. The new technologies of the nineteenth century made empires quite easy to acquire. As Brodie (1941: 106–7) argues: 'It is not an historical accident that the powerful resurgence of imperialism in the latter part of the nineteenth century coincided with the great development of the steamship.' But colonial rivalry also destabilized great power relations. The 'Scramble for Africa', the rivalry between Russia and Japan to control Korea and Manchuria, Spain's cession of Cuba and the Philippines to the US, Anglo-French rivalries in the Middle East, and Anglo-Russian hostilities in Iran and Afghanistan all played into both core–periphery and great power relations.

Although many important changes to military techniques, organization and doctrine took place in the centuries preceding the global transformation (Parker, 1988; Downing, 1992; Krause, 1992; Mann, 1993), these mainly occurred within the context of agrarian modes of power. The introduction of guns and gunpowder respectively from the thirteenth and fourteenth centuries certainly made a substantial difference to the nature of military power and the conduct of war. But the development of early gunnery was quite slow and not out of line with similar agrarian metalworking technologies such as church bells. All of the Eurasian empires acquired this technology, meaning that it changed the balance between them and their nemesis, the horse-mounted steppe barbarians, much more than it affected their relations with each other. Most powers used these technologies to considerable effect, perhaps most notably the Ottomans, who deployed enormous siege cannon in their conquest of Constantinople in 1453.

The configuration of global modernity generated a new mode of power baseline for achieving great power standing. Before the nineteenth century, military power was largely determined by population size and wealth, with territorial extent playing a supporting role. Great powers were those with sufficient manpower and resources to mobilize, equip and train large armies and/or navies. Variables like the quality of military leadership, logistics and training, and also, up to a point, the quality of weapons, often mattered as to who won or lost a particular battle or war. Great generals like Alexander, Hannibal or Napoleon could make a huge difference, as could the quality of training, as for example in the classical armies of Athens, Sparta and Rome. It was mainly organizational advantages that enabled the Europeans to conquer India during the late eighteenth century – there was no great gap in the technological level of equipment on either side (Headrick, 1981: 89–93 and 2010: 153). But overall, the material foundations for being a great power in the agrarian era were rooted in manpower and money. These two variables did not change quickly unless territorial expansion provided new resources. Indeed, because the agrarian foundations of military power were fairly stable and straightforward, including guns and gunpowder, they were relatively easy to copy.

During the nineteenth century, this formula collapsed. Manpower still mattered, so that a small country such as Belgium could not become a great power no matter how industrialized it was and even though it maintained imperial territories. So also did organization and training, with Prussia leading the way in developing professionally trained officers and a standing general staff (Osterhammel, 2014: 484). But the level of wealth, and the technological and organizational prowess necessary to support great power standing, could now come only from a rational state with an industrial economy buttressed by ideologies of progress. The transformation introduced by the French Revolutionary and Napoleonic Wars was social and political rather than technological. As Black (2009: 9; also see Broers, 2011; Gray, 2012: ch. 3) argues, the Napoleonic Wars were not 'industrial in any significant way'. There were, to be sure, some differences in the quality of naval and infantry weapons, but by and large all sides were fighting with similar eighteenth-century equipment. Rather, the French contribution to military modernity linked nationalism and popular sovereignty to the process of recruiting military manpower. This generated the *levée en masse*, which enabled the mobilization of very large and well-motivated armies (Broers, 2011).[1] During the nineteenth century as a whole, such military 'tasking' became much more sophisticated, so much so that, in 1899, it took the British just three months to provision, organize and transport a 100,000-strong army to South Africa to fight the Boer War (Black, 2009: 206). The brilliance of innovative generalship was also a factor in nineteenth-century wars. Napoleon made the best use of the weapons and forces available, and won a number of battles through superior tactics, strategy and motivation, but his military genius was a variable that could arise in any era. Mass mobilization was, however, manifestly modern, and profoundly changed the foundations of military power.

Mass mobilization remained a central element of modern military power until late in the twentieth century, but from the early nineteenth century it was accompanied by rapid and continuous advances in

---

[1] Nationalism was two-edged in that mobilizing the masses for war was also considered to be threatening to the stability and legitimacy of dynastic regimes (Kadercan, 2012). This was not just an issue for Europeans: the Qing dynasty in China was ethnically Manchu and feared the consequences of mobilizing its Han subjects against Japan (Paine, 2003: 128, 205, 240–1).

military technology. Within two decades of Napoleon's defeat, the firepower, range, accuracy and mobility of existing weapons began to improve markedly, with new types of weapons offering new military options appearing in quick succession. Only industrial economies could maintain this process of permanent, rapid innovation, and only industrial economies could afford to deploy the results on a large scale. Between the middle and end of the nineteenth century, the invention of machine guns lifted the potential rate of fire of infantrymen from around three rounds per minute for a well-trained musketeer to several hundred rounds per minute for the operators of a machine gun. This, in turn, required logistical developments to supply the prodigious amount of ammunition required. In the quarter century between 1860 and 1885 the weight of the biggest guns increased from 4.75 to 111 tons (Brodie, 1941: 213). Industrial techniques meant that, by 1860, the Woolwich Arsenal in London could produce 250,000 Miniéballs each day (Giddens, 1985: 225). These balls were used in rifles that were, in turn, used to pacify both domestic and international societies. The changing mode of organized violence, therefore, was significantly enabled by industrialization. Or to put this another way, a revolution in the means of production helped to generate a revolution in the means of destruction.[2]

One obvious consequence of the revolutions of modernity was to transform the pace, scale and cost of great power wars. As noted above, the French Revolutionary and Napoleonic Wars were largely fought with eighteenth-century kit, the main innovation being in forms of mobilization and tactics. The First World War, by contrast, was not only a war of production (who could produce the most troops and weapons), but also a war of technological innovation. Although some aspects of these dynamics were present in nineteenth-century wars in North America and Asia, the First World War was the first major conflict in which submarines, aircraft, tanks, machine guns and chemical weapons played leading roles. On land, the new firepower created a protracted and bloody stalemate on the Western front, only broken by the development of combined arms modes of warfare, including tanks (Gray, 2012: chs. 6–7). At sea, submarines came close to winning the

---

[2] In fact this was a mutually constitutive process, with imperatives for the mass production of standardized military goods also contributing to processes of industrialization (Lawrence, 1997: 17, 26).

battle of the Atlantic for Germany. The Second World War was similarly influenced by new military technologies, with aircraft and motor-
ized vehicles restoring combat mobility. The idea of the home front as a
strategic target meant that air power played a heightened role. Radar
made a big difference to the outcome of the Battle of Britain, while
submarines nearly won the battle of the Atlantic for Germany (and did
win a similar battle in the Pacific, where American submarines largely
eliminated the Japanese merchant marine). The first use of long-range
rockets and jet-powered aircraft in combat occurred and, while not
decisive in this war, laid down markers for what was to come.
Nuclear weapons capped the outcome of the war by introducing a
new scale of destructive power.

Some idea of the difference that new technologies and modes of
organization made to great power war can be seen from total casualty
figures: roughly 4 million for the French Revolutionary and Napoleonic
Wars, 15 million for the First World War, and 41 million for the Second
World War (Clodfelter, 2002). This roughly ten-fold increase has to be
seen against the background of the general three-fold increase in the
population of the West over roughly the same period (1820–1950)
(Maddison, 2001: 241). Military expenditure for a typical European
great power (Britain, France, Russia) increased by around a factor of
six between 1820 and 1910 (Singer et al., 1972; Singer, 1987), approximately in line with the increase in GNP in the core states during a similar
period (1830–1913) (Bairoch, 1981: 7; see also Eloranta, 2012: 108).
This surprising stability partly reflects the absence of major great power
wars during this period, meaning that economic growth could keep pace
with the rising costs of military equipment. During peacetime, the sharply
rising unit costs of iron and steam warships were offset by the fact that
fewer of these new types of ship were built (Brodie, 1941: 238).

This technological aspect of the global transformation still operates
in the contemporary world as it did during the nineteenth century. The
permanent RMA differentiates global modernity from previous periods
of world history. It defines one of the most crucial aspects of contemporary international relations, and is the main subject of the sub-field of
Strategic Studies. The following two sections look first at the unfolding
of military innovation and, second, at qualitative arms racing. We then
examine the impact of global modernity on who qualified as a great
power and how the process of continuous military innovation destabilized great power relations in a novel way. A final section surveys the

'defence dilemma' and the increasing dysfunctionality of great power war as consequences of both the costs of the permanent RMA, and its ever-rising powers of destruction.

The New Pace of Technological Innovation and Change

The emergence of global modernity had an enormous impact on the foundations of military power. Industrial production meant that mechanical weapons could be mass-produced, but the relentless innovation associated with industrialization also meant that what was produced was quickly superseded.[3] Each new generation of weapons represented marked improvements over their predecessors, and just as guns had made the crossbow obsolete, so aircraft and submarines made battleships obsolete. From the 1870s on, the acceleration of technological change not only played into arms competitions in Europe, but also created a gap between existing war experience and the emergent capabilities and implications of new weapons (Black, 2009: 134–50).

A good example of the pace and extent of change in military technology during the nineteenth century is the evolution in naval power. These changes underpinned not only the huge shift in the military balance between core and periphery illustrated by the victories of the steam sloop *Nemesis* over the Chinese discussed in Chapter 6, but also the destabilization of great power relations in the core. Although there were no major naval battles between Trafalgar (1805) and Jutland (1916), the technology of naval power underwent multiple transformations during that period. Many of these technologies were not put to a military test, but without keeping up with them, no state could claim to be a serious naval power. The pictures in Figure 8.1 graphically demonstrate the extent of these transformations starting with the relative stasis for the two centuries separating the *Sovereign of the Seas* and HMS *Victory*.

The transformation from wood and sail to steel and steam took just 50 years (see Brodie, 1941; Parkes, 1966; Black, 2009: 71–95). Across this half-century there was: a 33-fold increase in weapons range from

---

[3] A considerable literature exists on the history of military technology and weapons, including the impact of industrialization during the nineteenth century. Among them are: Brodie and Brodie, 1973; Bowen, 1977; McNeill, 1982; van Creveld, 1991; Krause, 1992.

(a)

(b)

Figure 8.1: The technological development of naval weapons, 1637–1906
(a) 1637 (*The Sovereign of the Seas*)
(b) Up to 1850 (HMS *Victory*)

(c)

(d)

Figure 8.1: (cont.)
(c) 1860 (HMS *Warrior*)
(d) 1871 (HMS *Devastation*)

(e)

Figure 8.1: (cont.)
(e) 1906 (HMS *Dreadnought*)

600 yards (*Victory*) to 20,000 yards (*Dreadnought*); a 26-fold increase in weight of shot from 32 pounds solid shot to 850 pounds explosive armour-piercing shell; more than a doubling of speed from 8–9 knots (*Victory*) to 21 knots (*Dreadnought*); and a shift from all sail (*Victory*), through single, double and triple expansion steam piston engines, to steam turbines (*Dreadnought*), permitting all-weather navigation for the first time. From the 1860s onward, each generation of warship made obsolete those that had preceded it. The metal-hulled *Warrior* was the most powerful warship of her day, able to sink any other ship afloat. But within a few years it would have been suicidal to take it into a serious engagement against more modern ships.

This kind of intense transformation in the nature of military power was not confined to the naval sphere, though it was perhaps most visible there. The parallel transformation on land started earlier than that at sea. From the 1840s onwards there were rapid improvements in both infantry weapons and artillery. Between 1840 and 1865, there was a shift away from single-shot, smoothbore, muzzle-loading infantry weapons (such as the musket), to repeating, breech-loading, rifled weapons, greatly increasing accuracy, range and rate of fire. One culmination of this was the introduction of machine guns during the 1860s. Artillery similarly transformed, moving from smoothbore, muzzle-loading cannon firing mostly solid shot, to rifled, breech-loading guns firing armour-piercing, explosive, cylindrical shells. Land-based artillery was usually smaller than naval, but again there were spectacular increases in range, accuracy and firepower based on improved metallurgy (especially better steels; see Brodie and Brodie, 1973: 124–31), explosives (for both propellants and warheads) and design. Better and cheaper steel not only improved guns, but also the armour plate that was adopted as a protection against them. The resulting duel between better guns and better armour continued until the middle of the twentieth century, though guns tended to hold the upper hand (Brodie, 1941: 175).

The improvements in technology that began to dominate understandings of military power in the middle of the nineteenth century were deeply embedded in wider industrial-technological transformations. The same types of metallurgical, engineering and design knowledge and skills that were necessary to produce typewriters could also produce machine guns. This not only meant that military technology was closely linked to the general state of scientific and technical knowledge, but also that there were two different aspects to the advance of military technology. First, there were many technologies that today would be referred to as 'dual-use', where the civil and military sectors used much the same things: railways, transport ships, telegraph, etc. Tinned food, for example, became available in 1812, transforming the logistics of feeding armies (Gray, 2012: loc. 2030). Alfred Nobel's invention of dynamite, ostensibly for use in mining, tunnelling and constructing, also became adopted for war-making purposes (Topik and Wells, 2012: 604). Second, there were technologies specific to the military for which there was no obvious commercial use: machine guns, heavy artillery, heavy armour plate, submarines, etc.

Dual-use technologies have their origins in the nineteenth century's RMA. The improved iron and steel that went into warship construction, armour and guns also went into civilian applications from steamships and railways, to bridges and industrial machinery. Railways built to haul people and goods could also transport armies and their equipment, transforming military logistics and strategy. Likewise steamships built for commercial purposes could be used as military transports, greatly increasing the range, speed and volume of military mobilizations: the speed and scale of the British expedition to South Africa in 1899 mentioned above would simply not have been possible in earlier times. Iron-built commercial steamships evolved ahead of warships. Early iron hulls that were functional for commercial purposes were not as useful for warships because the iron was too brittle to withstand the impact of cannon fire. Early commercial steamships were also driven by side-mounted paddle wheels that were again too vulnerable to damage (as well as reducing the number of guns that could be mounted down the side of the vessel). Naval interest in steam power for warships picked up with the introduction of the screw propeller at the end of the 1830s. The electric telegraph (emerging from the 1830s) and the radio (from the 1890s) were just as useful for speeding up military communications as they were for commercial, political and personal broadcasting.

This dynamic of interlocked civilian and military technological innovation was sustained through the twentieth century to the present day. The point here is not that twentieth- and twenty-first-century developments dwarf their nineteenth-century forebears in terms of range or destructive capacity. Obviously, as with nuclear weapons, they do. The point is that regardless of what the new technologies are capable of achieving, the process that underlies them and their consequences for relations between states are similar to the dynamics established during the nineteenth century and quite different from the dynamics that characterized older military relations. A new era of military relations began during the nineteenth century and we are still living in it.

Motor vehicles (emerging during the 1880s) and engine-powered, heavier-than-air flying machines (appearing at the turn of the century) had the same implications for military transport and communication as they did for civilian purposes. In addition, both technologies opened up possibilities for new types of weapon: tanks and bombers. Chemical weapons, such as incendiary 'Greek fire', were not unknown to agrarian societies, but the industrial versions were both more potent and on a larger scale, becoming a matter of concern from the 1890s. Initially, substances such as chlorine that provided basic inputs to civilian chemical industry were used as weapons, as during the First World War. Some technologies such as radar, nuclear fission, computers, satellites and the internet were the outcome mainly of military concerns, but they grew out of the general background of civilian science and technology, and quickly found major civilian as well as military applications.

Radar, emerging during the 1930s as an offshoot of earlier radio developments, found civilian uses from air-traffic control to weather forecasting. Nuclear fission, emerging during the 1930s and 1940s from a combination of scientific progress and military imperative, produced both reactors and bombs. Reactors were used not only for producing electricity, but also to power propulsion units in warships and ice-breakers. The first satellite was launched in 1957, ostensibly for scientific purposes, but this technology quickly became embroiled in Cold War competition between the US and the Soviet Union. Satellites were useful for military surveillance and potentially as weapons platforms, but they also developed a host of scientific and commercial functions including earth monitoring, weather, communications (civil and military) and navigation (satellite navigation and geo-positioning, also both civil and military).

The programmable electronic computer likewise emerged during the 1930s and 1940s, pushed by a combination of general technological and scientific advance plus a particular military need arising during the Second World War (code breaking). Computers found applications in business and science, and with the emergence of personal computers during the 1970s and 1980s, found their way into ever more aspects of public life. The increasing role of computers and computer networks in civilian and military life provided an opportunity for cyber weapons, which serves as the latest exemplar of dual-use technologies. At the time of writing this is still a new development, and definitions of cyber weapon and cyber security remain unclear (Hansen and Nissenbaum, 2009). What is clear is that dependence on computer networks creates opportunities for those who want to spy on, subvert, damage, manipulate and/or cripple the computers and networks of others. The technical skills for this are generic to the software and hardware industry. The motives may be individual (e.g. fun or status-seeking hackers), criminal (e.g. the hijacking of computers to serve as botnets for scam fraudsters), economic (e.g. industrial espionage), political (e.g. spying, cyber-attacks by activists and/or governments) and/or military (e.g. disrupting command and control networks or other strategic production facilities). To date, the most prominent examples of the latter are the *Stuxnet* worm, which came to light in 2010, and the *Flame* malware, exposed in 2012, both primarily directed against Iran's nuclear facilities, with the US and Israel considered to be the most likely initiators.

Although technological change often assumed dual-use form, military technology also had a distinctive cycle of innovation from which there was relatively little overlap into the civilian domain. The military's requirements in transportation and communication were, for the most part, not wildly different from those needed for civilian use, but the military had requirements for weapons and detection equipment that went well beyond civilian needs. This was already obvious by the middle of the nineteenth century, by which time the developments discussed above in heavy artillery, armour plate, machine guns and battleships were beginning to differentiate military from civilian technologies. A good early example of military-specific technological development is the submarine. The development of military submarines dates back to the late eighteenth century, but did not take off until the 1860s with their use in the American Civil War. The modern submarine emerged during the 1890s in the form that played a significant role during the First and Second World Wars (Brodie, 1941: 261–327).

As noted above, powered aircraft began as a dual-use technology, but their deployment during the First World War opened up a significant gap between civil and military requirements. The military needed fast, manoeuvrable machines for aerial combat, and heavy-duty long-range planes for bombing. During the interwar years there was a substantial improvement in aircraft technology, comparable to that in naval weapons from the late 1850s. Up to a point, general improvements in aircraft performance served both markets: more speed, longer range, better mechanical reliability, larger carrying capacity and improved navigation. The dual-use linkage remained strongest in relation to transportation, perhaps the best example being the conversion during the 1950s of a military tanker into the first commercially successful jet passenger liner: the Boeing 707. However, the military's need for fast, manoeuvrable fighters outpaced the civilian market, even though aerial racing was a popular sport during the 1920s and 1930s. The move from propellers to jets after the Second World War, and especially the move to supersonic jets during the 1950s, resulted in an almost exclusively military domain for fighters and bombers, as well as more specialized reconnaissance aircraft. The only exception to the military exclusivity of supersonic flight was the commercially marginal *Concorde* supersonic passenger liner, which operated from 1969–2003. Although some aspects of the technology behind today's advanced fighter jets and supersonic stealth bombers may find their way into civil aircraft, the planes themselves have no commercial utility. Perhaps most obviously, stealth technology runs directly against the grain of commercial aircraft, which have to be visible for safety reasons.

Like guns, and containing the same ancestry in gunpowder, rockets were a well-established technology of agrarian civilizations, having been in military use, especially in China, since the thirteenth century. In the late eighteenth century, Indian military rockets using metal casings, and in mass deployments, gave the British considerable trouble during their wars against Mysore. During the Napoleonic Wars, the British built on this Indian technology to develop the Congreve rockets, the largest of which were capable of carrying a 24-pound warhead for over a mile, albeit without much accuracy or reliability (Bowen, 1977: 116–18; McNeill, 1982: 220). These gunpowder rockets were essentially glorified fireworks. They were a useful form of artillery, but were superseded in the late nineteenth century by improved guns. Rockets played no significant role in the First World War.

Modern rocketry began to take off during the 1920s in the US (mostly through individual enthusiasts) and in the Soviet Union (mostly through state support). The German military became interested in rockets during the 1930s because of treaty restrictions on its access to artillery, culminating in the building of the first successful modern military rocket: the V-2. While the V-2 was not particularly cost-effective, it did provide a means of delivering explosives that, unlike aircraft, could not be shot down. Rockets extended the bombardment capability offered by artillery and aircraft. This role developed rapidly during the Second World War, but came to full fruition during the Cold War with the marriage of rockets and nuclear warheads, which solved the problem of cost-inefficiency and prompted a massive development of missiles by the Soviet Union, the US and other states.

Rocket technology was mainly for military purposes. However, space science developed a significant commercial sector around communications, navigation and related civilian purposes. Military dominance of rocketry remains, but is currently declining in significance. Recent developments towards space tourism, combined with other civilian uses, are making rocket technology increasingly dual-use.

Nuclear weapons arose from scientific breakthroughs in physics during the 1930s combined with the desire to develop fission bombs during the Second World War. The use of nuclear weapons against Japan in 1945 marked a step-level change in available powers of destruction. While the shift to industrial military technologies during the nineteenth century made available the unprecedented amounts of destructive power demonstrated during the First World War, military force was still a scarce commodity that needed to be carefully marshalled. Nuclear explosives unleashed a surplus capacity of destructive power, shifting the strategic imperative from how best to use such weapons to how to avoid fighting an all-out war with them. The marriage of nuclear weapons to increasingly accurate long-range missiles during the 1950s, and the intrinsic difficulty of building anti-missile defences, meant that the entire surface of the planet fell within range of weapons of mass destruction that could be delivered within half an hour (Buzan, 1987). The accumulation by the two superpowers (and a few other states) of tens of thousands of such warheads meant that, for the first time, humankind acquired the capability to commit species suicide. Although there was some thinking about using nuclear explosives for geo-engineering projects (such as digging canals), these were not implemented – the technology of nuclear explosives remains exclusively military.

This ongoing, often dramatic process of technological innovation has transformed both the nature of war, and the operation and structure of military organizations. The fact that technological innovation runs in both directions, civil to military and military to civil, reinforces the innovation process, especially in those states with responsive market mechanisms. Several of the innovations discussed above have moved military relations into a new dimension. The shift to global modernity has so far extended the military domain from two dimensions (land and sea surface) to six: submarines added the depths of the oceans; aircraft added the atmospheric envelope above the surface of the planet; satellites added earth orbital space; and digital technology added the virtual domain of cyberspace. Nuclear weapons did not add a new domain, but did transform the availability of destructive power, thereby changing the purpose and logic of war. The greater range, reach and scope of these weapons have transformed the geography of war, surmounting many barriers of distance and terrain, and opening up new strategic opportunities and dangers.

Global modernity has also transformed the military itself, not least by forcing its differentiation into domain-specific branches. During the twentieth century, the army and navy had to make way for a new service, the air force, as well as many new sub-branches. This brought with it modern problems of bureaucratization, inter-service rivalry and (lack of) interoperability. Military operations became considerably more complex, whether in the fields of logistics, strategic planning or battle management. New weapons make old weapons obsolete, as well as the tactics and strategies associated with them. The coming of iron and steam warships, for example, made centuries of experience associated with naval logistics and warfare under sail obsolete at a stroke. Machine guns, artillery, barbed wire and tanks likewise made horse cavalry obsolete, although this lesson took a long time to learn. Nuclear weapons arguably made all-out great power wars obsolete. At least in the West, they also opened the way for much greater civilian involvement in military and strategic thinking, both because they depended on scientists, and because the military could claim no expertise in how best to use them when they made war-avoidance the main priority (Buzan and Hansen, 2009).

Rapid and continuous military innovation, partly linked to innovations in civilian technology, partly with a specific military focus, is therefore a distinctive feature of global modernity. It first manifested in the mid-nineteenth century and has remained a core characteristic of military relations ever since. It underpinned three new problems of military relations. First, there was both the hope of gaining a rapid technological advantage and the fear of being caught at a strategically decisive disadvantage – these problems generated qualitative arms racing and arms control. Second, and related to this point, there was the concern that great power status could only be sustained by keeping up with new weaponry. Any failure to stay at the leading edge of military modernity would likely result in the loss of relative military power and status, and carry with it the danger of being defeated by rivals equipped with more potent weapons. Third, in some minds at least, routine escalations in destructive capabilities raised fears of military capabilities outrunning prudent policy-making and undermining the functionality of war.

Permanent Qualitative Arms Racing

Qualitative arms racing was certainly not unknown within earlier periods of world history. From iron swords (versus copper or bronze ones),

Figure 8.2: The Japanese super-battleship *Yamato*

through the chariot and the compound bow, to the gunpowder and guns already mentioned, military relations were periodically affected by qualitative innovations. But these were usually slow moving and infrequent. Quantity still mattered in the industrial era, but it was now accompanied by a strong qualitative element substantially based on technological innovation. In the military domain, the process of innovation generates two distinct cycles: first, the improvement of existing types; and, second, the displacement of existing types by new weapons. Both can be illustrated by elaborating further on the discussion of battleships begun above. The pictures in Figure 8.1 demonstrate a dramatic improvement in warships, culminating in the 1906 *Dreadnought*. The innovation in battleship technology continued for another 50 years with continuous improvements in size, speed, weaponry and armour. Perhaps the most spectacular battleships ever built were the Japanese *Yamato* class in the 1940s (see Figure 8.2).

Even a crude, like-for-like comparison of the *Yamato* with the *Dreadnought* (Table 8.1), leaving out radar, ship-carried aircraft,

Table 8.1: *Comparing the* Dreadnought *and* Yamato

	Dreadnought (1906)	*Yamato* (1940)
Displacement	17,000 tons	64,000 tons
Length	527 feet	839 feet
Speed	21 knots	27 knots
Main armament	10 × 12 inch guns	9 × 18 inch guns
Thickness of armour	3–12 inches	8–26 inches

secondary armament and other technologies not present on the latter, demonstrates the rapid nature of qualitative improvement.

Despite these increased capabilities, during the Second World War battleships proved vulnerable to attack by both aircraft and submarines. Many, including the *Yamato*, were sunk by bomb and torpedo, and few got the chance to engage with each other unmediated by aircraft (the *Bismarck*'s famous sinking of HMS *Hood* being one of the few exceptions). The place of battleships as the centrepiece of naval power was taken by aircraft carriers and nuclear-powered submarines, illustrating the second cycle of displacement as newer weapons succeeded older types. In contemporary navies, guns have been reduced to a vestigial role, largely replaced by missiles. How much longer aircraft carriers, or indeed any type of large surface vessel, can be defended against attack by long-range missiles and torpedoes is a question for navies everywhere.

Since the Second World War the costs of advanced weapons have been far more extreme than those for the early battleships. Since the 1950s, annual cost escalation rates for amphibious ships, surface combatants, attack submarines and nuclear aircraft carriers have ranged from 7–11%; during the same period, the annual cost escalation for US fighter aircraft has been circa 10% (Arena et al., 2006: xiv and 2008: 11). These figures compare with a general inflation rate (CPI) of 4.3%. A US nuclear attack submarine cost $484 million in 1967, but $2,427 million in 2005 (in 2005 US$) (Arena et al., 2006: 1). In a landmark article, Augustine (1975: 35–6) argued that the cost inflation in weapons would mean that, within a few decades, even the US would only be able to afford one plane, one tank and one ship. He noted that, between the First World War and the mid-1970s, the price of a tank had increased by a factor of 100 and that of a fighter aircraft by a factor of 1,000. Kolodziej (1987: 141–2) cites similar levels of inflation in military costs, supporting Augustine's concerns by noting how procurement numbers drop in inverse relation to a rise in unit costs. Arguably, both military aircraft and tanks, despite all their improvements, are on the brink of displacement. Tanks, like the battleship, are coming under pressure as it becomes more difficult to defend them against attack from lighter, cheaper infantry weapons. Long-range missiles have displaced many, though not all, of the functions of bombers, and anti-aircraft missiles have displaced some of the functions of fighters. Many types of manned military aircraft are coming under pressure from robotic drones.

The twin dynamics of improvements within type and displacement of existing types are defining features of the military component of global modernity. They operate both because of general advances in technology and because states seek an edge over their enemies and rivals. This means that standing still is not an option. Military forces that are not regularly upgraded will be ineffective against those that are upgraded, even in the absence of intentional arms racing. There is, therefore, a persistent technological pressure built into the military relations of global modernity. Such pressure was present during the earlier periods of world history, but it operated both slowly and sporadically, and did not generally dominate military power or political-military relations. This novel pressure can be accelerated by intense rivalries in which opponents actively try to accelerate military technological advance and deployment, as was the case between the US and the Soviet Union. But the general dynamic associated with permanent technological advances cannot be stopped.

Under conditions of global modernity, therefore, both the maintenance of the military status quo and arms racing are marked by qualitative improvements in military technology. There will always be opportunities to improve existing types of weapons. Quite regularly, there will also be opportunities to develop new types of weapons that displace older arsenals. These critical junctures can destabilize military relations by decisively altering the balance of military power. That was, and up to a point still is, the main driver behind the pursuit of anti-ballistic missile technologies. A cost-effective breakthrough in this area would render attack by long-range missiles obsolete, so offering an escape from the 'mutually assured destruction' logic of each side being vulnerable to attack by the nuclear-armed missiles of the other.

A sharp, sudden improvement to an existing type of weapon might also significantly alter the military balance. HMS *Dreadnought* was designed to do precisely this. By mounting ten heavy guns as opposed to the four typical of its predecessors, the ship was said to be worth three to five 'pre-dreadnought' battleships, thus rendering them obsolete. A similar effect can be seen in the move from propeller to jet-driven fighter aircraft in the mid-1940s. The twin cycles of improvement and displacement point to qualitative arms racing as a signature feature of the military relations of modernity. These cycles do not themselves mark changes in the prevailing mode of power. Rather, they mark increments, and sometimes jumps, of significant changes within the military sector that are linked to the new mode of power ushered in by the global transformation.

The historic turn to qualitative arms racing as a permanent feature of modern great power relations became visible during the 1840s, when the shift from wood and sail to iron and steam generated arguably the first modern qualitative industrial arms racing dynamics between Britain and France (Brodie, 1941: 38–85). Against the generally conservative British navy, with its huge investment in wood and sail, the French pushed the use of shell-firing guns (which were very effective against wooden ships), steam-powered warships (freed from the vagaries of the wind and tide) and armour plate (at least initially effective against shell fire). The French ambition was to use new technologies to offset the larger size of the British navy (Black, 2009: 57, 80–3). At the same time, the British feared that possession of a handful of the most modern warships could give France the ability to defeat a larger, but less modern, British navy, and so gain control of the English Channel. Given Britain's relatively weak army, this spurred both invasion panics and British naval innovation. The rivalry was more or less concluded by the launching of the French ironclad battleship *La Gloire* in 1859 (to which HMS *Warrior* was the reply). This played into Britain's relative advantage in iron and steam technology, with which France could not compete. Alongside companion advances in technology (steel, steam engines, explosives), this rivalry helped to propel the rapid development of steam and steel battleships discussed above. This first demonstration of the action–reaction dynamics of industrial arms racing set the pattern for all those that followed.

The same logic was replicated in the better-known Anglo-German naval race, which accelerated following the entry into service of the

Figure 8.3: The super-dreadnought HMS *Warspite* (1913)

Dreadnought in 1906. Although Britain had a comfortable lead over Germany in pre-dreadnought battleships, the launch of the *Dreadnought* rebooted the naval race between the two. The Germans converted their existing fleet-building programme into dreadnought-building. The race that ensued was concerned primarily with ensuring that Germany did not overtake Britain. By 1912, Germany had effectively lost the race to superior British dreadnought-building capacity. By the time of the First World War, 'super-dreadnoughts' such as HMS *Warspite* (see Figure 8.3) were twice the tonnage of the original *Dreadnought* and carried bigger 15-inch main guns instead of the 12-inch guns found in the first-generation dreadnoughts.[4]

The arms race between Britain and Germany did much to poison relations between the two countries in the run-up to the First World War (Marder, 1961). But although this arms race is generally understood as being one of the main causes of the First World War, its larger significance is as the first recognized major qualitative arms race of modernity in a key strategic weapons system.

---

[4] A move from 12-inch to 15-inch guns may not sound like much, but the key is in the weight and, therefore, power of the shells, where the move is from 517 kg to 879 kg, an increase of nearly 60%. A 16-inch shell weighs 1,225 kg, an 18-inch one 1,460 kg. See: http://pwencycl.kgbudge.com/G/u/Gun_Specifications.htm.

There is a close family resemblance between early qualitative naval arms races in the nineteenth century (and their equivalents for the weapons of armies in terms of improved artillery, infantry weapons and machine guns) and the arms races of the twentieth and twenty-first centuries. The same qualitative technological cycles of improvement and displacement marked the bomber, ballistic missile and anti-ballistic missile races during the Cold War, and the nascent rivalry currently underway between the US and China over control of the 'high frontier' in earth orbit, and the 'low' one in the East and South China Seas. This aspect of the global transformation put in place the pressure that remains central to the military life of great powers: to keep up with, and preferably lead, qualitative improvements in weapons systems. Achieving this can be done either by investing in military research and development or, for lesser powers, by buying the latest weapons from those that produce them. Failure to follow either strategy means exit from the ranks of significant military powers and vulnerability to defeat in war by better-equipped forces.

Arms Control

The qualitative element in military power that emerged as a major feature of the global transformation also opened up the general issue of what is now known as arms control: the process of attempting to restrict the manufacture, possession, deployment and/or use of specific types of weapons (Buzan, 1987: 227–88). Although the necessary condition for arms control – continuous innovation in military technology – was established during the nineteenth century, the actual practice of arms control among the great powers was slow to follow. One reason for this was that the nineteenth-century peace amongst the Western great powers meant that there were no major wars to expose the full potential of new military technologies. This great power peace was, for the most part, based on the capacity of Western powers to expand their empires into Africa and Asia. It was not until the First World War that the full horrors and potentials of industrial warfare became widely apparent, although they had been partially previewed during the Crimean War (1853–6), the Taiping Rebellion (1850–71) and the American Civil War (1861–5). The latter, for example, mobilized half of all white male Americans, of which a third lost their lives; the direct costs of the war are estimated at $6.6 billion (Belich, 2009: 331; see also Gray, 2012: ch. 4).

Nevertheless, the First Geneva Convention of 1864 and, later, the Hague Conventions of 1899 and 1907 (discussed in Chapter 7) contained a series of arms control measures that reflected responses to new military technologies. In conflicts between 'civilized' states, they banned bullets that flattened in the body (building on an earlier agreement on the non-use of so-called 'dum dum' bullets at the 1868 St Petersburg Conference), bombing from various kinds of aircraft, and the use of gases as weapons. They also restricted the deployment of mines and torpedoes. These agreements were the forerunners of later arms control and disarmament measures running from the Washington Naval Treaty (1922), which restricted the deployment of major warships, to the Nuclear Non-Proliferation Treaty (1968), and the various strategic arms agreements between the US and the Soviet Union during the Cold War. As noted in earlier chapters, nineteenth-century arms control agreements were, in part, a response to the activities of social movements (Clark, 2007: 61–82), foreshadowing the twentieth century's mass peace movements in favour of disarmament, arms control and the peaceful settlement of international disputes.

Along with qualitative arms racing, arms control also has its roots in the nineteenth-century global transformation (Shaw, 2002). Arms control was – and is – as much about restraining qualitative improvements in military technology, whether this was found in battleships, nuclear weapons or anti-ballistic missile technologies, as it was about restricting quantitative build-up. There were various motivations for this: preventing unnecessary expenditures and/or avoiding intense development and deployment rivalries (e.g. limits on battleship, intercontinental ballistic missile – ICBM – and warhead numbers); avoiding qualitative developments and deployments that might destabilize military relations or increase the risk of war (e.g. limiting the deployment of anti-ballistic missile (ABM) systems and space-based weaponry); and placing humanitarian markers against weapons that were considered to be beyond the pale (e.g. dum dum bullets, chemical and biological weapons, land mines). Also shared between the nineteenth century and contemporary international society is the contradiction between controlling arms on the one hand, and the tendencies of capitalism to diffuse innovation through trade, technology transfer and copying/stealing, on the other. As we noted in Chapter 6, Western powers were keen to keep modern weapons out of the hands of their colonial subjects. But arms manufacturers wanted to sell their weapons as widely as possible – in the post-mortems following the First World War, this earned them the label 'merchants of death' (Engelbrecht and Hanighen, 1934). Arms dealers were not above stoking up conflicts in order to expand their markets, selling expensive dreadnought battleships to Greece and the Ottoman Empire while they were at loggerheads with each other, as well as to rival South American states such as Argentina and Brazil.

Great Power Relations

A major consequence of this military transformation was, for a time, nearly to eliminate non-Western states as great powers or, to put this more precisely, to eliminate as great powers those polities that did not possess the new mode of power. By the end of the nineteenth century only the Ottoman Empire still retained great power status outside the core of Western states and, even then, the Ottomans held the title 'the sick man of Europe'. After a string of defeats by Russia, the Ottoman Empire had symbolic rather than practical status as a great power, dependent on support from Britain and other European great powers who saw it as a buffer against Russian expansionism. Japan, China and India had all been demoted, though of course Japan, as discussed in Chapter 7, soon returned to the ranks of the great powers. Indeed, the continuous change in the leading edge of military technology made it easier for new entrants like Germany, the US and Japan to acquire modern weapons without having to overcome the quantitative advantages in older types of weapons held by existing great powers (Brodie, 1941: 256–7).

The relative decline of Russia, Austria-Hungary and the Ottoman Empire during the later decades of the nineteenth century was a consequence of their relative lack of success in adapting to the global transformation. In this way, the nineteenth century pioneered the close link between great power standing on the one hand, and early, late and later developers on the other (Rosenberg, 2013). Successful adoption of the global transformation shaped entry into, and exit from, great power status (Hobsbawm, 1975: 94–102). This general process was far more important than specific instances of it, such as the rise of Germany. Important though the question of Germany's rise was – and is – for world history, it is just one example of a recurrent pattern established in the nineteenth century and maintained ever since: all rising powers are 'a problem' for all status quo ones, and vice versa.

How states stand in relation to each other in the context of global modernity is crucial in this regard. Over the past two centuries, Britain, Germany, Japan and Russia have risen and declined; the US has risen and, so far, held. In the contemporary world, these dynamics are continuing. As discussed in Chapter 7, China and India are closing the military power gap with the West. As they do so, it is not clear how much longer the US can maintain its hegemonic position. The rise of China, and the angst in the US about its primacy being challenged, are the latest iteration of the distinctive link between modernity and the instability of great power relations. The qualification for great power status established in the nineteenth century is what still determines both the power politics of modernity, and the 'polarity' and 'power transition' debates of the twentieth and twenty-first centuries.

The initial narrowing of the ranks of great powers to include only those with the new mode of power was a central aspect of the construction of a core–periphery global order discussed in Chapter 6. At the same time as narrowing the circle of great powers, the industrialization of military power destabilized relations among them by making relative power dependent on a rapidly changing portfolio of new technologies and their military applications. As set out in the previous section, great powers had to be able to produce their own modern weapons and keep up with the pace of technological change (Krause, 1992: 28). The rise into, and decline out of, the ranks of great powers could, and in some cases did, happen quickly as states took on, or failed to take on, the various aspects of the global transformation necessary for generating modern military power. At the same time, technological innovations destabilized relations even amongst great powers. The first to make a breakthrough to armoured warships, dreadnoughts, tanks, jet fighters, nuclear weapons or an effective anti-ballistic missile shield could obtain a temporary, but potentially decisive, military advantage over others. With the shift to global modernity, these innovations became fast, frequent and permanent. As a British MP speaking in 1864 about the naval developments sketched earlier in this chapter put it (in Brodie, 1941: 205):

The science of naval architecture and construction changes and progresses at so great a rate, that if we take ... three years to build an armour plated ship – I will not say that the ship will be obsolete when she is completed, but most undoubtedly we shall have commenced the construction of vessels which she could not venture to meet with any chance of success.

Fear of these qualitative military dynamics, and/or ambition based on them, became a notable feature of great power relations from the 1840s onwards. It forged the distinctly modern form of power politics that remains in place today.

The global transformation of the nineteenth century thus gave birth to the central military *problématique* of modernity that has obsessed IR, and more particularly the sub-field of Strategic/Security Studies: how to conduct military relations under conditions of permanent and rapid technological innovation. This *problématique* has two aspects. The most obvious, and the first to emerge, was how individual states could stay at the cutting edge of innovation so as to make themselves powerful and secure. It was abundantly clear, not least from Europe's nineteenth-century encounters in Africa, the Middle East and Asia, that falling behind meant both relegation from the ranks of great powers and military vulnerability to leading-edge polities. Here the main impetus was how to combat the fear of defeat under the new conditions imposed by global modernity. The second dynamic, to be discussed in the next section, was the increasing cost and danger of both preparing for, and fighting, great power wars.

Undermining the Functionality of War

As technological innovation unfolded, weapons became ever more powerful, destructive and costly.[5] This raised what might be called the *defence dilemma* (Buzan, 2007 [1991]: 217–33), in which fear of defeat was challenged by fear of military competition (because of its expense and its treadmill quality) and fear of war (because rising costs and destructiveness combined with ever more intense mobilizations of society, meaning that societies might be destroyed by the process of war regardless of whether they won or lost). The First World War was a catastrophe for all the states that engaged in it, apart from the US and Japan. Although it was still better to have won than to have lost, two empires (Ottoman and Austro-Hungarian) were removed from the

---

[5] The (in)famous 'weapons lethality index' ranks a longbow at 34, an eighteenth-century flintlock musket at 150, a First World War rifle at 13,000, and a Second World War machine gun at 68,000 (Robinson, 1978: 44–5). On this scale, an eighteenth-century 12 pounder field gun ranks 4,000, a modern howitzer 3,500,000, a heavy bomber with conventional weapons 210,000,000, and an ICBM with a one megaton nuclear warhead 210,000,000,000.

map, a third (Russian) underwent a social revolution, and the 'winners' (Britain and France) suffered huge casualties and economic forfeiture. The advent of nuclear weapons at the end of the Second World War merely made the defence dilemma incontrovertible: nuclear war could destroy all human life on the planet. Winning such a war would be meaningless, which meant that great power war no longer served as a rational policy instrument.

The defence dilemma was slower to become visible than the fear of defeat as a result of falling behind in military technology. The general peace within the West in the nineteenth century, during which Western powers busied themselves with core–periphery expansionism rather than core–core conflicts (Darwin, 2007: 222–37), meant that the full impact of industrialization on war was slow to become visible. To be sure, the impact of industrial weaponry on core–periphery relations was easily visible and, as noted in previous chapters, widely celebrated in the public life of colonial powers as a mark of cultural and racial superiority (Black, 2009: 196–7). The relatively swift wars around German uni-fication suggested the increasing importance of cutting-edge weaponry and modes of organization. So too did the Russo-Japanese war, which produced a quick and decisive outcome, and underlined the importance of logistics, especially railways, and the superiority of big guns in naval warfare (providing the lessons that produced HMS *Dreadnought*). Among the conflicts of the nineteenth century, the US Civil War offered a glimpse of the impact of industrialization on war: barbed wire, trenches, railways, armoured steam-powered warships, mass mobiliza-tion, long duration and high casualties.

The Great War of 1914–18 was the culmination of the uneven and combined development of global modernity (Rosenberg, 2013), and the industrialization of violence that had been unfolding for more than eight decades. Many of the weapons with which it was fought – dreadnoughts, submarines, tanks, poison gas, fighters, bombers and Zeppelins – had seldom, if ever, been used in major wars before. The generals did not know how to fight trench warfare, having prepared for a quick war of manoeuvre along the lines of the Franco-Prussian conflict of 1870. The First World War brought down empires, bankrupted great powers, fermented revolutions and produced unprecedented levels of destruction. To many it seemed that industrial war had outgrown the states that fought it, threatening to destroy European civilization itself. The slogan of 'the war to end war' was an attempt to conceptualize a conflict whose costs and casualties far exceeded any of the initial justifications for going to war. The Second World War replayed the pattern of new weaponry, vast costs and casualties, and political upheavals, and extended the range of destruction greatly through the use of mass bombing from the air. Its culmination in the use of nuclear weapons against Japan reinforced the thinking that powers of destruction had escalated beyond the point where they made great power wars rational. The risk was that there would be no meaningful winners, only a collection of devastated losers.

From the First World War onwards, therefore, the new mode of power opened up the defence dilemma. The defence dilemma created by the First World War was not strong or pervasive enough to prevent the Second World War, although it did play a role in Britain's war avoidance policy during the 1930s. It did not entirely remove the risk of war during the Cold War, but the doomsday logic of nuclear weapons made war avoidance a much stronger and more pervasive element (Mandelbaum, 1998/9). Five lines of analysis feed into the logic of the defence dilemma.

First is the historical memory of hugely destructive wars. This is strongest in Europe and Japan, where the damage was high, several countries were big losers, and even winners like Britain and France lost relative wealth and power. It is weaker in the US, which suffered much less, and was a big winner in terms of relative wealth and power. Historical memory seems to have had relatively little impact elsewhere, even in places such as Iran and Iraq, where mass casualty warfare has been felt quite recently. Both Russia and China suffered hugely during the Second World War, but like the US see themselves as winners who were empowered by their victory.

Second is the rising cost-ineffectiveness of war as a policy option. A case could be made that, up to 1945, world war remained a viable and rational option even given advances in military technologies. The Axis powers gambled losing a percentage of their population, wealth, status and territory against the possibility of becoming superpowers. They lost, but the big winners, the US and the Soviet Union, did become superpowers. As noted above, with the advent of nuclear weapons, the game of 'superpower chicken' ran a high risk that both players would drive their cars over the cliff.

Third is the fear that the modern destructiveness of war threatens the survival of the human species. At the height of the Cold War, the combined arsenals of the superpowers numbered many tens of thousands of warheads. If all of them had been used, the blast damage, fires and radioactive fallout might have extinguished human life. The possibility of such a conflagration generating a 'nuclear winter' by filling the atmosphere with smoke and dust underlined the point that the military technologies arising from modernity had provided humankind with the capacity to make itself extinct (Sagan, 1983/4). An all-out Third World War with nuclear weapons would make that self-extinction the principal consequence of the global transformation.

Fourth is the fear that the increasing technicalization of war undermines democratic control of it. In the early stages of industrial warfare, mass conscript armies made the state dependent on its citizens to go to war. Despite greater civilian involvement in deterrence strategy, nuclear weapons began to erode this dependence, because the possible need for rapid response against a first strike concentrated powers of decision within a small elite. By the 1970s, the professionalization of the military required to keep up with high-tech weaponry was eroding the conscript military, again disconnecting the use of force from wider publics. The latest development in this trend is the increasing application of robotics to weaponry, which moves policy-making around the use of force into the hands of elites, or conceivably, as is already the case in aspects of financial markets, into the hands of computer algorithms.

Fifth is the fear that the increasing technicalization of war will raise the possibility of unwanted or accidental war. New military technologies have compressed time and added to pressures on decision-makers. Within IR, this first became visible in the run-up to the First World War, for example in the ways that German decision-makers were pressured by railway timetables and the need to mobilize more rapidly than Russia if they were to avoid having to fight Russia and France at the same time. The Cuban missile crisis also provided a graphic demonstration of such time pressures, with very short missile flight times requiring fast decisions about how to respond before an attack crippled the decision-making process (Kennedy, 1969; Allison, 1971; Loth, 2014: 101–4). At the height of the Cold War, the attack warning systems of the two superpowers had become so automated and so interlocked as to raise fears that false readings could trigger dangerous and mutually reinforcing escalations, something that nearly took place on more than one occasion (Schlosser, 2013). After the end of the Cold War, this danger receded because there was no longer any need to keep nuclear weapons systems on a high stage of alert.

Although the twentieth century was marked by extreme warfare, both inflicted and threatened, it nonetheless saw a shift from great power war as a normal feature of interstate relations to great power war as a rare, last resort, or arguably an extinct practice. Key to this shift is the industrialization of violence, with its increased capacity for destruction unleashed by modernity, and the rising costs of both acquiring and using such weapons. The step-level change in destructive capability made by nuclear weapons made this logic obvious to all, but it was merely a dramatic manifestation of an underlying trend that became significant as early as the First World War.

Conclusion

The military relations of the global transformation were a central aspect of the new mode of power that came into being during the long nineteenth century and that still shapes core components of IR's contemporary agenda. First, the interrelationship between military relations and the new mode of power opened up a massive gap between the core and the periphery. This fed into inter-imperial competition in which overseas empires became part of the measure of great power standing. Down this path lay latecomer claims to 'a place in the sun' and the imperial rivalries that helped pave the way to the First and Second World Wars. Second, military modernity destabilized great power relations both by changing the criteria for attaining great power status and by inserting into great power relations a continuous qualitative arms dynamic. Third, the escalation in the cost and destructive capacity of weapons introduced the defence dilemma into international relations, moving war (especially great power war) from the centre to the margins of foreign policy options.

Seeing these three impacts as downstream consequences of the global transformation opens up a useful optic on issues in contemporary international relations. For one thing, it provides a common foundation for two dynamics that are usually dealt with separately in IR: the inequality between core and periphery on the one hand, and the volatility of great power relations within the core on the other. Both owe their origins to the global transformation. Seeing these dynamics as offshoots drawn from the same root is particularly important now that they are merging. The relative levelling off of power asymmetries noted in Chapter 7 means that what has been the periphery for nearly two centuries is once again becoming the home of great powers.

As global modernity extends, the power gap between core and periphery will matter less, and the core will expand. But while the problems of core–periphery inequality that were a feature of the last two centuries will have lower salience in years to come, the problems that military modernity posed for the core will not only remain, but also apply to a wider circle of powers. This is already apparent in the rise of China, a former peripheral state now widely seen as the principal challenger to the status of the US as the sole superpower. To some extent, the qualitative arms dynamic and the defence dilemma are beginning to govern this relationship. China is trying to strengthen its air, sea and space denial capabilities, while the US is trying to maintain its technological lead and its ability to project force and surveillance into China's region. At the same time, both because of their economic interdependence and shared fear of nuclear war, China and the US are keen to avoid outright military conflict.

As the differences between the former core and the former periphery even out, major technological differentiation of the kind that dominated core–periphery relations over the past two centuries will be further eroded. This process is perhaps most apparent in the slow but steady proliferation of nuclear weapons. Massive military inequality will be replaced by the more core-like dynamics of the past two centuries, in which technological competition takes place within a narrower range of policy options. As the current lead of the US in military technology shows, and as it has demonstrated in several conflicts, there will still be asymmetries of power. But the dynamics of the global transformation indicate that this gap will tend to narrow. As it does so, quantitative factors from population to numbers of weapons will reassert their influence. Big populations will once again be a major determinant of power, just as they were before the advent of modernity. That is why the discourse around the 'rise of the rest' is focused on China and India, and why the projected shrinking populations of Germany, Japan and Russia are reducing their influence in international affairs.

The closing of the power gap between core and periphery will raise the prominence of the power politics of global modernity with its continuous destabilization through technological innovation. That dynamic, however, will take place alongside the other core military dynamic resulting from the mode of power unleashed by global modernity – the defence dilemma – and its challenge to the functionality of war. The kind of world towards which this points is the subject of Chapter 9.

PART III

Implications

The configuration of industrialization, the rational state and ideologies of progress we have highlighted in previous chapters brought global modernity into being. It continues to serve as the basis for many aspects of contemporary international relations, shedding light on issues ranging from intervention to the changing nature of warfare. The contemporary world order is a historically specific configuration formed in the convulsions of the global transformation that became the dominant force in world politics during the nineteenth century. Future historians are likely to look back on the nineteenth, twentieth and twenty-first centuries as a single transformative period, examining the ways in which global modernity reconfigured social relations on a planetary scale. Because we make these observations from within this transformational process, it is difficult to know what conclusions future commentators will draw about when, or if, this transformation settled into a durable form. Thus while we can identify significant stages within the transformation process, we cannot say definitively whether that process is ongoing or over. The agrarian revolution took several thousand years before it settled into the classical world of city-states, kingdoms and empires that lasted for at least five millennia. The impact of the revolutions of modernity has been much quicker than previous macro-transformations. But whether they have reached a point of maturity or have instead generated a period of 'permanent revolution' is, as yet, unclear.

This final section of the book draws out the implications of the global transformation's first two centuries for the theory and practice of IR. Chapter 9 explores the main contours of the decentred global order that is emerging as the spread of the modern mode of power closes the gap that opened up during the nineteenth century. Chapter 10 looks at the consequences for IR of seeing the global transformation as the main determinant of contemporary international order.

9 | *From 'Centred Globalism' to 'Decentred Globalism'*

Introduction

We have argued that contemporary international order can be seen largely, although not completely, in terms of the downstream consequences of the configuration of power that fuelled global modernity. This argument implies that historical momentum (or 'path dependency' in more formal expression) matters a great deal to how the contemporary world is organized. Historical momentum represents an array of often contradictory events and does not infer an ability to predict the future. Human affairs are both complex and contingent – they are the quintessential 'open system'. Historical development is also subject to unpredictable, random events. Just think of the Cuban missile crisis, or what would happen if celestial mechanics pushed a large asteroid in our direction, or if machine intelligence emerged out of the geometric increases in computing power. The scope for human agency, random events and non-linear interactions is extensive.

Although we are not, therefore, in the predictions business, we do want to look forward and consider how the main vectors of the global transformation could play out. Some of the themes we have highlighted in earlier chapters are about change (e.g. the closing gap between core and periphery), while others are about continuity (e.g. the destabilizing impact of technological change on great power military relations). As developed in Chapters 6 and 7, we see three main stages within the global transformation to date. The first stage was *Western-colonial* international society, which lasted from the late eighteenth century until *c.*1945. The second stage was *Western-global* international society, which lasted from the end of the Second World War until the first decade of the twenty-first century. Both of these stages represented forms of *centred globalism*, with 'centred' meaning that development was highly uneven, with a mainly Western core dominant, and 'globalism' meaning that international order was combined on a planetary scale. Our label for the third stage of global modernity is *decentred globalism*. 'Decentred' refers to the ways in which the configuration that marks the global transformation is no longer concentrated in a small group of states, but is increasingly dispersed. Globalism marks both a basic continuity and an intensification of earlier phases of the global transformation in which the configuration of modernity assumes planetary scale. In the contemporary world, the mode of power that underpinned global modernity is both less unevenly concentrated and more combined than in previous stages of global modernity.

Our argument about the historical momentum of the global transformation can be summarized as follows:

- A global transformation emerged during the long nineteenth century and is still unfolding. During this period, a configuration of industrialization, rational statehood and ideologies of progress constituted a new mode of power that, in turn, established a new framework for how international relations was practised and conceived.

- This global transformation generated a new type of polity, a new form of political economy, and a variety of new actors including IGOs, INGOs and transnational corporations. It also destabilized great power relations and, as the new mode of power evolved, undermined much of the functionality of war.

- The global transformation was underpinned by a distinctive set of ideologies of progress. The tensions and interplay among and within these ideologies, and also between them and earlier symbolic schemas, still dominate much of the thinking and practice of international relations.

- The global transformation established massive, still ongoing, increases in both physical and social interaction capacity that generated an increasingly interdependent international order. Initially, the global transformation produced a highly unequal core–periphery international order. As global modernity intensified, the gap between core and periphery narrowed, first slowly and then more quickly. By the first decade of the twenty-first century, the modern mode of power was becoming more dispersed – the current international order is marked by decentred globalism.

Because we are within the transition to decentred globalism, it is difficult to assign a precise tipping point for the shift from Western-global
international society to decentred globalism. In other work, we have
argued that the onset of the global economic crisis in 2008 marked a
significant way-station within this process (Buzan and Lawson, 2014a:
457). In this chapter, we maintain the view that 2008 constitutes a
critical juncture after which the global distribution of power is evening
out. More generally, this chapter explores the main dimensions of the
emergent condition of decentred globalism. We examine the prospects
for cooperation and conflict within decentred globalism, as well as 'wild
cards' that might derail current trends. The final section establishes four
principles for the pursuit of international order under conditions of
decentred globalism.

The Material Conditions of Decentred Globalism

Since it is difficult to imagine further major breakthroughs in physical
interaction capacity, we expect future years to see only marginal
improvements in the ability to move goods, information and people
around the planet. Cost-efficiencies might improve with new technologies and there will certainly be major intensifications as the internet and
related technologies spread more widely and deeply. But for general
purposes, the current speeds and ranges of aircraft, ships and railways
are unlikely to increase greatly. The international system will remain
highly interdependent – in fact, it is likely to become ever more so. But
there will probably not be any breakthrough developments that have an
impact comparable to that of the first steamships, railways, telegraphs
and long-range jet aircraft.

If interaction capacity is largely a story of more of the same plus
intensification, the analysis of previous chapters opens up the possibility
of four major changes to the material conditions of contemporary
international society: the core will grow in relation to the periphery;
the distribution of power will become more dispersed; the regional level
of international relations will rise in importance; and the *problématique*
of interstate violence will no longer occupy such a central place within
international relations.

First, more states and peoples will acquire the configuration of power
associated with global modernity. The core will become both bigger
(absolutely and relatively) and less Western. Japan and the Asian Tigers

will no longer be exceptions; their experience will become the norm. The link between race and development first broken by Japan will increasingly fall away. At the same time, it seems likely that parts of Eastern and Southern Europe will either remain, or become, relatively underdeveloped compared to a more globally distributed leading edge. The periphery will shrink, but not disappear. The configuration of power that sustains global modernity is a destabilizing force that sets considerable challenges to states everywhere (Zarakol, 2011). As discussed in Chapter 5, over the past two centuries, many states have met these challenges through carrying out (often authoritarian) programmes of 'modernization'. Others have experienced some kind of revolutionary upheaval. The tensions between these dynamics are laid bare by the Arab uprisings of 2011, in which most elites in North Africa and the Middle East found a means by which to contain the challenges posed by their publics, often through violent repression. The turbulence that marked these uprisings illustrates the disruptive pressures that the configuration of global modernity continues to place on social orders around the world.

Second, and related to this point, *among* states (though not necessarily or even probably *within* them – more on this below) the distribution of power in the contemporary world will become less uneven and more diffuse. In general, the West will lose its privileged position in international society. This is already visible in the emergence of new sites of global governance (e.g. the G20), economic formations (e.g. the BRICs), and security institutions (e.g. the Shanghai Cooperation Organization). The evening-out of power is making it difficult for the US to hold on to its sole superpower status.

More specifically, and less obviously, this wider dispersal of power means that no state will be able to replace the US as sole, or even second, superpower. Although superpowers seem natural to modern IR, they are not. The age of superpowers was a particular consequence of the highly uneven distribution of power created by the Western-colonial phase of global modernity and sustained during its Western-global phase. During these two periods, states like Britain and the US amassed sufficient relative power to be world dominating. That level of capability is no longer possible. With many states becoming wealthy and powerful, no single polity will be able to accumulate sufficient relative power to dominate international society. Even giants such as China and India will be hemmed in both by the rise of each other and by other states. Nor are the established powers going away. There will be no modern 'fall of Rome'. The US will remain *primus inter pares* for some considerable time to come and, whatever their current troubles, the EU and Japan will remain substantial centres of power, wealth and influence. Superpowers should, therefore, be seen as a corollary of an international order defined by centred globalism. From having two superpowers in the Cold War period, we are now down to one whose position and legitimacy look increasingly tenuous. The rise (or return) of new powers will close the window in which superpowers have been a core component of international relations. The world of decentred globalism will have several great powers and many regional powers; it will not have any superpowers (Buzan, 2011).

Taken together, an expanding core and a widening diffusion of power suggest that the dominance of the West rests on increasingly thin foundations. The contemporary fascination with the rise of China, India, Brazil and other states spells the end of Western hegemony as the sources of the nineteenth-century power gap are reduced, if not completely eroded. As noted above, the West remains at the heart of the states system, retaining significant advantages in terms of power capabilities and institutional positions. But the hegemonic status of the West and its habit of claiming rights of global leadership no longer rest on the vast power superiority it enjoyed during the nineteenth and twentieth centuries. The world is returning to a more equal distribution of power akin to that which existed before the nineteenth century, except that in the twenty-first century the main centres of power are bound together in a tightly integrated international system. In this sense, the great divergence of the nineteenth century is becoming the great convergence of the twenty-first century (Darwin, 2007: 500–5).[1]

A more diffuse distribution of power and the absence of superpowers suggest that the third material feature of decentred globalism will be a world with several great powers operating in a more regionalized international order. The unnatural dominance of the US in the years following the Second World War was eroded first by the recovery of Europe and Japan, and later by the rise of both new powers (e.g. Brazil) and the revival of much older ones that had been temporarily eclipsed

---

[1] Readers interested in some striking visual representations of the shift from divergence to relative convergence should examine the wealth of maps, data and videos available at: www.gapminder.org.

by Western dominance (e.g. China and India). More recently it has been eroded by the decline of America's moral and political authority. Looking ahead, the power preponderance that enabled imperial powers to overwhelm other parts of the world during the nineteenth century is receding as global modernity expands. China is already a top-tier power and India is not far behind. There are also a number of substantial regional powers including Brazil, Turkey and Indonesia. The examples of Israel, South Africa, North Korea and Pakistan show that even quite modest powers can acquire nuclear deterrents. As several authors have suggested, these trends point to a world with a more diffuse distribution of power in which regional powers play a greater role (Kupchan, 1998 and 2012; Buzan, 2011; Acharya, 2014). The workings of the EU are one example of this shift to a more region-centred international society. Russia's annexation of Crimea in 2014, and the timid response of the West to Russia's actions, is another, altogether starker, indicator of how such a system might work.

Fourth, the spread of global modernity will both limit the cost-effectiveness of many types of war and relocate the central *problématique* of violence. By increasing the destructive capacity of weapons, most obviously, but not only, in the form of nuclear weapons, global modernity has made obsolete great power wars like those during the first part of the twentieth century. While accident and recklessness cannot be ruled out, the incentives for resort to total war amongst nuclear-armed great powers are close to zero. The spread of industrial weapons also makes wars of occupation like those of the colonial period cost-ineffective. When AK-47s, rocket-propelled grenades (RPGs) and shoulder-fired anti-aircraft weapons are ubiquitously available, sustained occupation against the will of a people is now both difficult to do and prohibitively expensive. The US discovered this in Vietnam, Iraq and Afghanistan, as did the Soviet Union in Afghanistan. The nature and availability of modern weapons will thus make marginal the traditional types of war between states that used to dominate world politics. War will not disappear, but it is no longer the driving force of great power relations and world politics that it once was.

In an international order characterized by decentred globalism, however, concern about a different species of violence is likely to become more prominent – and arguably has already done so in the current securitization of non-state actor (NSA) terrorism. This securitization has assumed renewed prominence since the 9/11 attacks on the US in

2001. But modern concerns about the dangers of terrorism can be traced back to the bombing and assassination campaigns carried out by anarchists in late nineteenth-century Europe, Bengali nationalists during the early part of the twentieth century, and those carried out by groups such as the Irish Republican Army (IRA), Euskadi Ta Askatasuna (ETA), Hamas and Hezbollah during the last quarter of the twentieth century. Despite the considerable impact of the 9/11 events, the power of NSA terrorist securitization is at first sight somewhat puzzling. First, terrorist acts have killed relatively few people when compared with other sources of death, ranging from car accidents to civil and interstate wars (Mueller and Stewart, 2012). In terms of raw numbers, terrorism is much more of a problem in the Middle East, Africa and parts of Asia than it is to people in the West. Second, there is nothing new about small groups being able to trigger large outcomes: the Russian and Cuban revolutions were initiated by a small number of committed activists, while a handful of Serbian nationalists were able to assassinate Archduke Ferdinand in Sarajevo in 1914, prompting the onset of the First World War. Third, such a focus occludes the ways in which states use terrorism for their own purposes, while at the same time, one of the consequences of the securitization of NSA terrorism is the more extensive surveillance of peoples everywhere by rational states.

These points notwithstanding, there is another driver pushing the securitization of NSA terrorism that is likely to make it a durable feature of decentred globalism: the idea that there is a dangerous conjuncture between deeply held ideologies on the one hand, and the availability of potent means of destruction on the other. On the ideological side, there is perceived to be both a *rising* degree of extremism, as underlined by instances of suicide bombing, and a *declining* degree of instrumentality in the goals of terrorist groups. In earlier periods such groups tended to fight for independence and/or a change in political system. Today, there is a concern that terrorists are unconstrained in their willingness to attack civilian targets, from marketplaces to trains and from hotels to planes. On the means of destruction side, the development and spread of applicable technologies are making powers of mass destruction available to small groups and networks (Rees, 2003). Until recently it required a substantial state to organize and command large-scale destructive technologies. In the contemporary world, it is argued that relatively small networks or even individuals can access viruses (electronic and biological), chemical weapons, and perhaps nuclear weapons (Rees, 2003). As demonstrated by the 9/11 attacks, the more integrated and interdependent infrastructure of a densely populated global economy provides a host of vulnerable targets. This offers the possibility of small terrorist groups being able to wield violence on a significant scale and pursuing targets without discriminating between combatants and non-combatants. The label 'global war on terror', however misjudged it might have been, acknowledges this perceptual shift in the *problématique* of violence.

This is also what differentiates concerns about NSA terrorism from concerns about state terrorism. States have always had access to the top-of-the-line means of destruction available at the time, and have wielded it against both state and civilian targets. Nothing has changed in this respect. NSAs have sometimes been able to exploit or trigger 'ripe' political opportunities, but they have not had access to, or the capacity to generate, the means of mass destruction. The contemporary securitization of NSA terrorism rests on the idea that such groups increasingly do, or will, have such capacity or access, and that the basic dynamic between states and terrorist organizations has therefore changed in a profound way.

The contemporary world is, therefore, witnessing a basic shift in the relationship of states and societies to the use of force. Rees (2003) is almost certainly right in thinking that the unfolding of the revolutions of modernity will continue to make large powers of destruction more easily and widely available to small groups of people. The fact that actual terrorist activity has so far been modest in its kill-rates is not, therefore, the best way to understand the force of NSA terrorist securitization. There is enough evidence that some networks are trying to get hold of mass destruction technologies to sustain political concerns (Bellany, 2007). One has only to imagine the impact of the obliteration of a city – any city, anywhere – by a terrorist nuclear attack to see why this securitization is sustained. How to govern a world where even small groups can wield large powers of destruction is not just a question of international politics, but for politics at all levels.

The Ideational Conditions of Decentred Globalism

We have argued that of the four ideologies of progress that emerged during the nineteenth century, two (liberalism and nationalism) remain potent both as ideas and in practice. One (socialism) has waned as a practice even though many of its guiding ideas and analysis remain potent. And one ('scientific' racism) has greatly diminished both as idea and practice. No new ideas of comparable weight have emerged to join them. Against this background, there are four ideational conditions that underpin decentred globalism: a relatively low degree of ideological division amongst the major powers; a shift towards geoeconomic competition rather than geopolitical conflict; a quite deep substrate of shared primary institutions; and a normative disposition towards regionalism.[2]

Reduced Ideological Divisions

Decentred globalism offers no single vision for how industrial capitalism, rational-bureaucratic states and ideologies of progress should be organized. Over the past two centuries, many forms of society have harnessed these sources of power: liberal, social democratic, socialist, colonial, post-colonial, fascist, and more. In the contemporary world, debates about how best to organize the revolutions of modernity tend to operate through attention to alternative modes of capitalist governance. As outlined in Chapter 5, following the market reforms in China in the late 1970s and the collapse of state socialism in Eastern and Central Europe between 1989 and 1991, capitalism has become pre-eminent. Almost every state organizes its economy through market logics and takes part in global regimes around trade, production and finance. China became a member of the WTO in 2001; Russia became a member in 2012. Rather than 'capitalism or not', the question in the contemporary world revolves about how to embed capitalism politically, with the main divide being between liberal and authoritarian modes of governance. We return to this point below.

As we also discussed in Chapter 5, almost every state in the contemporary world seeks to formally distinguish between states and markets. The universalization of market relations has meant a near worldwide conception of politics and economics as conceptually distinct spheres of activity. However poorly this relates to the actual experience of capitalist development and expansion, the conception of distinct spheres of

---

[2] The next sub-section and the following two draw heavily on Buzan and Lawson (2014b).

activity holds. Consequently, because China has made such strides towards accepting market conditionalities, there is much less sense of a zero-sum, existential, difference between it and the West than there was between the Soviet Union and the West, where the contestation was around the zero-sum equation of 'capitalism or not'. This points towards a future in which an array of politically diverse capitalist states both compete and cooperate with each other.

Although the universalization of capitalism has, therefore, narrowed the global ideological bandwidth, it has also meant that capitalism has become quite politically diverse. The literature on 'varieties of capitalism' stresses the importance of two modes of capitalism: 'liberal market economies' and 'coordinated market economies' (Hall and Soskice, 2001). Although based on clear empirical criteria, this typology has two faults. First, it is formed almost exclusively from the experience of Western states (McNally, 2012: 745–9). Second, the main point of differentiation does not include sufficient attention to the governance structures within which markets are embedded (Amable, 2003; Jackson and Deeg, 2006; Magaloni, 2006). We address the first of these lacunae by adding non-Western states to the analysis. We address the second through operationalizing our baseline definition of capitalism as marked by an ostensible separation between the political and economic spheres. This adds value to the economic criteria of the orthodox literature by stressing the ways in which different modes of capitalism are embedded politically. The result is not just two ideal-types of democratic capitalism (liberal and social democratic), but also two ideal-types of authoritarian capitalism (competitive authoritarian and state bureaucratic).

These four ideal-types of capitalist governance are oversimplifications intended to tease out differences for the purposes of analytical clarity and empirical comparison. They are best understood as occupying points on a continuum, one end of which is defined by the complete separation of economics and politics, the other by their complete union (see Figure 9.1). Since no known forms of capitalism meet either extreme condition, our four ideal-types do not reach either end of the spectrum. Liberal capitalism seeks to maximize economic autonomy, combine this with democratic governance and minimize the role of the state. Social democratic capitalism seeks to balance the market, the state and democracy. Competitive authoritarian capitalism favours state control over the market and constrains democratic governance. State bureaucratic capitalism attempts a complex, fluid,

Utopian free markets	Liberal democratic capitalism	Social democratic capitalism	Competitive authoritarian capitalism	State bureaucratic capitalism	Non-capitalist governance

Greater ------------- Claimed autonomy of economy from politics ----------- Less

Figure 9.1: Mapping ideal-types of capitalist governance

mix of state ownership and market relations, while rejecting democratic governance outright.

These ideal-types facilitate clarity when trying to characterize the political dynamics of varieties of capitalism. But there are two caveats to note about how they relate to the actual experience of states. First, many states are hybrids, containing features drawn from more than one category. Contemporary Russia is a mixture of state bureaucratic and competitive authoritarian capitalism. Most countries in Central America, and some in South America, combine competitive authoritarianism with aspects of market democracy. Somewhat counter-intuitively, the outlier to the post-2008 austerity regime favoured by both liberal democratic and social democratic states was the United States, which continued to pursue a policy of fiscal stimulus intended to break the liquidity trap and boost aggregate demand long after other democratic capitalist states wound down such programmes. These hybrid forms of capitalist governance muddy distinctions both within and between democratic and authoritarian groupings. Second, states often shift between categories over time. Chile under the Pinochet regime was a mixture of state bureaucratic and competitive authoritarian modes of capitalism; since the ending of military rule, it has instituted capitalism along a mix of liberal democratic and social democratic lines. This is far from being the only example of such movement in capitalist governance over time: change is the norm rather than the exception.

With these caveats in mind, individual states can be placed loosely along this continuum. As noted in Chapter 5: the US, the UK and other Anglophone countries represent liberal democratic capitalism; states in much of continental Europe, South America, India, Japan and South Korea exemplify social democratic capitalism; Russia, a number of states in the Middle East, sub-Saharan Africa, Central America and South-East Asia characterize competitive authoritarian capitalism; and China, Vietnam, most of the Gulf monarchies (including Saudi

Arabia) and some Central Asian states are the main bastions of state bureaucratic capitalism.

This continuum makes clear that capitalism is a near universal feature of contemporary international society and, because of the way it generates power, virtually a necessary condition for great power standing. If there was one overriding lesson from the Cold War, it was that non-capitalist economies could not compete with market economies over the long run, particularly when economies became more oriented around information and services. Each mode of capitalist governance has its strengths and weaknesses, generating a series of questions about its capacity for growth, its efficiency and its stability. Because capitalism turbo-charges change, it is always attended by trade-offs in terms of growth, inequality, efficiency and stability. Capitalism legitimizes itself by generating wealth in the form of growth and profits. But this wealth is unevenly distributed, something accentuated by the tendency of the rate of return on capital (particularly inherited wealth) to exceed growth in either income or output over the long term (Piketty, 2014). The result is the fostering of sometimes extreme inequality. The top 0.5% of the world's population owns over a third of its wealth and the world's 1,226 billionaires have a combined wealth of $4.6 trillion, more than the annual GDP of Germany (Bull, 2013: 15). The wealth of the richest individual in Mexico, Carlos Slim, is worth 6% of the country's GDP (Freedland, 2012: 195). At the same time, the bottom 68.4% of the world's population owns just 4.2% of its wealth and nearly 650 million people around the world are undernourished (Therborn, 2012: 14; Bull, 2013: 15). All forms of capitalist society are, therefore, compelled to maintain growth as a means of mediating the politics of inequality. If growth slows or reverses, and inequality remains, there is the risk of an ugly and potentially violent politics of redistribution coming to the surface. This is true across the spectrum: China is now as politically addicted to growth as the US. The four ideal-types of capitalist governance we highlight contain differing forms of these basic tensions.

It is not the case, therefore, that different forms of political economy will converge towards a single model of market democracy. That assumption rests on the argument that only democracy can contain the social forces unleashed by capitalism, provide capitalism with political and social legitimacy, and foster the high levels of creativity and innovation that underpin growth. As we explored in Chapter 5, state-led capitalism has its own advantages, not least in its ability to concentrate capital in strategic sectors and distort competition through subsidies and currency manipulation. This suggests that the contemporary world will be home to a range of capitalisms, a view supported by much of the literature on comparative capitalisms, which sees divergence rather than convergence as the norm (Jackson and Deeg, 2006: 30; Peck and Theodore, 2007; Brenner et al., 2009; Witt, 2010: 12; McNally, 2013: 7).

This diversity should come as no surprise. As discussed in Chapter 5, early analysts of capitalism did not see it as aligning with democracy. In the contemporary world, both democratic and authoritarian modes of capitalist governance face major challenges, most notably how to sustain growth while keeping both inequality and environmental damage in check. The narrower ideological bandwidth of the contemporary world does not, therefore, lead axiomatically to stable international order. The competition between varieties of capitalist governance is likely to be with us for some time.

Geoeconomics Rather than Geopolitics

If a world of decentred globalism will be marked by competing capitalisms, it is worth thinking carefully about how this competition will affect the emergent world order. In this respect, Luttwak's (1990) distinction between *geopolitics* and *geoeconomics* serves as a useful starting point. By geopolitics, Luttwak means zero-sum territorial competition in a military/political mode of relations among states. By geoeconomics, he means zero-sum competition for growth in an economic/political mode of relations among states where great power war is largely ruled out.

To capture the emerging world order, Luttwak's categories need to be differentiated into hard and soft types. *Hard geopolitics* means that intentional war is legitimate and expected (see also Mann, 2012: 14–15). We have already argued that such a situation is unlikely to be a feature of a world of decentred globalism. *Soft geopolitics* means that intentional great power war is marginalized, but territorial competition and military balancing/hedging remain, as is the case, for example, in contemporary East Asia. *Hard geoeconomics* means a zero-sum competition for profit within a largely political/economic modality; *soft geoeconomics* means a mix of zero-sum and positive-sum relations within a largely political/economic modality. While the former is a remote possibility, the latter is more plausible, particularly if a 'concert of capitalist powers' emerges that is able to manage inter-capitalist interaction. Taken together, the differentiation of hard/soft geopolitics and hard/soft geoeconomics captures well the international relations of varieties of capitalism in a decentred world order.

The last time there was a distribution of power that looked anything like decentred globalism was in the 1930s, and there is little doubt that the spectre of the 1930s will be rolled out by those looking to defend a US-led unipolar order. However, the analogy with the 1930s is largely false – contemporary international relations does not function like it did in the 1930s. At that time there were deep ideological differences among the great powers (communist, fascist, liberal), empire-building and racism were legitimate, and great power war and economic protection-ism were seen as mainstream policy choices. In the contemporary world, ideological differences amongst the great powers are comparatively narrow, empire and racism are illegitimate, and nuclear weapons have made great power war irrational. In addition, the version of capitalism that emerged victorious from the wars of the twentieth century was committed to global markets, not the regional blocs of the 1930s. Global economic governance (GEG) is far more institutionalized and the problems of international management are better (and differently) understood than in the interwar years (Drezner, 2012: 14). Even China, perhaps the most likely current candidate to seek to revise the way global markets operate, is firmly committed to existing global institu-tions and regimes (Deng, 2008; Johnston, 2008).

While there may be considerable disagreement about the specific rules and practices of GEG, there is much common ground between all types of capitalist governance when it comes to maintenance of the global trade, production and financial circuits on which their continued growth depends. There is, therefore, little or no reason to think that a world of decentred globalism will replay the conflicts of the 1930s. As a result, a return to hard geopolitics can be largely ruled out. However, as noted above in the case of East Asia, it may be that inter-capitalist competition will fuel soft geopolitical conflict. At its heart, capitalism is a hardnosed competition over accumulation and profits. Historically, as this book has shown, violence has played a central role in the extension and maintenance of markets around the world. This opens up three soft geopolitical possibilities.

The first is a situation in which authoritarian forms of capitalism become more extreme, abandoning the idea of a separation between the political and economic spheres. In this instance, elements of the 1930s scenario would be revived, although restrained by fears about the consequences of great power war, the illegitimacy of empire, and mutual dependence on world trade. This scenario is not impossible, but nor does it seem likely.

The second possibility is that the US and China fall into conflict because they mistakenly believe that they are engaged in a power transition crisis about who is to be the global superpower. The US will certainly have a lot of difficulty giving up this role (Weber and Jentleson, 2010); China remains divided about whether it wants such a role or not (Heath, 2012; Zhang, 2012; Shih and Yin, 2013). Neither country wants a war with the other, but their rivalry is already well established, and the right combination of carelessness, recklessness, miscalculation and mischance could pitch them into confrontation. Various pinch points are important here: whether or not China continues to buy US Treasuries; whether China seeks to promote the renminbi (RMB) as a reserve currency competing with the dollar; and whether soft geopolitical tensions in East Asia can be managed effectively. It is possible that the US 'pivot' towards Asia, combined with China's more assertive policies since 2008, could prompt a round of militarization (He and Feng, 2012; Womack, 2013). Although the US spends over five times more per year on its military than China, the latter's capacity is growing. On the back of its fast-growing GDP, China increased its military spending fourfold during the 2000s from \$33.5 billion per year in 2000 to \$129.3 billion in 2011, and did so without changing the proportion of GDP represented by defence expenditure (roughly 2%) (SIPRI, 2013).

Even if, as argued above, a system of decentred globalism prevents a build-up of power sufficient to elevate a single state to superpower status, a list of China's hard power assets is certainly striking (Shambaugh, 2013: 7–8, 157): the world's second largest economy, including four of the world's ten biggest banks by market capitalization; the world's second largest military budget; the world's biggest exporter; the world's highest foreign exchange reserves; the world's second largest recipient of FDI; and the world's leading producer. Between 2007 and 2012, China accounted for half of all global growth – China is now the EU's largest trading partner and accounts for two-thirds of the commerce between the BRIC states (Fenby, 2014: 5, 9). As China's rise gathers pace, soft geopolitical tensions in its region and with the US could escalate, though almost certainly not to the hard geopolitical levels experienced in the 1930s.

The third possibility is more of a question. Assuming both that authoritarian great powers do not become more authoritarian, and that China and the US manage to avoid open conflict, how important are the remaining ideological differences between democratic and authoritarian capitalists? In other words, will the greater ideological and practical homogeneity prompted by the universalization of capitalism moderate or override the antipathy between democracies and authoritarian regimes, or will political differences be sufficient to support either soft geopolitical rivalry or hard geoeconomic conflict?

The distinction between democracies and authoritarian regimes continues to play strongly in the global outlook of the US (Ikenberry and Slaughter, 2006; Halper, 2010). And there will certainly be concerns within democratic states that authoritarian countries will not play by the rules, for example by favouring their state-owned enterprises (SOEs) or manipulating their currencies. Current disputes range from the expansionary drives of large corporations, whether Google or Huawei, to currency policies, trade imbalances, cyber-warfare and industrial espionage. These tensions have to be managed within the fallout from the 2008 financial crisis, now widely acknowledged to be as severe as that of 1929, and the resulting weakening of both the global economy and GEG (Drezner, 2012: 14; Temin and Vines, 2013). The global decline in asset values in 2008 alone have been calculated at $50 trillion (Drezner and McNamara, 2013: 155), while cross-border capital flows are down 60% since 2008, and cross-border bank lending is down two-thirds since the crisis began (McKinsey Global Institute, 2013). Although most aspects of the global financial system have proved resilient, ongoing failures in the banking system, high levels of public debt, weak growth, limited credit flows and increasing capital controls constitute points of unease. These tensions lead, in turn, to a deeper concern that authoritarian states are not fully committed to capitalism, but are gaming the system in order to make short-term gains. In the medium term, liberal and social democratic states are hoping that authoritarian capitalist states will be forced to undergo political reforms. But even if such views are right, they are unlikely to be realized in the short term – authoritarian forms of capitalism will be part of the world of decentred globalism for quite some time.

A reversion to hard, zero-sum game, geoeconomics looks as implausible as a return to hard geopolitics. Many issues in international relations are mediated by deeply embedded and widely shared institutions, rules and regimes (Buzan, 2011: 19). These shared practices are reinforced by the need of all types of capitalist state to maintain the global economy (Ikenberry, 2011: 339–43). In short: hard geoeconomics is not an option because virtually every state is committed to global capitalism. Authoritarian states offer no systemic alternative for how global affairs might be organized. The US still retains substantial structural advantages over China and there are few signs that China is prepared to offer a global challenge to it. At the same time, authoritarian states show little desire for Chinese hegemony even as most democratic states continue to back US power (Shambaugh, 2013; Stokes, 2013). If there were a geopolitical, or even a hard geoeconomic, divide between authoritarian and democratic capitalists, authoritarian states would be weaker than their adversaries (Ikenberry, 2011: 343). The asymmetry of this scenario mitigates its likelihood.

The more likely scenario lies in the zone of soft geoeconomics in which capitalist powers both compete and cooperate with each other. A pragmatic version of this scenario could see the emergence of 'a concert of capitalist powers' in which great powers concentrate more on what they share than on what divides them. This is not, therefore, a scenario linked to the idea of a 'concert of democracies' (Ikenberry and Slaughter, 2006; Geis, 2013), a divisive notion rooted in the desire to maintain the role of the US as the sole superpower. Rather, it envisages a limited, pluralist system of great power management based not only on a shared desire for order, a shared set of interests, and a sense of shared fate in the face of common threats, but also recognition that capitalist competition will remain fierce, and political and cultural differentiation strong. A concert of capitalist powers would build on the existing substrate of rules, norms and institutions that constitute international society. Its focus would be on sustaining order in the global economy and on negotiating issues of shared fate, ranging from concerns about climate change to the proliferation of weapons of mass destruction (WMD). The shift from the G7/8 to the G20 could be a harbinger of just such a capitalist concert, as well as providing insights into the wider diplomacy of decentred globalism (Drezner, 2012: 9–12; Temin and Vines, 2013: 248–50).

Shared Primary Institutions

Buttressing the possible scenario of a concert of capitalist powers is the often under-appreciated substrate of consensus on many of the underlying norms, rules and principles (aka the 'primary institutions') of international society: the market, nationalism, diplomacy, international law, and suchlike (Bull, 1977; Buzan, 2014a). These primary institutions are mainly a legacy of Western hegemony, but many of them, most notably sovereignty and nationalism, have become so deeply embedded that they are now as global – and as local – as football. With the post-Cold War shift to more or less universal acceptance of the market, another powerful dimension has been added to this substrate of normative order. The operation of a global market creates pressures for shared standards in accounting, banking, fiscal and monetary policy, trade and corporate governance, and some degree of transparency is necessary for markets to function efficiently (Best, 2006; Seabrooke, 2006: 147). The degree of coordination and interoperability required by a global market means that states have to become more alike on questions of property rights, adherence to agreements, and restraints on the use of force. This contrasts with the pre-1989 world when ideological contestation over such issues was the norm. When the vast majority of states are capitalist, the institutions and rules required by the global market provide foundations on which a pluralist management of international society might be pursued.

If the primary institutions of a pluralist international society enjoy wide support among states, they also enjoy fairly wide public support. Most transnational actors want and need a stable legal framework through which to conduct interactions. Similar, and supportive, developments can be found within global civil society, where a dense web of transnational linkages plays a key role in deepening international society in issue-areas ranging from commercial law to the environment (Clark, 2007). The result is a set of primary institutions that are more robust and more widely accepted than in the past. It does not seem unreasonable to assume that most of these rules and principles will remain in place in a world of decentred globalism.

Such analysis is not meant to underestimate either differences of interpretation about these norms (such as over the right of non-intervention) or principles over which disagreements remain pronounced (such as the universal applicability of human rights). Emergent principles such as environmental stewardship could either add to the stock of disagreements or, depending on the circumstances, to the list of values held in common. But, all in all, there are deep and widely accepted rules that underpin contemporary international order. When combined with the diminution of ideological differences between states, and the likely shift from geo-political conflict to geoeconomic competition, this substrate of primary institutions provides the foundations on which a world of decentred globalism might be governed. The interaction culture of a soft geoeconomic order would be one of friends and rivals, not one of rivals and enemies.

A Normative Disposition Towards Regionalism

The material conditions of decentred globalism, particularly the absence of superpowers and the prominence of regional and great powers, point towards a more regionalized international order. The ideational foundations for a regionalized order start from the concerted anti-hegemonism associated with the rising powers as expressed in widespread calls for a more multipolar international system. Only in some parts of the EU (most obviously Britain and Eastern Europe), amongst some elites in the Middle East, and in Japan, India and some parts of South-East Asia where fear of Chinese power is most evident, is there sustained enthusiasm for the maintenance of US power. The relative decline of the US has made clearer what was already becoming obvious in the 1990s and 2000s, namely that the collapse of the Soviet project was not going to usher in a world homogenized along Western lines. Although nearly all states have accepted that some form of capitalism is the only way to compete economically, there are many cultural and political variations on this theme that could feed into a more regionalized world order. This variation is, in turn, sustained by a lack of consensus about issues as varied as human rights, freedom of sexual orientation and the role of religion in public life. This lack of consensus, allied to the anti-hegemonic sentiment and increasing capacities held by former peripheral states, means that regional formations are likely to gain salience vis-à-vis global institutions.

Speculations about the nature of a more regionalized international order have been around for a long time in the IR literature, and generally rest on the assumption of a world organized around three cores: the US, the EU and East Asia (Helleiner, 1994; Kupchan, 1998: 40–79). This picture does not capture well the dynamics of decentred globalism.

Regional organizations vary hugely in their quality and depth, ranging from the functionally elaborate layered sovereignty of the EU, to largely hollow and ineffectual organizations such as South Asian Regional Cooperation (SARC). The near ubiquity of such regional organizations, whether strong or weak, can be explained both as a fallback against the possible failure of globalization, and as a strategy to acquire more weight in a globalized world. The EU and the North American Free Trade Association (NAFTA) are the most obvious examples of this development. To them can be added Mercosur, the Association of Southeast Asian Nations (ASEAN), the Commonwealth of Independent States (CIS), the Southern African Development Community (SADC), the Shanghai Cooperation Organization (SCO), ECOWAS, the AU, and more. Although highly uneven in terms of their success and influence, these organizations do show how widespread the regionalizing impulse is. In the backwash of declining US leadership, and the coming realization that decentred globalism will be an order without superpowers, this impulse has every opportunity to develop further.

In some parts of the world, regional organizations may well become more prominent as a hedge against the erosion of centred globalism, providing political, economic and cultural comfort zones. In other places, local differences and particularisms may lead either to fragmentation or to absorption into super-regional constructs. The specific shape of decentred globalism is unpredictable. A decentred order will almost by definition be stronger regionally and perhaps super-regionally. But within this basic dynamic, the EU could get weaker and smaller or bigger and stronger. Russia might succeed or fail in its project to create a regional hegemonic simulacrum of the Soviet Union. Latin America could develop a single regional institutional structure, fragment, or become part of a US-dominated Western hemisphere system. South Asia might strengthen its currently weak regional institutions; more likely is that it will get drawn into a wider East Asian orbit, both attracted to and fearful of the rise of China. Super-regional schemes such as the Trans-Pacific Partnership (TPP) and the Transatlantic Trade and Investment Partnership (TTIP) could become influential or fail, leaving smaller regions dominant. None of these specific outcomes is predictable. What is predictable is that, in a world of decentred globalism, global-level IGOs, while continuing to play substantial roles, will be forced to share ground with both regional hegemons, and regional and super-regional institutional formations.

At the time of writing it is too early to tell what the impact will be of the 2008 financial crisis on the move towards regionalization. The crisis has asked serious questions of neoliberalism in general, and of financialization in particular. It has added to the weakening of American primacy and strengthened the hands of state actors in economic management. At the same time, however, GEG institutions have performed reasonably well (Drezner, 2012), while some of the most substantial regional organizations, most notably the EU, have been weakened. Quite what the balance will be between, on the one hand, the reconstruction of GEG along similar lines but with stronger financial controls, and on the other, a more hedged position with stronger regional and super-regional arrangements, remains to be seen.

The Challenges Facing Decentred Globalism

There are a number of reasons, therefore, to think that a world of decentred globalism might function reasonably well. But this is not to say that decentred globalism faces no challenges. Perhaps the main downside associated with a world without superpowers is that smaller states and peoples would be at risk of becoming the vassals of their regional power(s), having little or no recourse to outside support beyond disaster relief and other such one-off events. For some, it may be that the hegemonic dynamics of their local region offer a worse option than Western hegemony: Russia does not hesitate to bully its weaker neighbours; India's neighbours, especially Pakistan, vigorously resist its hegemony; anti-hegemonic historical memories weigh heavily on Japan and China in East Asia; the US has for some time been less than loved by its neighbours in the Americas; South Africa's influence in sub-Saharan Africa is resented by some of its neighbours and regional rivals; and in the Middle East, any move towards leadership by Egypt, Saudi Arabia or Iran would be deeply contested.

Some regions, most obviously the EU and North America, already possess robust intergovernmental organizations and practices that mediate such concerns. Other regions, such as South America, and to a lesser extent East Asia, also possess reasonably firm institutional frameworks. Yet other regions, such as West and Southern Africa, South Asia and the Middle East, contain only thin institutional frameworks that may not be able to mediate concerns about hegemony. Where such institutions are weak, a lot will depend on the distribution of power and the attitude of the powerful. Where the distribution of power is diffuse, as in the Middle East, perhaps the best that can be hoped for is a managed balance of power. Where power is concentrated, as in the former Soviet Union, and South and East Asia, much will depend on the behaviour of the relevant great and regional powers.[3]

Another potential downside of decentred globalism will, for some, be a weakening of the liberal project that has been fostered by Western pre-eminence. Liberals both in the West and elsewhere will lament the loss of hegemonic power that sustained their project and will fear the rise of various parochialisms, some possibly quite nasty. It is true that decentred globalism is likely to mean something of a retreat for liberal political and cultural agendas, if less so in the sphere of liberal economics. On both political and cultural grounds, there is substantial resistance to the liberal project around the world. For many people, liberal universalism is the latest twist in a history of Western imperialism that treats other cultures and political orientations as inferior. In this way of thinking, contemporary liberalism is old wine in new bottles, an updated 'standard of civilization' that represents an aggressive ideology rather than a tolerant viewpoint. Herein lies the root of contemporary contestation to Western hegemony, led by China (Halper, 2010). Although the Chinese government has accepted the strictures of the market, and thus the economic side of the liberal project, it is not buying into liberal culture and governance (Fenby, 2014: 28–52). A more decentred world order is likely to mean more such hybrid orders.

A third challenge is religion, which remains one of the most powerful bequests to modernity of earlier periods of world history. As we discuss in the next chapter, some modern thinkers saw religion as an anachronism that should have given way to secular ideologies of progress. But that has not happened. Instead, religions have fused with, and to some extent been empowered by, modernity. Within the West, evangelism went hand-in-hand with nineteenth-century imperialism and colonialism, and stood as a vital ingredient within the 'standard of civilization'. Some religious groups, most notably Quakers, played leading roles in INGOs ranging from the anti-slavery movement to the campaign for women's suffrage. Outside the West, religion also often contained a radical edge, playing a leading role in the Indian Revolt of 1857, and the Taiping (1850–64) and Boxer (1898–1901) Rebellions in China. For a time during the twentieth

---

[3] For a study of China in this regard, see Buzan (2014b).

century, religion seemed to have ceded considerable ground to secular ideologies, with liberalism, socialism and fascism holding sway within the framework of a Western-centred international order. Only in some conflicts, as in the dispute between India and Pakistan, between Catholics and Protestants in Northern Ireland, and in parts of the Middle East, did religion appear to retain a cardinal importance.

However, since the end of the Cold War, religion has made a concerted reappearance in international relations, from the impact of the American religious right on US foreign policy, the remobilization of Confucianism by the Chinese Communist Party, and of Hinduism by the Bharatiya Janata Party in India, to the influence of political Islam on Christian–Muslim violence in West Africa. Even in the ostensibly secularized space inhabited by contemporary Europe, religion continues to play an important role as a source of political allegiance (as in the various strains of Christian Democratic parties) and as a background reference to debates about human rights, humanitarian intervention and social justice. One of the core features of a decentred globalist world, therefore, is that religion will remain a powerful driver of behaviour both in the foreign policy of some states and in the actions of religiously motivated INGOs and networks. In a more regionalized world, religious belief could also play a significant role in the articulation of cultural difference and, on current trends, is likely to be a major factor in the legitimation of violence by non-state actors.

Beyond the three challenges highlighted above are wild cards that could affect the functioning of decentred globalism. Historically, wild cards have included the unintended consequences of new technologies, the side effects of new forms of energy production, disasters, diseases, and changes to the climate. If we had been writing this book during the 1960s, 1970s or 1980s, the wild card would likely have been nuclear war either obliterating humankind, or regressing it to the Stone Age. Such an event would have ended the global transformation, vindicating those who see the development of humankind's technological skills outpacing the development of its practical wisdom. Looking ahead, it is worth drawing attention to two factors that could impact on historical development over the coming decades: first, the possibility of an environmental crisis; and second, the possibility of a new mode of power that engenders a further major transformation.

Environmental crisis, whether natural or as an offshoot of the global transformation, covers a broad agenda from space rocks to new diseases, and from environmental degradation to the carrying capacity of the planet. If we look just at climate change, in theory, all states should share an interest in environmental stewardship; in practice, this is not the case (Falkner, 2012). Unrestrained growth in an ever more crowded planet with a rapidly changing environment speaks to a fundamental tension. If the Greenland and/or West Antarctic ice sheets were to undergo major melting, the global sea level would rise by up to 14 metres.[4] Such a rise would inundate many coastal areas, including a large number of the world's coastal (and 'global') cities such as London, New York and Shanghai. Some countries, most obviously Bangladesh, and anywhere else with a large area of popu-lated river delta, would face catastrophe.[5] The resultant evacuations, changes in geography and general disruption of both local and global political economies could rewrite the script of international relations in ways that are difficult to predict. Yet both the liberal democratic capitalists of the US and the state bureaucratic capitalists of China continue to stymie progress on environmental management because of fears that such management will compromise economic growth. China is now the world's largest energy user, consuming 38% of the world's coal, 48% of its cement and nearly 10% of its oil; it is home to 20 of the 30 most polluted cities on the planet (Lin, 2012: 17; McNeill and Engelke, 2014: 375).

Coming to terms with this issue may turn out to be the defining question for competing capitalist powers in a world of decentred global-ism. If they fail, and the climate warms by several degrees centigrade, then we will be living on a very different planet from that of the nine-teenth and twentieth centuries. We are probably moving past the point where significant temperature rises in the coming decades can be pre-vented, and there is still a great deal that we do not know about how feedback effects play into the release of greenhouse gases into the atmosphere, whether from melting permafrost or oceanic methane clathrates (IPCC, 2014). There could quite easily be an environmental fault-line that contains far-reaching consequences for how international relations is structured and practised.

[4] www.giss.nasa.gov/research/briefs/gornitz_09/ (accessed 25 October 2013).
[5] Interactive maps charting rising sea levels can be found at: http://ngm.national geographic.com/2013/09/rising-seas/if-ice-melted-map and http://flood.firetree. net/?ll=54.0000,-2.4000&zoom=2 (both accessed 25 October 2013).

The second wild card is the potential emergence of a new mode of power that supersedes the global transformation. Just as the British at the beginning of the nineteenth century did not know they were part of a new configuration of power that would reshape international order, so we may be unable to see where we stand in relation to developments that will look obvious to those on the other side of them. What would be big enough to count as a new era? One possibility would be the solving of the problem of production: a *Star Trek* scenario of 'replicators' able to produce anything on demand. The current hype around 3-D printing carries suggestions of such a revolution, involving a decentring of the whole productive process. Another might be the invention of an essentially limitless, reasonably cheap and environmentally friendly source of energy. Fusion power has been spoken of this way for a long time, but has yet to deliver. A third possibility would be the so-called 'singularity', in which either by electro-mechanical technologies or biomedical ones, or some combination of the two, entities are created that are more intelligent or long-lived than 'off the shelf' human beings (Kurzweil, 2005). It is easy to argue the case that such a development would transform pretty much everything in the human condition, though much more difficult to say what that transformation would look like. If this or other wild cards emerge during the coming decades, then international relations would lurch away from the template sketched in this chapter.

The Four Principles of Decentred Globalism

If we bracket these wild cards and assume a continued unfolding of the main lines of continuity and change suggested by the global transformation, what guidance does our analysis suggest?

We have argued for the probability of a world of decentred globalism in which there will be no superpowers, only great powers and regional powers, all situated in a global order in which regionalism is more prominent. Within this frame, capitalism would be a universally accepted framing for exchange, production and finance, but will be embedded in a variety of governance structures. At the global level there will be a well-grounded international society sharing a substantial substrate of primary institutions. This international society will be motivated mainly by norms of coexistence, but with significant elements of cooperation around collective problems (e.g. arms control, terrorism, climate change)

and projects (e.g. trade, big science). This emergent international order will be shaped by a more even global distribution of power among states and by increasingly influential elements within global civil society.

This combination makes a more pluralist mode of coexistence both possible and necessary. Decentred globalism will remain highly combined but much less uneven. It is both the successor to the Western-dominated era of the nineteenth and twentieth centuries and, in a way, the restoration of the classical order in which the distribution of power was relatively even. In the absence of a global superpower, a combination of shared rules and shared interests must be the foundation on which a cooperative international society is constructed. In our view, the following four principles represent the best way to start thinking about the international relations of a world of decentred globalism.

1. Global Non-Hegemony

In a world without superpowers nobody will have global primacy and none should seek or assume global hegemony. This principle will be particularly difficult for the US for two reasons: first, because it is used to, and deeply committed to, global primacy; and second, because it is a long-standing article of faith in the US that American values are universal (Buzan, 2008; Weber and Jentleson, 2010). The US might have difficulty giving rising powers (whether authoritarian or democratic) more influence over global governance. It might also struggle to adapt to life as just another great power, even if it remains first amongst equals. Against the odds, the US could seek to extend its period as sole superpower. The upside of this principle for Americans is that there is no particular need for the US to see off challengers to its sole super-power status, both because there won't be any and also because that status is indefensible in the context of the expansion of global modernity. The US in particular, and the West in general, will need to get used to the fact that they do not own the future.

The more ambitious nationalists in China might also have trouble with the principle of global non-hegemony (Westad, 2012; Shambaugh, 2013). They will have to accept that China will not replace the US as the global leader – it is not going to be 'China's turn' next. However remarkable China's resurgence over the past generation has been, the country faces a host of problems. At home, these range from rising inequality and environmental degradation to widespread capital mis-allocation and weak levels of innovation (Shambaugh, 2013; Fenby, 2014). At the same time, increasingly fractious publics are demanding less corruption, greater freedom of expression, enhanced labour rights, safer food and water, improved welfare provision and, in some cases, regional autonomy. Abroad, China will have to do a much better job than it does at present of living up to its rhetoric of peaceful rise (Buzan, 2014b). To the extent that majority opinion about China's exceptionalism is inwardly rather than outwardly referenced (the idea of 'Chinese characteristics' meaning that China is different from everyone else and should preserve that difference), accepting the limits of China's rise should not be as big a problem as it will be for those in the more universalistically inclined US to accept its relative decline. But it remains to be seen whether the rhetoric of a 'China Dream', heavily promoted by official figures since late 2012, has the capacity to generate a more outward-looking perspective. Although the notion has acted as a potent tool of elite and popular mobilization, it often appears to outside observers as a vague set of aspirations rather than as a coherent statement of collective identity (Schell and Delury, 2013; Callahan, 2014).

Global non-hegemony is not just about accepting that there will be no more superpowers. It is also about placing the period of Western hegemony into the past, while safeguarding the more useful parts of its legacy that already enjoy a wide consensus. A sound place to start is the burying of racism, the contemporary residues of the 'standard of civilization' and Western cultural arrogance more generally. The West was the first recipient of the configuration of power that enabled global modernity, but it will not be the last. As we have shown, the sources of Western power were not derived from endogenously sourced genius – they were the result of international connections and dynamics. The ongoing intensification of combined development means that those dynamics are now embedding the modern mode of power in many societies around the world.

The big question is whether a decentred world order could engender the levels of global management required to deal with collective problems. Some argue that system management under a hegemon is more efficient than the alternatives (e.g. Temin and Vines, 2013), and the US has certainly used this idea in reaping seigniorial rights over the international system. Yet the recent history of system management under a waning Western-global international order, and a declining and increasingly self-centred sole superpower, has caused as many problems as it has solved. It is time to give a more decentred system a try.

Grounds for optimism can be found in the degree to which a number of primary institutions in international society are held in common. As highlighted earlier in this chapter, these shared institutions provide an important resource for the maintenance of international order. The reduced management capacity caused by decentred globalism would be balanced, at least to some extent, by a reduced agenda of things that would need to be managed. A world without a global hegemon would feature less Western interference and, as a result, would face fewer problems that arise from such interference. Tensions over hegemonic interference would decline if regions were, for better or worse, more in charge of their own affairs.

2. Responsible Great Powers

If there will be no single leader in world politics, then international order depends on the great powers conducting themselves in a responsible manner. While it is the case, as argued above, that contemporary international society has some robust qualities, this should not be taken for granted – there is no teleological imperative to a further deepening of primary institutions (Bull, 1977: 40–52). The effectiveness of international society is particularly bound up with the great powers of the day. To be a responsible great power means to uphold the basic principles of social order: restraint on the use of force, respect for agreements, acknowledgement of the rights and status of smaller powers, a greater role for regional powers as management partners, and observing sovereignty and other ground-rules of international order (Bull, 1977: 53–7, 228–9; Hurrell, 2007).

These maxims of great power responsibility highlight the shortcomings of claims of exceptionalism (Holsti, 2011). What Ruggie (2004: 3–4) nicely labels 'American exemptionalism' – the US using both its sense of exceptionalism and its role as hegemon to exempt itself from many of the rules it wants others to observe – will not stand in a world of decentred globalism. What is required is a general attitude of pluralism, self-restraint and tolerance, and a willingness to take joint action on shared problems. In the absence of a superpower to either follow or oppose, the previous section argued that a concert of capitalist powers could emerge with the capacity to manage competition amongst integrated but diverse models of political economy. What Gray (2012: loc. 2368) notes about the nineteenth-century Concert of Europe also applies to a twenty-first-century concert of capitalist powers: its master rule is that no great power should take unilateral action without a prior attempt to secure the consent or tolerance of the others; each great power is 'obliged to be sensitive to the legitimate defensive concerns of others' (see also Mitzen, 2013). Such a concert would have to take a less ambitious view of GEG than was the case under the Washington Consensus. But it might also extend existing cooperation on big science projects, such as high-energy physics, astronomy, space exploration, disease control, and defence of the planet against collisions with space rocks.

A concert of capitalist powers would be a pluralist order: one in which there was respect for, or at least tolerance of, difference, alongside a responsible attitude towards the maintenance of a coexistence international society (Jackson, 2000). After the collapse of state socialism and the fall of the Washington Consensus, international society should cultivate a degree of ideological humility in which each of the four varieties of capitalist governance experiments with its own forms of political economy. Time will determine which of these forms of political economy is best able to deliver the good life.

Yet a world of capitalist powers will certainly be competitive and there is no reason to think that the long-standing tension between capitalism and a fragmented, 'anarchic' international political structure will disappear. Nationalism, sovereignty and territoriality remain widely held values. But an acceptance of pluralism is perfectly compatible with international order – in fact, diversity of polity forms is the historical norm rather than an aberration (Phillips and Sharman, forthcoming; see also Ferguson and Mansbach, 1996). Since all capitalist powers have an interest in keeping the global economy functioning efficiently, their relations will be cooperative as well as competitive. In such a system, the logic of *raison de système* will feature strongly. To this end, all great powers need to be aware of the substrate of ideas and institutions on which they agree, and to build on this: (a) a coexistence international society in which different modes of capitalist governance take part in 'soft geoeconomics'; and (b) a cooperative international society capable of handling joint projects such as world trade and big science, and collective action problems such as climate change and nuclear proliferation.

The discipline of IR could make a modest contribution here. Although IR shares some terminology with public policy discourses (e.g. balance of power, interdependence, globalization), it has conspicuously failed to integrate the term *international society* into policy discussions. Public policy is dominated, unfortunately, by the term *international community*, which, aside from being used to represent widely different meanings (Buzan and Gonzalez-Pelaez, 2005), creates a much higher, and significantly more unrealistic, expectation of shared values and affectivities than is actually found in international relations. The distinction between *society* as plural and negotiated, and *community* as affective and identity-based, is a useful one. Wider use of the term *international society* in both IR and within policy circles would be a closer reflection of how the world actually operates. And that, in turn, would help to create more realistic expectations about the nature of responsible great power behaviour and what is possible in a world of decentred globalism.

Pluralism is not, therefore, a cause for despair. The range of ideological difference amongst great powers in the contemporary world is quite narrow. At the same time, all great powers share significant principles and interests. What these amount to collectively is much better understood as a society than as a community, and IR should make concerted efforts to move the concept of international society into the public domain.

3. Regionalization Alongside Globalization

In a world of decentred globalism with no superpowers and a relatively wide distribution of power, regionalization may be as strong a tendency as globalization. Great powers are likely to have their local spheres of influence and, up to a point, these might be reinforced by cultural and historical differences between regions. The EU, NAFTA, Mercosur, Russia and its 'near abroad', and other such formations are harbingers of this trend. Regional formations can serve three functions in a world of decentred globalism, standing as: bastions for retaining local distinctiveness; fall-backs if global cooperation weakens; and platforms from which to practise pluralist international relations more effectively.

Great powers are often crucial to the regions in which they sit; in a world of decentred globalism, great powers need to pay as much attention to their regions as to each other. China and Japan need to think more about their relations with each other, South-East Asia and India, and less about their interactions with the US. And the US needs to think more about its hemisphere, and less about Asia and the Middle East. Both powers face the difficult task of conducting a mutual de-escalation in which China threatens its neighbours less, and the US threatens China less. More generally, in looking to their regions, great powers should prioritize the creation of stable, consensual and legitimate regional international societies, although some, like Russia, might seek to construct regional hegemonies.

Great powers cannot help but have a considerable impact on the character and extent of regional order. As discussed above, part of being a responsible great power is the cultivation and exercise of legitimate leadership. This again raises the tricky question of hegemony. It is possible that hegemony will become obsolete at the global level only to reappear in regions. Without superpowers to meddle and mediate, regional powers will, for better or worse, have a stronger hand in their locales. The corollary of this, as we pointed out in the previous section, is that those states disgruntled with their regional hegemons will have less chance of outside assistance. The development of a system of regional international societies is still very much a work in progress. It is an experiment whose stability and outcome is unclear.

4. Shared Fates Mean Common Security

The existence of shared problems and shared fates is not in doubt. Even the two superpowers during the Cold War acknowledged that they had a mutual interest in survival. A central component of responsible great power behaviour is the recognition of common problems that require collective action because they generate shared fates. Shared fates require a turn towards the principle of common security: security 'with' rather than security 'against'. Security is usually understood as 'security against'; 'security with' only enters the equation in the form of alliances or 'coalitions of the willing' (Porter and Brown, 1991: 109; Buzan and Hansen, 2009: 136–8). This approach of security 'against' makes little to no sense when facing shared threats such as climate change, biological and digital viruses, the proliferation of weapons of mass destruction, space rocks, and the management of the global economy.

There will, of course, continue to be territorial disputes and differences of opinion about issues deep enough to legitimize a resort to military means. But in the absence of threats of either great power war, or any great power striving to replace the US as the sole superpower, national security agendas no longer have the existential quality they once had. The security agenda has shifted to shared problems and shared fates. Security 'with' is now more important than security 'against'.

Conclusion

Taken together, these four principles chart a path through an international order characterized by decentred globalism. From the perspective of those pursuing universalist political visions these principles are likely to be unsatisfactory. In our view, however, they offer a relatively judicious guide to the conduct of international relations in a world without Western hegemony. The four principles outlined above offer the prospect of managing competition between integrated but diverse models of political economy. The task is to ensure that the four main modes of capitalist governance engage in peaceful competition rather than overt conflict, cooperating well enough to maintain the foundations of international order. Such peaceful competition will show soon enough whether one mode of political economy is superior to the others, or whether each of them simply contains a different balance of strengths, weaknesses and socio-political preferences.

10 | *Rethinking International Relations*

Introduction

In the nine preceding chapters we have done four things. First, we established the central components and importance of the global transformation (Chapter 1); second, we examined the relative lack of attention paid by IR scholarship to the global transformation (Chapter 2); third, we tracked many of the most important themes and concerns of contemporary IR from their origins in the nineteenth century to the present day. These included:

- globalization and the shrinking of the planet (Chapter 3);
- the pervasive impact of ideologies of progress (Chapter 4);
- the transformation of political units through imperialism, revolution and capitalism (Chapter 5);
- the construction of a Western-colonial international society and its development into a Western-global international society (Chapters 6 and 7);
- the impact of the global transformation on great power competition, military competition and war (Chapter 8).

Finally, we used the historical framing of the global transformation to rethink aspects of contemporary world politics, paying particular attention to the shift from centred globalism to an international order characterized by decentred globalism (Chapter 9).

We have argued that much of the form and content of contemporary international relations has its origins in the global transformation, and that the nineteenth century is therefore close kin to the twentieth and twenty-first centuries in a way that earlier centuries are not. We are manifestly *not* saying that everything of importance to IR has its origins in the long nineteenth century. But the configuration of industrialization, the rational state and ideologies of progress not only introduced the main dynamics that underpin modern international relations, it also continues to serve as the basis for many important aspects of contemporary international affairs. The contemporary international order is neither natural nor eternal. It is a historically specific and highly unusual configuration formed in the convulsions of global modernity.

From this perspective, mainstream IR has put far too much emphasis on the historical continuity of its basic forms and processes and shown far too little awareness of how historically recent many of these forms and processes are. A central theme of our argument is that IR needs to start thinking about the nineteenth century more in the way that historical sociologists, world historians and economic historians do already.

The task of this chapter is to set out the implications that follow from this argument. We think that these are substantial and that the payoff would be extensive. Global modernity provides a common starting place for much of IR's contemporary agenda. Up to a point, it provides an antidote to the often lamented fragmentation of the discipline (e.g. Holsti, 1985) by showing how sub-fields in IR – IR theory, Strategic/Security/War Studies, IPE, Foreign Policy Analysis, Diplomatic Studies, etc. – relate to each other and form part of a cohesive whole. The following discussion probes the implications of the global transformation for how IR thinks about six key elements of its agenda: power, security, globalization, ideational structure, periodization and history. Our argument is that all of these elements look quite different when viewed from the perspective of the global transformation. We close by examining the consequences for IR as a discipline of incorporating global modernity into its framing.

Implications for Thinking About Power

IR has long been concerned with the issue of power as a basic driver of world politics. Since the seminal works of Waltz (1979), Gilpin (1981) and Keohane (1984), neo-realists and neoliberal institutionalists have been particularly concerned with the *distribution* of power. Waltz defined the distribution of power as a central element of system structure, and the only element that was likely to change. For better or worse, his formulation, and the polarity theory it generated, has been influential within both IR theory and the sub-field of international security (e.g. James and Brecher, 1988; Hopf, 1991; Kapstein and

Mastanduno, 1999; Waltz, 2000; Mearsheimer, 2001; Brooks and Wohlforth, 2008; Wohlforth, 2009).

This book has introduced the idea of the *mode of power* – the social sources of power – and argued that this is a deeper concern than issues of power distribution. The mode of power changes less frequently than the distribution of power, but has a more profound effect on international order when it does so. Indeed, the mode of power is *generative* of the distribution of power, combining material and ideational relations that establish new ways in which power is practised and conceived. As we have examined during this book, the global transformation was a configuration of three dynamics (industrialization, rational statehood and 'ideologies of progress'), which together generated a new basis for how power was constituted, organized and expressed. This configuration was the source of a power gap that was both unusually big and unusually difficult to close. Such a shift in the mode of power also transformed the units of, and main actors within, the international system. The meaning of sovereignty and territoriality, and the economic and political practices associated with them, were profoundly altered by the global transformation. Empires were initially reinvigorated by the new mode of power, only to be undermined by the struggle of those in the periphery who used modern ideologies (such as nationalism and socialism), modern weapons and modern tactics against them.

The global transformation therefore changed not just the distribution of power (by making the West more powerful than other parts of the world), but also the dominant mode of power (the social sources of power that produce political, economic, military and ideological formations). IR has much to say about the changing distribution of power, but it seldom examines changes to the underlying mode of power. The closest it gets to such a discussion is in debates about the impact of nuclear weapons on the state, the balance of power and war (e.g. Herz, 1957 and 1968). However, even nuclear weapons constitute a change *within* a mode of power rather than comprising a change *of* the mode of power. Because IR does not look in any systematic way at global modernity, it has failed to take into account the basic shift in the mode of power that was constitutive of changes to the ordering principles of modern international society.

In the preceding chapters we developed two examples to illustrate this point: the opening and maintenance of a large gap between core and periphery; and the destabilization of great power relations.

First, the new mode of power associated with global modernity enabled the West to dominate key aspects of international relations, projecting new forms of organization and new ideas that destabilized existing social orders. From around the middle of the nineteenth century, the global international system began to operate through a bifurcated, core–periphery structure. This analysis yields two broader contentions: first, during the initial period that marks the appearance of a new mode of power, sizeable power gaps will be opened between those who harness the new mode of power and those who do not; and second, these power gaps will be much more difficult to close than those that occur within a single realm of social life. The first claim rests on the fact that any new mode of power introduces resources that massively favour those in possession of them. The second claim rests on the difficulties that most societies have in accommodating a new mode of power. Such accommodations require radical changes that are not only difficult to make in their own right, but are actively inhibited by both domestic elites and external powers, each seeking to preserve their existing advantages. As we explored in preceding chapters, these effects were particularly strong during the early phases of global modernity. They linger on in many parts of the contemporary world.

Second, global modernity destabilized great power relations both by changing the criteria for being a great power and by adding the requirement for continuous upgrading in military technology. As demonstrated in Chapter 8, during the global transformation, acquiring power changed from the accumulation of territory, population and specie to harnessing a new mode of power that allowed a handful of states to dominate populations and territories much larger than their own. The present rise (more accurately described as a return) of China and India attracts great interest because they combine the configuration of global modernity with territorial heft and large populations. As the configuration that sustains global modernity becomes more widespread, the raw effect of population size and territorial capacity is being reasserted. As the modern mode of power evens out, only large states will be able to be great powers.

Adding the mode of power to IR's analytical apparatus thus adds considerable depth to how the discipline approaches the subject of power. During the modern period, it is changes in the mode of power that drive both power transition and power distribution dynamics, not the other way around. The extension of global modernity generates not a rise of rest/fall of West scenario, but one in which the West remains powerful while other states 'catch up'. The differential embedding of the mode of power that fuelled Western domination for much of the nine-teenth and twentieth centuries is fading away, but the West will not disappear in the way that Rome, Byzantium, the Mughals and the Ottoman Empire did. It remains one amongst several centres of power, and quite likely *primus inter pares* for some time to come.

Implications for Thinking About Security

If changes in the mode of power are more fundamental than changes in the distribution of power, this has four consequences for understanding security. Three of these relate to what might be called the traditional security agenda, which privileges military-political relations as the main, or even only, element in security. The fourth focuses on the widening of security beyond the military-political sphere into the eco-nomic, environmental and societal sectors (Buzan and Hansen, 2009).

The first (and fastest) military consequence of global modernity was the way in which the new mode of power generated the distinctive modern security *problématique* of qualitative arms competition between core states, with a consequent destabilization of great power relations. In parallel, global modernity opened up a substantial military gap between core and periphery, underpinning the creation of an extremely hierarchical international society. This was a temporary, if long-lasting, dynamic, strong in the first (Western-colonial) and second (Western-global) phases of global modernity, weaker in its third (decen-tred globalism). As outlined in Chapter 8, a key development in the closing of the gap between core and periphery has been the spread of both light infantry weapons and nuclear weapons.

The second (somewhat slower) military consequence of global mod-ernity was the 'defence dilemma' generated by the continuous, rapid escalation of destructive power enabled by new technologies. As dis-cussed in Chapter 8, new weapons were a major concern for those thinking about military security. Weapons were problematized in terms of their cost, their moral implications, their destabilizing effects on military relations (mainly by creating options for disarming first strikes), and their implications for war as a policy tool. Initially, the escalation in the cost and destructive power of modern weapons was not sufficient to threaten the regular practice of great power war.

However, after the First World War, and especially after the introduc-tion of nuclear weapons during the Second World War, this aspect of military modernity raised the question of whether new weaponry was making the traditional functions of war obsolete. Great power war looked neither prudent nor cost-effective in the context of the destruc-tiveness and diffusion of modern weaponry. In the contemporary world, great power war is no longer a rational option.

The third (much slower) military consequence of global modernity was the placing of significant powers of destruction in the hands of small groups, networks and individuals. Terrorism has been a concern since at least the late nineteenth century, but 9/11 has become the contemporary signifier for the elevation of this dynamic to the forefront of securitization. The global war on terror has, unwisely, raised non-state actors to the peer status of 'enemy'. As we pointed out in the previous chapter, although terrorism is a far greater concern to the inhabitants of Iraq, Pakistan, Afghanistan, Lebanon, Kenya, Nigeria and many other states in the global South than it is to people in the West, there is a widespread concern about small groups acquiring big weapons that, in turn, arises from three distinctive features of modernity: the creation of ever more destructive weapons; the relative ease of access to these technologies as they get older and as technological know-how spreads; and the higher vulnerabilities created by modern concentrations of people in cities and transportation systems. When these are combined with extremist attitudes, political disenfranchisement, economic dispar-ity and cultural alienation, a new dimension of security is opened up.

The fourth consequence of global modernity for security arises from the intensification of societal interdependence, which generates a distinctive, non-military security agenda: human, environmental, economic, identity based, etc. (Buzan et al., 1998; Sheehan, 2005; Williams, 2008; Buzan and Hansen, 2009: 187–282; Owens, 2012). In part, this expansion of the security agenda is a result of the obsoles-cence of great power war. But it is also a consequence of the mode of power that underpins global modernity. Owens (2012), for example, shows how the notion of human security has its roots in the emergence of a distinct notion of 'the social', which she locates in nineteenth-century ideas of household governance as concerned with 'pacification' and 'domestication'. The increase in productive capacity unleashed by modernity has placed considerable stress on the planetary environment. As we showed in earlier chapters, coal was a key component of the first industrial revolution, while oil and natural gas were central to 1 second industrial revolution. By the end of the nineteenth centu_,, around half of the world's energy was produced through fossil fuels; by 2010, fossil fuels provided 80% of global energy use (McNeill and Engelke, 2014: 365–6). This dependence on fossil fuels is matched by other causes of human-induced climate change: from 1945–2011, there was an eightfold increase in carbon emissions (IPCC, 2014; McNeill and Engelke, 2014: 411). These longer-term developments, allied to disasters like those at the Chernobyl and Fukushima Daiichi nuclear power plants, have generated a basic interdependence of shared fate – environmental changes alter the conditions of life for peoples in ways that are deeply threatening. At the same time, economic interdependence, combined with the instabilities of global capitalism, can inflict war-like pain on societies around the world. Global modernity also transmits cultural flows that destabilize existing identity frames and, sometimes, empower nativist sentiments. As the planet has become more intensely interdependent, security has shifted from a narrow, contained sphere of military relations to a wide, everyday set of concerns (Buzan and Hansen, 2009).

Such a widening of the security agenda is one of the most important unintended consequences of global modernity. Liberals hoped that economic interdependence would both reduce the incentives to annex territory, and raise the costs of war. Both of these hopes have, to a substantial extent, been realized. What liberals did not expect was that the rolling back of interstate military security would be replaced by a wider and, in some ways, more intrusive security agenda arising from the character of modern society itself. Both the change in the character of military threats, and the shift to a wider security agenda, are traceable to the global transformation. This wider security agenda is therefore not going away.

Implications for Thinking About Globalization

Globalization is an essentially contested concept, but a useful working definition is provided by Held et al. (1999: 16):

a process (or set of processes) which embodies a transformation in the spatial organization of social relations and transactions – assessed in terms of their extensity, intensity, velocity and impact – generating transcontinental or interregional flows and networks of activity, interaction and the exercise of power.

In other words, globalization focuses on the scale and intensity of international orders. It is about a shift from a world in which contact between social orders was light and slow to an era in which peoples and places are intensely connected. Over the long term, economies tend to be connected more widely and deeply (and earlier) than political, military and cultural relations (Buzan and Little, 2000: 213, 315, 339, 366, 372, 381–2). This is the case, at least in part, because the interaction capacity requirements for economic relationships are lower than those required for military and political relations.[1] As we discussed in earlier chapters, trading systems linked distant parts of the world long before they engaged in regular military or political contact. In the contemporary world, there is a world economy without there being a world polity or single-world society. The economic sector is the leading edge of globalization.

It is possible to view globalization from different vantage points: short (twentieth century), medium (since the nineteenth century), long (since around 1500) and very long (all of human history). IR tends to employ the short vantage point, seeing globalization as a twentieth-century phenomenon. Clark (1997: 33), for example, argues that 'the ushering in of the twentieth century marked the beginning of globalised international relations'. While Held et al. (1999: 414–52) acknowledge that globalization can be found in different eras, they also favour the short vantage point on the grounds that post-Second World War globalization has been particularly intense and has taken place within all sectors. In our view, the short perspective captures well some recent developments. However, it fails to give a satisfactory answer to significant questions over when, where and how the really big changes that underpin contemporary globalization began. Our answer to these questions can be found in Chapters 1, 3 and 5.

At the opposite end of the spectrum is the very long-term vantage point, in which globalization emerged from the original human migrations out of Africa and the settling of the planet (Fagan, 1993). From this vantage point, globalization has been an almost

---

[1] Cultural relations have a dual quality in relation to interaction capacity. As we have argued, because ideas are easy to carry, cultural traffic spread across Eurasia for many centuries before the global transformation, even when interaction capacity was low. But this traffic tended to be slow moving. The rapid, mass contact between cultures that is a feature of modernity depends on high levels of interaction capacity.

permanent, if episodic, feature of historical development. For advocates of the long-term view (Buzan and Little, 2000), globalization is marked by a quantitative increase in economic (trading), cultural (mostly religious) and political (mostly imperial) relations rather than featuring a qualitative leap in interaction capacity. The culmination of this process is the emergence of a global web of interrelations that, once it assumed planetary extent, became deep as well as broad. The problem with this perspective is that it diminishes the analytical bite of globalization, reducing it to a descriptive term that fails to delineate the distinctively modern features of globalization. Indeed, such a perspective effectively reduced globalization, or proto-globalization, to *interconnections*, omitting the particular characteristics of *interdependence* that have fuelled many of the dynamics we have explored in this book.

The long view focuses on the opening up of the sea-lanes from Europe to Southern Africa, the Indian Ocean, the Americas, and across the Pacific between 1487 and 1522 (Wallerstein, 1974; McNeill, 1991; Christian, 2004; Crosby, 2004). This opening up established regular connections between the continents and expanded the international system to planetary scale. It precipitated the death of most of the native populations and civilizations of the Americas, inaugurated a transfer of flora, fauna, commodities, people, ideas and diseases, and led to a thin but significant global economy in commodities ranging from silks and silver to spices and slaves. The impact of this cluster of macro-historical processes was limited by the scope of agrarian technology, but it paved the way for the intensification of the global economy and the mass human migrations that accompanied it during later periods. The drawback with this perspective is that, in many ways, globalization after 1500 was more symbolic than real, affecting relatively few parts of the world. While a thin form of globalization may be said to have emerged around this time, the qualitative leaps associated with the global transformation are a far richer means by which to unpack the main properties of globalization.

Our position, therefore, occupies the medium vantage point, which while not absent from IR is a minority view (Gellner, 1988; Hirst and Thompson, 1996; Ferguson, 2004). Chapter 3, for example, emphasized the changes in physical and social interaction capacity that underpinned globalization during the long nineteenth century. These changes marked the beginning of a quantitative *and* qualitative leap in interaction capacity that produced radically different social orders from those found in preceding periods. Chapter 5 emphasized the emergence of transnational firms and financial capitalism during the last quarter of the nineteenth century. Chapter 6 discussed the extensive migrations that scattered people around the world during the long nineteenth century. And, as Lenin (1975 [1916]: 90) amongst others pointed out, during the late nineteenth century, the extension of the market, the expansion of inter-imperialist competition and advances in both technology and transportation meant that the international system reached global scale and therefore became 'closed' (see also Mackinder, 1996 [1904]). From then on, only redivision and intensive development were possible. These changes were, in turn, the antecedents to a number of dynamics in the twentieth century that tend to preoccupy globalization theorists, such as the extension of financial capitalism, the emergence of the internet, and the increasing role of diasporas. Our case is that the really big breakthrough to globalization, not just measured in terms of speed, intensity, scale and volume, but also in terms of the depth of changes that accrued from these intensified interactions, took place during the long nineteenth century. The medium view also captures the shift from stratificatory to functionally differentiated social orders that we have characterized as a central feature of modernity. This period was when the international sphere became both deeply interdependent and increasingly differentiated in terms of economic, political, military, legal and cultural relations.

From this perspective, the short vantage point is best seen as the downstream effects of dynamics that began in the nineteenth century. The long view is not wrong, but is limited because the major changes in quantitative and qualitative interaction capacity took place well after 1500. The very long view is even more limited, occluding the shift in scale and intensity wrought by later historical periods. During the global transformation, as we have shown, practically everything studied by globalization theorists changed, and changed deeply. The centrality of the global transformation to globalization is one of the main reasons for giving it more prominence in IR. Without doing so, as argued in Chapter 9, the discipline risks mischaracterizing the dynamics that shape both the content and trajectory of contemporary world politics. It also risks missing an opportunity to share a common discourse with neighbouring disciplines. The medium-term view should be the starting point for analysis of globalization.

Implications for Thinking About Ideational Structure

As argued in Chapter 4, the global transformation was as much ideational as material, and the ideational transformation instituted by global modernity was no less comprehensive and dramatic than its material revolution. Just as material technologies such as horses and sailing ships were marginalized by railways, steamships and the telegraph, so too were old ideas pushed to the margins by new schemas, most notably liberalism, socialism, nationalism and, for nearly a century, 'scientific' racism. In various combinations and permutations, these four 'ideologies of progress' have dominated the ideational landscape of international relations for the past two centuries.

Dynasticism was the clearest ideational loser of global modernity.[2] Wars over dynastic rights remained common up to the beginning of the nineteenth century, but as Clark (2005: 71–84; see also Holsti, 1991: 71–89) notes, the balance of power began to challenge dynastic principles after the Treaty of Utrecht (1713), becoming formally enshrined as an institution of international society in the Treaty of Vienna (1815) (Reus-Smit, 1999: 134–40). Great power conferences, like that in Berlin in 1884–5 to manage the partition of Africa, provide archetypal examples of the institution of balance of power in action. Like the balance of power, the logic and legitimacy of great power interests strengthened as the dynastic principle weakened. The principle of great power management also became more evident following the Treaty of Vienna and the Concert of Europe, establishing a practice that was maintained in the League of Nations after 1919 and the UN Security Council after 1945 (Holsti, 1991: 114–37; Jarrett, 2013: 369–72). As argued in Chapter 4, the emergence of nationalism corroded dynasticism, providing a new principle of political legitimacy. Nationalism both sacralized territory and shifted the moral purpose of political units from dynastic hierarchy to sovereign equality. The shift from dynastic to modern nation-states that took

---

[2] There are, as ever, exceptions to this rule. In Saudi Arabia, for example, dynasticism has persisted – the country operates more like a family firm than as a rational state. And almost everywhere, family genealogy remains important, whether these families take the name Gandhi, Kennedy, Kim or Rothschild. The hold of such families over the 'commanding heights' of some contemporary polities and economies has led Piketty (2014) to label this tendency 'patrimonial capitalism'.

place during the nineteenth century thus carried with it ideational changes central to the conduct of international relations.

Other ideational schemas had a more mixed experience. Patriarchy was, in many ways, reconstituted during the long nineteenth century (McClintock, 1995; Towns, 2009). The term 'feminism' only emerged during the latter part of the nineteenth century (Offen, 2010b: 5), and it was not until the second half of the twentieth century that feminists exerted a full-spectrum challenge to gendered sources of inequality (Goedde, 2014: 609–31). Empire was first reinvigorated and then destabilized by global modernity. As we showed in Chapter 4, the nineteenth century saw both the ending of the Atlantic trade in slaves and the rearticulating of racism in 'scientific' form. European imperialists were responsible for the mass extermination of peoples in the periphery, and the early-to-middle decades of the twentieth century saw fascists introduce such policies into the core. The revulsion that followed helped prompt the institutionalization of the human rights regime and wide acceptance of the notion of human equality as a primary institution of international society. If racism continued as a private, and sometimes public, practice, its wider legitimacy was greatly diminished. Post-colonial movements acted as the vanguard of this wider movement, even as the 'standard of civilization' was reconstituted in the post-war development project (Anghie, 2006), a dynamic we explored in Chapter 7.

As we pointed out in the previous chapter, the ideological bandwidth of contemporary international relations is much narrower than at any time over the past two centuries. Rather than systemic, at times existential, conflicts between rival social orders, international relations is now marked by competing 'varieties of capitalism'. This is not to say that there are no significant ideational differences in the contemporary world. But it is to say that recent years have seen no major new ideational schemas that compare to those unleashed during the long nineteenth century. Indeed, the contemporary world appears to be just as interdependent ideationally as it is materially.

One curiosity, at least for some, is the enduring place of religion in the contemporary world – over three-quarters of the world's population adheres to a major religion (Goedde, 2014: 646). Many modern thinkers in the West, including nineteenth-century figures such as Marx and Nietzsche, expected modernity to herald 'the death of God'. Yet, as we discussed in the previous chapter, religion remains an important feature of the contemporary international landscape, and has recaptured some of its force as a motivation for political violence. In a world marked by decentred globalism, religion looks likely to remain a prominent feature of both state behaviour and INGO activity.[3] Such a dynamic illustrates how some very old ideational schemas have withstood the challenge of global modernity, if only by being transformed by it (Turner, 2013).

Like the material aspects of the global transformation, the ideational component of global modernity has thus now permeated the whole planet. There are still marked differences in the way, and the degree to which, ideologies of progress have been embedded in social orders around the world. But as with industrial technologies, these differences are much less pronounced than they were at the beginning of the process. The remaining differences are largely within the confines of varieties of capitalism rather than being about capitalism or not. This is not to say that no significant differences or sources of turbulence remain within world politics. But because only modernity can generate the power and wealth necessary to sustain social orders in the contemporary world, all states have to find ways of coming to terms with its mode of power.

Implications for Thinking About Periodization

Taking the global transformation into account provides a much clearer narrative of the historical emergence of modern international relations as well as a superior take on the main contours of contemporary international order.

To start with the latter point first, if contemporary scholarship tends to agree that the world *is* changing, there is considerable disagreement about *how* it is changing. Commentators variously locate this change in a 'power shift' from West to East (Quah, 2011), a trade in superpower status between the United States and China (Halper, 2010; Yan, 2011), or in a transition from an era of bipolarity to one of unipolarity (Brooks and Wohlforth, 2008), multipolarity (Ikenberry, 2011; Kupchan, 2012)

---

[3] The wider argument here, which we do not have the space to consider, is the ways in which *all* human communities, 'modern' or otherwise, contain forms of the sacred and magical. For a discussion of this issue, see Geertz (1973) and Tambiah (1990).

or even non-polarity (Haass, 2008). These analyses are joined by attention to a smorgasbord of dynamics that are said to be disrupting the smooth functioning of international order: globalization, US militarism, dynamics of revolution and counter-revolution, finance capital, climate change, the rise of non-state actors, new security threats, the dislocating effects of ICTs, and more.

The problem with most of these analyses is that they either possess a weak account of how the contemporary international order came into being, or ignore this process altogether. This neglect means that many commentators have oversimplified, narrow understandings of the emergent world order. It also means that commentators tend to mischaracterize disruptive social forces, seeing them as recent when in fact they are rooted in nineteenth-century dynamics, and assessing them in isolation rather than as interrelated components within a set of transformative dynamics unleashed by global modernity.

This book has outlined an alternative account of the formation of modern international relations. As discussed in Chapter 9, the contemporary world is witnessing the third stage of global modernity. The opening phase, lasting from the early part of the nineteenth century until around 1945, was marked by the opening of a massive power gap between a relatively small group of Western states (plus Japan) and a much larger group of polities that were dominated by these states. This power gap fostered what we have called *Western-colonial* international society. The second phase lasted from 1945 until *c.*2008. During this period, decolonization changed the form of international society from Western-colonial to *Western-global,* but had little impact, at least initially, on some aspects of the core–periphery structure characteristic of the first stage of global modernity, particularly economic inequality and, to some extent, military inequality. The third phase of global modernity, *decentred globalism,* is marked by the relative (if not absolute) decline of the West and the more sustained closing of the power gap begun during the post-Second World War period. The core of industrial, rational states is getting bigger; the periphery of states who lack, or who have been denied, access to these sources of power is shrinking. As argued in Chapter 9, as global modernity unwinds, no state will attain superpower status.

In this narrative, the same configuration that enabled the 'rise of the West' is now enabling the 'rise of the rest' (Zakaria, 2009). And it is this development that provides the often-unseen backdrop to accounts of contemporary global turbulence. Contemporary commentators are right to say that profound changes are underway. But they are wrong to see this primarily in terms of superpower rivalry, continental power shifts or changes in polarity. The changes go far deeper than this, affecting the very sources of power on which international order rests. Decentred globalism provides a foundation for international affairs quite unlike the core–periphery global order of the past two centuries. It also provides a backdrop quite unlike the world before the nineteenth century, in which there were many centres of power, but these were only lightly and slowly connected with each other. The optic provided by the global transformation provides a sounder basis for thinking about the development, shape and content of international order than analysis that fails to root contemporary concerns in an account of global modernity.

Implications for Thinking About IR and History

The global transformation raises three issues about the relationship between IR and history: first, an ontological question about the implications of big disjunctures for how IR is studied; second, an awareness of the ways in which the nineteenth century affects contemporary international relations; and third, the question of what benchmark dates should be used to organize the study and teaching of IR.

1. Disjunctures in IR

As noted in Chapter 2, some commentators argue that the global transformation represents a disjuncture on such a scale that it cannot meaningfully be compared with earlier periods in world history. For example, Fred Halliday (2009: 19) claims that IR has to theorize modern international relations in quite different ways from earlier types of international order. This position feeds into a more general set of concerns around whether different historical periods are comparable in that they are constituted by different ways of knowing and are, thereby, out of tune with contemporary discourses, vocabularies and concerns (Skinner, 1988). Such a view challenges a number of positions in mainstream IR, most obviously neo-realism (e.g. Waltz, 1979), which claims a more or less timeless comparability of international politics across time and place.

In this book we have made the case that the global transformation did constitute a major disjuncture, albeit an uneven, gradual, multilinear one rather than a 'big bang', sustained by a mode of power that was radically different from those available in previous periods of world history. Do we thereby commit ourselves to the view that denies comparability across history? To answer that question would require another book and a much deeper foray into the philosophy of knowledge than we have space for here. What we can say is that we recognize the importance of the question. At a minimum, mainstream IR needs to problematize comparability by paying more attention to continuities and changes across major disjunctures. We have argued that the configuration of power that sustained the global transformation distinguishes the last two hundred years from earlier periods of world history. This opens up the possibility that the concepts and analytical tools we have used to assess global modernity are not easily transportable to other times and other places.

However, we have also made the point that global modernity was uneven and messy, and that there are a range of important continuities between the current era and previous ones. Notions of sovereignty preceded modernity, at least in Europe, by several centuries, yet the high point of sovereignty as a ground rule of international society did not peak until the end of the twentieth century (Lawson, 2008). The Axial Age religions preceded modernity, in some cases by more than two millennia; these too have survived and adapted to the global transformation. Gender relations remain dismally unequal across world history. And certain basic techniques of statecraft (divide and rule, diplomacy, balancing, etc.) appear in one guise or another across much of recorded history.

In this way, even as we have emphasized the disjunctive dimensions of the global transformation, we have also recognized some of the continuities between the modern period and its predecessors. Lurking behind this stance is a broader question about the conduct of any such comparative exercise. On the one hand, those (like Waltz) who make comparisons across world historical time need to justify the basis on which they do so – merely assuming 'like-units' on the basis of superficial similarities will not stand. On the other hand, those who deny macro-comparability (like Halliday) need to set out the defining characteristics of the periods where they do think meaningful comparisons can be made. Our view is that this is not a zero-sum game. Given the contextual, situated nature of historical knowledge (Kratochwil, 2006), easier comparisons are likely to be made within periods that share the same basic characteristics. That is why we have stressed the kinship of the nineteenth, twentieth and twenty-first centuries. But this does not rule out comparative work across apparently distinct periods of world history. Such comparisons are necessarily more limited and conditional, and have to be based on clear justifications of the criteria on which they are conducted. Even if we always take our contexts with us as we conduct macro-historical comparisons, and even if there is always the risk of anachronism in any such exercise, this does not rule out the possibility of carrying out meaningful work into apparently remote times.[4] The cultivation of such a historical sensibility is to make a start at tackling the question of what can and cannot be compared across time and place.

2. Legacy Issues from the Global Transformation

Our argument is that the global transformation has left an easily recognizable imprint on the contemporary world: an intensely interdependent world economy; a dominant form of modern statehood; global communication and transportation systems; a prevailing set of ideologies of progress; a wide set of intergovernmental organizations; a growing body of international law; a closed, global-scale international system, and more.

In addition to these general legacies are a host of specific issues bequeathed by global modernity, many of which are central to the day-to-day operations of contemporary international relations. Among those we have discussed are:

- The strongly felt resentment to, and resistance against, the legacies of racism and colonialism maintained from the nineteenth and twentieth centuries.
- The deep hostility between China and Japan, and Korea and Japan, stemming from Japan's appropriation of the modern mode of power and its subsequent attempt to foster an imperial project in East Asia.

---

[4] The same goes for 'remote places', albeit with similar caveats: that immersion in other ways of life is not straightforward, requiring deep immersion rather than a 'Lonely Planet' approach to such an enterprise. For more on this issue, see Lawson (2012).

- The defence dilemma and the ongoing problem of permanent technological change as a security issue.
- The 'development project' with all of its attendant disagreements about the allocation of responsibilities between core and periphery.
- The particular history of Israel and the late-colonial project of Zionism.

There are many other issues we could have discussed, ranging from border disputes in Africa, the Middle East and South Asia that stem from arbitrary or vague colonial boundaries, to the absence of a dominant regional great power in the Middle East (Lustick, 1997). The key point is that a substantial agenda in contemporary international relations, in addition to many of its underlying dynamics, has its roots in the global transformation. Even the basic geopolitical terminology of much of the discussion of contemporary IR has nineteenth-century origins, from the idea of 'the West', to framings such as 'the Middle East' and 'Latin America' (Osterhammel, 2014: 78–86). It is worth scholars and students of IR being aware of just how much of the discipline's contemporary agenda, both general and particular, originates in the global transformation. Starting from, and with, global modernity would provide a much surer basis for effective comparative work than IR's current foundations permit.

3. Benchmark Dates in IR

Benchmark dates are used in every discipline that engages with history as a means of placing boundaries around research and teaching, identifying turning points and simplifying analysis. In short: benchmark dates are as important as theories – both serve as lenses that foreground some things, while marginalizing others.

We noted in Chapter 2 how the main benchmark dates in IR jump from 1648 to 1919, and why this is a problem. Elsewhere we have argued that introducing the global transformation into IR changes the make-up of the existing benchmark dates around which much of the discipline organizes its research and teaching (Buzan and Lawson, 2014a). The nub of the argument is that IR has allowed itself to drift into a set of five benchmark dates that are largely defined by major wars and their outcomes: 1500, 1648, 1919, 1945, 1989. It is not uncommon in IR to use major wars to periodize history and many would agree with

Gray's (2012: loc. 605) claim that: 'Our modern world has been made, unmade and remade pre-eminently by the threat and use of organized force.' The first of the orthodox benchmark dates, 1500, is the exception to the 'defined by war' convention – it marks the making of a global-scale system by the opening of intercontinental sea passages. However, this date is the least used of the 'big five'. Importantly, 1648 has iconic status as the benchmark date that stands for the founding of a modern system of sovereign states – this makes IR the only social science that locates modernity in the seventeenth century rather than the nineteenth century. Our contention is that the current set of benchmark dates in IR over-privileges the experience of modern Europe and focuses the discipline too tightly around wars and their settlements.

Making the global transformation more front-and-central to IR places two question marks against the practice of privileging major wars as benchmark dates. One question is why some major wars and their settlements are featured prominently (1648, 1919, 1945, 1989) and others relegated to the background (1713, 1815). The other is more fundamental: why is the particular kind of crisis signified by major wars favoured over other types of change, whether in crisis form (economic depressions, revolutions) or as longer-term transformations (market expansion, state formation, the rise and decline of major organizing ideas, etc.)? Because the global transformation emerged largely between big multipower conflicts (the Atlantic Revolutions and the First World War) and was mainly a case of long-term transformation, it does not register within IR's orthodox schema. This leaves a long gap between 1648 and 1919 in which, by implication, nothing of major consequence for IR took place. We hope to have demonstrated in this book why such an assumption is somewhere between flawed and fraudulent.

Once the idea that IR's benchmark dates must be determined by major wars is abandoned, a range of possibilities opens up for thinking about how to reorient the subject. The 'empty' nineteenth century contains a host of significant events that bear comparison with IR's orthodox set of benchmark dates in terms of their importance to the development of international order. Drawing from our previous chapters, one might choose:

- 1776: The American Revolution introduces popular sovereignty as a source of foreign policy, and strengthens republicanism as an alternative to dynasticism.

- 1789: The French Revolution unleashes republicanism and popular sovereignty against dynasticism and aristocratic rule, while making use of novel organizing vehicles such as the *levée en masse*.
- 1840: This date roughly signifies when the cloth trade between India and Britain was reversed, illustrating the turnaround of trade relations between Europe and Asia, and the establishment of an unequal relationship between an industrial core and a commodity-supplying periphery.
- 1842: The First Opium War sees the British defeat the greatest classical Asian power, helping to establish a substantial inequality in military power between core and periphery.
- 1857: The Indian Revolt causes Britain to assume formal control of the subcontinent, while serving as a forerunner to later anti-colonial movements.
- 1859: The launching of the French ironclad warship *La Gloire* opens the era of industrial arms racing in which permanent technological improvement becomes a central factor in great power military relations.
- 1862: The British Companies Act marks a shift to limited liability firms, opening the way to the formation of transnational corporations as significant actors in international society.
- 1865: The International Telecommunications Union becomes the first standing intergovernmental organization, symbolizing the emergence of permanent institutions of global governance.
- 1866: The opening of the first transatlantic telegraph cable begins the wiring together of the planet with instantaneous communication.
- 1869: The opening of the Suez Canal marks the beginning of geo-engineering on a planetary scale.
- 1870: The unification of Germany serves as an indication of the new standing of nationalism as an institution of international society, as well as highlighting a central change in the distribution of power.
- 1884: The Prime Meridian Conference establishes world standard time, serving to facilitate the integration of trade, diplomacy and communication.
- 1905: Japan defeats Russia, becoming the first non-Western, non-white imperial great power.

Using these and similar events as benchmark dates would help to locate IR within a series of macro-historical debates that are germane to

contemporary international relations: the emergence and institutional
ization of a core–periphery international order that was first established
during the global transformation; the ways in which global modernity
served to intensify inter-societal interactions, but also amplify differences between societies; the closeness of the relationship between war,
industrialization, rational state-building and the 'standard of civilization'; the central role played by ideologies of progress in legitimating
practices ranging from scientific advances to coercive interventions; and
the centrality of dynamics of imperialism and revolution to the formation of contemporary international order.

Closer attention to these dates would also foster more balanced
analysis by integrating economic, cultural and technological transformations alongside military-political events, helping to reduce IR's
tendencies towards parochialism and West-centrism. Indeed, once the
range, depth and magnitude of the changes initiated during the nineteenth century is understood, it becomes clear that the orthodox
benchmark dates within the twentieth and twenty-first centuries are
not self-defining and free-standing events. They represent a series of
responses to forces unleashed during the nineteenth century that are
still working themselves out. As we have argued repeatedly in this
book, if IR is to gain a better grasp of its core areas of enquiry, the
historical pivot of the nineteenth century needs to become more central
to its field of vision.

Pursuing this line of thinking leads to a major change in IR's orthodox
set of benchmark dates. There are, in effect, three types of benchmark
date operating within IR:

1. Point-in-time events that are seen as turning points (e.g. 1929, 1989,
   2008).
2. Relatively short, sharp, transition periods, often featuring major
   wars and symbolized by the dates of the treaties that settle them
   (e.g. 1713, 1815, 1919, 1945).
3. Tipping points for transformative processes that are decades, possibly centuries, in duration (e.g. 1500, 1648, and the various attempts
   to capture the global transformation). In this understanding, benchmark dates represent clusters of events that open up enquiry into a
   range of nested dynamics.

In our previous work (Buzan and Lawson, 2014a), we prioritized the
third type of benchmark date, downgrading the significance of 1648,

1919 and 1989, and proposing a symbolic tipping-point date of 1860 to take into account the peak of the first stage of the global transformation between 1840 and 1870. We rank 1860 alongside 1500 and 1942 as the primary benchmark dates for IR, each representing a cluster of changes that, taken together, transformed the way in which international relations was conceived and practised. Our argument in this book suggests that 2008 might be another important turning point in international affairs. However, in our earlier work, we instituted a 'thirty-year rule' for assessing critical junctures lest presentism override hindsight. We will therefore have to wait some time before seeing whether our argument about 2008 stands up. More generally, a rearticulation of IR around a more considered, open set of benchmark dates would generate both more acute historical antenna and a more deeply formed contemporary agenda. Rethinking its benchmark dates in the light of the nineteenth-century global transformation would also put IR in a stronger position to exchange ideas with neighbouring disciplines in the social sciences and history, a point we return to in the next, final section of the book.

Implications for Thinking About IR as a Discipline

Making the global transformation more front-and-central to IR's substantive agenda affects the discipline's self-understanding in three ways: how it understands its origins and history; what attitude it takes towards its theoretical perspectives and divisions of labour; and how it relates to neighbouring disciplines in the social sciences and history.

IR's Understanding of its Origins and History

As indicated in Chapter 2, we broadly accept the Carvalho et al. (2011) critique of the 1919 founding myth of IR. There is some substance to this myth in terms of when the discipline became self-conscious and when chairs in, and departments of, IR came into being. But the idea of pristine creation out of the horrors of the First World War obscures IR's deeper, and in some cases darker, roots. Seeing IR as founded in 1919 constitutes the discipline as a 'noble' cause (Vitalis, 2010), with its gaze fixed firmly on how to understand and solve the problem of war. What is forgotten is the strands of thinking – liberal, realist, Marxist, colonial, racist, geopolitical, strategic, legal, historical, normative – about the, as yet, unlabelled 'international relations' that emerged in the period preceding the First World War and that fed into the formalization of the discipline (Bell, 2007; Vucetic, 2011; Hobson, 2012; Armitage, 2013; Ashworth, 2013).

As noted in Chapter 2, this thinking included strands of thought with direct links to a broad set of themes: the dynamics of great power politics and the balance of power; the rise of positive international law and intergovernmental organizations; the links between colonial administration, the mandate system and later debates about development and underdevelopment; the prominence of racism in conceptualizing and practising world politics; the interplay between trade, finance, production and war; the relationship between imperialism and nationalism; and the formalization of strategy and geopolitics as ways of systematizing foreign policy. One aspect of IR's coming to terms with the global transformation is to acknowledge how deeply the origins of the discipline are rooted in nineteenth-century debates.

IR's Attitude Towards its Internal Theoretical Perspectives

IR has long been considered as a fragmented discipline (Holsti, 1985; McKinlay and Little, 1986). Taking the global transformation into account will not cure this fissiparous tendency. But it does offer significant opportunities for all of the main approaches to the subject, both individually and collectively. A rearticulating of IR around the dynamics of the global transformation means examination of how industrialization, the rational state and ideologies of progress have generated the configuration within which much of contemporary international relations works, but which few IR theories accommodate.

Realists need to think more about the mode of power and not just about its distribution. Doing so will give them a richer and more productive view of the concept they take to be their core concern. It might even motivate them to question one of their key dictums that, as Gilpin (1981: 211) puts it, 'the nature of international relations has not changed fundamentally over the millennia'. The concept of mode of power identifies a qualitative difference in the type, form and sources of power – these qualities matter more than issues of raw capabilities. Qualitative differences in power create a deeper form of differentiation than quantitative power, affecting both the ways in which great powers interact with each other and the utility of war as an instrument of policy.

As explored above, these dynamics are re-envisioning the contemporary security agenda towards a broad range of concerns, requiring a deeper appreciation of both power relations and the sources of insecurity in modern societies.

In addition, neo-realists need to think harder about polarity theory. If we are right that we are heading for a world without superpowers, then polarity theory is in trouble, because it rests on there being globally operating and globally competing superpowers. A world of only great and regional powers would represent a quite different structure from a world with one or more superpowers. It would not be multipolarity as conventionally understood.

In some ways, liberals are well placed to take the great transformation on board. Liberalism already includes some aspects of the global transformation within its purview, not least the increasingly dense sphere of international relations occupied by IGOs and INGOs, and the emergence of the modern global economy (Ikenberry, 2001 and 2009). However, liberals could do more to address the question of *why* it was that IGOs and INGOs emerged when they did. Can this be explained only by the increasing density, interconnectedness and functional differentiation of the international system, or does one also need to look to the rise of the rational state, and the changing ideational environment of sovereignty, diplomacy and international law? There are also other aspects of the agenda opened up by global modernity that liberals should do more to embrace. Since the 1970s, IR has drifted into a division of labour in which realists study the use of force and liberals focus on issues of international cooperation (Caporaso, 1995). The wider security agenda generated by the global transformation has disrupted this cosy, and unconvincing, division of labour. Liberalism cannot – and should not – divorce itself from issues of security. Despite the hopes and pretensions of its classical thinkers, liberalism is not an alternative to security. To the contrary, contemporary security issues, ranging from human security to the vulnerabilities of interdependence, make liberal thought an important component of the security agenda.

Constructivists might take a lead from Reus-Smit (1999 and 2013) by focusing on the ideational shift that unfolded during the nineteenth century. As we have argued, the ideational landscape of world politics was profoundly altered by global modernity. Nearly all of the big ideas that have helped to shape the modern world rose to prominence during the long nineteenth century, and nothing equivalent to them has emerged since this time. This offers an opportunity for constructivists to carry out research into large-scale ideational transformations rather than serve a residual role by filling in the niches left by realist and liberal approaches.

The opportunity for the English School is, in some ways, similar to that for constructivists in that both approaches examine the interplay between ideational formulations and social practices. For the English School, the main point of interest is the impact of global modernity on the primary institutions of international society. Mayall (1990) has already pioneered such a study by exploring the rise of nationalism and the market during the nineteenth century, although he did not do so through a framework rooted in the global transformation. This task needs to be approached more systematically. The English School has not said nearly enough about racism, colonialism and imperialism as primary institutions during the period in which modernity emerged (partial exceptions include Keene, 2002; Keal, 2003; and Suzuki, 2009). Nor has it said nearly enough about the conditions that lie behind the rise, development and sometimes obsolescence of both primary and secondary institutions (partial exceptions include Buzan, 2004; and Holsti, 2004). The English School has a good claim to be the founding site for using 'the standard of civilization' in the analysis of international relations (Gong, 1984), but has not subsequently featured this concept as much as it might. Finally, the English School could build on work that traces the emergence of global civil society back to the configuration that enabled the global transformation (Clark, 2007).

Many critical approaches already use the global transformation, or aspects of it, as the starting point of their analysis. For most Marxists, global modernity marked a sea change in modern history, and Marxian-inspired approaches are right to see industrial capitalism as a central driver of modern international order. Several ideas associated with Marxian approaches have featured prominently in our analysis, most notably the analytical tool of uneven and combined development, and the deployment of 'core–periphery' as a means of conceptualizing the structure of international order during the first two stages of the global transformation. In similar vein, our emphasis on colonialism and racism as constitutive features of modern international order will be familiar to post-colonial scholarship, as will our analysis of the many legacies fostered by them. We have also made wide use of the term 'standard of civilization', which post-colonial scholarship rightly sees as fundamental to the emergence and maintenance of a hierarchical international order. More generally, our narrative of global modernity is written within the spirit of coeval histories envisaged by Said (1994) and others (e.g. Gruffydd Jones, 2006: 12–13; Krishna, 2006: 89). We see the construction of such narratives as fundamental to the development of debates about the global origins and outcomes of modernity. We also see these narratives as fundamental to recovering previous suppressed histories, not least those around race and colonialism. We are aware that, in carrying out our historical reconstruction, we have not presented an epistemological challenge to existing social scientific concepts and categories (Mitchell, 1998; Chakrabarty, 2000; Bhambra, 2007; Seth, 2007 and 2013; Mignolo, 2011). Although sensitive to this point, and to the broader issues raised by the politics of knowledge production, that task would require another book for which we are not the best qualified authors. Our aim in this book is something different: to offer a historical interpretation that is of use across IR's epistemological spectrum.

Feminists work within most of the above approaches, and their unifying concern with studying gender under conditions of patriarchy might fruitfully be examined more closely in relation to the global transformation. We have only touched upon the many ways in which patriarchy was redefined and, in many cases, reinvigorated by global modernity (McClintock, 1995; Towns, 2009 and 2010). Similarly, we have not done enough to show how these dynamics have been reinscribed and, to some extent, challenged in contemporary societies.[5] We can only deploy the standard cop-out line: not everything can go into one book. What we do hope is that we have provided a general framework within which future work can be mobilized.

IR and the Wider Social Sciences

The final issue we want to raise concerns IR's relationship with cognate disciplines. Here, as with other issues, insights from the global transformation offer considerable advantages, most obviously the generation

---

[5] The challenges are recent, but potentially important. Since 1991, nearly 50 states have introduced quota legislation to raise the numbers of women in national legislatures, while 90% of the world's states now contain a 'national women's machinery', albeit of widely differing qualities (Towns, 2010: 2–3).

of an interdisciplinary conversation that is less parochial and intellectually richer than existing dialogues.

IR has long been criticized for the narrowness of its intellectual agenda (e.g. Buzan and Little, 2001). At the same time, the discipline has been chided for its US-centrism. Since its formal institutionalization after the First World War, IR has been dominated by the Anglosphere, and especially since 1945 by the US IR community, which in sheer numbers and resources constitutes much of the discipline. An ostensibly international discipline has thus far been too closely bound up with primarily American concerns and methods, and dominated by American journals and organizations (Hoffman, 1987; Wæver, 1998; Shilliam, 2011; Tickner and Blaney, 2012).[6] Yet IR as a discipline is now also visibly subject to the logic of decentred globalism. Although the US (specifically) and the Anglosphere (in general) remain core parts of the discipline, and English its dominant tongue, IR is expanding rapidly in many parts of Europe, Asia, Latin America, the Pacific and Africa, and taking on more independent forms as it does so. One of the advantages of taking the global transformation more seriously is that it offers the chance to address this decentring of the discipline by acknowledging and embracing the global origins and outcomes of modernity. As we have shown in this book, the modern international order emerged from interactions between promiscuous, geographically variegated social forces. The contemporary world remains a site of ceaseless, multidirectional encounters. IR as a discipline is finally catching up with these dynamics by itself becoming both more global and more decentred.

Beginning the study of international relations with the global transformation provides a wider, more empirically accurate reading of both the emergence of modern international order and the shape of contemporary world politics. An account rooted in macro-history moves away

---

[6] One of the peculiarities of US IR is its closeness to Political Science, a discipline that favours the formulation of testable hypotheses that are usually evaluated through cross-case co-variation – a research programme that often goes under the label 'neo-positivism' (Jackson, 2011: 43). IR in other countries sometimes reproduces this trend, especially where there are many US-trained PhDs. But the discipline can and does have other roots: for example, in Britain, History, International Law and Political Theory; in Germany, Sociology; in China and Japan, History and Diplomatic Studies; and in France, Sociology and International Law. Even in the US, there are now strong strands of IR that pursue methods and concerns outside those favoured by neo-positivists.

from both 'comfort stories' that explain Western power through unidirectional accounts of metropolitan superiority (e.g. Jones, 1981), and the hegemony of neo-positivist methods. The long hold of neo-positivism has weakened IR's relationship with history (Hobson and Lawson, 2008). Neo-positivists of all stripes mine history for their data, using the past as a predetermined site for the empirical verification of abstract claims. As we showed in Chapter 2, the nineteenth century is no exception in this regard, being used as an uncontested background narrative that is coded within pre-existing theoretical categories (Lustick, 1996). The difficulty with such an approach is that it fosters a selection bias in which history is reduced to a role in which it is already filled in as the fulfilment of neo-positivism's theoretical abstractions. As such, neo-positivism is ahistorical, using history to code findings, mine data or as a source of *post factum* explanations rather than as a tool of effective theory-building (Smith, 1999; Isacoff, 2002; Lawson, 2012).

Our view is that IR needs to restore historical and historical socio-logical approaches as desirable methods in their own right, while at the same time cultivating methodological and epistemological pluralism (Jackson, 2011). This will both fit with the increasing globalization of the discipline, and facilitate desirable, indeed necessary, communication across disciplinary boundaries. IR should take its place as a 'historical social science' that aims to write new narratives of global modernity. These narratives, whether they concentrate on macro-dynamics or more granular accounts of particular events and processes within global modernity, will better reflect the origins and development of modern international order. The benefits of such a reorientation would be to move IR towards conversations already taking place throughout the social sciences on shared areas of concern: market exchanges, the experiences and legacies of colonialism, technological changes, state practices, cultural performances, and more. Taking the global trans-formation as its starting point would enable IR to exploit its comparative advantage of looking at the international dimensions of these shared issue-areas, an advantage helped by the relative paucity of Sociology's international imagination (Hobson et al., 2010).[7] This would also allow

---

[7] Linklater (2011) argues that process sociology can, when combined with the English School concept of international society, do much to repair the sociological deficit regarding the international. Rosenberg (2013) argues that uneven and combined development provides a distinctive *social* theory of the international.

for a reorientation of IR as a genuinely international discipline, using diverse vantage points within a common experience (global modernity) as a means of decentring and pluralizing the discipline's operating assumptions (Tickner and Blaney, 2012). This would, in turn, enable IR to develop a clearer view of how international order has developed and, as a result, a clearer view of where the downstream momentum of the global transformation is taking us. An IR enterprise constituted along these lines is much more likely to resonate with a world of decentred globalism.

There are two main benefits, therefore, to reformulating the discipline around the global transformation: first, constructing superior accounts of the formation and embedding of modern international order; and second, fostering a genuinely international discipline more likely to contribute useful insights to a world of decentred globalism. We do not underestimate the difficulties of turning the IR supertanker towards such an agenda. Academic specialization reinforces orthodoxy by encouraging scholars to pursue narrow, professionalized expertise (itself a product of the nineteenth century!). The result is that many scholars lose sight of, and perhaps even interest in, wider debates such as those highlighted in this book. Our aim is to contribute to a literature that understands the need to think outside the narrow bandwidth of much contemporary IR and to join the fertile debates taking place in cognate disciplines about the emergence and development of the modern international order. An IR that understood the extent to which its main concerns were rooted in the global transformation would itself have undergone a transformation. It would have integrated (rather than just tolerated) IPE. It would have rediscovered its links to International Law and Sociology. It would have put Political Science into its place as merely one of its constitutive disciplines, and at the same time given equal weight to its ties to Historical Sociology, Economic History and World History. By taking these steps, IR would have set itself up to become the intellectual space in which synthesizing debates across the social sciences could and should take place.

Bibliography

Abernathy, David B. (2000) *The Dynamics of Global Dominance*, New Haven: Yale University Press.

Abrahamian, Ervand (1993) *Khomeinism*, Berkeley: University of California Press.

Abu-Lughod, Janet (1989) *Before European Hegemony*, Oxford University Press.

Acemoglu, Daron and James A. Robinson (2012) *Why Nations Fail*, London: Profile.

Acharya, Amitav (2014) *The End of American World Order*, Cambridge: Polity Press.

Adorno, Theodor and Max Horkheimer (1979 [1944]) *Dialectic of Enlightenment*, London: Verso.

Agamben, Giorgio (1995) *Homo Sacer: Sovereign Power and Bare Life*, Palo Alto: Stanford University Press.

Alba, Richard and Roxane Silberman (2002) 'Decolonization Immigrations and the Social Origins of the Second Generation: The Case of North Africans in France', *International Migration Review*, 36(4): 1169–93.

Albert, Mathias and Barry Buzan (2011) 'Securitization, Sectors and Functional Differentiation', *Security Dialogue*, 42(4–5): 413–25.

Albert, Mathias, Barry Buzan and Michael Zürn (eds.) (2013) *Bringing Sociology to International Relations: World Politics as Differentiation Theory*, Cambridge University Press.

Alexandrowicz, C. H. (1967) *An Introduction to the History of the Law of Nations in the East Indies (16th, 17th, and 18th Centuries)*, Oxford: Clarendon Press.

  (1973) *The European-African Connection: A Study in Treaty Making*, Lieden: A. E. Sijthoff.

Allen, Robert (2009) *The British Industrial Revolution in Global Perspective*, Cambridge University Press.

Allison, Graham (1971) *Essence of Decision: Explaining the Cuba Missile Crisis*, Boston: Little, Brown & Co.

Amable, Bruno (2003) *The Diversity of Modern Capitalism*, Oxford University Press.

Anderson, Benedict (1983) *Imagined Communities: Reflections on the Origin and Spread of Nationalism*, London: Verso.

Anderson, Claire (2000) *Convicts in the Indian Ocean*, Basingstoke: Macmillan.

Anderson, Perry (1974) *Lineages of the Absolutist State*, London: Verso.

Angell, Norman (1910) *The Great Illusion: The Relation of Military Power to National Advantage*, London: William Heinemann.

Anghie, Antony (1999) 'Finding the Peripheries: Sovereignty and Colonialism in Nineteenth-Century International Law', *Harvard International Law Journal*, 40(1): 1–80.

    (2004) *Imperialism, Sovereignty and the Making of International Law*, Cambridge University Press.

    (2006) 'Decolonising the Concept of "Good Governance"', in: Branwen Gruffydd Jones (ed.), *Decolonizing International Relations*, Plymouth: Rowman & Littlefield, 109–30.

Annan, Kofi (2012) *Interventions: A Life in War and Peace*, London: Allen Lane.

Ansorge, Josef (2013) 'Writing Exceptions to the Laws of War', unpublished manuscript.

Ansorge, Josef and Tarak Barkawi (2014) 'Utile Forms: Power and Knowledge in Small War', *Review of International Studies*, 40(1): 3–24.

Anwar, Muhammad (1995) '"New Commonwealth" Migration to the UK', in: Robin Cohen (ed.), *The Cambridge Survey of World Migration*, Cambridge University Press, 274–8.

Arena, Mark, Irv Blickstein, Obaid Younossi and Clifford A. Grammich (2006) *Why Has the Cost of Navy Ships Risen? A Macroscopic Examination of the Trends in U.S. Military Aircraft Costs over the Past Several Decades*, Santa Monica: RAND.

Arena, Mark, Obaid Younossi, Kevin Brancato, Irv Blickstein and Clifford A. Grammich (2008) *Why Has the Cost of Fixed-Wing Aircraft Risen? A Macroscopic Examination of the Trends in U.S. Military Aircraft Costs over the Past Several Decades*, Santa Monica: RAND.

Arendt, Hannah (1963) *On Revolution*, London: Penguin.

Armbruster, Chris (2010) 'One Bright Moment in an Age of War, Genocide and Terror? On the Revolutions of 1989', in: George Lawson, Chris Armbruster and Michael Cox (eds.), *The Global 1989: Continuity and Change in World Politics*, Cambridge University Press, 201–18.

Armitage, David (2000) *The Ideological Origins of the British Empire*, Cambridge University Press.

    (2013) *The Foundations of Modern International Thought*, Cambridge University Press.

Armstrong, David (1993) *Revolution and World Order*, Oxford University Press.

(1998) 'Globalization and the Social State', *Review of International Studies*, 24(4): 461–78.

Armstrong, David, Lorna Lloyd and John Redmond (2004) *International Organisation in World Politics*, 3rd edn., Basingstoke: Palgrave Macmillan.

Arnold, David (2000) *The Cambridge History of India*, Cambridge University Press.

Arrighi, Giovanni (2010) *The Long Twentieth Century*, London: Verso.

Ashworth, Lucian M. (2013) 'Mapping a New World: Geography and the Interwar Study of International Relations', *International Studies Quarterly*, 57(1): 138–49.

Augustine, Norman R. (1975) 'One Plane, One Tank, One Ship: Trend for the Future?', *Defense Management Journal*, 11(2): 34–40.

Aydin, Cemil (2007) *The Politics of Anti-Westernism in Asia*, New York: Columbia University Press.

Badiou, Alain (2001) *Ethics*, London: Verso.

Bain, William (2003) *Between Anarchy and Society: Trusteeship and the Obligations of Power*, Oxford University Press.

Bairoch, Paul (1981) 'The Main Trends in National Economic Disparities Since the Industrial Revolution', in: Paul Bairoch and Maurice Lévy-Leboyer (eds.), *Disparities in Economic Development since the Industrial Revolution*, London: Macmillan, 3–17.

(1993) *Economics and World History: Myths and Paradoxes*, New York: Harvester Wheatsheaf.

Ballantyne, Tony and Antoinette Burton (2012) 'Empires and the Reach of the Global', in: Emily S. Rosenberg (ed.), *A World Connecting, 1870–1945*, Cambridge, MA: Belknap Press, 285–434.

Barkawi, Tarak (2011a) 'Defence Diplomacy in North–South Relations', *International Journal*, 66(3): 597–612.

(2011b) 'State and Armed Force in International Context', in: Alejandro Colás and Bryan Mabee (eds.), *Mercenaries, Pirates, Bandits and Empires*, London: Hurst & Co, 33–54.

Barkey, Karen (2008) *Empire of Difference*, Cambridge University Press.

Barnett, Michael (2011) *The Empire of Humanity*, Ithaca: Cornell University Press.

Barnett, Michael and Martha Finnemore (2004) *Rules for the World: International Organizations in Global Politics*, Ithaca: Cornell University Press.

Barrett, Ward (1990) 'World Bullion Flows 1450–1800', in: James D. Tracey (ed.), *The Rise of Merchant Empires*, Cambridge University Press, 224–54.

Barry, Brian (1973) *The Liberal Theory of Justice*, Oxford University Press.

Bartleson, Jens (1995) *A Genealogy of Sovereignty*, Cambridge University Press.

Bass, Gary (2008) *Freedom's Battle: The Origins of Humanitarian Intervention*, London: Vintage.

Bayart, Jean-François (1993) *The State in Africa: The Politics of the Belly*, London: Longman.

Bayly, C. A. (1983) *Rulers, Townsmen and Bazaars: North Indian Society in the Age of British Expansion, 1780–1870*, Oxford University Press.

(2004) *The Birth of the Modern World, 1780–1914*, Oxford: Blackwell.

(2011) *Recovering Liberties: Indian Thought in the Age of Liberalism and Empire*, Cambridge University Press.

Bayly, Christopher and Tim Harper (2005) *Forgotten Armies: Britain's Asian Empire and the War with Japan*, London: Penguin.

Beck, Colin (2011) 'The World-Cultural Origins of Revolutionary Waves', *Social Science History*, 35(2): 167–207.

Beeson, Mark (2009) 'Developmental States in East Asia: A Comparison of the Japanese and Chinese Experiences', *Asian Perspective*, 33(2): 5–39.

Belich, James (2009) *Replenishing the Earth: The Settler Revolution and the Rise of the Anglo-World, 1783–1939*, New York: Oxford University Press.

Bell, Duncan (2007) *The Idea of Greater Britain: Empire and the Future of World Order 1860–1900*, Princeton University Press.

(2010) 'John Stuart Mill on Colonies', *Political Theory*, 38(1): 34–64.

(2012) 'The Project for a New Anglo Century: Race, Space and Global Order', in: Peter Katzenstein (ed.), *Anglo-America and Its Discontents*, London: Routledge, 33–56.

(2013) 'Race and International Relations: Introduction', *Cambridge Review of International Affairs*, 26(1): 1–4.

(Forthcoming) 'What is Liberalism?', *Political Theory*.

Bellamy, Alex (2010) *Global Politics and the Responsibility to Protect*, London: Routledge.

Bellany, Ian (ed.) (2007) *Terrorism and Weapons of Mass Destruction: Responding to the Challenge*, Abingdon: Routledge.

Benjamin, Walter (1999) *Illuminations*, London: Pimlico.

Bentley, Jerry H. (1993) *Old World Encounters: Cross-Cultural Contacts and Exchanges in Pre-Modern Times*, Oxford University Press.

Benton, Lauren (2002) *Law and Colonial Cultures: Legal Regimes in World History, 1400–1900*, Cambridge University Press.

(2010) *A Search for Sovereignty: Law and Geography in European Empires, 1400–1900*, Cambridge University Press.

Benton, Lauren and Jeppe Mulich (Forthcoming) 'The Space Between Empires: Coastal and Insular Microregions in the Early Nineteenth-Century

World', in: Paul Stock (ed.), *The Uses of Space in Early Modern History*, New York: Palgrave Macmillan.

Berdal, Mats and Monica Serrano (eds.) (2002) *Transnational Organized Crime and International Security: Business as Usual?*, Boulder, CO: Lynne Rienner.

Berlin, Isaiah (1969) *Four Essays on Liberty*, Oxford University Press.

Bernal, Martin (1987) *Black Athena*, London: Free Association Books.

Best, Jacqueline (2006) 'Civilizing through Transparency: The International Monetary Fund', in: Brett Bowden and Leonard Seabrooke (eds.), *Global Standards of Market Civilization*, Abingdon: Routledge, 134–45.

Bhahba, Homi (1990) *Nation and Narration*, London: Routledge.

Bhambra, Gurminder (2007) *Rethinking Modernity: Postcolonialism and the Sociological Imagination*, Basingstoke: Palgrave Macmillan.

  (2013) 'The Possibilities Of, and For, Global Sociology', *Political Power and Social Theory*, 24: 295–314.

Bilgin, Pinar (2012) 'Globalization and In/Security: Middle Eastern Encounters with International Society and the Case of Turkey', in: Stephan Stetter (ed.), *The Middle East and Globalization*, Basingstoke: Palgrave Macmillan, 59–76.

Bisley, Nick (2004) 'Revolution, Order and International Politics', *Review of International Studies*, 30(1): 49–69.

Black, Jeremy (2009) *War in the Nineteenth Century 1800–1914*, Cambridge: Polity Press.

Blackburn, Robin (1997) *The Making of New World Slavery*, London: Verso.

Blanning, T. C. W. (ed.) (2000) *The Nineteenth Century*, Oxford University Press.

Blumi, Isa (2012) *Foundations of Modernity*, London: Routledge.

Blyth, Mark (2002) *Great Transformations: Economic Ideas and Institutional Change in the Twentieth Century*, Cambridge University Press.

  (2013) *Austerity: The History of a Dangerous Idea*, Oxford University Press.

Bobbitt, Philip (2002) *The Shield of Achilles*, London: Allen Lane.

Boli, John and George M. Thomas (eds.) (1999) *Constructing World Culture: International Non-Governmental Organizations Since 1875*, Stanford University Press.

Bowden, Brett (2009) *The Empire of Civilization: The Evolution of an Imperial Idea*, University of Chicago Press, Kindle edn.

Bowen, Daniel (ed.) (1977) *Encyclopedia of War Machines*, London: Octopus Books.

Branch, Jordan (2012) 'Colonial Reflection and Territoriality: The Peripheral Origins of Sovereignty', *European Journal of International Relations*, 18(2): 277–97.

(2014) *The Cartographic State: Maps, Territory and the Origins of Sovereignty*, Cambridge University Press.

Braudel, Fernand (1977) *Afterthoughts on Material Civilization and Capitalism*, Baltimore: Johns Hopkins University Press.

(1985) *The Perspective of the World: Civilization and Capitalism 15th–18th Century*, Vol. III, London: Fontana.

Brenner, Neil, Jamie Peck and Nik Theodore (2009) 'Variegated Neoliberalization: Geographies, Modalities, Pathways', *Global Networks*, 10(2): 182–222.

Brenner, Robert (1976) 'Agrarian Class Structure and Economic Development in Pre-Industrial Europe', *Past and Present*, 70(1): 30–75.

(1985) 'The Agrarian Roots of European Capitalism', in: T. H. Aston and C. H. E. Philpin (eds.), *The Brenner Debate*, Cambridge University Press, 213–327.

Breuilly, John (1993) *Nationalism and the State*, Manchester University Press.

Brewer, John (1990) *The Sinews of Power: War, Money, and the English State, 1688–1783*, Cambridge, MA: Harvard University Press.

Broadberry, Stephen (2014) 'Accounting for the Great Divergence', unpublished manuscript.

Brodie, Bernard (1941) *Sea Power in the Machine Age*, Princeton University Press.

Brodie, Bernard and Fawn M. Brodie (1973) *From Crossbow to H-Bomb*, Bloomington: Indiana University Press.

Broers, Michael (2011) 'Changes in War: The French Revolutionary and Napoleonic Wars', in: Hew Strachan and Sibylle Scheipers (eds.), *The Changing Character of War*, Oxford University Press, 64–78.

Brooks, Stephen and William Wohlforth (2008) *World Out of Balance*, Princeton University Press.

Brown, Michael E. (ed.) (1996) *Debating the Democratic Peace*, Cambridge, MA: MIT Press.

Bukovansky, Mlada (2002) *Legitimacy and Power Politics: The American and French Revolutions in International Political Culture*, Princeton University Press.

Bull, Hedley (1977) *The Anarchical Society: A Study of Order in World Politics*, London: Macmillan.

(1984a) 'The Revolt Against the West', in: Hedley Bull and Adam Watson (eds.), *The Expansion of International Society*, Oxford University Press, 217–28.

(1984b) 'Introduction', in: Hedley Bull (ed.), *Intervention in World Politics*, Oxford: Clarendon Press, 1–6.

Bull, Hedley and Adam Watson (eds.) (1984a) *The Expansion of International Society*, Oxford University Press.

(1984b) 'Conclusions', in: Hedley Bull and Adam Watson (eds.), *The Expansion of International Society*, Oxford University Press, 425–35.

Bull, Malcolm (2013) 'Help Yourself', *London Review of Books*, 21 February: 15–17.

Burbank, Jane and Frederick Cooper (2010) *Empires in World History*, Princeton University Press.

Butler, Judith (1990) *Gender Trouble*, London: Routledge.

Buzan, Barry (1981) 'Change and Insecurity: A Critique of Strategic Studies', in: Barry Buzan and R. J. Barry Jones (eds.), *Change and the Study of International Relations: The Evaded Dimension*, London: Pinter, 155–72.

(1987) *An Introduction to Strategic Studies*, Basingstoke: Macmillan.

(1995) 'Focus On: The Present as a Historic Turning Point?', *Journal of Peace Research*, 32(4): 385–98.

(2004) *From International to World Society?* Cambridge University Press.

(2007 [1991]) *People, States and Fear*, Colchester: ECPR Press.

(2008) 'A Leader Without Followers? The United States in World Politics after Bush', *International Politics*, 45(5): 554–70.

(2010) 'Culture and International Society', *International Affairs*, 86(1): 1–25.

(2011) 'A World Order Without Superpowers: Decentred Globalism', *International Relations*, 25(1): 1–23.

(2012) 'How Regions were Made, and the Legacies of that Process for World Politics', in T. V. Paul (ed.), *International Relations Theory and Regional Transformation*, Cambridge University Press, 22–46.

(2014a) *An Introduction to the English School of International Relations*, Cambridge: Polity Press.

(2014b) 'The Logic and Contradictions of "Peaceful Rise/Development" as China's Grand Strategy?', *Chinese Journal of International Politics*.

Buzan, Barry and Mathias Albert (2010) 'Differentiation: A Sociological Approach to International Relations Theory', *European Journal of International Relations*, 16(3): 315–37.

Buzan, Barry and Ana Gonzalez-Pelaez (2005) 'International Community after Iraq', *International Affairs*, 81(1): 31–52.

(eds.) (2009) *International Society and the Middle East: English School Theory at the Regional Level*, Basingstoke: Palgrave Macmillan.

Buzan, Barry and Lene Hansen (2009) *The Evolution of International Security Studies*, Cambridge University Press.

Buzan, Barry and George Lawson (2013) 'The Global Transformation: The Nineteenth Century and the Making of Modern International Relations', *International Studies Quarterly*, 57(3): 620–34.

(2014a) 'Rethinking Benchmark Dates in International Relations', *European Journal of International Relations* 20(2): 437–62.

(2014b) 'Capitalism and the Emergent World Order', *International Affairs*, 90(1): 71–91.

Buzan, Barry and Richard Little (2000) *International Systems in World History*, Oxford University Press.

(2001) 'Why International Relations Has Failed as an Intellectual Project and What to Do About It', *Millennium*, 30(1): 19–39.

(2010) 'The Historical Expansion of International Society', in: Robert A. Denemark (ed.), *International Studies Encyclopedia*, Oxford: Blackwell.

Buzan, Barry and Ole Wæver (2003) *Regions and Powers: The Structure of International Security*, Cambridge University Press.

Buzan, Barry, Ole Wæver and Jaap de Wilde (1998) *Security: A New Framework for Analysis*, Boulder, CO: Lynne Rienner.

Buzan, Barry and Yongjin Zhang (eds.) (2014) *International Society and the Contest Over 'East Asia'*, Cambridge University Press.

Cairncross, Frances (2001) *The Death of Distance 2.0*, London: Texere.

Calhoun, Craig (2007) *Nations Matter*, London: Routledge.

(2012) *The Roots of Radicalism*, University of Chicago Press.

Callahan, William A. (2014) 'China's New World Order: The China Dream, the American Dream and the World Dream', paper presented at the Association for Asian Studies Annual Conference, Philadelphia, March.

Calvert, Peter (1984) *Revolution and International Politics*, New York: Pinter.

Caporaso, James A. (1995) 'False Divisions: Security Studies and International Political Economy', *Mershon International Studies Review*, 39(1): 117–22.

Cardoso, Fernando and Enzo Faletto (1979) *Dependency and Development in Latin America*, Berkeley: University of California Press.

Carroll, William K. (2010) *The Making of a Transnational Capitalist Class*, London: Zed.

Carruthers, Bruce (1996) *City of Capital: Politics and Markets in the English Financial Revolution*, Princeton University Press.

Carvalho, Benjamin de, Halvard Leira and John Hobson (2011) 'The Big Bangs of IR: The Myths That Your Teachers Still Tell You about 1648 and 1919', *Millennium*, 39(3): 735–58.

Castells, Manuel (1996) *The Rise of the Network Society*, Oxford: Blackwell.

Castles, Stephen, Hein de Haas and Mark J. Miller (2014) *The Age of Migration: International Population Movements in the Modern World*, 5th edn., Basingstoke: Palgrave Macmillan.

Cerny, Phil (2010) *A Theory of Transnational Neopluralism*, Oxford University Press.

Chakrabarty, Dipesh (2000) *Provincializing Europe*, University of Chicago Press.

Chase-Dunn, Christopher (2013) 'Response to Barry Buzan and George Lawson', *International Studies Quarterly*, 57(3): 635–6.

Chaudhuri, K. N. (1985) *Trade and Civilization in the Indian Ocean*, Cambridge University Press.

Chibber, Vivek (2003) *Locked in Place: State Building and Late Industrialization in India*, Princeton University Press.

(2013) *Post-Colonial Theory and the Spectre of Capital*, London: Verso.

Chin, Gregory and Fahimul Quadir (2012) 'Rising States, Rising Donors and the Global Aid Regime', *Cambridge Review of International Affairs*, 25(4): 493–506.

Chirot, Daniel (1985) 'The Rise of the West', *American Sociological Review*, 50(2): 181–95.

Christensen, Jens (1998) 'Internettets Verden' [The World of the Internet], *Samvirke*, 4 (April): 106–12.

Christian, David (2004) *Maps of Time*, Berkeley: University of California Press.

Clark, Ann Marie (1995) 'Non-Governmental Organizations and their Influence on International Society', *Journal of International Affairs*, 48(2): 507–25.

Clark, Ian (1989) *The Hierarchy of States: Reform and Resistance in the International Order*, Cambridge University Press.

(1997) *Globalisation and Fragmentation: International Relations in the Twentieth Century*, Oxford University Press.

(2005) *Legitimacy in International Society*, Oxford University Press.

(2007) *International Legitimacy and World Society*, Oxford University Press.

(2011) *Hegemony in International Society*, Oxford University Press.

Clodfelter, Michael (2002) *Warfare and Armed Conflicts: A Statistical Reference to Casualty and Other Figures, 1500–2000*, 2nd edn., London: McFarland & Co.

Cockett, Richard (1995) *Thinking the Unthinkable*, London: Fontana.

Cohen, Raymond and Raymond Westbrook (eds.) (2000) *Amarna Diplomacy: The Beginnings of International Relations*, Baltimore: Johns Hopkins University Press.

Collier, Paul (2007) *The Bottom Billion*, Oxford University Press.

Collins, Michael (2011) *Empire, Nationalism and the Postcolonial World*, London: Routledge.

Connell, Raewyn (2007) *Southern Theory*, Cambridge: Polity Press.

Connolly, William (1991) *Identity/Difference*, Minneapolis: University of Minnesota Press.

Connor, Walker (1994) *Ethnonationalism*, Princeton University Press.

Cook, Helena (1996) 'Amnesty International at the United Nations', in: Peter Willetts (ed.), *The Conscience of the World: The Influence of Non-Governmental Organisations in the UN System*, London: Hurst, 181–213.

Cooper, Frederick and Ann Laura Stoler (1997) *Tensions of Empire*, Berkeley: University of California Press.

Cooper, Robert (2002) 'The New Liberal Imperialism', www.guardian.co.uk/world/2002/aor/07/1/print, accessed 17/5/2010.

Cox, Robert (1986) 'Social Forces, States and World Orders: Beyond International Relations Theory', in: Robert Keohane (ed.), *Neo-Realism and its Critics*, Princeton University Press, 204–54.

(1987) *Production, Power and World Order*, New York: Columbia University Press.

Crawford, Neta (2002) *Argument and Change in World Politics: Ethics, Decolonization, and Humanitarian Intervention*, Cambridge University Press.

Crosby, Alfred W. (2004) *Ecological Imperialism: The Biological Expansion of Europe, 900–1900*, Cambridge University Press.

Crouch, Colin (2011) *The Strange Non-Death of Neoliberalism*, Cambridge: Polity Press.

Curtin, Philip D. (1984) *Cross-Cultural Trade in World History*, Cambridge University Press.

Darwin, John (2007) *After Tamerlane: The Rise and Fall of Global Empires, 1400–2000*, London: Penguin.

(2009) *The Empire Project*, Cambridge University Press.

(2012) *Unfinished Empire: The Global Expansion of Britain*, London: Allen Lane.

Davidson, Neil (2012) *How Bourgeois Were the Bourgeois Revolutions?* London: Haymarket.

Davies, Thomas (2013) *NGOs: A New History of Transnational Civil Society*, London: Hurst.

Davis, John P. (1971 [1905]) *Corporations: A Study of the Origin and Development of Great Business Combinations and of their Relation to the Authority of the State*, 2 vols., New York: Burt Franklin.

Davis, Mike (2002) *Late Victorian Holocausts*, London: Verso.

(2006) *Planet of Slums*, London: Verso.

Davis, R. E. G. (1964) *The World's Airlines*, Oxford University Press.

Deleuze, Gilles (1994) *Difference and Repetition*, London: Athlone.

Deng, Yong (2008) *China's Struggle for Status*, Cambridge University Press.

Derrida, Jacques (2001 [1967]) *Writing and Difference*, London: Routledge.

Deudney, Daniel (2007) *Bounding Power*, Princeton University Press.

Deudney, Daniel and John Ikenberry (2009) 'The Myth of the Autocratic Revival', *Foreign Affairs*, 88(1): 77–93.

De Vries, Jan (2008) *The Industrious Revolution*, Cambridge University Press.

(2013) 'Reflections on Doing Global History', in: Maxine Berg (ed.), *Writing the History of the Global*, Oxford University Press, 32–47.

Diamond, Jared (1998) *Guns, Germs and Steel*, London: Vintage.

(2005) *Collapse: How Societies Choose to Fail or Survive*, London: Penguin.

Dikötter, Frank (1992) *The Discourse of Race in Modern China*, London: Hurst.

Dirks, Nicholas B. (2011) *Castes of Mind*, Princeton University Press.

Dodge, Toby (2013) 'Intervention and Dreams of Exogenous Statebuilding: The Application of Liberal Peacebuilding in Afghanistan and Iraq', *Review of International Studies*, 39(5): 1189–212.

Donnelly, Jack (1998) 'Human Rights: A New Standard of Civilization?', *International Affairs*, 74(1): 1–23.

Downing, Brian (1992) *The Military Revolution and Political Change*, Princeton University Press.

Drayton, Richard (2000) *Nature's Government: Science, Imperial Britain and the 'Improvement' of the World*, New Haven: Yale University Press.

Drezner, Daniel and Kathleen McNamara (2013) 'International Political Economy, Global Financial Orders and the 2008 Financial Crisis', *Perspectives on Politics*, 11(1): 155–66.

Drezner, David W. (2012) 'The Irony of Global Economic Governance: The System Worked', Working Paper, New York: Council on Foreign Relations.

Du Bois, W. E. B. (1994 [1903]) *The Souls of Black Folk*, New York: Dover.

Duffield, Mark (2007) *Development, Security and Unending War: Governing the World of Peoples*, Cambridge: Polity Press.

Duncan, Richard (2012) 'A New Global Depression', *New Left Review*, 77(Sept./Oct.): 5–33.

Eichengreen, Barry (1996) *Global Capitalism*, Princeton University Press.

Eisenstadt, S. N. (2000) 'Multiple Modernities', *Dædalus*, 129(1): 1–29.

Eley, Geoff (2002) *Forging Democracy: The History of the Left in Europe, 1850–2000*, Oxford University Press.

Elias, Norbert (1978) *What is Sociology?*, London: Hutchinson.

Elman, Colin (2004) 'The Louisiana Purchase and America's Rise to Regional Hegemony', *American Political Science Review*, 98(4): 563–76.

Elman, Colin and Miriam Findius Elman (1995) 'Correspondence: History vs. Neo-Realism', *International Security*, 20(1): 182–93.

Eloranta, Jari (2012) 'The Economic History of War and Defense', in: Robert Whaples and Randall E. Parker (eds.), *Routledge Handbook of Modern Economic History*, New York: Routledge, 105–15.

Engelbrecht, H. C. and F. C. Hanighen (1934) *Merchants of Death*, New York: Dodd, Mead & Co.

Ertman, Thomas (1997) *Birth of the Leviathan*, Cambridge University Press.

Escobar, Arturo (1995) *Encountering Development*, Princeton University Press.

Evans, Peter (1979) *Dependent Development*, Princeton University Press.

(1995) *Embedded Autonomy*, Princeton University Press.

Fagan, Brian M. (1993) *World Prehistory: A Brief Introduction*, 2nd edn., New York: HarperCollins.

Falkner, Robert (2012) 'Global Environmentalism and the Greening of International Society', *International Affairs*, 88(3): 503–22.

Fenby, Jonathan (2014) *Will China Dominate the 21st Century?*, Cambridge: Polity Press.

Ferguson, James (2006) *Global Shadows: Africa in the Neoliberal World Order*, Durham, NC: Duke University Press.

Ferguson, Niall (2001) *The Cash Nexus: Money and Power in the Modern World*, London: Allen Lane.

(2004) *Empire: How Britain Made the Modern World*, London: Penguin.

(2010) 'Crisis: What Crisis?', in: Niall Ferguson, Charles S. Maier, Erez Manela and Daniel J. Sargent (eds.), *The Shock of the Global: The 1970s in Perspective*, Cambridge, MA: Belknap Press, 1–23.

Ferguson, Yale H. and Richard W. Mansbach (1996) *Polities: Authority, Identities, and Change*, Columbia: University of South Carolina Press.

Finnemore, Martha (2003) *The Purpose of Intervention*, Ithaca: Cornell University Press.

Fligstein, Neil (2001) *The Architecture of Markets*, Princeton University Press.

Forbes, R. J. (1955) *Studies in Ancient Technology*, vol. 2, Leiden: Brill.

Foucault, Michel (2002 [1969]) *The Archaeology of Knowledge*, London: Routledge.

Frank, Andre Gunder (1966) 'The Development of Underdevelopment', *Monthly Review*, 18(4): 17–31.

(1998) *ReOrient*, Berkeley: University of California Press.

Frank, Andre Gunder and Barry Gills (eds.) (1993) *The World System: 500 Years or 5000?*, London: Routledge.

Freeden, Michael (1996) *Ideologies and Political Theory: A Conceptual Approach*, Oxford University Press.

(2005) *Liberal Languages*, Princeton University Press.

Freedland, Chrystia (2012) *Plutocrats*, London: Penguin.

Frieden, Jeffry (2006) *Global Capitalism: Its Rise and Fall in the Twentieth Century*, New York: W. W. Norton.

Frieden, Jeffry and Anthony Lake (eds.) (2000) *International Political Economy: Perspectives on Global Power and Wealth*. Boston: St. Martin's Press.

Friedman, Milton (1962) *Capitalism and Freedom*, University of Chicago Press.

Gallagher, John and Ronald Robinson (1953) 'The Imperialism of Free Trade', *The Economic History Review*, 6(1): 1–15.

Galtung, Johan (1971) 'A Structural Theory of Imperialism', *Journal of Peace Research*, 1(3/4): 206–31.

Gareis, Bernhard and Johannes Varwick (2005) *The United Nations: An Introduction*, trans. Lindsay P. Cohn, New York: Palgrave Macmillan.

Geertz, Clifford (1973) *The Interpretation of Cultures*, New York: Basic Books.

Geis, Anna (2013) 'The "Concert of Democracies": Why Some States are More Equal than Others', *International Politics*, 50(2): 257–77.

Gellner, Ernest (1983) *Nations and Nationalism*, Oxford: Blackwell.

(1988) *Plough, Sword and Book: The Structure of Human History*, London: Paladin.

(1992) 'Nationalism Reconsidered and E. H. Carr', *Review of International Studies*, 18(4): 286–93.

Giddens, Anthony (1985) *The Nation-State and Violence*, Cambridge: Polity Press.

(1990) *The Consequences of Modernity*, Cambridge: Polity Press.

Gilpin, Robert (1981) *War and Change in World Politics*, Cambridge University Press.

(1987) *The Political Economy of International Relations*, Princeton University Press.

Gilroy, Paul (1993) *The Black Atlantic: Modernity and Double Consciousness*, London: Verso.

Glenny, Misha (2009) *McMafia: Seriously Organised Crime*, London: Vintage.

Go, Julian (2011) *Patterns of Empire*, Cambridge University Press.

(Forthcoming) 'Where is "the Global" in Historical Sociology?', in: Julian Go and George Lawson (eds.), *Global Historical Sociology*.

Goedde, Petra (2014) 'Global Cultures', in: Akira Iriye (ed.), *Global Interdependence: The World After 1945*, Cambridge, MA: Belknap Press, 535–678.

Goldgeier, James M. and Michael McFaul (1992) 'A Tale of Two Worlds: Core and Periphery in the Post-Cold War Era', *International Organization*, 46(2): 467–91.

Goldstone, Jack (2002) 'Efflorescences and Economic Growth in World History', *Journal of World History*, 13(2): 328–89.

Gong, Gerrit W. (1984) *The Standard of 'Civilisation' in International Society*, Oxford: Clarendon Press.

(2002) 'Standards of Civilization Today', in: Mehdi Mozaffari (ed.), *Globalization and Civilization*, New York: Routledge, 77–96.

Goody, Jack (1996) *The East in the West*, Cambridge University Press.

(2009) *The Eurasian Miracle*, Cambridge: Polity Press.

Gorman, Daniel (2012) *The Emergence of International Society in the 1920s*, Cambridge University Press.

Gorski, Philip (2000) 'The Mosaic Moment: An Early Modernist Critique of Modernist Theories of Nationalism', *American Journal of Sociology*, 105(5): 1428–68.

(2003) *The Disciplinary Revolution: Calvinism and the Rise of the State in Early Modern Europe*, University of Chicago Press.

Gramsci, Antonio (1971 [1929–35]) *Selections from the Prison Notebooks*, ed. and trans. Quintin Hoare and Geoffrey Nowell-Smith, London: Lawrence and Wishart.

(1988 [1929–33]) 'Passive Revolution, Caeserism, Fascism', in: David Forgacs (ed.), *The Antonio Gramsci Reader*, London: Lawrence and Wishart, 246–74.

Grant, A.F., Arthur Greenwood, J.D.I. Hughes, P.H. Kerr and F.F. Urquhart (1916) *An Introduction to International Relations*, London: Macmillan.

Gray, Colin S. (2012) *War, Peace and International Relations: An Introduction to Strategic History*, 2nd edn., London: Routledge, Kindle edn.

Grovogui, Siba (1996) *Sovereigns, Quasi Sovereigns, and Africans*, Minneapolis: University of Minnesota Press.

Gruffydd Jones, Branwen (2006) 'International Relations, Eurocentrism and Imperialism', in: Branwen Gruffydd Jones (ed.), *Decolonizing International Relations*, Plymouth: Rowman & Littlefield, 1–19.

Guzzini, Stefano (ed.) (2013) *The Return of Geopolitics in Europe?*, Cambridge University Press.

Haass, Richard (2008) 'The Age of Nonpolarity', *Foreign Affairs*, 87(May–June): 44–56.

Hacking, Ian (1990) *The Taming of Chance*, Cambridge University Press.

Haggard, Stephen (1990) *Pathways from the Periphery*, Ithaca: Cornell University Press.

Hall, Peter A. and David Soskice (eds.) (2001) *Varieties of Capitalism*, Oxford University Press.

Hall, Rodney Bruce (1999) *National Collective Identity*, New York: Columbia University Press.

Hall, Stuart (1992) *Formations of Modernity*, Cambridge: Polity Press.

Halliday, Fred (1999) *Revolution and World Politics*, Basingstoke: Macmillan.

  (2002a) 'The Middle East and the Politics of Differential Integration', in: Toby Dodge and Richard Higgott (eds.), *Globalization and the Middle East*, London: Chatham House, 33–56.

  (2002b) 'For an International Sociology', in: Stephen Hobden and John Hobson (eds.), *Historical Sociology of International Relations*, Cambridge University Press, 244–64.

  (2009) 'The Middle East and Conceptions of "International Society"', in: Barry Buzan and Ana Gonzalez-Pelaez (eds.), *International Society and the Middle East*, Basingstoke: Palgrave Macmillan, 1–23.

  (2010) 'Third World Socialism: 1989 and After', in: George Lawson, Chris Armbruster and Michael Cox (eds.), *The Global 1989: Continuity and Change in World Politics*, Cambridge University Press, 112–34.

Halper, Stefan (2010) *The Beijing Consensus*, New York: Basic Books.

Halperin, Sandra (2013) *Re-Envisioning Global Development*, London: Routledge.

Hameiri, Shahar (2010) *Regulating Statehood: State Building and the Transformation of the Global Order*, Basingstoke: Palgrave Macmillan.

Hannaford, Ivan (1996) *Race: The History of an Idea in the West*, Baltimore: Johns Hopkins University Press.

Hansen, Lene and Helen Nissenbaum (2009) 'Digital Disaster, Cyber Security, and the Copenhagen School', *International Studies Quarterly*, 53(4): 1155–75.

Harvey, David (1990) *The Condition of Postmodernity*, Oxford: Blackwell.

  (2011) *The Enigma of Capital*, London: Profile.

Hatton, Timothy J. and Jeffery G. Williamson (1998) *The Age of Mass Migration: Causes and Economic Impact*, Oxford University Press.

He, Kai and Huiyin Feng (2012) 'Debating China's Assertiveness: Taking China's Power and Interests Seriously', *International Politics*, 49(5): 633–44.

Headrick, Daniel R. (1981) *The Tools of Empire: Technology and European Imperialism in the Nineteenth Century*, New York: Oxford University Press.

  (1988) *The Tentacles of Progress: Technology Transfer in the Age of Imperialism*, Oxford University Press.

  (2010) *Power over Peoples: Technology, Environment, and Western Imperialism, 1400 to Present*, Princeton University Press.

Heath, Timothy R. (2012) 'What Does China Want? Discerning the PRC's National Strategy', *Asian Security*, 8(1): 54–72.

Held, David, Anthony McGrew, David Goldblatt and Jonathan Perraton (1999) *Global Transformations*, Cambridge: Polity Press.

Helleiner, Eric (1994) 'Regionalization in the International Political Economy: A Comparative Perspective', *Eastern Asia Policy Papers No. 3*, University of Toronto.

Herz, John H. (1957) 'The Rise and Demise of the Territorial State', *World Politics*, 9(4): 473–93.

(1968) 'The Territorial State Revisited', *Polity*, 1(1): 12–34.

Hewitt, Nancy A. (2010) 'Re-Rooting American Women's Activism: Global Perspectives on 1848', in: Karen Offen (ed.), *Globalizing Feminisms, 1789–1945*, London: Routledge, 18–25.

Hibou, Béatrice (ed.) (2004) *Privatising the State*, London: Hurst.

Hill, Christopher (1975) *The World Turned Upside Down*, London: Pelican.

Hinsley, F. H. (1982) 'The Rise and Fall of the Modern International System', *Review of International Studies*, 8(1): 1–8.

Hintze, Otto (1975 [1906]) 'Military Organisation and the Organisation of the State', in: Felix Gilbert (ed.), *The Historical Essays of Otto Hintze*, Oxford University Press, 178–215.

Hirschman, Albert O. (1977) *The Passions and the Interests: Political Arguments for Capitalism Before its Triumph*, Princeton University Press.

Hirst, Paul and Grahame Thompson (1996) *Globalisation in Question*, Cambridge: Polity Press.

Hobsbawm, Eric (1959) *Primitive Rebels: Studies in Archaic Forms of Social Movement in the 19th and 20th Centuries*, New York: W. W. Norton.

(1962) *The Age of Revolution, 1789–1848*, London: Abacus.

(1975) *The Age of Capital, 1848–1875*, London: Abacus.

(1986) 'Revolution', in: Roy Porter and Mikuláš Teich (eds.), *Revolutions in History*, Cambridge University Press, 5–46.

(1987) *The Age of Empire, 1875–1914*, London: Abacus.

(1990) *Nations and Nationalism Since 1780*, Cambridge University Press.

(2011) *How to Change the World*, London: Little, Brown and Co.

Hobson, John (2004) *The Eastern Origins of Western Civilization*, Cambridge University Press.

(2010) 'Back to the Future of Nineteenth Century Western International Thought?', in: George Lawson, Chris Armbruster and Michael Cox (eds.), *The Global 1989: Continuity and Change in World Politics*, Cambridge University Press, 23–50.

(2012) *The Eurocentric Origins of International Relations*, Cambridge University Press.

Hobson, John and George Lawson (2008) 'What is History in International Relations?', *Millennium*, 37(2): 415–35.

Hobson, John, George Lawson and Justin Rosenberg (2010) 'Historical Sociology', in: Robert A. Denemark (ed.), *The International Studies Encyclopaedia*, Oxford: Wiley-Blackwell.

Hodgson, Marshall G. S. (1993) *Rethinking World History: Essays on Europe, Islam and World History*, Cambridge University Press.

Hoerder, Dirk (2011) 'Migrations', in: Jerry Bentley (ed.), *The Oxford Handbook of World History*, Oxford University Press, 269–87.

(2012) 'Migrations and Belongings', in: Emily S. Rosenberg (ed.), *A World Connecting, 1870–1945*, Cambridge, MA: Belknap Press, 433–589.

Hoffmann, Stanley (1961) 'International Systems and International Law', *World Politics*, 14(1): 205–37.

(1987) 'An American Social Science: IR', in: Stanley Hoffmann (ed.), *Janus and Minerva: Essays in International Relations*, Boulder: Westview, 3–24.

Holbraad, Carsten (1970) *The Concert of Europe*, London: Longman.

Holsti, Kalevi J. (1985) *The Dividing Discipline*, Winchester, MA: Allen & Unwin.

(1991) *Peace and War: Armed Conflict and International Order, 1648–1989*, Cambridge University Press.

(1992) *International Politics*, 7th edn., Upper Saddle River, NJ: Prentice-Hall.

(2004) *Taming the Sovereigns: Institutional Change in International Politics*, Cambridge University Press.

(2011) 'Exceptionalism in American Foreign Policy: Is It Exceptional?', *European Journal of International Relations*, 17(3): 381–404.

Hopf, Ted (1991) 'Polarity, the Offense–Defense Balance, and War', *American Political Science Review*, 85(2): 475–93.

Howard, Michael (1976) *War in European History*, Oxford University Press.

Hugill, P. J. (1993) *World Trade Since 1431: Geography, Technology and Capitalism*, Baltimore: Johns Hopkins University Press.

Hurrell, Andrew (2007) *On Global Order: Power, Values and the Constitution of International Society*, Oxford University Press.

Ikenberry, John (2001) *After Victory: Institutions, Strategic Restraint and the Rebuilding of Order after Major War*, Princeton University Press.

(2009) 'Liberal Internationalism 3.0: America and the Dilemmas of Liberal World Order', *Perspectives on Politics*, 7(1): 71–86.

(2011) *Liberal Leviathan*, Princeton University Press.

Ikenberry, John and Anne-Marie Slaughter (2006) *Forging a World of Liberty Under Law: U.S. National Security in the 21st Century*, Princeton: Princeton Project Papers, Woodrow Wilson School of Public and International Affairs.

Inayatullah, Naeem and David Blaney (2004) *International Relations and the Problem Difference*, London: Routledge.

Intergovernmental Panel on Climate Change (IPCC) (2014) *Fifth Assessment Report*, www.ipcc.ch/report/ar5/index.shtml.

International Air Transport Association (IATA) (2012) *2012 Annual Review*, Beijing: IATA.

International Monetary Fund (IMF) (2013) *World Economic Outlook Database*, www.imf.org/external/pubs/ft/weo/2013/02/weodata/index. aspx.

International Organization for Migration (2013) 'Global Estimates and Trends', www.iom.int/cms/en/sites/iom/home/about-migration/facts-fig ures-1.html. Accessed 29 October 2012.

Iriye, Akira (2004) *Global Community: The Role of International Organizations in the Making of the Contemporary World*, Berkeley: University of California Press.

Isacoff, Jonathon B. (2002) 'On the Historical Imagination of International Relations', *Millennium*, 31(3): 603–26.

Israel, Jonathan (2010) *A Revolution of the Mind*, Princeton University Press.

(2012) *Democratic Enlightenment*, Oxford University Press.

Jackson, Gregory and Richard Deeg (2006) 'How Many Varieties of Capitalism? Comparing the Comparative Institutional Analyses of Capitalist Diversity', Köln: Max Planck Institute for the Study of Societies, Discussion Paper 06/2.

Jackson, Patrick (2000) *The Global Covenant: Human Conduct in a World of States*, Oxford University Press.

(2011) *The Conduct of Inquiry in International Relations*, London: Routledge.

Jacob, Margaret (1997) *Scientific Culture and the Making of the Industrial West*, Oxford University Press.

Jacques, Martin (2010) *When China Rules the World*, London: Allen Lane.

Jahn, Beate (2005) 'Kant, Mill and Illiberal Legacies in International Affairs', *International Organization*, 59(4): 177–207.

James, Patrick and Michael Brecher (1988) 'Stability and Polarity: New Paths for Enquiry', *Journal of Peace Research*, 25(1): 31–42.

Jarrett, Mark (2013) *The Congress of Vienna and Its Legacy*, New York: I. B. Tauris.

Joas, Hans (2003) *War and Modernity*, Cambridge: Polity Press.

Johnson, Allen W. and Timothy Earle (2000) *The Evolution of Human Societies*, Stanford University Press.

Johnston, Alastair Iain (2008) *Social States: China in International Institutions*, Princeton University Press.

Joll, James (1982) 'The Ideal and the Real: Changing Concepts of the International System, 1815–1982', *International Affairs*, 58(2): 210–24.

Jones, Charles (1987) *International Business in the Nineteenth Century: The Rise and Fall of a Cosmopolitan Bourgeoisie*, Brighton: Wheatsheaf Books.

Jones, D. M. (2001) *The Image of China in Western Social and Political Thought*, Basingstoke: Palgrave Macmillan.

Jones, Eric (1981) *The European Miracle: Environment, Economies and Geopolitics in the History of Europe and Asia*, Cambridge University Press.

Jones, Raymond (2011) *The Battle of Adwa*, Cambridge, MA: Harvard University Press.

Jönsson, Christer and Martin Hall (2005) *Essence of Diplomacy*, Basingstoke: Palgrave Macmillan.

Judt, Tony (2008) *Reappraisals: Reflections on the Forgotten Twentieth Century*, London: William Heinemann.

Kadercan, Burak (2012) 'Military Competition and the Emergence of Nationalism: Putting the Logic of Political Survival into Historical Context', *International Studies Review*, 14(3): 401–28.

Kapstein, Ethan B. and Michael Mastanduno (eds.) (1999) *Unipolar Politics*, New York: Columbia University Press.

Kaufmann, Chaim D. and Robert A. Pape (1999) 'Explaining Costly International Moral Action: Britain's Sixty-Year Campaign Against the Atlantic Slave Trade', *International Organization*, 53(4): 631–68.

Kayaoğlu, Turan (2010) *Legal Imperialism: Sovereignty and Extraterritoriality in Japan, the Ottoman Empire, and China*, Cambridge University Press.

Keal, Paul (2003) *European Conquest and the Rights of Indigenous Peoples: The Moral Backwardness of International Society*, Cambridge University Press.

Kedourie, Elie (1960) *Nationalism*, London: Hutchinson & Co.

Keene, Edward (2002) *Beyond the Anarchical Society*, Cambridge University Press.

(2013) 'International Hierarchy and the Origins of the Modern Practice of Intervention', *Review of International Studies*, 29(5): 1077–90.

Kennedy, Paul (1989) *The Rise and Fall of the Great Powers*, London: Fontana.

(2007) *The Parliament of Man*, London: Penguin.

Kennedy, Robert (1969) *Thirteen Days: A Memoir of the Cuban Missile Crisis*, New York: W. W. Norton.

Keohane, Robert O. (1984) *After Hegemony: Cooperation and Discord in the World Political Economy*, Princeton University Press.

Kerr, P. H. (1916) 'Political Relations Between Advanced and Backward Peoples', in: A. F. Grant, Arthur Greenwood, J. D. I. Hughes, P. H. Kerr and F. F. Urquhart, *An Introduction to the Study of International Relations*, London: Macmillan, 141–82.

Keylor, William R. (2001) *The Twentieth Century World*, 4th edn., Oxford University Press.

Khazanov, Anatoly M. (1984) *Nomads and the Outside World*, Cambridge University Press.

Kissinger, Henry (2003) *Diplomacy*, New York: Touchstone.

Knox, MacGregor (2001) 'Mass Politics and Nationalism as Military Revolution', in: MacGregor Knox and Williamson Murray (eds.), *The Dynamics of Military Revolution*, Cambridge University Press, 57–73.

Knutsen, Torbjorn (1997) *The History of International Relations Theory*, 2nd edn., Manchester University Press.

Kohli, Atul (2004) *State-Directed Development*, Cambridge University Press.

Kolodziej, Edward A. (1987) *Making and Marketing Arms: The French Experience and Its Implications for the International System*, Princeton University Press.

Koselleck, Reinhart (2000 [1959]) *Critique and Crisis*, Cambridge, MA: MIT Press.

Koskenniemi, Martti (2001) *The Gentle Civilizer of Nations: The Rise and Fall of International Law, 1870–1960*, Cambridge University Press.

Kratochwil, Friedrich (2006) 'History, Action and Identity', *European Journal of International Relations*, 12(1): 5–29.

Krause, Keith (1992) *Arms and the State: Patterns of Military Production and Trade*, Cambridge University Press.

Krippner, Greta (2011) *Capitalizing on Crisis*, Cambridge, MA: Harvard University Press.

Krishna, Sankaran (2006) 'Race, Amnesia and the Education of International Relations', in: Branwen Gruffyd Jones (ed.), *Decolonizing International Relations*, Plymouth: Rowman & Littlefield, 89–108.

Kumar, Krishnan (2001) *1989: Revolutionary Ideas and Ideals*, Minneapolis: University of Minnesota Press.

Kunitake, Kume (2009) *Japan Rising: The Iwakura Embassy to the United States and Europe*, Cambridge University Press.

Kupchan, Charles A. (1998) 'After Pax Americana: Benign Power, Regional Integration, and the Sources of Stable Multipolarity', *International Security*, 23(2): 40–79.

(2012) *No-One's World*, Oxford University Press.

Kurzman, Charles (2008) *Democracy Denied, 1905–1915*, Cambridge, MA: Harvard University Press.

Kurzweil, Ray (2005) *The Singularity is Near*, New York: Viking.

Lach, Donald F. (1965) *Asia in the Making of Modern Europe*, Vol. I: *The Century of Discovery*, University of Chicago Press.

(1977) *Asia in the Making of Modern Europe*, Vol. II: *A Century of Wonder*, University of Chicago Press.

Lach, Donald F. with Edwin J. Van Kley (1993) *Asia in the Making of Modern Europe*, Vol. III: *A Century of Advance*, University of Chicago Press.

Lacher, Hannes and Julian Germann (2012) 'Before Hegemony: Britain, Free Trade and Nineteenth-Century World Order Revisited', *International Studies Review*, 14(1): 99–124.

Lake, David (1993) 'Leadership, Hegemony, and the International Economy: Naked Emperor or Tattered Monarch with Potential?', *International Studies Quarterly*, 37(4): 459–89.

Lake, Marilyn and Henry Reynolds (2008) *Drawing the Global Colour Line*, Cambridge University Press.

Landes, David (1969) *The Unbound Prometheus: Technological Change and Industrial Development in Western Europe from 1750 to the Present*, Cambridge University Press.

(1998) *The Wealth and Poverty of Nations*, New York: W. W. Norton.

Lane, David (1996) *The Rise and Fall of State Socialism*, Cambridge: Polity Press.

Latham, Robert (1997) 'History, Theory and International Order', *Review of International Studies*, 23(4): 419–43.

Lawrence, Philip K. (1997) *Modernity and War: The Creed of Absolute Violence*, Basingstoke: Macmillan.

Lawson, George (2005) *Negotiated Revolutions: The Czech Republic, South Africa and Chile*, London: Ashgate.

(2008) 'A Realistic Utopia? Nancy Fraser, Cosmopolitanism and the Making of a Just World Order', *Political Studies*, 56(4): 881–906.

(2010) 'The "What", "When" and "Where" of the Global 1989', in: George Lawson, Chris Armbruster and Michael Cox (eds.), *The Global 1989: Continuity and Change in World Politics*, Cambridge University Press, 1–20.

(2012) 'The Eternal Divide? History and International Relations', *European Journal of International Relations*, 18(2): 203–26.

(Forthcoming) *Anatomies of Revolution*, Ann Arbor: University of Michigan Press.

Lawson, George and Luca Tardelli (2013) 'The Past, Present and Future of Intervention', *Review of International Studies*, 39(5): 1233–53.

Layne, Christopher (1993) 'The Unipolar Illusion: Why New Great Powers Will Rise', *International Security*, 17(4): 5–51.

Lebow, Richard Ned (2010) *Forbidden Fruit: Counterfactuals and International Relations*, Princeton University Press.

Legro, Jeffrey (2005) *Rethinking the World*, Ithaca: Cornell University Press.

Lenin, V. I. (1975 [1916]) *Imperialism: The Highest Stage of Capitalism*, Peking: Foreign Languages Press.

Levine, Philippa (ed.) (2004) *Gender and Empire*, Oxford University Press.

Levitsky, Steven and Lucan Way (2010) *Competitive Authoritarianism: Hybrid Regimes After the Cold War*, Cambridge University Press.

Lin, Justin Yifu (2012) *Demystifying the Chinese Economy*, Cambridge University Press.

Lingelbach, William Ezra (1900) 'The Doctrine and Practice of Intervention in Europe', *Annals of the American Academy of Political and Social Science*, 16(1): 1–32.

Linklater, Andrew (2010) 'Global Civilizing Processes and the Ambiguities of Interconnectedness', *European Journal of International Relations*, 16(2): 155–78.

(2011) *The Problem of Harm in World Politics*, Cambridge University Press.

Little, Richard (2007) 'British Neutrality Versus Offshore Balancing in the American Civil War', *Security Studies*, 16(1): 68–95.

(2013) 'Intervention and Non-Intervention in International Society: Britain's Reponses to the American and Spanish Civil Wars', *Review of International Studies*, 39(5): 1111–29.

(2014) 'Eurocentrism, World History, Meta-Narratives and the Convergence of International Societies', in: Shogo Suzuki, Yongjin Zhang and Joel Quirk (eds.), *International Orders in the Early Modern World: Before the Rise of the West*, London: Routledge.

Losurdo, Domenico (2011) *Liberalism: A Counter History*, trans. Gregory Elliott, London: Verso.

Loth, Wilfried (2014) 'States and the Changing Equations of Power', in: Akira Iriye (ed.), *Global Interdependence: The World After 1945*, Cambridge, MA: Belknap Press, 9–199.

Lovell, Julia (2011) *The Opium War: Drugs, Dreams and the Making of China*, London: Picador.

Lundestad, Geir (2005) *East, West, North, South: Major Developments in International Relations Since 1945*, 5th edn., Oxford University Press.

Lustick, Ian S. (1996) 'History, Historiography and Political Science: Multiple Historical Records and the Problem of Selection Bias', *American Political Science Review*, 90(3): 605–18.

(1997) 'The Absence of Middle Eastern Great Powers: Political "Backwardness" in Historical Perspective', *International Organization*, 51(4): 653–83.

Luttwak, Edward (1990) 'From Geopolitics to Geoeconomics', *The National Interest*, 20: 17–23.

McClintock, Anne (1995) *Imperial Leather: Race, Gender and Sexuality in the Colonial Context*, London: Routledge.

McDaniel, Tim (1991) *Autocracy, Modernization and Revolution in Russia and Iran*, Princeton University Press.

MacDonald, Paul (2014) *Networks of Domination*, Oxford University Press.

Mackinder, Halford (1996 [1904]) 'The Geographical Pivot of History', in: Halford Mackinder, *Democratic Ideals and Reality*, Washington, DC: National Defense University, 175–94.

McKinlay, R. D. and Richard Little (1986) *Global Problems and World Order*, London: Pinter.

McKinsey Global Institute (2013) *Financial Globalization: Retreat or Reset?*, London: McKinsey and Co.

Mackintosh-Smith, Tim (2002) *The Travels of Ibn Battutah*, London: Picador.

McNally, Christopher (2012) 'Sino-Capitalism', *World Politics*, 64(4): 741–76.

(2013) 'How Emerging Forms of Capitalism are Changing the Global Economic Order', East-West Center: Asia-Pacific Issues No. 107.

McNeill, J. R. and Peter Engelke (2014) 'Into the Anthropocene: People and Their Planet', in: Akira Iriye (ed.), *Global Interdependence: The World Since 1945*, Cambridge, MA: Harvard University Press, 363–533.

McNeill, William H. (1982) *The Pursuit of Power*, University of Chicago Press.

(1991) *The Rise of the West: A History of the Human Community*, 2nd edn., University of Chicago Press.

Macpherson, C. A. (1962) *The Political Theory of Possessive Individualism*, Oxford University Press.

Maddison, Angus (2001) *The World Economy: A Millennial Perspective*, Paris: Development Centre of the OECD.

(2005) *Growth and Interaction in the World Economy*, Washington, DC: AEI.

(2007a) *Chinese Economic Performance in the Long Run*, Paris: OECD.

(2007b) *Contours of the World Economy*, Oxford University Press.

Magaloni, Beatriz (2006) *Voting for Autocracy*, Cambridge University Press.

Magubane, Zine (2005) 'Overlapping Territories and Intertwined Histories', in Julia Adams, Elisabeth S. Clemens and Ann Shola Orloff (eds.), *Remaking Modernity: Politics, History, and Sociology*, Durham, NC: Duke University Press, 92–108.

Mandelbaum, Michael (1998/9) 'Is Major War Obsolete?', *Survival*, 40(4): 20–38.

Mann, Michael (1986) *The Sources of Social Power*, Vol. 1: *A History of Power from the Beginning to AD 1760*, Cambridge University Press.

(1988) *States, War and Capitalism*, Oxford: Blackwell.

(1993) *The Sources of Social Power*, Vol. 2: *The Rise of Classes and Nation States, 1760–1914*, Cambridge University Press.

(2004) *Fascists*, Cambridge University Press.

(2005) *Incoherent Empire*, London: Verso.

(2012) *The Sources of Social Power*, Vol. 3: *Global Empires and Revolution, 1890–1945*, Cambridge University Press.

(2013) *The Sources of Social Power*, Vol. 4: *Globalizations, 1945–2011*, Cambridge University Press.

Marder, Arthur J. (1961) *From the Dreadnought to Scapa Flow: The Royal Navy in the Fisher Era, 1904–1919*, Vol. 1: *The Road to War 1904–1914*, Oxford University Press.

Marx, Karl (1853) 'The Future Results of British Rule in India', *The New York Daily Tribune*, No. 856, 9 August.

Massey, Douglas S., Joaquin Arango, Graeme Hugo, Ali Kouaouci, Adela Pellegrino and J. Edward Taylor (1998) *Worlds in Motion: Understanding International Migration at the End of the Millennium*, Oxford University Press.

Mayall, James (1990) *Nationalism and International Society*, Cambridge University Press.

(2000) *World Politics: Progress and its Limits*, Cambridge: Polity Press.

Mayer, Arno (1971) *Dynamics of Counterrevolution in Europe*, London: Harper & Row.

(2010) *The Persistence of the Old Regime*, London: Verso.

Mazower, Mark (2009) *No Enchanted Palace*, Princeton University Press.

(2012) *Governing the World*, London: Allen Lane.

Mead, Walter Russell (1995/6) 'Trains, Planes and Automobiles: The End of the Postmodern Movement', *World Policy Journal*, 12(4): 13–31.

Mearsheimer, John (1990) 'Back to the Future', *International Security*, 15(1): 5–56.

(2001) *The Tragedy of Great Power Politics*, New York: W. W. Norton.

Mehta, Uday (1999) *Liberalism and Empire: A Study in Nineteenth Century British Liberal Thought*, University of Chicago Press.

Meier, Charles S. (2012) 'Leviathan 2.0', in: Emily S. Rosenberg (ed.), *A World Connecting, 1870–1945*, Cambridge, MA: Belknap Press, 29–282.

Meijer, Fik and Onno van Nijf (1992) *Trade, Transport and Society in the Ancient World*, London: Routledge.

Metcalf, Thomas R. (2007) *Imperial Connections: India in the Indian Ocean Arena, 1860–1920*, Berkeley: University of California Press.

Meyer, John W., John Boli, George M. Thomas and Francisco O. Ramirez (1997) 'World Society and the Nation-State', *American Journal of Sociology*, 103(1): 144–81.

Mignolo, Walter (2011) *The Darker Side of Modernity*, Durham, NC: Duke University Press.

Mill, John Stuart (1859) 'A Few Words on Non-Intervention', www.liberta rian.co.uk/lapubs/forep/forep008.pdf.

Miller, David (1997) *Principles of Social Justice*, Cambridge, MA: Harvard University Press.

Miller, Manjari Chatterjee (2013) *Wronged by Empire*, Stanford University Press.

Mitchell, Timothy (1998) *Colonizing Egypt*, Cambridge University Press.

Mitzen, Jennifer (2013) *Power in Concert: The Nineteenth Century Origins of Global Governance*, University of Chicago Press.

Modelski, George and William R. Thompson (1996) *Leading Sectors and World Powers: The Coevolution of Global Politics and Economics*, Columbia: University of South Carolina Press.

Mokyr, Joel (2009) 'The Intellectual Origins of Modern Economic Growth', *Journal of Economic History*, 65(2): 285–351.

Morefield, Jeanne (2004) *'Covenants without Swords': Idealist Liberalism and the Spirit of Empire*, Princeton University Press.

Morgenthau, Hans J. (1967) 'To Intervene or Not to Intervene', *Foreign Affairs*, 45(3): 425–36.

(1978) *Politics Among Nations*, 5th edn., New York: Knopf.

Morphet, Sally (1996) 'NGOs and the Environment', in: Peter Willetts (ed.), *The Conscience of the World: The Influence of Non-Governmental Organisations in the UN System*, Washington, DC: Brookings Institution, 116–47.

Morris, Ian (2010) *Why the West Rules for Now*, London: Profile.

(2013) *The Measure of Civilization*, London: Profile.

(2014) *War: What is it Good For?* London: Profile.

Morton, Adam David (2010) 'Mexican Revolution, Primitive Accumulation, Passive Revolution', *Latin American Perspectives*, 37(1): 7–34.

Motyl, Alexander (1999) *Revolutions, Nations, Empires*, New York: Columbia University Press.

Moyn, Samuel (2010) *The Last Utopia: Human Rights in History*, Cambridge, MA: Belknap Press.

Mueller, John and Mark G. Stewart (2012) 'The Terrorism Delusion: America's Overwrought Response to September 11', *International Security*, 37(1): 81–110.

Mulgan, Geoff (2013) *The Locust and the Bee*, Princeton University Press.

Mulich, Jeppe (2013) 'Microregionalism and Intercolonial Relations: The Case of the Danish West Indies, 1730–1830', *Journal of Global History*, 8(1): 72–94.

Muthu, Sankar (2003) *Enlightenment Against Empire*, Princeton University Press.

National Science Foundation (2012) 'R&D: National Trends and International Comparisons', in: *Science and Engineering Indicators 2012*, Arlington, VA, NSB 12-01, www.nsf.gov/statistics/seind12/c4/c4s8.htm.

Neal, Larry (1990) *The Rise of Financial Capitalism: International Capital Markets in the Age of Reason*, Cambridge University Press.

Neff, Stephen C. (2010) 'A Short History of International Law', in: Malcolm D. Evans (ed.), *International Law*, Oxford University Press, 3–31.

Neocleous, Mark (2003) 'Off the Map: On Violence and Cartography', *European Journal of Social Theory*, 6(4): 409–25.

Neumann, Iver and Halvard Leira (eds.) (2013) *International Diplomacy*, 4 vols., Thousand Oaks, CA: Sage.

Neumann, Iver and Einar Wigen (2013) 'The Importance of the Eurasian Steppe to the Study of International Relations', *Journal of International Relations and Development* 16(3): 311–30.

Newbury, Colin (2003) *Patrons, Clients, and Empire: Chieftaincy and Overrule in Asia, Africa, and the Pacific*, Oxford University Press.

Nexon, Daniel (2009) *The Struggle for Power in Early Modern Europe*, Princeton University Press.

Nexon, Daniel and Thomas Wright (2007) 'What's at Stake in the American Empire Debate', *American Political Science Review*, 101(2): 253–71.

Nisbet, Robert (1969) *Social Change and History*, Oxford University Press.

North, Douglass C., John Joseph Wallis and Barry R. Weingast (2009) *Violence and Social Orders: A Conceptual Framework for Interpreting Recorded Human History*, Cambridge University Press.

Nozick, Robert (1984) *Anarchy, State and Utopia*, New York: Basic Books.

O'Brien, Patrick (1988) 'The Costs and Benefits of British Imperialism, 1846–1914', *Past and Present*, 120(1): 163–200.

(2004) 'Colonies in a Globalizing Economy, 1815–1948', LSE Department of Economic History, Working Papers of the Global Economic History Network, No. 08/04.

O'Brien, Robert and Marc Williams (2007) *Global Political Economy: Evolution and Dynamics*, Basingstoke: Palgrave Macmillan.

O'Donnell, Guillermo (1973) *Modernization and Bureaucratic Authoritarianism*, Berkeley: University of California Press.

Offen, Karen (ed.) (2010a) *Globalizing Feminisms, 1789–1945*, London: Routledge.

(2010b) 'Was Mary Wollstonecraft a Feminist?', in: Karen Offen (ed.), *Globalizing Feminisms, 1789–1945*, London: Routledge, 5–17.

Olson, William C. and A. J. R. Groom (1992) *International Relations: Then and Now*, London: HarperCollins.

Onuf, Nicholas (2004) 'Humanitarian Intervention: The Early Years', *Florida Journal of International Law*, 16(4): 753–87.

Onuma, Yasuaki (2000) 'When was the Law of International Society Born? An Inquiry of the History of International Law from an

Intercivilizational Perspective', *Journal of the History of International Law*, 2(1): 1–66.

Orford, Anne (2011) *International Authority and the Responsibility to Protect*, Cambridge University Press.

Organisation for Economic Co-operation and Development (OECD) (2012) *Looking to 2060: Long-Term Global Health Prospects*, OECD Economic Policy Papers No. 03, www.keepeek.com/Digital-Asset-Man agement/oecd/economics/looking-to-2060-long-term-global-growth-pro spects_5k8zxpjsggf0-en#page1.

Organski, A. F. and Jacek Kugler (1980) *The War Ledger*, University of Chicago Press.

Osiander, Andreas (2001a) 'History and International Relations Theory', in: Anja V. Hartmann and Beatrice Heuser (eds.), *War, Peace and World Orders in European History*, London: Routledge, 14–24.

(2001b) 'Sovereignty, International Relations, and the Westphalian Myth', *International Organization*, 55(2): 251–87.

Osterhammel, Jürgen (2014) *The Transformation of the World: A Global History of the Nineteenth Century*, trans. Patrick Camiller, Princeton University Press.

Ó Tuathail, Gearóid (1996) *Critical Geopolitics: The Politics of Writing Global Space*, Minneapolis: University of Minnesota Press.

Ó Tuathail, Gearóid, Simon Dalby and Paul Routledge (eds.) (1998) *The Geopolitics Reader*, London: Routledge.

Owens, Patricia (2012) 'Human Security and the Rise of the Social', *Review of International Studies*, 38(3): 547–67.

Özkirimli, Umut (2010) *Theories of Nationalism*, New York: St Martin's Press.

Paige, Jeffery (2003) 'Finding the Revolutionary in the Revolution: Social Science Concepts and the Future of Revolution', in: John Foran (ed.), *The Future of Revolution*, London: Zed, 19–29.

Paine, S. C. M. (2003) *The Sino-Japanese War of 1894–1895*, New York: Cambridge University Press.

Paine, Thomas (2004 [1776]) *Common Sense*, London: Penguin.

Palan, Ronen (2002) 'Tax Havens and the Commercialization of State Sovereignty', *International Organization*, 56(1): 151–76.

Panitch, Leon and Sam Gindin (2012) *The Making of Global Capitalism*, London: Verso.

Parker, Geoffrey (1988) *The Military Revolution*, Cambridge University Press.

Parkes, Oscar (1966) *British Battleships*, London: Seeley Service & Co.

Parmar, Inderjeet (2012) *Foundations of the American Century*, New York: Columbia University Press.

Parthasarathi, Prasannan (2011) *Why Europe Grew Rich and Asia Did Not*, Cambridge University Press.

Pasha, Mustapha Kamal (2013) 'The "Bandung Impulse" and International Relations', in: Sanjay Seth (ed.), *Postcolonial Theory and International Relations*, London: Routledge, 144–65.

Pearson, Michael (2003) *The Indian Ocean*, London: Routledge.

Pearton, Maurice (1982) *The Knowledgeable State: Diplomacy, War and Technology Since 1830*, London: Burnett Books.

Peck, Jamie and Nik Theodore (2007) 'Variegated Capitalism', *Progress in Human Geography*, 31(6): 731–72.

Pejcinovic, Lacy (2013) *War in International Society*, Abingdon: Routledge.

Phillips, Andrew (2011) *War, Religion and Empire*, Cambridge University Press.

(2012) 'Saving Civilization from Empire', *European Journal of International Relations*, 18(1): 5–27.

(2013) 'From Global Transformation to Big Bang', *International Studies Quarterly*, 57(3): 640–2.

Phillips, Andrew and J.C. Sharman (Forthcoming) *International Order in Diversity: War, Trade and Rule in the Indian Ocean*, Cambridge University Press.

Philpott, Daniel (2001) *Revolution in Sovereignty*, Princeton University Press.

Pietsch, Tamson (2013) 'The Floating University of 1926', paper presented at 'International Relations, Capitalism and the Sea' workshop, Birkbeck College, London, 16 September.

Piketty, Thomas (2014) *Capital in the Twenty-First Century*, Cambridge, MA: Belknap Press.

Pincus, Steven (2009) *1688: The First Modern Revolution*, New Haven: Yale University Press.

Pitts, Jennifer (2005) *A Turn to Empire: The Rise of Imperial Liberalism in Britain and France*, Princeton University Press.

Pocock, J.G.A. (1975) *The Machiavellian Moment*, Princeton University Press.

Pogge, Thomas (1989) *Realizing Rawls*, Ithaca: Cornell University Press.

Polanyi, Karl (2001 [1944]) *The Great Transformation*, Boston: Beacon Press.

Pollard, A.F. (1923) 'The Balance of Power', *Journal of the British Institute of International Affairs*, 2(2): 51–64.

Pomeranz, Kenneth (2000) *The Great Divergence*, Princeton University Press.

Porter, Gareth and Janet W. Brown (1991) *Global Environmental Politics*, Boulder, CO: Westview Press.

Porter, Theodor (1995) *Trust in Numbers: The Pursuit of Objectivity in Science and Public Life*, Princeton University Press.

Potts, Lydia (1990) *The World Labour Market: A History of Migration*, London: Zed.

Prebisch, Raúl (1950) *The Economic Development of Latin America and Its Principal Problems*, New York: United Nations.

Quah, Danny (2011) 'The Shifting Distribution of Global Economic Activity', CEI Working Paper, LSE, May.

Quijano, Anibal (1992) 'Coloniality and Modernity/Rationality', *Cultural Studies*, 21(2–3): 22–32.

(2000) 'Coloniality of Power and Eurocentrism in Latin America, *International Sociology*, 15(2): 215–32.

Rancière, Jacques (2006) *Hatred of Democracy*, London: Verso.

Rathbun, Brian C. (2010) 'Is Anyone Not an International Relations Liberal?', *Security Studies*, 19(1): 2–25.

Rawls, John (1971) *A Theory of Justice*, Cambridge, MA: Harvard University Press.

Rees, Martin (2003) *Our Final Century*, London: Heinemann.

Reinhart, Carmen M. and Kenneth S. Rogoff (2009) *This Time is Different: Eight Centuries of Financial Folly*, Princeton University Press.

Rejai, Mostafa and Cynthia H. Enloe (1969) 'Nation-States and State-Nations', *International Studies Quarterly*, 13(2): 140–58.

Reno, William (1999) *Warlord Politics and African States*, Boulder, CO: Lynne Rienner.

Reus-Smit, Christian (1999) *The Moral Purpose of the State*, Princeton University Press.

(2001) 'Human Rights and the Social Construction of Sovereignty', *Review of International Studies*, 27(4): 519–38.

(2013) *Individual Rights and the Making of the International System*, Cambridge University Press.

Riello, Giorgio (2013) *Cotton: The Fibre that Made the Modern World*, Cambridge University Press.

Riley, Dylan and Manali Desai (2007) 'The Passive Revolutionary Route to the Modern World: Italy and India in Comparative Perspective', *Comparative Studies in Society and History*, 49(4): 1–33.

Roberts, Andrew (2006) *A History of the English-Speaking Peoples*, London: HarperCollins.

Robinson, Julian Perry (1978) 'The Neutron Bomb and Conventional Weapons of Mass Destruction', *Bulletin of the Atomic Scientists*, 34(March): 42–5.

Robinson, William I. (2004) *A Theory of Global Capitalism*, Baltimore: Johns Hopkins University Press.

Rosenau, James N. (1966) 'Pre-Theories and Theories of Foreign Policy', in: R. Barry Farrell (ed.), *Approaches to Comparative and International Politics*, Evanston, IL: Northwestern University Press, 27–92.

Rosenberg, Emily (2012) 'Transnational Currents in a Shrinking World', in: Emily S. Rosenberg (ed.), *A World Connecting, 1870–1945*, Cambridge, MA: Belknap Press, 813–996.

Rosenberg, Justin (1994) *The Empire of Civil Society*, London: Verso.

(2006) 'Why is There No International Historical Sociology?', *European Journal of International Relations*, 12(3): 307–40.

(2010) 'Problems in the Theory of Uneven and Combined Development. Part II: Unevenness and Multiplicity', *Cambridge Review of International Affairs*, 23(1): 165–89.

(2013) 'Kenneth Waltz and Leon Trotsky: Anarchy in the Mirror of Uneven and Combined Development', *International Politics*, 50(2): 183–230.

Rosenthal, Jean-Laurent and R. Bin Wong (2011) *Before and Beyond Divergence*, Cambridge, MA: Harvard University Press.

Rostow, W. W. (1960) *The Stages of Economic Growth: A Non-Communist Manifesto*, Cambridge University Press.

Roy, Tirthankar (2012) *India in the World Economy*, Cambridge University Press.

Ruggie, John G. (1982) 'International Regimes, Transactions and Change: Embedded Liberalism in the Postwar Economic Order', *International Organization*, 36(2): 379–415.

(1983) 'Continuity and Transformation in the World Polity: Towards a Neo-Realist Synthesis', *World Politics*, 35(2): 261–85.

(1993) 'Territoriality and Beyond: Problematizing Modernity in International Relations', *International Organization*, 47(1): 139–74.

(2004) 'American Exceptionalism and Global Governance: A Tale of Two Worlds?', Working Paper No. 5, Corporate Social Responsibility Initiative, Harvard University, April.

Rupert, Mark (1990) 'Producing Hegemony: State/Society Relations and the Politics of Productivity in the United States', *International Studies Quarterly*, 34(4): 427–56.

Ryan, Alan (2013) *The Making of Modern Liberalism*, Princeton University Press.

Sagan, Carl (1983/4) 'Nuclear War and Climatic Catastrophe', *Foreign Affairs*, 62(2): 257–92.

Said, Edward W. (1978) *Orientalism*, New York: Pantheon.

(1994) *Culture and Imperialism*, London: Vintage.

Salter, Mark B. (2002) *Barbarians and Civilization in International Relations*, London: Pluto Press.

Sandel, Michael (1998) *Liberalism and the Limits of Justice*, Cambridge University Press.

Sassen, Saskia (2001) *The Global City*, 2nd edn., Princeton University Press.

(2006) *Territory, Authority, Rights*, Princeton University Press.

(2008) 'Two Global Geographies for Remittances: States Formalize One But Not the Other', *Migrant Remittances*, USAID, 5(2), http://pdf.usaid. gov/pdf_docs/PNADN334.pdf.

(2010) 'The Return of Primitive Accumulation', in: George Lawson, Chris Armbruster and Michael Cox (eds.), *The Global 1989: Continuity and Change in World Politics*, Cambridge University Press, 51–75.

(2014) *Expulsions: Brutality and Complexity in the Global Economy*, Cambridge, MA: Harvard University Press.

Sassoon, Donald (2010) *One Hundred Years of Socialism*, London: I. B. Tauris.

Sayer, Derek (1985) 'The Critique of Politics and Political Economy', *Sociological Review*, 33(2): 221–53.

Schell, Orville and John Delury (2013) *Wealth and Power: China's Long March to the Twenty-First Century*, New York: Random House.

Schlosser, Eric (2013) *Command Control: Nuclear Weapons, the Damascus Incident, and the Illusion of Safety*, London: Penguin.

Schmidt, Brian (1998) *The Political Discourse of Anarchy: A Disciplinary History of IR*, New York: SUNY Press.

Schroeder, Paul (1994) *The Transformation of European Politics, 1763–1848*, Oxford University Press.

Schwartz, Herman (2000) *States and Markets*, Basingstoke: Macmillan.

(2009) *Subprime Nation*, Ithaca: Cornell University Press.

Schwarz, Bill (2011) *The White Man's World*, Oxford University Press.

Schwarzenberger, Georg (1955) 'The Standard of Civilization in International Law', in: George W. Keeton and Georg Schwarzenberger (eds.), *Current Legal Problems*, London: Stevens and Sons, 212–34.

Scott, Andrew (1982) *The Revolution in Statecraft: Intervention in an Age of Interdependence*, Durham, NC: Duke University Press.

Scott, James (1999) *Seeing Like a State*, New Haven: Yale University Press.

(2012) *Two Cheers for Anarchism*, Princeton University Press.

Scupin, Hans-Ulrich (2011) 'History of International Law: 1815 to World War I', *Max Planck Encyclopedia of Public International Law*, www.mpepil.com, accessed 13/6/2012.

Seabrooke, Leonard (2006) 'Civilizing Global Capital Markets: Room to Groove?', in: Brett Bowden and Leonard Seabrooke (eds.), *Global Standards of Market Civilization*, Abingdon: Routledge, 146–60.

Seary, Bill (1996) 'The Early History: From the Congress of Vienna to the San Francisco Conference', in: Peter Willetts (ed.), *The Conscience of the World: The Influence of Non-Governmental Organisations in the UN System*, London: Hurst, 15–30.

Seth, Sanjay (2007) *Subject Lessons: The Western Education of Colonial India*, Durham, NC: Duke University Press.

(ed.) (2013) *Postcolonial Theory and International Relations*, London: Routledge.

Sewell, William (2004) 'The French Revolution and the Emergence of the Nation Form', in: Michael Morrison and Melinda Zook (eds.),

Revolutionary Currents: Nation Building in the Transatlantic World, 1688–1821, Lanham, MD: Rowman & Littlefield, 91–125.

Shambaugh, David (2013) *China Goes Global: The Partial Power*, Oxford University Press.

Shaw, Martin (2002) *Theory of the Global State*, Cambridge University Press.

Shaxson, Nicholas (2011) *Treasure Islands*, London: Bodley Head.

Sheehan, Michael (2005) *International Security: An Analytical Survey*, Boulder, CO: Lynne Rienner.

Shih, Chih-yu and Yin Jiwu (2013) 'Between Core National Interest and a Harmonious World: Reconciling Self-Role Conceptions in Chinese Foreign Policy', *Chinese Journal of International Politics*, 6(1): 59–84.

Shilliam, Robbie (2009) 'The Atlantic as a Vector of Uneven and Combined Development', *Cambridge Review of International Affairs*, 22(1): 69–88.

(2011) 'The Perilous but Unavoidable Terrain of the Non-West', in: Robbie Shilliam (ed.), *International Relations and Non-Western Thought*, London: Routledge, 12–26.

(2013) 'Intervention and Colonial-Modernity: Decolonising the Italy/ Ethiopia Conflict Through Psalms 68:31', *Review of International Studies*, 39(5): 1131–47.

(Forthcoming) 'Europe, Freedom, Colonial Amnesia', in: Julian Go and George Lawson (eds.), *Global Historical Sociology*.

Short, John Phillip (2012) *Magic Lantern Empire: Colonialism and Society in Germany*, Ithaca: Cornell University Press.

Silver, Beverly and Giovanni Arrighi (2003) 'Polanyi's Double Movement', *Politics and Society*, 31(2): 325–55.

Simmel, Georg (1978 [1900]) *The Philosophy of Money*, London: Routledge.

Simpson, Gerry (2004) *Great Powers and Outlaw States: Unequal Sovereigns in the International Legal Order*, Cambridge University Press.

Singer, Charles, E. J. Holmyard, A. R. Hall and Trevor I. Williams (eds.) (1954) *A History of Technology*, Vol. 1: *From Early Times to the Fall of Ancient Empires*, Oxford: Clarendon Press.

(eds.) (1956) *A History of Technology*, Vol. 2: *The Mediterranean Civilizations and the Middle Ages c. 700 B.C. to c. A.D. 1500*, Oxford: Clarendon Press.

Singer, J. David (1987) 'Reconstructing the Correlates of War Dataset on Material Capabilities of States, 1816–1985', *International Interactions*, 14(2): 115–32.

Singer, J. David, Stuart Bremer and John Stuckey (1972) 'Capability Distribution, Uncertainty, and Major Power War, 1820–1965', in Bruce Russett (ed.), *Peace, War, and Numbers*, Beverly Hills: Sage, 19–48.

Singer, J. David and Melvin Small (1972) *The Wages of War 1816–1965*, New York: Wiley.

Singer, Max and Aaron Wildavsky (1993) *The Real World Order: Zones of Peace/Zones of Turmoil*, London: RIIA.

SIPRI (2013) *SIPRI Military Expenditure Database*, http://milexdata.sipri.org/result.php4.

Skinner, Quentin (1988) 'Meaning and Understanding in the History of Ideas', in: James Tully (ed.), *Meaning and Context: Quentin Skinner and his Critics*, Princeton University Press, 29–67.

Smaje, Chris (2000) *Natural Hierarchies: The Historical Sociology of Race and Caste*, Oxford: Blackwell.

Smith, Anthony D. (1991) *National Identity*, London: Penguin.

   (1998) *Nationalism and Modernism*, London: Routledge.

Smith, Derek D. (2006) *Deterring America: Rogue States and the Proliferation of Weapons of Mass Destruction*, Cambridge University Press.

Smith, Thomas (1999) *History and International Relations*, London: Routledge.

Sohrabi, Nader (1995) 'Historicizing Revolutions: Constitutional Revolutions in the Ottoman Empire, Iran, and Russia, 1905–1908', *American Journal of Sociology*, 100(6): 1383–447.

Sørensen, Georg (2006) 'Liberalism of Restraint and Liberalism of Imposition', *International Relations*, 20(3): 251–72.

Spence, Jonathan (1996) *God's Chinese Son*, New York: W. W. Norton.

Spivak, Gayatri Chakravorty (1988) *In Other Worlds*, London: Routledge.

Spruyt, Hendrik (1994) *The Sovereign State and its Competitors*, Princeton University Press.

Stasavage, David (2011) *States of Credit*, Princeton University Press.

Stavrianos, L. S. (1990) *Lifelines from Our Past*, London: I. B. Tauris.

Stedman Jones, Daniel (2012) *Masters of the Universe: Hayek, Friedman and the Birth of Neoliberal Politics*, Princeton University Press.

Steinmetz, George (2007) *The Devil's Handwriting*, University of Chicago Press.

Stern, Philip J. (2011) *The Company-State: Corporate Sovereignty and the Early Modern Foundations of the British Empire in India*, Oxford University Press.

Stokes, Doug (2013) 'Achilles' Deal: Dollar Decline and US Grand Strategy After the Crisis', *Review of International Political Economy* (online first version).

Strandsbjerg, Jeppe (2008) 'The Cartographic Production of Territorial Space', *Geopolitics*, 13(2): 335–58.

Streeck, Wolfgang (2011) 'The Crises of Democratic Capitalism', *New Left Review*, 71(Sept./Oct.): 5–29.

Streets, Heather (2010) *Martial Races: The Military, Race and Masculinity in British Imperial Culture, 1857–1914*, Manchester University Press.

Sugihara, Kaoru (2013) 'The European Miracle in Global Perspective', in: Maxine Berg (ed.), *Writing the History of the Global*, Oxford University Press, 129–44.

Suzuki, Shogo (2005) 'Japan's Socialization into Janus-Faced European International Society', *European Journal of International Relations*, 11(1): 137–64.

(2009) *Civilization and Empire: China and Japan's Encounter with European International Society*, London: Routledge.

Sylvest, Casper (2005) 'International Law in Nineteenth-Century Britain', *British Yearbook of International Law*, 75: 9–70.

Taliaferro, Jeffrey (2004) *Balancing Risks: Great Power Interventions in the Periphery*, Ithaca: Cornell University Press.

Tambiah, Stanley J. (1990) *Magic, Science, Religion and the Scope of Rationality*, Cambridge University Press.

Tammen, Ronald et al. (2001) *Power Transitions*, New York: CQ Press.

Tardelli, Luca (2013) 'When Elites Fight: Elites and the Politics of U.S. Military Interventions in Internal Conflicts', PhD dissertation, LSE.

Taylor, Peter J. (2004) *World City Network*, London: Routledge.

Taylor, W. Cooke (1840) *The Natural History of Society in the Barbarous and Civilized State*, London: Brown, Green and Longmans.

Temin, Peter and David Vines (2013) *The Leaderless Economy*, Princeton University Press.

Teschke, Benno (2003) *The Myth of 1648*, London: Verso.

Therborn, Goran (2012) 'Class in the 21st Century', *New Left Review*, 78(Nov./Dec.): 5–29.

Thompson, E. P. (1968) *The Making of the English Working Class*, London: Penguin.

Thompson, Mark R. (2004) *Democratic Revolutions*, London: Routledge.

Thomson, David (1990) *Europe Since Napoleon*, London: Penguin.

Thomson, Janice (1994) *Mercenaries, Pirates and Sovereigns*, Princeton University Press.

Tickner, Arlene and David Blaney (eds.) (2012) *Thinking International Relations Differently*, London: Routledge.

Tilly, Charles (1975) 'Reflections on the History of European State Making', in: Charles Tilly (ed.), *The Formation of Nation-States in Europe*, Princeton University Press, 3–83.

(1990) *Coercion, Capital and European States, AD 990–1992*, Oxford: Blackwell.

Tinker, Hugh (1974) *A New System of Slavery*, Oxford University Press.

Tiryakian, E. A. (1999) 'War: The Covered Side of Modernity', *International Sociology*, 14(4): 473–89.

Tombs, Robert (2000) 'The Triumph of Liberalism', in: T. C. W. Blanning (ed.), *The Nineteenth Century*, Oxford University Press, 10–46.

Tooze, Adam (2007) *The Wages of Destruction*, London: Penguin.

Topik, Steven C. and Allen Wells (2012) 'Commodity Chains in a Global Economy', in: Emily S. Rosenberg (ed.), *A World Connecting, 1870–1945*, Cambridge, MA: Belknap Press, 593–812.

Towns, Ann (2009) 'The Status of Women as a "Standard of Civilization"', *European Journal of International Relations*, 15(4): 681–706.

(2010) *Women and States*, Cambridge University Press.

Trimberger, Ellen Kay (1978) *Revolution from Above*, New Brunswick: Transaction.

Trotsky, Leon (1997 [1932]) *The History of the Russian Revolution*, London: Pluto.

Turner, Adair (2011) 'Reforming Finance', Clare Distinguished Lecture in Economic and Public Policy, Cambridge, UK, February.

Turner, Bryan (2013) *The Religious and the Political*, Cambridge University Press.

United Nations (1991) *World Urbanization Prospects*, New York: UN Department of International Economic and Social Affairs.

United Nations Department of Economic and Social Affairs, Population Division (1999) *Briefing Packet: 1998 Revision World Population Estimates and Projections*, New York: United Nations.

(2007) *World Population Prospects: The 2006 Revision*, www.un.org/esa/population/publications/wpp2006/wpp2006.htm.

(2009) *Trends in International Migrant Stock: The 2008 Revision* (United Nations database, POP/DB/MIG/Stock.Rev2008).

(2011) *International Migration Report 2009: A Global Assessment*, www.un.org/esa/population/publications/migration/WorldMigrationReport 2009.pdf.

(2013) *Trends in International Migrant Stock: The 2013 Revision – Migrants by Destination and Origin*, http://esa.un.org/unmigration/TIMSO2013/migrantstocks2013.htm.

van Creveld, Martin (1991) *Technology and War from 2000 BC to the Present*, London: Brassey's.

van Zanden, Jan Luiten (2004) 'Estimating Early Modern Economic Growth', International Institute of Social History Working Paper, www.iisg.nl/research/jvz-estimating.pdf.

Verosta, Stephen (2011) 'History of International Law, 1648–1815', *Max Planck Encyclopaedia of Public International Law*, www.mpepil.com.

Vincent, John (1974) *Non-Intervention and International Order*, Princeton University Press.

Vitalis, Robert (2005) 'Birth of a Discipline', in: David Long and Brian Schmidt (eds.), *Imperialism and Internationalism in the Discipline of International Relations*, Albany: SUNY Press, 159–81.

(2010) 'The Noble American Science of Imperial Relations and its Laws of Race Development', *Comparative Studies in Society and History*, 52(4): 909–38.

Vucetic, Srdjan (2011) *The Anglosphere: A Genealogy of a Racialized Identity in International Relations*, Palo Alto: Stanford University Press.

Wæver, Ole (1997) 'Figures of International Thought: Introducing Persons Instead of Paradigms?', in: Iver B. Neumann and Ole Wæver (eds.), *The Future of International Relations: Masters in the Making?*, London: Routledge, 1–37.

(1998) 'The Sociology of a not so International Discipline: American and European Developments in International Relations', *International Organization*, 52(4): 687–727.

(2005) 'European Integration and Security: Analysing French and German Discourses on State, Nation, and Europe', in: David R. Howarth and Jacob Torfing (eds.), *Discourse Theory in European Politics*, Basingstoke: Palgrave Macmillan, 33–67.

Wallace, Michael and J. David Singer (1970) 'Intergovernmental Organization in the Global System, 1816–1964: A Quantitative Description', *International Organization*, 24(2): 239–87.

Wallerstein, Immanuel (1974) *The Modern World-System*, Vol. 1: *Capitalist Agriculture and the Origins of the European World-Economy in the Sixteenth Century*, London: Academic Press.

(1979) *The Capitalist World Economy*, Cambridge University Press.

(1983) *Historical Capitalism with Capitalist Civilization*, London: Verso.

(1984) *The Politics of the World Economy*, Cambridge University Press.

(2004) *World Systems Analysis*, Durham, NC: Duke University Press.

(2011a) *Centrist Liberalism Triumphant, 1789–1914*, Berkeley: University of California Press.

(2011b) *The Second Era of Great Expansion of the Capitalist World Economy, 1730s–1840s*, Berkeley: University of California Press.

Waltz, Kenneth N. (1979) *Theory of International Politics*, Reading, MA: Addison-Wesley.

(2000) 'Structural Realism After the Cold War', *International Security*, 25(1): 5–41.

Walzer, Michael (2004) *Politics and Passion*, New Haven: Yale University Press.

Watson, Adam (1984) 'New States in the Americas', in: Hedley Bull and Adam Watson (eds.), *The Expansion of International Society*, Oxford University Press, 127–41.

(1992) *The Evolution of International Society*, London: Routledge.

(1997) *The Limits of Independence: Relations Between States in the Modern World*, London: Routledge.

Weber, Max (1978a [1922]) *Economy and Society, Vol. 1*, Berkeley: University of California Press.

(1978b [1922]) *Economy and Society, Vol. 2*, Berkeley: University of California Press.

(2001 [1905]) *The Protestant Ethic and the Spirit of Capitalism*, London: Routledge.

Weber, Steven and Bruce W. Jentleson (2010) *The End of Arrogance: America in the Global Competition of Ideas*, Cambridge, MA: Harvard University Press.

Weiner, Amir (2003a) 'Introduction: Landscaping the Human Garden', in: Amir Weiner (ed.), *Landscaping the Human Garden*, Stanford University Press, 1–18.

(ed.) (2003b) *Landscaping the Human Garden*, Stanford University Press.

Wendt, Alexander (1999) *Social Theory of International Politics*, Cambridge University Press.

Westad, Arne (2005) *The Global Cold War*, Cambridge University Press.

(2012) *Restless Empire: China and the World Since 1750*, London: Bodley Head.

Wight, Martin (1977) *Systems of States*, Leicester University Press.

(1991) *International Theory: The Three Traditions*, ed. Brian Porter and Gabriele Wight, Leicester University Press/Royal Institute of International Affairs.

Willetts, Peter (ed.) (1996) *The Conscience of the World: The Influence of Non-Governmental Organisations in the UN System*, London: Hurst.

Williams, David (2004) *Defending Japan's Pacific War: The Kyoto School Philosophers and Post-White Power*, Abingdon: Routledge.

(2013) 'Development, Intervention and International Order', *Review of International Studies*, 39(5): 1213–31.

Williams, Michael C. (2005) *The Realist Tradition and the Limits of International Relations*, Cambridge University Press.

Williams, Paul D. (ed.) (2008) *Security Studies: An Introduction*, 2nd edn., Abingdon: Routledge.

Wilson, Charles (1968) *The Dutch Republic*, New York: McGraw-Hill.

Witt, Michael A. (2010) 'China: What Variety of Capitalism?', Singapore: INSEAD Working Paper 2010/88/EPS.

Wohlforth, William C. (2009) 'Unipolarity, Status Competition, and Great Power War', *World Politics*, 61(1): 28–57.

Wolf, Eric (1997) *Europe and the People Without History*, Berkeley: University of California Press.

Womack, Brantly (2013) 'Beyond Win-Win: Rethinking China's International Relationships in an Era of Economic Uncertainty', *International Affairs*, 89(4): 911–28.

Wong, R. Bin (1997) *China Transformed*, Ithaca: Cornell University Press.

Woodruff, William (1966) *Impact of Western Man: A Study of Europe's Role in the World Economy, 1750–1960*, London: Macmillan.

Woollacott, Angela (2006) *Gender and Empire*, New York: Palgrave Macmillan.

World Bank (n.d.) *Global Bilateral Migration Database*, http://data.world bank.org/data-catalog/global-bilateral-migration-database.

Woytinsky, W.S. and E.S. Woytinsky (1955) *World Commerce and Governments: Trends and Outlook*, New York: Twentieth Century Fund.

Yan, Xuetong (2011) *Ancient Chinese Thought, Modern Chinese Power*, Princeton University Press.

Yearbook of International Organizations 1994–5, Volume 3: Subject Volume, 12th edn., Munich: K. G. Saur.

Young, Iris Marion (1990) *Justice and the Politics of Difference*, Princeton University Press.

Yurdusev, A. Nuri (2009) 'The Middle East Encounter with the Expansion of European International Society', in: Barry Buzan and Ana Gonzalez-Pelaez (eds.), *International Society and the Middle East*, Basingstoke: Palgrave Macmillan, 70–91.

Zakaria, Fareed (2009) *The Post-American World and the Rise of the Rest*, London: Penguin.

Zarakol, Ayşe (2011) *After Defeat: How the East Learned to Live with the West*, Cambridge University Press.

Zeiler, Thomas W. (2014) 'Opening Doors in the Global Economy', in: Akira Iriye (ed.), *Global Interdependence: The World After 1945*, Cambridge, MA: Belknap Press, 203–361.

Zhang, Feng (2009) 'Rethinking the "Tribute System": Broadening the Conceptual Horizon of Historical East Asian Politics', *The Chinese Journal of International Politics*, 2(4): 545–74.

(2012) 'Rethinking China's Grand Strategy: Beijing's Evolving National Interests and Strategic Ideas in the Reform Era', *International Politics*, 49(3): 318–45.

Zhang, Yongjin (2001) 'System, Empire, and State in Chinese International Relations', *Review of International Studies*, 27 (Special Issue): 43–63.

Zimmern, Alfred (1928) 'The Prospects of Democracy', *Journal of the Royal Institute of International Affairs*, 7(3): 153–91.

Žižek, Slavoj (1989) *The Sublime Object of Ideology*, London: Verso.

Index

CAMBRIDGE STUDIES IN INTERNATIONAL RELATIONS